AUSTRALIA'S FEW

and the

BATTLE OF BRITAIN

AUSTRALIA'S FEW
and the
BATTLE OF BRITAIN

KRISTEN ALEXANDER

Pen & Sword
AVIATION

First published in 2014 by NewSouth Publishing
University of New South Wales Press Ltd, University of
New South Wales, Sydney NSW 2052, Australia.

Reprinted in this format in 2015 by
PEN & SWORD AVIATION
An imprint of
Pen & Sword Books Ltd
47 Church Street
Barnsley, South Yorkshire
S70 2AS

ISBN 978 1 47383 379 1

Typeset by Josephine Pajor-Markus

Printed and bound in England
By CPI Group (UK) Ltd, Croydon, CR0 4YY

Pen & Sword Books Ltd incorporates the Imprints of Aviation, Atlas,
Family History, Fiction, Maritime, Military, Discovery, Politics, History,
Archaeology, Select, Wharncliffe Local History, Wharncliffe True Crime,
Military Classics, Wharncliffe Transport, Leo Cooper, The Praetorian Press,
Remember When, Seaforth Publishing and Frontline Publishing

For a complete list of Pen & Sword titles please contact
PEN & SWORD BOOKS LIMITED
47 Church Street, Barnsley, South Yorkshire, S70 2AS, England
E-mail: enquiries@pen-and-sword.co.uk
Website: www.pen-and-sword.co.uk

For my dear friend
Jill Sheppard

Contents

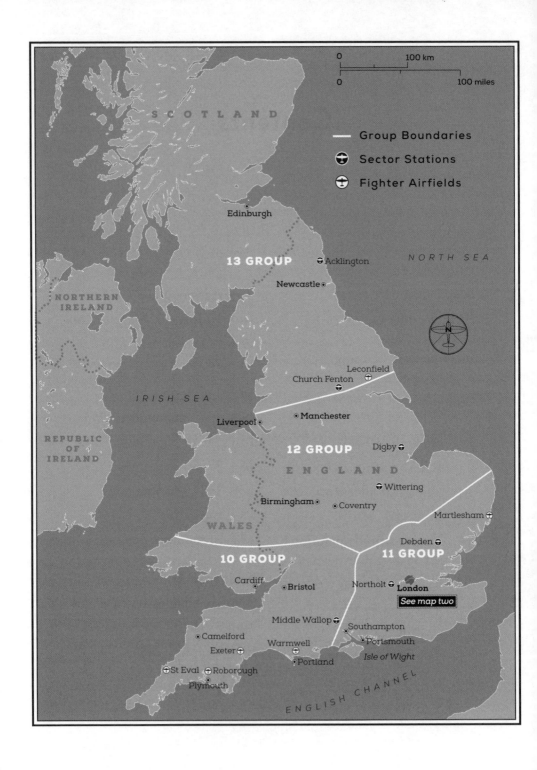

Map 1: Fighter Command during the Battle of Britain, 1940. Diane Bricknell

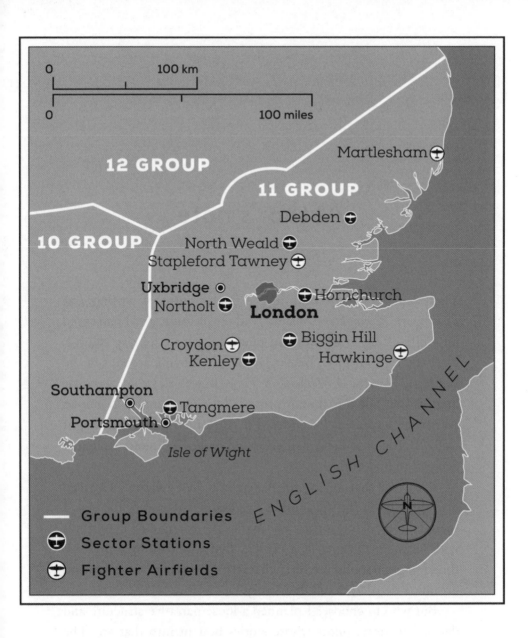

Map 2: 11 Group during the Battle of Britain, 1940. Diane Bricknell

Author's note

There had been little time in the final months of writing *Jack Davenport: Beaufighter Leader* to read for pleasure, and I had saved up a pile of old favourites and new books for a literary splurge. Near the top was H.E. Bates's lyrical and moving account of the Battle of Britain, *A Moment in Time*. It was as fresh as on my first reading but this time it provoked a new thought. When an Australian appeared, I wondered if Australian pilots had fought in the Battle or if Bates had exercised inclusive literary licence. I decided to find out.

I learned that '30 or so' Australians had fought.[1] Thirteen died during the Battle, another five before the end of the war. I spent hours looking at their photographs – young men in uniform with clear eyes gazing at a camera that would forever preserve their images but obscure their characters, personalities, hopes and dreams. I decided to tell their story.

But who to choose? I planned a loose narrative structure and decided to select pilots whose stories best fit into that arc. The first to die. The last. Death – or at least an untimely exit – in each phase of the Battle. A survivor. But I also wanted a broad spread of backgrounds and experiences. State school, private school. Catholic, Protestant. RAAF trained, short service commission, Royal Air Force Volunteer Reserve. Married or affianced and single. The natural pilot. The one who struggled or failed to impress in training but later astounded.

Bill Millington, John Crossman, Ken Holland, Dick Glyde, Jack Kennedy, Stuart Walch, Des Sheen and Pat Hughes all met my loose criteria. They were as young as their fictional counterparts: their ages ranged from 20 to 26, with the youngest and eldest coincidentally sharing a birthday. The majority were born in 1917. Those men may have been young, but most possessed a maturity that belied their age and they rank among 'The Few'. It is a privilege to tell of their part in Britain's defence.

For the general narrative and framework of the Battle of Britain, I have drawn on the official account of the RAF's Air Historical Branch, which was first published in 1947 and republished in 2000. Daily casualty numbers differ depending on the source. I have deferred to those compiled by Derek Wood and Derek Dempster in *The Narrow Margin*. The Battle of Britain Historical Society's website has been a key resource for casualty lists.

For background biographical material, Kenneth G. Wynn's *Men of the Battle of Britain: A Biographical Directory of 'The Few'* has been invaluable, as has the assistance of Geoff Simpson, historical advisor to and trustee of the Battle of Britain Memorial Trust and editor of the forthcoming third edition of Wynn's biographical directory. Where possible, I have included the given names of the squadron friends, wartime associates and instructors of Australia's 'Few'. Unfortunately, squadron records and other sources did not always record given names, and our diarists often included only rank and surname.

Throughout, I have cited victory tallies. At the time, a 'destroyed' had to be verified by someone who had seen the downed aircraft, such as another pilot or a person on the ground like a member of the observer corps or Home Guard. Even so, there is much debate about overall numbers, because often more than one pilot contributed to the destruction of an enemy aircraft. For squadron claims I have drawn on their operations record books. For individual scores, I have deferred to the forensic post-war work of Christopher Shores and Clive Williams in their *Aces High* and in the former's *Those Other Eagles*.

In the interests of consistency and readability, where appropriate, I have corrected spelling and 'improved' punctuation in quoted extracts. For ease of reading, I have not used the 24-hour clock.

In recent years there has been some softening of how the men of the Battle of Britain are collectively referred to, but 'The Few' is more appropriately capitalised within quote marks and I too have adopted this style.[2]

Modern aviation literature refers to the German fighter types as the Bf109 and 110, but Allied pilots knew the aircraft as Messerschmitts and would call them 'Mes'. Contemporary sources such as combat reports, operations record books and squadron diaries use the 'Me' prefix. In deference to the pilots, I also use it.

The RAF was split into functional units called commands. Of these, key to Britain's defence were Bomber Command, which controlled the bombing force; Coastal Command, which was dedicated to maritime defence and protection of supply lines; and Fighter Command, which was responsible for Britain's fighter operations. Fighter Command was divided into a number of groups which had operational responsibilities for specific areas of the United Kingdom. 11 Group covered London and the south of England, 12 Group defended central England as well as central and north Wales, and 13 Group covered England's north and Scotland. 10 Group, which formed on 1 June 1940, became operational on 8 July and assumed responsibility for southwest England and south Wales.

Author's note

Measurement conversions are messy, especially in quoted text, and so for ease of reading I have used the imperial form.

	Imperial	Metric
Length	1 inch	2.5 centimetres
	1 foot / 12 inches	30.5 centimetres
	1 yard / 3 feet	91.4 centimetres
	1 mile / 5280 feet	1.6 kilometres
Weight	1 pound / 16 ounces	453.6 grams
	1 stone / 14 pounds	6.4 kilograms
Capacity	1 gallon	4.5 litres

Introduction:
Naming 'The Few'

Even before it had been won, Winston Churchill immortalised those who fought and died in the Battle of Britain. On 15 August 1940, the Luftwaffe – the German air force – was determinedly trounced on a day that would become known to the Germans as Black Thursday. Five days later, Churchill addressed the House of Commons. He iterated the country's 'gratitude' which 'goes out to the British airmen' who were 'turning the tide of the World War by their prowess and by their devotion'. He thanked all 'British airmen' and acknowledged his nation's debt to them. 'Never in the field of human conflict was so much owed by so many to so few.'[1] He did not exclude the valiant airmen of Bomber and Coastal commands, but despite this 'The Few' came to stand collectively for the men of Fighter Command.

In 1946, an Air Ministry order determined that 'issues of silver-gilt rose emblems denoting a clasp to the 1939–45 Star may be made to flying personnel who flew in fighter aircraft engaged in the Battle of Britain between 10 July 1940 and 31 October 1940'.[2] The aircrew entitled to the Battle of Britain clasp comprised pilots, gunners, observers and radar operators, and their aircraft were the Supermarine Spitfire, Hawker Hurricane, Bristol Blenheim fighter, Boulton Paul Defiant, Gloster Gladiator, Bristol Beaufighter and Fairey Fulmar. Qualifying criteria varied over the years, but ultimately the only men to receive it were those who had flown at least one authorised operational sortie with specified Fighter and Coastal command and Fleet Air Arm squadrons.

Fifteen years after the Battle, Flight Lieutenant John Holloway, a serving Royal Air Force (RAF) officer who had been a sergeant wireless fitter with 615 Squadron during the Battle of Britain, began collecting autographs of clasp recipients and set about compiling a list of those he needed. In 1961, the 2937 names were published as an appendix to Wood and Dempster's *The Narrow Margin*. This list, however, was not definitive. The 60th anniversary edition of Wynn's authoritative *Men of the Battle of Britain* records 2917 men. The RAF's website lists 2918. The Christopher Foxley-Norris Memorial Wall at the National Memorial to 'The Few' at Capel-le-Ferne, in Kent, commemorates 2939 airmen. The Battle of Britain Monument, in London, and the Battle of Britain Historical Society honour 2936 men. Geoff Simpson, however, believes the figure might be at least 2940 and considers further research might reveal even more claims.[3]

How many of those entitled to the clasp were Australian? Again, an exact number cannot be agreed upon. John Herington, the official historian of the Royal Australian Air Force's (RAAF) activities in Europe during the Second World War, noted in 1954 that 'some 30 Australians' served in Fighter Command during the Battle. By 1957, the Medals Section of RAAF Overseas Headquarters determined that 29 Australians were eligible. John Holloway acknowledged 21. The Australian War Memorial's online encyclopaedia states 25, and the RAF claims 26. Wood and Dempster list 27, both the Battle of Britain Monument and the Battle of Britain Historical Society record 32, and Patrick Bishop, in his *Fighter Boys: Saving Britain, 1940*, notes 33. After exhaustive research for his 1990 publication *A Few of 'The Few': Australians and the Battle of Britain*, Dennis Newton determined that 37 Australians fought in the Battle, but on 15 September 2011, a Battle of Britain honour board unveiled at RAAF Base Edinburgh, South Australia, recorded 36 names. New Zealand historian Adam Claasen followed Newton's lead and accepted 37. Whatever the total, recent research indicates that one acknowledged Australian was Irish. With no conclusive total, the RAAF's

Office of Air Force History follows Herington's lead and refers to '30 or so' Australians.[4]

But why the inconsistencies? For a start, of the Australian pilots and one air gunner entitled to the clasp, none served with the RAAF during the Battle of Britain. Scattered throughout a handful of squadrons, they all served with the RAF or the Royal Air Force Volunteer Reserve. Although some Australians had trained as cadets at 1 Flying Training School, Point Cook, Victoria, before the war, they had been discharged from the RAAF and removed from the air force list at the completion of their courses.

Further complicating matters is the issue of Australian identity. The term 'Australian citizen' did not exist until 1949, when the Nationality and Citizenship Act came into force. Those airmen who had been born in Australia carried passports designating them British subjects and they were listed as British on their service records. In addition, the different family circumstances, national ties and varying degrees of 'Australianness' make it difficult in some cases to conclusively state that someone was Australian.

Eight of the '30 or so' exemplify the great range of 'Australianness'. Bill Millington, whose family hailed from Newcastle-upon-Tyne, Northumberland, migrated to Adelaide, South Australia, as a child because of his father's health problems. William Millington considered his son British, as did Bill, who was 'proud of my country and its people, proud to serve under the Union Jack'. Bill never lost his Geordie accent. Nevertheless, he was fond of his new homeland and, soon after joining the RAF, started a 'collection of souvenirs from down under'.[5]

John Crossman, born in Mackay, Queensland, but raised in Newcastle, New South Wales, was the son of an Englishman, and his Australian mother was of German descent. Although he loved England and even learned the names of northern stars, he suffered pangs of homesickness and believed there was nothing to compare to the beauty of the Southern Cross.[6]

Dick Glyde of Perth, Western Australia, had Australian parents but an English lineage that could be traced to 1225. He enjoyed a carefree Australian childhood with holidays on the family property but was educated according to the English tradition.

Although Jack Kennedy's paternal grandfather was Irish, he had married an Australian in Australia. Jack and his parents were Australian born. Once he joined the RAF, however, he appeared little interested in maintaining an Australian connection. Although allowed to keep his RAAF uniform he adopted that of the RAF. He lost his accent, and when he met the woman who would become his fiancée she assumed he was British. Jack planned to stay in England after his short service commission expired and, when war was declared, believed he was defending his homeland.[7]

Stuart Walch's great-grandfather travelled to Van Diemen's Land – now Tasmania – in 1842. Stuart grew a dashing RAF-style moustache and collected cigarette cards of service aircraft, but his heart was still in Hobart, the city of his birth. Like many young men of the day he smoked, and he carried his cigarettes in a case emblazoned with his school's badge. During his free time, he made a point of keeping in touch with The Hutchins School's 'old boys' and Britain-based Australian friends.

Des Sheen of Canberra, Australian Capital Territory, had British-born parents and considered himself a British subject but was an Australian at heart. Like Jack Kennedy, Des was issued with an RAAF uniform as a cadet at Point Cook, but he wore his proudly for some years. Given the relative scarcity of the 'dark blue Australian uniform' in the early months of the war, Des was said to look 'rather unique'. He did, however, don RAF kit as occasion demanded – for instance, when the King presented him with his Distinguished Flying Cross (DFC). Des paid homage to Australia with a boomerang painted on the cockpit of a succession of Spitfires. He always spoke with a laconic Australian drawl, and, in later life, his British friends, not quite appreciating the origins of his accent, referred to him as the 'Cockney group captain'.[8]

Pat Hughes, a descendant of a First Fleet convict, had deep Australian roots and a strong love of New South Wales's Monaro region, where he spent his boyhood. Like Stuart Walch, he grew a moustache when he joined the RAF, but his was not the Ronald Coleman type usually sported by young officers. It was 'rather dirty looking but nevertheless fierce', adopted more to keep women at bay than to fit in. Pat had lost his Australian accent by the time he came to 234 Squadron in November 1939 but continued to wear his RAAF uniform for some months.[9]

Ken Holland had an Australian father and English mother. After migrating to England when he was 16, he seemed intent on keeping his new life and Australian past separate. He was adamant that he did not want his uncle, who had travelled to the United Kingdom, to visit, and he cultivated the impression that he was an orphan. Even so, he spoke of Australia whenever he was offered the chance.[10]

'The Few' varied as much in background, skills, personality, behaviour, character and appearance as any handful of liquorice allsorts. There was a prevailing belief in the inter-war years that prospective fighter pilots possessed qualities that set them apart. RAF selectors were on the lookout for a certain delicacy of touch in their candidates, as fighter pilots had to be instantly responsive to the demands of both the aircraft and the aerial situation. They needed good eyesight as well as experience with guns and shooting. If they had no trade or technical qualifications, some sort of technical knowledge or experience with motorcars or motorcycles was always desirable. It was commonly believed that sportsmen, horsemen, sailors and pianists, as well as those who grew up on farms or who had hunted, possessed the perceived attributes of a fighter pilot. Selectors also considered those with prior military experience as suitable and were impressed by young men who displayed keenness, determination and leadership ability.

Mirroring their British and Allied counterparts, Bill Millington, John Crossman, Ken Holland, Dick Glyde, Jack Kennedy, Stuart Walch, Des Sheen and Pat Hughes were socially adept and good solid students – some even brighter than average – and most revelled in a healthy athleticism. All possessed characteristics believed to mark the embryo fighter pilot. They, and others entitled to the Battle of Britain clasp born or raised under the Southern Cross, were part of the unique band of 'The Few'.

Prologue

'I go forth into battle, light of heart'

In June 1940, Bill Millington sat down to write the hardest letter of his life. 'My dear parents …' But how to go on? With an invasion expected at any time and his new friends flying regular sorties to France, it would not be long before the 22-year-old joined them on operations. He had no fear of dying. 'I go forth into battle, light of heart.' He acknowledged that he might not survive combat and wanted to salve the grief of those he loved in case he failed to return.

Bill was penning a 'last letter' to his parents, to be delivered only in the event of his death. He wanted to give them a sense of his passion for flying, which 'meant more to me than just a career or means of livelihood', his joy in the 'companionship of men and boys with similar interests, the intoxication of speed, the rush of air and the pulsating beat of the motor [which] awakes some answering chord deep down which is indescribable'. He wanted to tell them of his commitment to defending the land of his birth. And he wanted to assure them that 'since leaving home I have endeavoured to live up to those standards dictated by honour and chivalry' which they and he held so dear, 'and am sure that I have not failed you'. He accepted that he might die in battle but had no regrets. 'I would not have it otherwise.'

There was no more to say. After signing it 'Farewell, your loving son, Bill', he folded the page, slipped it into an envelope and addressed it to his mother. He wrote firmly on the top left-hand corner, 'To be forwarded in the event of fatal accident'.[1]

1

Australia's 'Few'

Bill Millington: 'Scout Law was his creed'

Eight-year-old Willie Millington arrived at the Port of London on 1 July 1926. He, his mother, Elizabeth, and four sisters had been living in a two-storey terrace in Newcastle-upon-Tyne. Within hours they would leave England for a new life in South Australia. Third-class tickets in hand, they boarded the SS *Balranald*.

Life had not been easy for the Millingtons. Willie's father, William Henry Millington Sr, had been born with a fallen bowel. His health declined over the years and affected his work: by the mid-1920s, the former commercial traveller was employed as a clerk. William developed breathing difficulties and his condition became so bad that his doctor recommended a warm climate with dry air.[1]

A relative who had settled in Adelaide suggested the city. After much deliberation, William embarked on the SS *Ormonde* on 5 February 1926. He found a home and employment as a sales-man, and arranged for Elizabeth and Queenie, Marjorie, Eileen, Audrey and Willie to follow. At 11 a.m. on 11 August, the SS *Balranald* reached Adelaide's Outer Harbour.[2] Willie leaned over the deck rail and breathed in the Australian air. It was his ninth birthday, and his new life was about to begin.

The Millingtons initially lived in Woodville, then in Mills-wood. William saved hard and in March 1927 bought his own home in Edwardstown. Willie originally enrolled in Westbourne Park Primary School but in January 1928 transferred to Edwards-town Primary School.[3]

As he grew older, Willie came to be known as Bill. He was gregarious and valued friendships. His sister Eileen remembered that he was 'interested in what was going on all over the world – had several pen friends'. At school, he was popular with pupils and teachers alike. Fair haired and freckle faced with a cheeky cleft chin, he had a boyish smile that endeared him to Thomas Nevin, Edwardstown Primary's headmaster.[4] That smile remained throughout his adult-hood, as did his open-faced, cheery demeanour.

Bill was a small boy and never filled up or out. Even by the time he reached 21 he was only 5 feet 6 inches tall and weighed 10 stone 4 pounds. He was an active child, enjoying seaside trips and playing soccer. He later took up tennis, squash, golf, football and sailing. He helped his father in the garden – often sharing a cup of tea and sandwich served on a silver tray after a hard day's work – and took pride in planting prize dahlias. He loved animals, and snaps of the family collie, Prince, found their way into his photo collection. He was mechanically adept and as an adult was more than capable of reconditioning an old motorbike. He was mad about aeroplanes and took his camera to Parafield and Ceduna aerodromes. But photos weren't enough. Eileen recalled that he 'always wanted to fly', and he regularly insisted that he would join the air force and make flying his career.[5]

Although an average student, Bill was considered an exemplary pupil. In 1930, he enrolled at Adelaide Technical High School because he thought the technical focus would provide skills he would need when he learned to fly. In 1931, he attained the Intermediate standard, passing six subjects and obtaining a ranking of 20th in the school merit list. In addition, he was assessed as a capable scholar, diligent in 'habits of industry', excellent in punctuality, neat and courteous, and of 'correct' speech with legible handwriting. As far as leadership qualities were concerned, however, he was rated as 'retiring'.[6]

Bill never deviated from his desire to be a pilot, but his school records indicate he was also interested in a career as a mechanical draughtsman or in chemistry. When he was 14 he took a job with Gilbert Engineering as he believed this sort of work would stand him in good stead when he eventually applied for one of the flying services. His headmaster insisted he maintain his studies, so in February 1932 he embarked on the school's program of special guidance. He later left Gilbert's and was employed as a commercial traveller at G. & R. Wills & Co. Ltd, a wholesale warehouse and commodity agent.[7]

Bill asked his father if he could learn to fly, but William Millington would not give his underage son permission, so when he wasn't dreaming of flying, Bill channelled his energies into scouting, graduating from cub to scout and then rover, and winning many achievement badges. He was connected with both the Forestville and the Torrensville rover crews and joined the Boy Scouts Association's soccer league.[8] He wasn't a bad player either. On 4 August 1934, when South Eastern Division defeated North Western Division by seven goals to one, Bill was declared one of the best on the field.

His friends were his fellow scouts and rovers. Together, they enjoyed camping, bushwalking and rabbit shooting in the Adelaide Hills and messing about in boats. Bill's devotion to scouting was based on more than just friendship with like-minded fellows and exciting excursions. 'Although not deeply religious', his sister Eileen recalled, 'he had strong moral principles and Scout Law was his creed'. He strove to be trustworthy; loyal to King, Empire and Country; helpful; friendly, cheerful and considerate; thrifty, courageous and respectful.[9]

Much of what Bill did exemplified Scout Law. For example, in January 1939, he and his rover crew braved record-breaking temperatures to fight bushfires raging around Adelaide. Within a week, the danger passed and the fundraising began. Bill attended a dance which raised £9, went to a fire relief concert and enjoyed a charity midget-car meeting.[10]

Bill joined the Royal Australian Naval Reserve as a cadet on his 18th birthday, later serving in the Signals Branch.[11] About the time of his 21st birthday, he realised war was imminent and decided to do his part. As he was of age and could learn to fly if he wanted to, he applied for an RAAF cadetship. Regardless of his years as a scout and rover, his training as a naval reserve cadet and his social ease and gregariousness, he missed out. Undeterred, he decided to go to England and join the RAF. While he saved for his passage, he sat for and passed his paymaster's examination but nearly failed the medical because of the poor state of his teeth. After a sound repair job by the family dentist, he waited to be offered a commission as a sub-lieutenant in the naval reserve.

Bill soon hit upon a way to combine a career in the air with a naval life: he would join the Royal Navy and later transfer to its Fleet Air Arm, which had the principal tasks of defending naval shore establishments and facilities, as well as undertaking offensive operations from aircraft carriers.[12] He joined the Royal Aero Club of South Australia and took flying lessons at Parafield. Tuition was expensive, and by the end of 1938 he had accrued just 5 hours 15 minutes' dual instruction on Moths. In January 1939 he notched up only 2 hours 50 minutes. As the year advanced, he abandoned the lessons.

He remained active with his rover crew and learned wireless and code in his spare time. The naval commission came through but he declined it. War continued to threaten, and he remained convinced that his homeland needed him, Eileen recalled. He was 'determined to do his part'. He had not saved enough for the voyage so his mother helped out. (Bill promised to pay her back as soon as he joined the RAF.)[13] He handed in his notice and left work on 29 April to start packing.

John Crossman: 'mad about planes from the time he could walk'

John Crossman was stricken by a passion for all things aviation. His mother recalled that 'he was mad about planes from the time he could walk'.[14] His father regularly brought home pieces of balsa-wood so he could make model aeroplanes from scratch, but John wanted to see the real thing up close. He had his chance when Charles Kingsford Smith, one of Australia's aviation heroes, embarked on a barnstorming tour of Australia. He landed at the Newcastle Aero Club at Broadmeadow in late November 1932, and 14-year-old John begged his father to take him to see Smithy.

Together they headed to Broadmeadow. Ted and John looked over the Fokker F.V11b/3 trimotor monoplane in which Smithy, Charles Ulm and Americans Jim Warner and Harry Lyon had made the first trans-Pacific flight, in 1928. The 'Old Bus' could fit 16 joyriders at a time, and more if children perched on a parent's lap. Eyes aglow with excitement, John watched as Smithy thrilled passenger after passenger. Soon it was his turn, but rather than sit in *Southern Cross*'s fuselage, he climbed into the cockpit with the great man. He was hooked, and within an instant his balsa models weren't enough. He wanted to fly just like Smithy, and chattered about his future aviation career all the way home. Hoping to gauge his wife's feelings, Ted told her he was thinking of giving their son a taste of the air. She retorted, 'Over my dead body'. Ted sheepishly admitted it was too late. And indeed it was. John's mother realised 'there was no holding him'. Her son was 'one of those youngsters whose spirit had been caught and held by flight'.[15]

John was tall, dark haired, dark eyed and of slim build. Even at an early age it was clear he would grow into a handsome man. He had a strong likeness to his father, George Edward Crossman, known as Ted, who was born in Taunton, in Somerset, England, the only son in a family of four daughters. As a youth Ted was apprenticed to an engineering business. On 24 October 1912, he set sail on the SS *Orama*, working his passage to Australia. His first job was in the Queensland sugar mills before he moved south to Newcastle and the shipbuilding industry. There he met and fell in love with Gladys Dallas, known as Mick. They eloped in 1917.[16] Mick was entranced by Ted's stories of Queensland so applied in his name for a position as a junior engineer at Colonial Sugar Refining Co.'s Homebush sugar mill.

Shortly after, he was working at the Mossman mill, located about 500 miles further north.[17] Mick was heavily pregnant, so she returned to Mackay for her confinement. John Dallas Crossman was born on 20 March 1918. Twins followed, but died in infancy. The family was completed by Joan's arrival in November 1922. John started infants' school at Mossman. When Ted and Mick decided to return to Newcastle he enrolled at Cooks Hill Primary and later at Newcastle Boys' High School.

John may have looked like his father, but their characters were very different. Ted had helped support his family from the age of 11. When he lost his father, two years later, he was the family breadwinner and developed a seriousness that belied his years. He worked hard, was a careful saver and soon owned his own home. He was also a strict disciplinarian and did not believe in sparing the rod.[18] There was little spent on luxuries, especially during the Depression. He had 13 jobs during those hard years, chasing positions all around Sydney and Newcastle. Although he was never out of work before landing a job as chief draughtsman at Lysaght's, it had been a worrying struggle to ensure his family's financial security.

John, however, had a more relaxed, generous and spendthrift nature. He swam, loved music, collected stamps, was generous with gifts he could ill afford and read voraciously. His deft fingers easily carried out electrical work. He always had a crowd of friends. Everyone liked John. And why wouldn't they? He was happy, frequently laughing and always saw the funny side of things, like the time he was at a party and stepped outside for a walk in the dark. He told his friend he knew the grounds like the back of his hand but apparently had not looked at his hands recently, as he fell over twice within 5 minutes of uttering his assurances.[19]

His passion for flying and all things aviation increased as he grew older.[20] Whenever he could, he spent the day at the aerodrome watching local and visiting pilots and their aircraft, adding snaps of them to his photo albums. He travelled to Victoria to visit the RAAF station and flying school at Point Cook – located southwest of Melbourne – and added more photographs to his collection.

Despite John's friendly, outgoing nature, his teachers considered him 'a quiet, unassuming, capable lad with whom it was a pleasure to come into contact', but he wasn't the best scholar. He consistently received bad marks in history, was lucky to pass Latin, had a long way to go in French, was inaccurate and careless in maths, and was only fair in the sciences. Realising he would need better results if he wanted to join the air force, he pulled up his socks, but good marks in Latin eluded him even though he spent extra time working on his translations. When he sat for the Intermediate Certificate, in October 1933, he failed Latin but was awarded B passes in six subjects and one A.[21]

John left school and applied for a vacancy at A. Goninan & Co. of Broadmeadow, but the position was given to someone else. There was, however, an opening for a clerk in the accountancy section, and he started there on 30 April 1934. Over the next few years he dealt with all aspects of the cashbook, the debtors' and creditors' ledger, and cheques and invoices. His employers found him to be 'of gentlemanly demeanour, [and] temperate habits' and acknowledged that he gave 'every satisfaction by the diligent discharge' of his duties.[22]

John did whatever he could to enhance his chances of selection by an air force recruitment board. He signed up on 4 December 1934 as a senior cadet with the 1st Field Company Royal Australian Engineers (Militia), as prior service always went down well. (He served until 20 March 1936, resigning because it interfered with his studies.) He was examined by the Australian Institute of Industrial Psychology, which deemed him 'eminently suited for a career in the air force as you possess not only a high level of general intelligence but also the requisite practical abilities'. He also acquired a reference from the rector of St Philip's Anglican Church, who believed that John would 'give satisfaction' and 'prove dependable in any work he undertakes'.[23]

Ted Crossman urged his son to enrol in night classes in accounting at the Metropolitan Business College. John acquiesced but, perhaps thinking a recruitment board would value practical skills over accountancy, took up mechanics in his spare time. He knew his efforts to improve himself would make him a better candidate when he eventually applied to the air force, but he realised an existing ability to fly would be even more in his favour so he kept nagging his father. Even though Ted introduced John to the ecstasy of flight, he did not want him to pursue an aviation career. He adamantly refused to give permission for his underage son to take private lessons.[24]

Ken Holland: an unwanted child

Kenneth Christopher Holland was a well-built lad of medium height, fair skinned with sun-tipped blond, wavy hair and good looking in a fresh-faced way. He had grown up in the coastal suburbs of Sydney, ranging around the Bondi area, scampering over the rocky outcrops and plunging into the surf like any other boy. When not at the beach he took pot-shots at rats with his air rifle. Ken's apparently carefree existence, however, was clouded by constant poverty, his father's continuing shell shock from his service in the Great War, and the bitter knowledge that he was an unwanted child.[25]

On 16 December 1916, Sergeant Harold Holland came down with a heavy cold and an infection of the larynx. He was on his way to a field hospital in France when he was caught in an artillery attack. After a month or so, he began to complain of general weakness, loss of weight and loss of voice, and was shaky.[26] He was shell shocked. Assessed as employable only in a base environment, he was transferred on 17 February 1917 to Westham Camp, Weymouth, on England's Dorset coast, a holding facility for casualties no longer requiring hospitalisation but not fit enough to rejoin their units. It is not known whether Harold met Dorset-born Ina Christopher, an assistant florist, during his convalescence or earlier while on leave. Either way, it was a whirlwind romance and they married on 23 April 1917.

A medical board on 7 August 1918 declared Harold 'temporarily unfit for General Service for more than six months but fit for Home Service'. He embarked two days later and arrived in Australia on 5 October 1918. He took a house in Bronte, a coastal suburb of Sydney, and later moved to nearby Bondi. Ina was on her way to Australia when he was medically discharged, in February 1919. Although receiving a small pension, Harold resumed his old work as a commercial traveller on commission, and Ina fell pregnant. Harold was far from well and his earnings were erratic. The couple struggled. Ken's birth, on 29 January 1920, was not a happy event.[27]

Harold's health deteriorated. His working hours and commission fluctuated. He experienced frequent headaches and shortness of breath. His dream-filled nights were broken by restless sleeping from which he would wake with a start in a cold sweat. He was so physically debilitated that, although he was energetic enough in the morning, he 'was not much use' in the afternoon. He could not afford to buy his own home, so his family moved from one house to another. Always breathless, Harold would have had few opportunities to play with his growing son or take him out and about as any father would.[28] Even so, Ken made the most of life. After all, many of the families in the Bondi area during the Depression lived in poverty.

The young lad entered Randwick Intermediate High School in 1933. After three years he gained his Intermediate Certificate with A passes in English and French and B passes in history and Latin, but he failed mathematics. Living in a beachside suburb, he was a keen and strong swimmer, and in October 1935 he joined the Tamarama Surf Life Saving Club as a junior member. As soon as he turned 16 – the minimum age for candidates – he began working towards the Royal Life Saving Society's bronze medallion.[29]

Ken became interested in aviation, unable to resist the aerial fever sweeping over Australia during his childhood as record upon aerial record was made and then broken. He went to the pictures whenever he could afford a ticket. He liked poetry and confidently scattered French phrases in conversation and throughout his diaries, indicating a touch of – or pretension towards – intellectualism. His diaries were also littered with capitals, exclamation marks and underlining which demonstrated a natural joie de vivre. But it is not too much of a stretch to see that Ken's home life, Harold's chronic illness – which never improved – and the knowledge he was a burden on his family would have left their mark on his natural vibrancy. And it is not hard to see how he would have been drawn to another father figure, in the form of Major Hugh Ivor Emmott Ripley.

Ripley, born in Yorkshire in 1884, was the third son of a baronet. Known to all as Toby, he was educated at Marlborough College and admitted to the Royal Military College, Sandhurst, in January 1903. He was awarded the Sword of Honour and granted a commission in the Worcestershire Regiment in August 1904. Gassed in France during the Great War, he wanted to live in a mild climate. He settled in Hobart, Tasmania, arriving in February 1923, and by 1930 was living in Bondi. He joined the Tamarama Surf Life Saving Club and was a well-liked, generous supporter who often staked the refreshments at functions. Regardless of the age difference, Ken grew close to Toby, who appeared to him all that a father should be. More than that, Toby gave Ken a glimpse of a different life and a means to escape his own. Ken begged the older man to take him to England. In May 1936, they boarded the RMS *Comorin* and arrived in London on 12 June. Next stop was Camelford, in Cornwall, where Toby had purchased Melorne, a large house near the railway station.[30]

Ken was baptised in the Parish Church of St Materiana, Tintagel, on 13 September 1936.[31] Within a fortnight he and Toby were travelling first class back to Sydney. When they arrived, Ken told his parents he wanted to live in England permanently under Toby's guardianship. It was an attractive proposition. Ken had no job and only limited employment prospects. The most coveted positions in offices and the banking system were out of reach because he had failed maths, and once he turned 16 the Hollands lost the pension component relating to an underage dependant as well as the child endowment. Finances were already tight and would not improve if he couldn't contribute to the family income. How then could Harold and Ina refuse to allow their son to travel to England under the patronage of a wealthy man who offered to fund his further education? They couldn't and they didn't. After all, they hadn't wanted him in the first place.

Dick Glyde: 'work among the ... most wonderful machines'

In July 1928, Richard Lindsay Glyde's Aunty Lon walked into her nearest stationer to purchase *The Wonder Book of Aircraft* for her nephew, an only child born on 29 January 1914 and known as Dick from an early age.[32] The book contained official RAF photos as well as others that had appeared in *Flight*, a popular English weekly covering civil and service aviation stories, which depicted rugged-looking pilots and the latest aircraft performing aerobatics. Even better, it had chapters on how to fly and about life in the RAF that made service aviation seem fun and glamorous. Dick was entranced.

Inspired by the RAF's life of 'adventure, travel and work among the newest and most wonderful machines in the world', young Dick biked the 2 miles or so from his home at Mount Lawley, Perth, to Maylands Aerodrome and watched the aerial comings and goings. From 1929, Western Australia's first 'airliners' arrived there weekly, and Sundays soon became known as flying days. Dick and a friend saved up to take a joyride in a 14-passenger de Havilland DH66 Hercules, the largest aeroplane in Australia at the time. On the days he could not ride to the aerodrome, with a bit of luck a southwest breeze would bring the sound of aircraft revving their engines to his ears or he'd watch one of the metallic birds soar through the blue above.[33]

Dick attended South Perth State School until July 1925, when he transferred to Highgate State School. He then enrolled at Guildford School WA (Church of England Grammar School) on 10 January 1927. He was keen on cricket and played in the school's Second XI. In 1929 he was in the athletics team and at one stage was the sport activities captain in School House. Dick didn't devote all his time to the playing fields. He was also a house prefect, and in the school's first inter-house music competition, in

December 1928, he and a friend contributed to School House's victory with a violin duet that was well received. He was bright and in 1929 passed his junior university examination in eight subjects.[34]

Dark-haired Dick had clear brown eyes and possessed an honest, penetrating gaze beneath thick dark brows. He was of slim build and average height, was strong and fit and sported a healthy-looking tan acquired on Guildford's playing fields. Holidays were spent with relations on a 1000-acre wheat and sheep property near Three Springs, about 200 miles north of Perth. There was horse riding on tap, a gravel tennis court and ample opportunity to ride a bike or just roam the paddocks. He was expected to pitch in with the farm chores, but nothing too strenuous for a young lad who had the freedom to wander as he chose.[35]

Frank and Phillis Glyde wanted their son to spend three years at Guildford, but he 'was unable to study for the Leaving Certificate as the economic depression necessitated my removal from school' in 1930 at the end of the first term. He joined the Perpetual Trustee Co. (WA) as a junior, assisting with the mail, running inter-departmental messages, changing the blotting paper on executives' desks and keeping their inkwells full.[36]

An office environment was a stark contrast to the wide spaces of Three Springs, and Dick champed at the fustiness of menial duties. Out of the office he played sport and dreamed of a life in the air. As the boy grew into a man, his interest in *The Wonder Book of Aircraft*'s glamorous pilots was supplanted by the exploits of the Great War airmen. His hero was James Byford McCudden VC, a leading British ace – that is, someone who had been credited with five or more aerial victories – who had never been defeated in combat. It wasn't long before Dick decided to escape from Perpetual Trustees. He wanted a flying career for himself and confided to a friend that he was thinking of joining the air force.[37]

Jack Kennedy: 'a decent sort of presence'

John Connolly Kennedy was born on 29 May 1917. Named after his father, he was known as John within the family but as Jack at school and later in the air force. He was the only son in a staunchly Catholic family. His father was employed by a successful bookmaker when he met Frances Storey, of Footscray, Melbourne. They married at St Paul's Roman Catholic Church in Dulwich Hill, Sydney, on 31 August 1916. Beryl completed the family on 27 August 1921, soon after they had moved to Bellevue Hill.

Jack was a handsome lad and lost none of his good looks when he shot up to 6 feet and filled out to be a solidly built young man. He was tall, broad shouldered and well tanned, with dark brown hair. Any girl would fall for him, but he was not interested in romance. For him, sport was all, and his father encouraged him to participate in a variety of outdoor activities.

John Kennedy's employer diversified into real estate, specialising in city property. After he died, John, who had progressed from clerk to manager, took over the property business. Sales were down during the Depression and his income reduced by 50 per cent during the hardest years. The Kennedys felt the strain as they learned to manage with less, but, no matter the sacrifice, Jack's and Beryl's schooling was never affected.[38]

In about 1925, Jack enrolled at St Charles's junior school, which was run by the Franciscan Order. In 1930, he proceeded to Waverley College, the senior school, run by the Christian Brothers. He became a significant character at Waverley. In 1932, he was in the school's Intermediate A rugby union team, winners of the senior class competition. Two years later, he graduated to a forward's position in the First XV. He was selected for the Representative XV and played at venues as far afield as Goulburn, Wagga Wagga and the Royal Military College, Duntroon, in Canberra, becoming one of that select band considered by the school to be 'stamped with a certain brand of quality'. He was a champion gymnast and played cricket, lawn tennis and hand ball. He also excelled as an athlete and was a member of the school's 1934 athletics team. In that year's J.F. Hennessy Cup events he gained first place in the broad jump, second in the hop, step and jump and third in the shot put. His parents were proud of him.[39]

Jack loved swimming, and his father regularly took him to the local swimming baths. He looked like an Olympic champion as he executed faultless dives. On one occasion, the perfect image was shattered when he hit his head and cracked a front tooth. It was repaired with a gold cap, and at least one school friend remembered it as a unique feature. Jack had always been a cheeky lad, with a good sense of humour and a warm laugh, but the accident left a shadow. As he grew older, he became self-conscious and tried to hide the gold tooth when he spoke. He rarely sported an open smile in photographs.[40]

The Kennedys were a strong Catholic family, and Jack demonstrated a strong faith and commitment to his school's spiritual life. He displayed sound character traits and had a good sense of responsibility, especially towards his sporting commitments. He was made a prefect in his fourth and Leaving Certificate years. He was sensible, softly spoken, had a 'decent sort of presence' and was well liked. More importantly, from the perspective of sister Beryl, he was a good brother who was always protective of her.[41]

Jack was bright and did well in his Intermediate Certificate. When he sat for the leaving exams in 1934 he gained B passes in five subjects and a lower standard pass in one. It would have been natural to follow in his father's professional footsteps, but the real estate business had not recovered by the time he left school. As it happened, Jack's godfather was a partner in Bray & Holliday, which by 1925 was Sydney's largest shop-fitter, with a client list including David Jones, Grace Brothers and Farmers. Pat Bray wanted his godson to join the company. Although Jack did not see his future in a commercial environment, he accepted – reluctantly – his godfather's offer of employment. He enrolled in accountancy studies at night, as these would lead to advancement, but he was bored. He found everything about the business world stultifying and soon realised he did not want a desk job. He never displayed any overt enthusiasm for aviation, but somehow, perhaps as an antidote to the tedium of an office job, he decided he would rather sit in the cockpit of an aeroplane than spend his working life with Bray & Holliday.[42]

Stuart Walch: 'one of the best footballers and oarsmen in the school'

Stuart Crosby Walch was born into a successful family enterprise that had strong ties with country and community. J. Walch and Sons opened its doors on New Year's Day 1846, and the company prospered.[43] As well as books and stationery, they stocked sporting goods and musical instruments and had a successful publishing arm. Stuart's father, Percival, joined the company when he left school and took over as managing director in 1915. He and his wife, Florence, whom he had married in 1908, lived in Sandy Bay, an affluent area where many of Hobart's social elite resided. Following Nancy and Brenda, born in 1909 and 1911 respectively, their third child and long-awaited son was born on 16 February 1917.

Like other boys in the Walch family before him, Stuart was educated at The Hutchins School. He enrolled in 1927 when he was ten.[44] Like many of Australia's oldest private schools for boys, Hutchins is modelled on long-established English schools such as Rugby and Winchester. Like Waverley and Guildford, Hutchins espoused the traditional values of academic excellence and the development of faith and social conscience, and considered a rigorous sporting program an important mechanism to help develop a lad's character.

Equally competent at his studies and sports, Stuart thrived. He was a popular boy and was remembered as 'one of the best footballers and oarsmen in the school'. He rowed in two school crews and in 1934 was in the winning Head of the River crew. He also received the Parents' Association Shield for the inter-house football competition at Hutchins's 1934 prize-giving ceremony.[45]

While Stuart excelled on field and river, he harboured a secret desire. In June 1933, the Hutchins football and tennis teams were invited to play a series of matches with Trinity and Malvern grammar schools in Melbourne. The tennis team was defeated, but the footballers were victorious against both host schools, with Stuart scoring one goal against Trinity. Over the next few days the boys enjoyed the sights of Melbourne and environs, including a trip to Geelong Grammar School, where they were 'deeply impressed by the beauty of the school chapel and the necessity of having a chapel of our own'. After an excellent lunch en route, the tourists called in at the Point Cook air base, where they were shown through the hangars and watched a Bristol Bulldog going through its paces.[46] The visit played on Stuart's mind. He decided to apply for the air force when he was old enough but told no one of his newfound interest in aviation.

Stuart took his Leaving Certificate exams in December 1934 and received passes in five subjects. His father wanted him to join the family business, so Stuart joined J. Walch and Sons as a clerk. He turned 18 in February 1935, played cricket and football with the Hutchins School Old Boys' Association team and mingled with Hobart society at its bridge parties, dances, fundraisers and celebrations. Although not featured as much as his sister Brenda, his name was a regular in published guest lists in the *Mercury*'s social pages. Tall, with a dark complexion, brown eyes and dark brown hair, he was confident in social situations and was invited to the most exclusive parties and dances.[47]

Like Jack Kennedy, Stuart chafed at the confines of an office. He had little interest in publishing and preferred the outdoors. On 27 March 1935, he joined the 40th Battalion (Militia).[48] He trained on the .303 Vickers machine guns, Lewis guns, rifles, revolvers and mortars and received a solid grounding in range finding and map and terrain reading. As well as a chance to escape the office, military service would be a good thing to have under his belt. He had not forgotten his schoolboy visit to Point Cook and the aerial display put on by the Bristol Bulldog. And so, when the RAAF advertised cadetships, he applied.

Des Sheen: 'as game as they are made'

Canberrans took the day off work or escaped from household duties on Monday 9 May 1927 so they could witness the Duke and Duchess of York open Parliament House. It was an occasion full of colour and pomp, punctuated by the impressive forces' march past, the boom of the royal salute, Dame Nellie Melba's rendition of 'God Save the King' and formal guards of honour. Nine-year-old Desmond Frederick Burt Sheen was in the crowd enjoying the day's events. He was excited by the aerial pageant and couldn't believe his luck when one of the RAAF's DH9s landed in a paddock near his home. From that moment, he was hooked. He thought, 'That's for me … I decided as soon as I was old enough I would join the air force'.[49]

Soon after migrating to Australia from Lambeth, in London, Des's father, Walter, a plasterer, took a job with the Howie Brothers construction firm and was sent to Canberra in 1911. His skills were put to good use on the capital's first Commonwealth Bank and hospital. Construction slowed after the outbreak of war, so Walter left Canberra. He was working in the Jenolan Caves district, in the Blue Mountains, when he met Harriet Marchant, who hailed from Semley, Wiltshire. Walter followed the work to

Sydney, and he and Harriet married in the Methodist Church at Waverley on 29 December 1916. Des was born on 2 October 1917, and on 13 December 1922 his younger brother, Gordon, joined the family.

Walter worked on a number of building sites in Sydney and Jervis Bay. Back in Canberra construction was gaining pace, and so he returned with his young family. The Sheens initially lived at Westlake, an early Canberra suburb, in a timber cottage located a short distance from the tunnel that was being constructed for the capital's sewerage system. Each night, the cottage was shaken by strong blasts which were so loud that Harriet and Walter had to stuff cotton wool into their sons' ears to protect them from the noise. Des's earliest education was at Mortdale Public School, in Sydney's south, but after the move to Canberra he enrolled at Telopea Park School in February 1924.[50] About this time, the Sheens moved to the Causeway.

Des's fascination with flying continued as famous aviators came to Canberra, touching down in paddocks near his school. He was enthralled by their presence, their machines and the glamour of their record-breaking achievements, particularly those of Bert Hinkler, who arrived in Canberra less than 12 months after the royal visit as part of a grand aviation tour following his daring solo flight from England. Even with the rain on 14 March 1928, a crowd of about 5000 awaited Hinkler's arrival. The *Canberra Times* reported that, after 'circling round like a bird', he 'made a beautiful landing' in his Avro Avian a stone's throw from Telopea Park School. Two days later, Hinkler visited Des's school. The children listened in delight as their new hero spoke of his own school days and advised them to '"play the game", to study and work, and not to forget that sport was a valuable help in building up character'. According to the reporters, at the end of his speech, the children 'shot a cloud of paper aeroplanes at him', but 'their marksmanship was poor'.[51]

Amy Johnson, the first woman to fly solo from England to Australia, and Jean Batten, who, in 1934, after two failed attempts, succeeded in flying solo from England to Australia and broke Johnson's 1930 record while she was at it, also influenced him. Both included Canberra in their aerial tours, but Des counted Batten's visit especially as an inspirational memory.[52]

He may have dreamed of taking to the skies himself, but life on the ground had much to offer an active lad. Judging by his burgeoning interest in sport during his school years, it seems Des heeded Hinkler's advice, growing into a noted athlete. He also started his football career with the school rugby league teams and was later regarded as a fair player and one of his school's best half-backs. The 1932 season was a great success, with Des's team surprising their supporters as no one expected them to be quite as good as they were. He was one of the four best players and was even tipped to form a solid backbone for the senior team if he did not leave school.[53]

Des did not spend all his time at football training. Like Dick Glyde, he learned to play the violin. He was not a natural and found his sporting commitments a good excuse to wriggle out of lessons, later quipping it was no great disappointment, as he had broken so many fingers on the football field he couldn't continue his musical career. He did not altogether lay aside the violin, however. His daughter recalled him playing 'pretty roughly' at a 'mess do'. Des also briefly trod the boards. Leaving the acting parts to those with a stronger claim, he provided the scene-setting narration for the Telopea Park School Dramatic Society's 1932 end-of-year production of three extracts from Shakespeare's *Julius Caesar*.[54]

He sat for his Intermediate Certificate that year, gaining solid B passes, but could not go on to study for the Leaving Certificate as he had to contribute to the family income. Shortly after his 15th birthday, he joined the public service as a messenger in the Prime Minister's Department. Des may have abandoned the classroom and school team, but he did not give up sport entirely. He played soccer, and in 1933, his team, the Federal Rovers, was awarded the winner's medal. He joined the South City rugby league team and was soon acknowledged as a 'half back in the making and, although very light of build, is as game as they are made'. Critics expected big things of him.[55]

Des did not enjoy the public service, but it was the Depression and he could not leave a steady job. He had never forgotten Bert Hinkler, Jean Batten and Amy Johnson. Nor did he forget the DH9s and Gipsy Moths which had landed near his home and school. Throughout his boyhood and youth he was enthralled by 'all those old string bags, some tied together with bits of wire'. Nothing would turn him from his childhood dreams. 'My ambition had always been the flying service.' Time passed slowly as he ran messages until he was old enough to join the RAAF.[56]

Pat Hughes: 'a bright spark and a practical joker'

Pat Hughes was brought up in the Monaro, an area of pastoral and mining riches at the foot of New South Wales's Snowy Mountains. To him, it was a land 'unrivalled in the magnificence and grandeur of its beauty', lying under a sky 'unmatched in its clearness and depth of colour'. In 'An Autumn Evening', written for the magazine of his Sydney school after he had left the area, a man he dubbed 'the watcher' sat on a jutting crag of a mountain, looking with 'wondering awe' into the distant blue and giving an 'involuntary exclamation' as the 'slanting rays of the setting sun' revealed the scene before him. It is not hard to imagine that Pat was writing about himself, transported to the country of his childhood. He remembered the clean, fresh air and the 'gracious hand of autumn' that 'caressed the countryside and decorated it in the purest gold and brown'. He saw in his mind's eye the 'faint blue peaks and domes and ridges' of the nearby mountains. In a time when the Nazi Party was gaining more power in Germany and war was predicted, Pat named one of those summits Peace Mountain.[57]

As the 19th century drew to a close, Pat's father, Percival Clarence Hughes, took up a teaching post at the Upper Cowra Creek school. He taught in a number of local one-room schools over the years, including those at Jerangle and Peak View. Percy had a sense of humour and keen intelligence. He gained a reputation as a literary talent, penning poetry and stories for local papers and the *Bulletin*. He was also renowned as a reader and was so engrossed in his books he was often late for school. Percy married local girl Caroline Vennell in 1895 and moved to Peak View. Their first child, Muriel (known as Midge), was born in 1896. A new addition to the family appeared regularly – four within the first five years of marriage – and Caroline proved a loving mother to her ever-increasing brood.[58]

Percy took on the Peak View post office and ran it out of his home. Percy and Caroline's youngest son, Paterson Clarence Hughes, known as Pat, was born on 19 September 1917. Pat's RAAF service record states that he was born at or near Numeralla, near Cooma, but his nephew Greg noted his place of birth as Peak View.[59] He was the 11th of 12 children. Elizabeth, the youngest, died in infancy. Pat took after his mother in looks, but it was Percy who seemed to influence his son the most. Although Percy's birth name was Percival, 'Paterson' was recorded on his marriage certificate. (Pat later named his father as 'Paterson Clarence Hughes' on his own wedding certificate.) He was known as Percy all his life, so it is a mystery as to why he changed his name.[60] Perhaps he was paying homage to fellow poet and co-contributor to the *Bulletin* A.B. 'Banjo' Paterson. Whatever the reason, his new name meant so much that he gave it to his youngest son.

Like his father, Pat was happy to settle down with a good

book whenever he had the opportunity and would become lost in it. He inherited his father's sense of humour, but his took a more mischievous bent: he was remembered by an old school friend as 'a bright spark and a practical joker'.[61] Pat also had a flair for words. His schoolboy essays displayed a poetical turn of phrase, and his adult letters and diary sparkled with wit, humour and an eye for detail. In the privacy of his diary, however, wit often turned to sarcasm or malice.

Even with 21 years' difference between eldest and youngest – and with some leaving home before his birth – Pat and his six sisters and four brothers were close. He especially looked on William, born in 1911, as a mentor. Midge was the first to leave, marrying in Annandale, Sydney, in 1916. She and her husband, Tom Tongue, eventually moved to Kiama, on the coast of New South Wales, and always welcomed her large family when they visited. Those holidays at her seaside home were much-anticipated and long-treasured times.[62]

Percy relinquished the post office and taught at Cooma Public School for a few years. He took up bookkeeping at Dromore station but from 1921 worked as a labourer. By 1928, he was at Bulong, on Cooma's Mittagang Road. He and his family lived on the property, and Pat retained fond memories of it. In 1930, Percy, Caroline and those still living at home relocated to Sydney, where Percy worked as a labourer.[63] After a short residence in Ashfield West, they moved to Haberfield.

As a labourer, Percy would have worked sporadically during those hard years, and with three school-age children when they first arrived in Sydney, money was tight. On occasion, Pat's brother William and sister Valerie helped out with the family's rent, and Caroline juggled intermittent wages and government endowment payments to pay the bills as she stretched her budget to ensure her brood were well fed. She was a good cook and always kept the pantry stocked for large family meals. Her youngest child especially had a hearty appetite and never let his mother's good cooking go to waste.[64]

Pat had attended Cooma Public School but registered at Petersham Public High School after the move to Sydney. His conduct and attendance were respectable and he was made a prefect in 1932 and vice-captain in 1933. He enjoyed sport and devoted his leisure time to field, court and pool. He played fourth-grade tennis in 1931 and was in the premier team of the fourth-grade rugby league competition, moving up to first grade in 1932–33. He also swam for the school and was in the life-saving class, gaining proficiency and first aid certificates, and the Royal Life Saving Society's bronze medallion.[65]

At just over 5 feet 11 inches tall, with a solid frame to match his height, grey eyes, brown hair and a medium complexion, Pat grew into a good-looking young man. He was tempted to over-eating, but sport usually kept the inevitable weight increase at bay. He developed an early fascination with electricity and spent hours constructing crystal radio sets and tuning in to programs from around the world. Academically, he possessed above average intelligence. He attained second place among the school's 106 students who had sat for the Intermediate Certificate, receiving A passes in four subjects and B passes in maths and business principles.[66]

Pat enrolled at Fort Street Boys' High School in February 1934 and remained for eight months. Although he obtained satisfactory passes in all subjects during his short time there and his Intermediate results indicated he would have done well if he sat for the Leaving Certificate, he left to take up employment as a junior stock clerk with A. Saunders Watchmaker, Jewellers, and Optician, in George Street, Sydney (whose shop front, incidentally, had been designed by Bray & Holliday).[67]

Who knows if Saunders's took advantage of Pat's mathematical and business skills? What is known is that Pat did not see himself as a clerk forever. An old friend, Jock Goodwin, recalled that 'Pat was always interested in flying as a schoolboy' and had constructed balsa-wood model aeroplanes in his bedroom. He was also an avid reader of the exploits of the premier Great War pilots from both sides of the conflict, including Oswald Boelcke, and Edward 'Mick' Mannock, who he considered 'the best of all the British pilots in the war'. As he grew older, his fascination for models and admiration of his aerial heroes translated to something more substantial. He wanted to take to the air himself, and his brother William encouraged him to join the air force. He did not need much persuasion. After all, he believed it would 'be the thing in [a] couple of years'. He found his way to Sydney Airport, where he took 'two passenger flights' with enough time in the air – in his mind at least – to qualify as flying experience.[68]

2

RAAF cadets

'Admirably adapted to the hazardous life of an airman'

The RAAF regularly advertised cadetships for training at 1 Flying Training School, Point Cook, welcoming applications from candidates who would have attained their 18th birthday by a certain date but were less than 22 years old and had achieved the Intermediate Certificate or similar qualification, with physics, elementary science and mathematics as compulsory subjects. After completing their cadetships, the new pilots could be appointed to short service commissions of four years in the RAAF or five in the RAF.

Once his mind was made up to join the RAAF, Dick Glyde needed a few years' savings behind him, as the cost of physical training gear, winter and summer underwear, evening shoes, dinner jacket, grooming items and the civilian clothes a cadet was expected to have was steep. In addition, the active cadet had to participate in a range of sports, including cricket, football, golf, tennis, baseball and swimming, which all required appropriate kit. He worked at Perpetual Trustees for three years and, with a healthy bank balance, applied for a cadetship in 1933.

Armed with birth certificate, academic qualifications, and character and educational references, Dick faced an interview board and elaborated on his sporting achievements. He was asked his reasons for wanting to join the air force and was assessed for 'intelligence, accuracy, general alertness, quickness of observation', 'personality' and 'general promise of fitness for service'. In late 1933 he was advised that he had been selected for training. After dreaming of flying for so long, he was on his way.[1]

Dick joined 1 Flying Training School's 15 Course, in January 1934, shortly before his 20th birthday. Within two weeks, he was in the air, initially as a passenger and then at the controls under the watchful eyes of an instructor. He was the first on his course to solo, after 5 hours of dual instruction.[2]

Dick had little time to experience the joy of solo flight, as he was discharged medically unfit for further service on 5 March 1934. His conduct and character up to that time had been good, but a medical examination picked up a slight spinal curvature. It was not debilitating – he had not even noticed it. But it was enough to bar him from further service training.[3]

Over 1000 young men responded to the 1935 advertisements for RAAF cadetships. Pat Hughes, Des Sheen, Stuart Walch and Jack Kennedy were among the elite called for interview. Not all anxiously awaited the results. When Jack was escorted from the interview room, he was patted on the back and told, 'You'll do all right, son'. He was so close mouthed he had not even hinted to his family that he was keen on aviation and they had no idea he had applied for a cadetship. When the letter from Air Board arrived they were completely surprised. Even so, they shared his excitement at the news that he was going to join the RAAF. His sister, Beryl, was exhilarated: her brother was going to fly! Jack may have kept his aviation interest a secret but there was something about his personality, even at school, that indicated he was well suited to the life of a pilot. Perhaps it was his prowess as a tough rugby forward that led to the opinion that he was 'admirably adapted to the hazardous life of an airman, being utterly devoid of fear and cool and resourceful in every emergency'.[4]

Pat Hughes entertained no doubts that he would be accepted by the RAAF. He had a strong sense of self that ranged from a false but comedic modesty – when one of his siblings presented the world with another welcome addition he thought the newest member of his family had better be 'strong and healthy to stand up to the shock of having an uncle like me' – to supreme confidence. He was certain he would be offered a cadetship. How could the RAAF resist taking on someone who was 'above the average in intelligence' and 'honest', whose 'conduct and attendance have been satisfactory'? Not to mention all that flying experience – those two joy flights – and the ability to drive a car as testament to his technical qualifications. He may have had only a 'fair' personality but he was 'a good type' and 'might develop' some 'general promise of fitness for service'. The RAAF couldn't possibly let such a promising candidate go, so when he was formally advised in December 1935 that he would join 19 Course in January 1936 (subject to dental treatment), he headed the first entry in his new diary 'The Chronicles of Hughes Junior: Air Cadet in Air Force (naturally)'.[5]

'Broken to discipline'

'17 January 1936. Fateful day. Left home.' Pat Hughes's family and friends accompanied him to Sydney's Central Railway Station (which was opposite his former workplace) and loaded him and luggage onto the 8.20 p.m. train for Melbourne. Goodbyes within a close family were difficult enough at the best of times, and Pat hoped the train would be late, allowing him a few extra moments with 'the best family in the world'. But 'fate was unkind'. As he settled into his carriage, 'the train wheels rattled in furious rhythm to my own thoughts and what jumbled ones they were … I don't think I fully realised just what it meant to be enrolled in the Royal Australian Air Force'. Anticipating what his future career would bring, Pat admitted, 'This is one day that I guess the outward calm of yours truly deserted me'.[6]

Point Cook's cadets came from diverse backgrounds, and as Pat looked over his fellow trainees on 20 January they seemed to be 'a very motley crowd'. His initial assessment, however, was far from accurate. As well dressed as anyone wanting to make a good impression on the first day of the rest of their lives, none looked particularly motley, including Des Sheen, finally released from servitude in the prime minister's office. But perhaps Pat was referring to himself when he disparaged the appearance of the freshly minted cadets. For one thing, a spattering of acne marred his face. For another, his salary was not large and he would have had difficulty affording the full range of accoutrements required by the RAAF. It had been all family hands on deck to help outfit him. His sister-in-law Ruby – who had married his brother Fred in 1927 – was a theatre costume designer. She could sew anything from overcoats to pyjamas and soon found herself responsible for part of Pat's wardrobe, including a warm dressing gown. Gordon Olive of Brisbane saw nothing of the homespun about Pat. He noticed a 'big, well-built fellow with more boisterous life in him than anyone I have ever met. [He] just loved life and lived it at high pressure'.[7]

The new cadets were assigned their quarters, allotted positions in the mess, introduced to their instructors and allocated to flights. Pat initially missed his close family, but he soon found that 'homesickness is going, even though very slowly and I am surprisingly making several good friends'.[8] Recognising that the cadets hailed from all strata of society and that few would have had any experience of military training, the instructors launched into a levelling process that would ultimately develop strong bonds and air force spirit among a bunch of disparate personalities. Pat and his new friends learned to salute, and their drill corporal brooked no defiance. They were also at the mercy of the good or ill will of their instructors. The cadets' uniforms may have given them cachet in the Melbourne shops – as Pat discovered on weekend leave – but at Point Cook they soon found they were 'the lowest form of animal life in the commissioned ranks, both mentally and morally'. This was reinforced by institutionalised 'fagging', where the juniors were expected to be lackeys for the seniors, running their messages and cleaning their rooms.

There were constant rules, supervision and prescribed activity. Pat and his course mates crammed in 2 hours of compulsory sport each day. He did not at first appreciate having his precious free time impinged upon, but when he was assured of a place in the football team, he was 'very proud and pleased as the rugby players are treated as tough lads you know, and anyway, it is something to do'.

It wasn't long before the cadets became fed up with hours of drill, and by 24 January, Pat had had enough of 'the damn corporal who by the beard of the prophet had the callousness to drill me for 7 hours 5 minutes. Woe's my middle name'. And he was not the only one. 'Abject misery is stamped forever it seemed on some faces.' Things did not improve. But three days later, after the cadets endured another '4 hours of backache and drill', Pat started to see the sense in it: 'It all goes in being a man, but it was hard to take today. Positively the worst day so far'.

Before Pat knew it, the days of 'abject misery' had passed and he found himself 'being broken to discipline'. With tongue firmly in cheek, he recorded that despite the 'rules and rubbish we hope to emerge into a clearer and happier atmosphere … to take our place amongst that highly honoured body of men who pass under the grouping of officers of the RAAF'. In the meantime, 'we show as much good nature as possible and try very hard to succeed'. And they would have to try, as their course load, with its 23 textbooks, was heavy, though not particularly arduous.[9] As well as flying instruction, they would be examined in ground subjects, including airmanship, law and discipline, theory of flight, meteorology, signals, air navigation, semaphore and armament. They worked 14 hours a day, 80 hours a week, as the training school strove to produce officer pilots in one year to the same standard as the RAF's short service commission pilots who had undertaken a two-year course at the RAF (Cadet) College, located at Cranwell, Lincolnshire.

In Pat's eyes, at least, things were looking up by 28 January, 'a heartening day, life is becoming less complex. The living is good. The people are good, the privileges are few but enough and life seems fair'. By the end of the month, they had learned 'to carry and march ourselves in the air force manner'.

'The brunt of it fell upon our nude bodies'

From 1923, in an effort to create a more professional standing for its officer corps, the RAAF recruited graduates from the Royal Military College, Duntroon, on secondment and eventual permanent transfer. Those officers drew on their army training to influence the development of a service ethos at Point Cook. They brought with them significant army traditions, including the Sword of Honour, awarded at graduation to the best cadet, and the appointment of cadet under-officers who assumed leadership responsibilities such as the daily discipline of cadets – Stuart Walch would be appointed one. The weekly formal dining session, which Pat Hughes dubbed the 'stiff-backed ceremony of dinner night', was another such tradition. On those occasions, all officers wore their mess uniform and dined with the cadets. The president and vice-president presided, the King was toasted, and the cadets were served a five-course meal and allowed beer.[10] The novelty of this tradition soon wore off, especially as the cadets could not leave the anteroom – which resembled a gentlemen's club – until the president had retired, thus curtailing their already limited study time.

While the pomp and ceremony became for Pat, at least, a 'complete dreary routine', away from the table there was general encouragement of energetic behaviour to let off steam. Dick Cohen, one of the senior cadets from 18 Course – which had started in July 1935 and now overlapped 19 Course – recalled the usual sorts of silly games, 'cock-fighting' and early morning high-speed motorcycle races round the oval. Pat was not one for standing back from pranks and misdeeds. For instance, there was the time he and his friends debagged one of their fellow cadets and threw the unfortunate victim's trousers over the rafters of the anteroom. On another occasion, 'everyone tried to get drunk … but the beer ran out'. And one day, Pat 'tore things up generally'. It was 'juniors versus seniors in the anteroom. Blood and thunder and plenty of wrecking of rooms'.[11]

One tradition imported from Duntroon was livelier. Point Cook's initiation ceremony had been practised since at least 1931. Over the years, it evolved to include elements of bullying and became less about fun and acceptance and more of a secondary selection process. Those whom the seniors did not consider suitable were identified and either hounded out, repressed or toughened up. The rationale was that if a cadet could not cope with the harsher extremes of horseplay he could not cope with air force life or the future stresses of an operational squadron. Harsh, but it was condoned and considered an important part of service life.[12]

The initiation for 19 Course was held on the night of 31 January 1936. The 'seniors devised a very complicated ceremony, and needless to say', noted Pat, 'the brunt of it fell upon our nude bodies'. The seniors daubed the juniors' naked bodies with so much duco that Pat thought the supply would have been 'pretty low after it'. Then, they were paraded to the lily pond for 'a splash in the muddy murk', after which the bedraggled cadets were herded inside and, 'standing each in his turn, on a table in the anteroom ... had to sing a song, preferably disgusting'. Pat could not carry a single tuneful note but 'needless to say passed easily'.[13]

'Today was the day I flew splendidly'

Initiation ceremony over, it was time to get down to the serious business of learning to fly. Pat's course was divided into two flights. One, which included Pat, trained on de Havilland Moths. The other, which included Des Sheen, took to the air in Avro Cadets. The Moth had come on strength in 1930 and proved adequate, but the Avro Cadet, recently arrived from England, was considered to be one of the most efficient trainers of the time. Des took his first instructional flight on 3 February. He practised taxiing and discovered the effects of the controls. The next day he moved onto straight and level flying. He had little trouble with the Avro Cadet; he thought flying came naturally to him and the Avro 'very pleasant to fly'.[14]

It was a good thing he learned to fly so easily. The trainees were fully aware that they were allowed a certain number of hours' dual before going solo. If not deemed natural pilots, they were scrubbed. Two weeks before he soloed, Pat Hughes confessed to his diary that his 'flying was worse than terrible. I don't know what's the matter. I can't even fly straight much less land a plane safely'. Pressure was not exclusively the province of the instructors. When 20 Course lined up for their first flights, Pat, perhaps recalling his own difficulties, did not expect much from them: 'We will see some fun, perhaps. They may even be worse than we were'.[15]

Neither Des's nor Pat's individual flying evaluations exist. However, Jack Kennedy's first term assessment does. Along with Stuart Walch, Jack joined 20 Course on 15 July 1936, and his course notes give an indication of the stresses involved for any cadet taking to the air for the first time. Flight Lieutenant

Wallace Hart Kyle was Jack's first instructor. Kyle, a Western Australian who had graduated from Cranwell and returned to Australia on an exchange with the RAAF, had high standards. He initially found Jack 'a bit dull. Jerky with control at present. Fair effort at straight and level'.[16] His judgement of Jack's second flight was not much better. During the 45-minute session, he was 'very heavy handed and footed', and Kyle noted 'not much progress at present'. Jack had not improved by his third flight, when Kyle found him 'definitely slow and forgetful. Swings like hell taking off'. But all was not lost. Kyle considered that Jack was 'very keen'.

Jack progressed seemingly one step forward, two steps backward over the next weeks. After a few days out of the air, his take-off was better and he made a fair attempt at turns. He soon displayed further improvement on take-off, but his medium turns were only fair and he was still jerky with the controls. He continued to forget some of the basics, but Kyle discerned a 'great improvement on both landings and take-off, even if tail a little high'. But progress was short lived. Kyle recorded that Jack was 'very rough and hamfisted'. He 'tried to taxi with brake full on', and his 'judgement in approaches very low. Unless some improvement is shown soon I'm afraid he won't make it'.

Kyle must have spoken to Jack about his progress, because within a few days the cadet's low flying was 'quite accurate', his landings were good, and although he displayed erratic gliding speeds on approach he was getting better. More positive comments followed, but Kyle thought Jack's judgement was 'still hopeless'. The ups and downs continued. On the same day as a 'great improvement' on a flight with Kyle, another instructor considered Jack was 'rushing into turns. Judgement poor. Holding off too high'.

Kyle's early assessments indicated his doubts about any natural ability that Jack might possess, but within a few weeks he

41

found that Jack was 'really flying quite accurately' with 'very good landings'. Kyle then decided that, after 9 hours 40 minutes' dual – carried out over 17 sessions within a month – it was time Jack took the controls on his own. Kyle thought his pupil's effort a 'very good first solo'. The excitement must have gone to Jack's head, because his next flight, with Kyle back in the instructor's seat, saw him overshoot the designated landing point twice. Overall, this flight was 'not quite so good', and although Jack 'used his engine intelligently' Kyle 'thought it wise not to send him solo again today'.

Jack's assessments do not indicate the euphoria he must have felt when he finally flew solo, but Pat Hughes recorded his. On 11 March 1936, he began that day's diary entry 'Solo' and wrote, 'Today was the day I flew splendidly'. He 'did some corker landings in succession' with Squadron Leader Francis Bladin, the officer in charge, Cadet Squadron. 'Then, to my delirium', Bladin climbed out. 'I flew off and around for 20 minutes and it is quite unnecessary and impossible to tell how I felt. I went mad, whistled, sang and almost jumped for joy.'[17]

As with Jack, his newfound skill then seemed to abandon him. The next day was 'hellish', so bad that 'flying with an instructor after going solo seemed a blessing'. He couldn't do a thing right. 'One damn bump after another. Tried some forced landings to such a reckless extent the poor old instructor couldn't say a word. I damn near hit a fence about 20 times.'[18]

The pressure was on to solo by 10 hours. How did the cadets fare? Gordon Olive soloed after 5 hours 20 minutes. Des Sheen took 8 hours 20 minutes. Pat's nervousness got the better of him and he had to endure his instructor's presence for 14 hours 45 minutes. Interestingly, given Pat's predictions about the capability of the 20 Course juniors, the fastest to solo did so after 4 hours. Stuart Walch, however, took 11 hours 5 minutes, and Jack Kennedy was right on the course average of 9 hours 40 minutes.[19]

By 10 March, eight from 19 Course had flown solo, and with the exception of six pupils flying training was progressing well. Instructors were able to discriminate between apprehension and lack of talent, but they made it clear that unless the six picked up their game, their days were numbered. And so they were. Des Sheen recalled that they, and one more, 'were very rapidly eliminated'.[20]

Once the solo barrier was smashed the cadets started to come into their own. Pat Hughes was overtaken by an almost overweening trust in his own ability. Less than a month after his solo, he 'felt rather confident' so 'screamed' his Moth 'flat out at 150 miles an hour and tore around a couple of loops'. It was a 'great' feeling. 'The thought that perhaps the wings may fall off is quite exhilarating even though disturbing.' He was willing to take the risk, however. 'I'm young and unmarried.'[21]

'Vale cadet'

Training accidents were inevitable. Point Cook had had its fair share of fatal ones over the years, and on 16 April 1936, the 19 Course cadets experienced their first service death. Although it was a 'fearful day, blowy and gusty', flying training went ahead. Nineteen-year-old Norman Chaplin of Ormond, in Melbourne, who had already notched up 25 flying hours, had been flying solo and practising aerobatics when one of his Moth's wings crumpled as he came out of a loop. As his fellow trainees watched, Chaplin jumped from the diving aircraft, but his parachute did not open fully. He was fatally injured and died shortly afterwards.[22]

Chaplin, 'a quiet gentlemanly lad', was well liked by his class mates. Pat Hughes recorded Chaplin's death bluntly: 'Bloody awful. First death. Boys are taking it pretty badly'. That night, the officers, who had witnessed many training deaths, 'put on a show in the mess', and although Pat considered 'it has taken the sting out of things, the thought of Chaplin's death still hangs around'. In a touching conclusion to his diary entry, he wrote, 'Vale Cadet'.[23]

When a Wapiti crashed into high-tension wires in August 1935, throwing free the instructor before bursting into flames and incinerating the cadet, one of his course mates recalled that it didn't seem to have any adverse effects.[24] That was the way it was for 18 Course, 19 Course, and every other course. After the initial shock, there was no time to dwell on the accident because the instructors kept the dead cadet's class mates constantly on the go. Just as they drilled them into a ready acceptance of the strictures of service life, so too did they school their charges to recognise that fatalities were inevitable. The young man's death would be marked and honoured, but the official attitude was to carry on and leave it behind.

It was business as usual the day after Chaplin's death, with flying tests, formation flying, stall turns and loops. This stance was reinforced on operational squadrons when empty seats at the table were filled and the committee of adjustment removed personal kit from quarters. Some squadrons did not even record a combat death in their daily summaries. Des Sheen learned to be pragmatic: 'Most squadrons had accidents and we lost a couple of pilots in various ways but I think we all accept that as quite normal really. Way of life'.[25]

Even so, Pat Hughes still appeared to be rattled. He 'flew like a mad woman's hair on a windy day – all over the place', then 'broke up at about 3000 feet, about 150 miles per hour in a vertical dive. Stall turns, loops, frightened hell out of Jackson ... Just gives me an idea of the riskiness of air fighting'. It was almost as if he were pushing himself to the limits of safety.

Chaplin was buried with full ceremonial honours on 18 April, and by Monday 20 April, after a weekend off during which the cadets acted the goat by playing chariot races with the easy chairs in the mess, Pat thought 'the effects of Chaplin's death are wearing off completely. The boys are coming through OK'. Perhaps so, but Pat managed to have an 'unlucky' outing the next day. After chasing another trainee out to sea, he careened down to 'the deck' and 'turned up on my nose in A7-40', or, as the casualty report had it, landed 'out of wind in bumpy conditions'.[26] Was he still shaken by Chaplin's death or again pushing the limits? However long it took to get over, Pat and his friends were becoming inured to the prospect of service death and the possibility of their own. As Pat put it, 'What's what is what'.

'Try and do something special'

Pat continued to push the boundaries. He bought a cane-handled feather duster and hid it in his suitcase. 'When the corporal was searching the bags for beer ... I opened mine and the duster sprung out. Frightened hell out of the corporal. Thought it was a bloody cobra!' A few days later, he expected 'a drill for not cleaning my room or polishing my floor tonight but I'm too damn tired'. The next week, he 'strained a poor old Moth by climbing to 9000 feet up above the clouds ... I span down ... for about 4000 feet and then did stall turns without my engine'. It was 'tough on the plane', but even so, 'I must try it as soon as possible again'.

Pat felt frustrated at the training syllabus, his progress, the strictures of RAAF rules and life in general. He vented his irritation as rowdily as possible. On one occasion a 'pillow fight and a bucket of water helped liven somebody else's dreary existence' and was followed the next day, after Pat had been bored witless during an early session on signals, by his spending the 'entire morning playing practical jokes on friends', and afterwards 'a concerted attack on the water supply in the form of a glorious water fight'. He would hide the bedclothes of a course mate for the sheer hell of it, and on occasion he was so pent up that, feeling like 'the proverbial ball of muscle', he would head into the mess 'to start a fight'.

With so much vibrant but disruptive energy, it is no wonder Pat was eventually charged with 'conduct to the prejudice of good order and air force discipline' after he was caught talking during a lecture and, even when checked by his instructor, continued to disrupt the class. He was confined to barracks for three days to cool his heels.[27] He didn't have a high opinion of the 'fat, illiterate little swine' who laid the charge, but 'I suppose I deserved it'. He was not, however, impressed with the punishment: 'Can't read the papers, have to report like a paroled convict', and he couldn't appear in the anteroom until meals began. However, he facetiously noted that he was able to take advantage of the extra 10 minutes this restriction afforded him to 'sit down and meditate on my crimes'.

By 10 June 1936, the junior term for 19 Course was drawing to a close. After a three-week mid-course break, they graduated to the Wapiti.[28] Pat, who was 'itching to start flying again', considered them 'colossal big things like farmhouses. About as big and as clumsy'. When he had his opportunity to give them a go, he found they were 'kind old aeroplanes' but could 'get bloody cranky if we do anything we shouldn't'. Pat's Wapiti solo was a mixed success. He considered it a 'stinking effort but the flight lieutenant who tested me was pretty decent so I'm off in less than 2 hours, which is supposed to be pretty good'.

After covering the basics during their junior term, the cadets had to apply the theory and their earlier experiences to the processes of war. They began formation flying in earnest, went 'under the hood' – where a canvas hood was pulled over the cockpit – to learn instrument flying so they could fly at night or through thick cloud, and mastered the art of high-altitude flying. They also practised dive-bombing and air-to-ground gunnery. Even with the emphasis on training for prospective warfare, and given an increasingly more threatening political situation in Europe, Des Sheen, for one, was oblivious to a likely war.[29]

Towards the end of their course, the cadets were given the choice of joining the RAAF or the RAF. At his cadetship interview, Pat Hughes had nominated the RAAF because he preferred service in Australia, but by mid-August he was reconsidering: 'Talked heaps about going to England. I think I have made my mind up to go and try and do something special'. But he was confused. 'I'm damned if I know what I'm going to do!' He was still undecided by 27 August, when he was 'nearly talked … into going to England again tonight. Painted a fascinating picture of easy life, beer and women'. But it seemed as if personal choice might not come into it. The RAF had started expanding vigorously in response to the increasing threat from Nazi Germany, and by October 1936, Australia had agreed to increase its short service commission commitment for embarkation in 1937 to 50 a year.[30] The 19 Course cadets were the first to feel the impact of this decision. 'They say 25 cadets are going', recorded Pat, 'so it looks as though I might be going against my will. But speaking of wills, I think it is willed that I would (go to England, I mean)'.

In October, when a final decision was imminent, Pat mused that 'I would like to go [to Blighty] very much, travel and all that but being away from home for so long appears to be the worst part'. Des Sheen had no doubts. He wanted to go to England to fly. He felt it 'was a good time to go and see a bit of the world and see the old country'.[31]

The cadets completed their training by 27 November 1936. The air work standard was considered to be a 'fair average', with fewer below average pupils than in the previous course, and overall the ground work standard was considered above average. Des, with 73.2 per cent, was 16th on the course and was given an above average rating in 'proficiency as pilot on type'. Pat may have considered Mannock to be the best of the Great War pilots, but he failed to take out the Mannock Cup in the flying competition for the best all-round pupil. After 37 hours 15 minutes' solo on the Wapiti (on top of 17 hours 55 minutes' dual), he was assessed as only 'average' and would benefit from 'occasional checking'. He received 78.7 per cent for qualities as a pilot and 74.4 per cent for war organisation and tactics, but only 60.0 per cent for qualities as an officer. He was recommended to fly 'medium types' of aircraft and ranked 28th in the class. Overall, he was considered 'energetic and keen' but with 'no outstanding qualities'.[32]

On 9 January 1937, Pat Hughes, Des Sheen and their fellow graduates destined for the RAF (including Gordon Olive and Richard Power, who would also fly in the Battle of Britain) boarded the elderly P&O liner RMS *Narkunda*. Six months later, on 17 July, Jack Kennedy – 27th in his course, with 66.7 per cent – arrived at No. 5 Wharf at Pyrmont, in Sydney. He was accompanied by his parents, his sister, Beryl, his grandmother, a friend of his mother's and an old school friend. He bade them farewell and boarded the Orient Royal liner RMS *Orama*. Twelve other New South Welshmen from 20 Course also embarked, and Beryl Kennedy remembered waving ribbons at the ship as it slowly moved from the wharf. Stuart Walch – 14th in his course, with 71.7 per cent – and those from other states would join them in a few days.[33] The Point Cook boys' great adventure had begun.

3

The great adventure

Fighter training 'was my choice'

In Des Sheen's opinion, Australia was a good place to learn to fly and he had been taught by experienced instructors. Accordingly, he and his fellow pilots bound for England expected to receive operational postings when they arrived. The RAF, however, considered that the cadets had been trained on obsolescent aircraft by men lacking in flying experience.[1] To make up for the seeming deficiencies, the RAF sent the Australians to advanced training schools after a two-week stint at RAF Uxbridge, the home of Fighter Command's 11 Group, about 20 miles from London. There they learned to drill all over again, were taught the administrative duties young officers would be expected to carry out and experienced mess protocol RAF-style.

After Uxbridge, Des Sheen, who had been issued with RAF service number 39474, was sent to 3 Flying Training School, Grantham, in Lincolnshire. There he was introduced to the Hawker Hart light bomber and Audax (a Hart variant). He then went to 9 Flying Training School, Thornaby, north Yorkshire, on 22 March 1937, where he was tutored on the Hawker Fury fighter. Despite the RAF's perception of the quality of the RAAF's syllabus, he did not see too many differences between his training at Point Cook and at Thornaby: 'The system was the same ... It was just based on the same principles'.[2]

During the advanced program, instructors assessed their students' personality traits and skills to channel them towards fighter, bomber or other more prosaic but essential flying duties. Budding fighter pilots were audacious, had nerve and were disciplined enough to fly the rigid formations favoured by the air force at the time. A demonstrated aerobatic ability hinted at a nascent capacity to operate in all dimensions. Great War aerial combat experiences had shown how vital it was to be able to look up, down, in front and behind seemingly all at the same time. Fighter pilots had to judge distance, speed and time. They had to anticipate the enemy and position themselves to the greatest advantage. Above all, they had to trust their aircraft as well as their instinct and ability.

Instructors also had to discern whether a trainee had the 'killer instinct'. A clinical ability to overlook the humanity of an enemy pilot separated the successful operational pilot and potential ace from the merely competent. It could not be taught. It could be acquired only during combat. Even so, instructors would have been on the lookout for young men of focus, coordination and determination, a good eye, lightning reactions and a healthy aggression displayed on the sporting field.

After comparing the relative merits of the bomber and fighter aircraft during advanced training, Des realised he was attracted to fighters. He thought they were 'lively and energetic and manoeuvrable, a bit more exciting'. On 30 June 1937, he was posted to 72 Squadron and attached to B Flight. Located at Church Fenton, halfway between York and Leeds, in Yorkshire, the squadron was equipped with the Gloster Gladiator biplane. Des was 'quite happy to be given a posting as a fighter pilot'. Fighter training 'was my choice'. Even though the Gladiator was outmoded, Des thought it 'a lovely little aeroplane ... It was a beautiful aeroplane to fly and very manoeuvrable and I liked it'.[3] He became so fond of K6143 that he commissioned a watercolour of it in flight.

In December 1938, another Australian joined 72 Squadron. Like Des, Squadron Leader Ronald Lees had graduated from Point Cook. He had accepted a short service commission in the RAF on 18 March 1931 and one week later received a posting to 29 Squadron. In May 1935, while Des was counting the months until he turned 18 and could apply for RAAF training, Lees had been sent to 4 Flying Training School, Abu Sueir, as an instructor and during 1937 had spied on secret Luftwaffe training activities in Egypt. Des and his new commanding officer enjoyed a bond other than a common training experience: Lees had developed his aerial zeal after seeing Bert Hinkler in Adelaide during the record-breaking pilot's round-Australia tour in 1928.[4]

Fighter Command's complement of pilots hailed from all parts of the former empire, and almost every squadron had at least one pilot representing Britain's allies. 'We had people from England, Canada, there was myself and a New Zealander', Des recalled. There was always 'a lot of hilarity and a lot of fun'. Those of different nationalities worked together 'extremely well'. In such an affable squadron – Des endeared himself to the ground crew when he took a group of them for their first flight – there was little conflict, and what there was, was mainly good natured: 'There was a lot of taking the mickey out of each other, but it was all very friendly. Good sports'.[5]

After spending 12 months together at Point Cook, Des Sheen and Pat Hughes had parted company after their brief stint at RAF Uxbridge. While Des found his way to Grantham, Pat, who had been issued with RAF service number 39461, made his way to Lincolnshire along with Gordon Olive and settled into 2 Flying Training School, Digby. The school was equipped with the rugged two-seat Avro Tutor initial trainer, Harts, Audaxes and Furies. Pat perfected his flying skills but maintained his reputation as a joker, including the time he and some friends erected a toilet – complete with pedestal, seat, cistern and chain – outside a pub. The landlord was none too pleased and the local constabulary were called in. Thanks to Olive's quick talking, Pat avoided being hauled away. But Pat wasn't overly grateful for his friend's intervention. He believed a cell would have been warmer than the accommodation at Digby and demanded to be locked up.

Pat wanted to be a fighter pilot, but at the end of his advanced training he was disappointed to learn he had been categorised on bombers. Most would have been happy with such a posting, because bomber squadrons were considered the 'sexy' postings – pilots accepted the prevailing belief that success in any future war would hinge on a sound bomber offensive. Even if they weren't happy with their posting they would not usually dispute it. Des Sheen, for example, knew he had little choice and so was prag-matic about it: 'I would have gone to bombers'. Pat did not bow to the inevitable. He successfully appealed and in June 1937 was sent to 64 Squadron, a fighter unit located at RAF Martlesham Heath, Suffolk's oldest airfield.[6] There he familiarised himself with the Hawker Demon fighter. A variant of the Hart light bomber, it was designed as an interim fighter until dedicated high-performance aircraft could be brought on line.

While Pat and Des Sheen enjoyed their first few months in operational squadrons, Jack Kennedy and Stuart Walch were aboard the RMS *Orama*. After landing in England, they both reported to RAF Uxbridge on 26 August 1937. They were sworn in as members of the RAF. Des and Pat had kept their RAAF uniforms, but Jack could not wait to put his in mothballs. He was fitted for a dress uniform by a Savile Row tailor who presented the sort of account you would expect from a top-flight establish-ment. Jack took it to the station adjutant's office and borrowed the 'officer deceased' stamp. He inked it up and pressed down firmly. The tailor was evidently wise to this sort of trick: he had obtained next-of-kin details at Jack's first appointment. He forwarded the invoice to John Kennedy, who paid it.[7]

Jack was issued with service number 40052 at Uxbridge, and Stuart, who also donned the RAF uniform, received number 40063. From there, their training paths diverged. Jack was posted to 1 Flying Training School, Leuchars, in Scotland, arriving on 6 September. On 19 December, he was sent to 65 Squadron at RAF Hornchurch, an important 11 Group station in Essex, within easy striking distance of London. There, like Des Sheen, he flew the Gladiator. When he arrived he again met Gordon Olive, who had completed his advanced training at Digby. They were both posted to A Flight. Jack fitted in well with his new friends and discovered a more laid-back atmosphere than that at Point Cook. There was lots of flying practice, including formation flying and aerobatics. Just over 12 months earlier, he had been assessed as 'self-satisfied and too sure of himself. Needs constant checking'. He had improved so much that he was dubbed '*The* Kennedy'.[8]

Meanwhile, Stuart was briefly sent to RAF Northolt, another key 11 Group station near London, before arriving at 11 Flying Training School, Wittering, in Cambridgeshire, on 18 September 1937. Wittering had a number of Hawker Hinds, Harts, Audaxes and Furies among its complement of training aircraft. Next stop was 151 Squadron, based at 11 Group's RAF North Weald, near Epping, in Essex, which was equipped with the Gloster Gauntlet. After arriving on 8 January 1938, Stuart lost no time in acquainting himself with the fighter aircraft.

He began collecting Players' cigarette cards, which featured pictures of RAF aircraft and accompanying technical details. He purchased an album to mount his collection and glued in the cards. Then, he 'marked with an X the aircraft I have merely flown for a short time', like the Hind, and indicated 'the ones I have had experience on', such as the Gauntlet. He sent the album to his young niece back in Australia with a brief note: 'Dearest Ann, I

Stuart Walch's Players' cigarette card album. Courtesy of Ann Walter via John Walch

thought you might like to have this album of aircraft of the Royal Air Force'. He suggested to Ann that 'Gramps would like to see it too'. He dispatched photos to his parents so they would have some sense of his air force life. Percival Walch proudly hung one on his office wall.[9]

'The things they can do with an aeroplane'

On 18 May 1938, Pat Hughes joined his old Point Cook comrade Des Sheen in Yorkshire, when 64 Squadron transferred there from Martlesham Heath. They arrived just in time for the preparations for Empire Air Day, taking place at the end of the month.

In the week preceding Church Fenton's open day, the Australians practised 'thrilling displays' in 'their high-speed fighting planes'. Their exercises were covered by the local press, and Des was photographed with his squadron friends standing in front of their Gladiators.

The station's 'absorbing and spectacular' displays on 28 May attracted an estimated crowd of 15 000. Special trains from Leeds were laid on, and the crowds flocked to see the work of their local squadrons as well as a high-profile visitor, the Hurricane, 'one of the latest fighting planes', which had recently 'created a sensation' when it flew from Edinburgh to Northolt 'at an average speed of 410 miles per hour'. The program opened with formation flying, followed by aerobatics and a mock attack by three Demons. After a Hind was put through its aerobatic paces, nine of 64 Squadron's 'most skilful and daring pilots' carried out a dive-bombing exercise, squadron formation, air drills and a series of target attacks. A reporter summed up the exciting displays well: 'The things they can do with an aeroplane have to be seen to be believed'.

Next came Des Sheen and 72 Squadron, whose contribution to the day's excitement included aerobatics, three Gladiators attacking an Armstrong-Whitworth Whitley bomber and an air drill by five machines. At the conclusion of the day's breathtaking events, 30 of Church Fenton's fighters joined a formation of several hundred aircraft from the south of England and the Midlands that visited Leeds and York.[10]

'Preparations for mobilisation'

As well as providing an exciting day out, the 1938 Empire Air Day programs showed the public what Britain's air force could do. Hitler had recently pronounced – not for the first time – that Germany needed more living space (*Lebensraum*), and his eyes turned initially towards Austria and Czechoslovakia. An opinion poll had revealed that a third of Britons believed war was imminent. With the annexation of Austria – Anschluss – in March 1938 and Hitler's increasingly strident demands that the Germans in the Sudetenland be returned to Germany, it seemed their foresight had some basis. Des Sheen was one of those who concluded that Europe was fast reaching a war footing. He realised the inevitability of conflict was 'beginning to be in people's minds', and 'very soon things did get pretty dicey'.[11]

The RAF kept a close eye on Germany's mounting aggression. Shortly after Jack Kennedy's 21st birthday, on 29 May 1938, the Hornchurch squadrons participated in a week-long full-strength war mobilisation exercise. It included alerts, air raid drills, mock air attacks and interception exercises, and 132 hours of night flying, which the squadron diarist believed was a record for fighter squadrons. They flew to RAF Aldergrove, in Northern Ireland, on 12 July for their annual two-week armament training camp, and each pilot expended an average of 6400 rounds from his Gladiator's four Browning guns. On 5 August, as their ground crew acquainted themselves with their recently issued gas masks, Jack and his fellow pilots united with other fighter squadrons, Bomber Command, the observer corps and anti-aircraft units in a new round of home defence exercises.[12]

War seemed closer than ever, and in September the Sudeten crisis, which had dominated the news for months, came to a head. As Germany looked set to invade Czechoslovakia, over 38 million gas masks were distributed to Britain's civilian population. Squadron personnel were recalled from leave. At Church Fenton, Des Sheen was promoted to flying officer on 19 September, and 72 Squadron's shiny Gladiators and 64 Squadron's silver Demons were covered in camouflage paint. Des, Pat Hughes and their confreres were grounded, 'owing to the grave international situation': flying was curtailed so 'preparations for mobilisation may be carried out'.[13]

Similar activity took place throughout Fighter Command. Down south at Hornchurch, 65 Squadron's Gladiators were daubed in drab brown and green. The station didn't have the appropriate machinery to load the ammunition belts, so Jack Kennedy and the other pilots helped the ground staff do it by hand. An intelligence officer came from Fighter Command and spoke about German aircraft, training exercises were taken more seriously, and Jack and his friends studied battle tactics closely. Flights took it in turns to be on readiness. Each day, one of Hornchurch's three squadrons was put 'on duty', flying above and around the airfield with live ammunition, prepared to intercept enemy aircraft.

As late as 29 September, the general population believed war would be declared on 1 October. When the Munich Agreement, a non-aggression pact with Germany, was announced and British prime minister Neville Chamberlain affirmed 'peace for our time', a relieved nation rejoiced. The RAF, however, did not relax. The Luftwaffe was already well equipped, and many of its pilots had – or were gaining – combat experience in Spain. In a sense, this period of uneasy peace was a blessing for the RAF, which took advantage of it to continue readying for war. But as the international crisis eased, squadrons were taken off alert, and on 3 October, Pat Hughes and 64 Squadron again embarked on a full training program.[14]

Looking back, Des Sheen was not convinced of the efficacy of his pre-war combat training, which consisted of constant practice of six rigid formation attacks. The most simple was fighter attack number one, in which the pilots moved from the 'vic', or v-shaped formation, into line astern – one behind the other – and fired in turn at the enemy bomber which was supposed to obligingly wait for them. After breaking away, they would reposition. The other strike formations were increasingly more complicated, with one modern commentator dismissing fighter attack number six, which dictated how the whole squadron dealt with nine enemy bombers, as 'so complex that it would be tedious and futile to describe it'. Des recalled that they were drilled to strike at large bomber formations and their attacks 'were designed for that purpose', but when the bombers were accompanied by 'escorts of 109s all those tactics were quite useless'.[15]

'A taste for scholarship'

In 1934, while the future Point Cook cadets had been continuing their education, or, in the case of Des Sheen, running messages in the prime minister's office, Dick Glyde had been consulting a physician. After his discharge from the RAAF in March 1934 because of a spinal curvature, he had rejected the apparent inevitability of never flying again. With steely determination he carried out the specialist's recommended exercise program, and within four months the defect had been 'completely remedied'. Another opportunity to fly would present itself, and Dick would be ready. In the meantime, proving there was nothing wrong with his back, he took to the dance floor at Guildford School's May ball and the St George's College ball.[16]

Reverend Robert Evelyn Freeth MA, the headmaster of Dick's alma mater – by that stage known as Guildford Grammar School – advertised for a temporary assistant master in the preparatory school. On 13 July 1934, Dick sent in an application along with his RAAF discharge papers, which attested to his good character. Without a Leaving Certificate he was not an obvious choice for even a junior teacher, but he had some merit. Freeth had long made a practice of placing responsibility in the hands of his captains, prefects and house sporting captains. He relied on them to virtually run the school out of hours, and senior boys held considerable disciplinary power. As a house prefect Dick had supervised the younger boys in their homework and ensured lights out at bedtime. This, along with his growing maturity, would have put him in good stead as a junior master. His sporting interests also would have made him an attractive candidate. Moreover, in his application, he mentioned that he was interested in obtaining additional qualifications as 'it is my desire to commence teaching as a career' and he had 'lately acquired a taste for scholarship which was lacking during my school days'.[17]

There is no evidence that Dick enrolled in any academic program, and his promptness in remedying the spinal problem indicated little desire to dedicate his life to teaching. It seems he simply framed his application to suit a potential employer. Even so, he did promise that 'should my application receive favourable consideration' he would be 'interested in every branch of my work' and would 'at all times further the interests of the school'. Freeth was desperate to fill the vacancy. He engaged Dick on a temporary basis just four days after his former pupil penned the application and thanked him for 'coming to our rescue at such short notice'.[18]

Dick continued to put in appearances at Perth's social occasions, such as the Bankers' ball at Government House, a masked costume dance and the Karrakatta Club ball. Off the dance floor, he played sport and, in addition to schoolboy cricket and track events, added tennis, football, shooting, swimming, boxing and riding to his athletic repertoire.[19] He also joined the Old Guildfordians' A2 grade hockey team. In one 'clean, fast and skilful game' in which the old boys were the underdogs, they beat Christian Brothers' College three to nil and Dick was deemed the best player. They later carried off the 1935 Premiership Cup.

His life was full, but he still found time to keep his promise to Freeth to further the interests of the school. In the past, Guildford, like other private schools, had had a strong cadet corps, but by the time Dick enrolled it had been all but abandoned. Recently, however, the military authorities had urged schools to revive their units, so Freeth committed to resurrecting Guildford's. It wasn't long before Dick, too, became involved, and his commission as a provisional lieutenant in the Australian Senior Military Cadets 5th Military District was gazetted on 30 April 1935.

The training syllabus included shooting, squad and guard drill and Lewis gun instruction. Dick had no military experience so borrowed some books from Freeth. He was put in charge of rifle exercises, and his cadets were successful in the 5th Division's 1935 Memorial Trophy competition, excelling in drill and physical training and taking the prize in the shooting section. He participated in a number of ceremonial events, including the guard of honour for the governor's visit to the school on the 1935 speech day, and he sat on the board of examiners for cadet promotions.[20]

Freeth was pleased with Dick's work and extended his employment beyond an initial review period. But circumstances at Guildford began to change. Student numbers fell during the Depression years and Freeth was forced to reduce expenditure. As 1936 advanced, he had to make more sacrifices. He told Dick that his employment would cease at the end of the first term. Dick understood and left Guildford Grammar with warm feelings towards Freeth. After all, his job had been only temporary, and regardless of his declaration that he wanted to undertake teacher training he still hankered after an air force career. The cadets were 'very sorry to lose … the services of Mr Glyde who spent a great deal of his time and energy in the interests of the corps'.[21]

'A good average pilot'

Dick soon found a job with the Temperance and General Life Assurance Society as an insurance agent, but he had no intention of staying long. During his time at Guildford, he had reapplied to the RAAF. Regardless of a clean bill of health, an active sporting interest and his work with the cadets, he was rejected.[22] He decided to give up on the RAAF; he would sail to England and join the RAF.

He celebrated his 23rd birthday on 29 January 1937, and on 20 February he boarded the British steam merchant *Brookwood*. He arrived at the Port of London on 15 April and within days set off for the Air Ministry at Adastral House to apply for a short service commission. After impressing the recruitment board, the Western Australian was ushered to his medical. The RAF doctors found no lingering signs of the spinal defect. Soon afterwards, Dick was advised that he had been accepted by the RAF, and as Pat Hughes and Des Sheen reached the end of their advanced training, he was posted to Hanworth, Surrey, on 24 May 1937, for initial training on Blackburn B-2 and Hart trainers.[23]

Over the next two or so months he notched up 50 hours' flying time, during which he learned, among other things, basic flight skills, cross-country navigation and aerobatics. Next stop was 24 (Training) Group, on 9 August 1937, where he was granted a short service commission in the General Duties Branch of the RAF for four years (with effect from 24 May 1937), with RAF service number 39983. Days later, he boarded the train to 3 Flying Training School, South Cerney, in east Gloucestershire – the school had recently relocated from Grantham – arriving on 23 August. Like Stuart Walch and Jack Kennedy, who would arrive at their flying training schools the following month, he was to join an advanced course.

As many failed advanced training as those did on elementary courses. Dick worked hard, and shortly after his final exams he read the results pinned to the lecture room noticeboard. Dick's instructor thought he had achieved a 'good all round result'. He acknowledged that his pupil was 'a natural disciplinarian' and considered him to be 'a good average pilot'.

Dick was authorised to wear his flying badge on 2 November 1937. Wings sown onto his tunic breast, he headed to 1 Anti-Aircraft Co-operation Unit, Farnborough, in Hampshire, on 26 March 1938. As a staff pilot on one of the towed target flights, he trailed drogues behind his aeroplane so anti-aircraft batteries could practise firing on them. It was necessary but uninspiring work, and Dick did not enjoy it. He transferred to RAF Stranraer, on the southern shore of Scotland's Loch Ryan, and was appointed liaison officer with the army.[24] This was short lived, and on 24 October 1938 he was posted to 87 Squadron, which was located at RAF Debden, in north Essex, about 40 miles north of London. He was to become a fighter pilot, like his hero McCudden and the glamorous airmen in *The Wonder Book of Aircraft*.

'Flies fighters'

RAF Debden was a well-appointed station, and Dick Glyde enjoyed the amenities offered, including fine grass tennis courts and hockey, football and rugby fields; in summer, the thwack of leather against willow was heard on the cricket pitch. He corresponded regularly with the secretary of the Old Guildfordians, who kept Dick's former school friends and pupils apprised of his activities. 'They have a good golf course [at Debden] and, better still, a fine variety of "old and mild" at the local tavern'. The secretary also recounted details of a recent outing on horseback where Dick obviously suffered from lack of practice. Apparently, 'Saffron Walden is an old Cromwellian town, but unfortunately the ground is a little hard when one falls from a horse'.

Dick's squadron had been under strength when he arrived and had only partially converted from Gladiators to Hurricanes. The Old Guildfordians soon read that 'in his spare time [Dick] flies fighters and aeroplanes in general'.[25] In truth, however, it was some time before Dick took the controls of 87 Squadron's new Hurricanes. He was allowed to study the manuals, sit in the cockpit and run his hands and eyes over the instrument panel and controls, but until he had flown at least 10 hours in a Gladiator, he was not permitted to fly one of the RAF's most advanced fighter aircraft.

Dick was allocated to B Flight and his flight commander
was Flight Lieutenant Robert Voase Jeff, with whom he shared a
billet.[26] Once he had acquired the requisite hours on the Gladiator he flew the Hurricane as often as possible. Squadron training
was constant and focused on aerobatics and formation flying in
which they rehearsed the RAF's basic fighter attacks. The pilots
also practised instrument flying as well as intercepts and attacks
on British aircraft and, occasionally, on French bombers during
joint exercises.

'Letter writing was never a strong point of mine'

Meanwhile, Jack Kennedy was honing his skills as *The* Kennedy
at Hornchurch, but when flying was not on the agenda he found
plenty of things with which to amuse himself. He kept up his
swimming and became involved in water polo, adding a few tro-
phies to his collection.[27] He acquired a black Lagonda sports car
and took it for spins in the countryside.

Like Dick, Jack fell into the rhythm of squadron life, but while
Dick was happy to tell family and friends of his experiences, Jack
hardly ever put pen to paper; he was having too good a time.
His parents constantly urged him to write, but Jack's letters home
were so infrequent that John Kennedy wrote to Stanley Bruce,
Australia's high commissioner to Great Britain, complaining that
he had not heard from his son. Bruce could do nothing about
the recalcitrant correspondent, so in desperation John turned to
the minister for Air, James Fairbairn, for information about the
well-being and whereabouts of his son. Although Fairbairn had
no responsibility for RAF officers he contacted the RAAF liaison
officer, who extracted a promise from Jack that he would write
to his family at once and reported that he 'regrets not doing so
before'. In addition, 'his commanding officer has been requested
to remind Kennedy periodically to write to his parents'. But Jack

did not write. His reluctance to pick up a pen, however, was not unusual. Pat Hughes joked to his family that 'letter writing was never a strong point of mine', but 'every now and then, when George RI can spare my time, I splash some ink in the direction of the Great South Land'. It wasn't from any great desire to share his news, however. It was 'mainly to serve as a reminder to the home folks that despite the colossal number of the family at home, there's still another one somewhere'.[28]

Pat thrived on squadron life. He ate well and enjoyed parties in the mess – but not necessarily the resultant hangovers that required copious doses of tomato juice the following morning. He submitted to the raucous voice of his batman echoing up to his room proclaiming that tea was ready and even 'got into the poisonous habit' of drinking it. It wasn't surprising that he was much too busy to write home and did so only when his mother told him there was a lot of sibling 'gnattering' about overdue letters.[29]

'The very best squadrons in the land'

Squadron Leader F. Victor Beamish, who had been posted to 64 Squadron as commanding officer in December 1937, was strongly committed to disciplined flying and over the next few months had the squadron practising fighter affiliation with searchlight battalions, night and formation flying, battle climbs and fighter exercises. Beamish's pilots were impressed by his attitude to training, and Pat especially became adept at formation flying.[30]

On 12 December 1938, Pat heard that the squadron would receive the fighter variant of the Bristol Blenheim, the Blenheim 1F. By 17 January 1939, the squadron was fully re-equipped. The pilots carried out fighter attack affiliation exercises over the next few weeks, and in April led seven squadrons in a massed flight over the Midlands. As usual, Pat couldn't find time to write home and was guilty of tardy congratulations on the marriage of his brother Charles and new sister-in-law Heather.[31]

Pat had been promoted to flying officer on 19 November 1938.[32] With promotion came responsibility. He often took on his flight commander's duties but was still as boisterous as ever. He enjoyed wild parties, and when he won a raw duck in the Christmas sweep he painted a swastika on its chest and hung it over the front doors of the mess. The weather was so icy it stayed there for three days without spoiling. He finally took it down and presented it to his batman.

If anything dampened Pat's spirits it was the Yorkshire weather. He had not adapted to the bitter northern climate and dreamed of the Australian sun. The thought of his sister Marjorie enjoying a summer holiday with Midge and her husband, Tom, at Kiama as he endured England's bleak 1938–39 winter almost gave him 'apoplexy'. He tried hard not to think of the scorching summer temperatures but was 'so damned cold I fear I shall crawl into a sleeping bag like a bear and hibernate'. He managed to 'gather my fleeing sanity together by thinking hard of things far removed from beaches and sun' by sucking on bits of sleet as they settled on his tongue.[33] But this did not always work. He felt that 'after living in an atmosphere of perpetual rain or smoke and fog' his soul was 'slowly shrivelling within me, my senses are becoming dulled to all normal beauties of life and I find myself becoming a terrific cynic'. He viewed the local families as 'either terribly county or else strict church goers'. The highlights were the odd game of tennis with 'the fair widows of the district', but their attractions were overshadowed by tedious 'evenings at home which consist of my slowly sipping a glass of muck after struggling through an incredibly indigestible dinner'. Then, the hostess would 'spring to her feet, clap her hands and exclaim, "I know let's play sardines" – Ye gods, our existence is limited'. But there was 'one consolation'. Pat knew full well he was 'in one of the very best squadrons in the land and we do tons and tons of flying in all kinds of weather so that keeps all the boys more or less occupied'.[34]

Stuart Walch was also in a fine squadron and was just as hard working as Pat. He increased his flying hours in the Gauntlet until 1 December 1938, when 151 Squadron's first Hurricane arrived. Some time later, the Hobart *Mercury* reported that Stuart 'was the first member of his squadron to fly a Hurricane fighter', but this assertion is not supported by the squadron's operations record book. That honour belonged to 151 Squadron's new commanding officer, Squadron Leader Edward Mortlock 'Teddy' Donaldson, who collected Hurricane L1724 from the Hawker Aircraft Company. Stuart's claim to being the first to fly 151 Squadron's Hurricanes might be unsubstantiated, but he was 'highly regarded by his senior officers'. He flew the Gauntlet until February 1939, and the squadron's conversion to Hurricanes was completed by 3 March.[35]

4

War

'Permish to join RAFVR'

Two years before Stuart Walch first flew the Hurricane, Ken Holland had been working towards his bronze medallion. He passed the examination on 20 December 1936, and then in early 1937, with his parents' permission, he severed his Australian ties and sailed to Toby Ripley's homeland. With Toby at his side, he traded the beaches of Bondi and Tamarama for the Cornish coastline, where he revelled in the trappings of a young gentleman of leisure. He swam at the nearby beaches and took up hunting, shooting, tennis and golf. Ken was an affectionate and personable young man and soon made friends, but Toby was the centre of his new life, becoming much more than just a father figure. He was his mentor and confidant.

Ken couldn't live a life of ease in Camelford forever, and the question of what he would do soon arose. He fixed on a career in aviation, but even though he had turned 17 on 29 January, he was too young to enlist in the recently created Royal Air Force Volunteer Reserve. Even if he had been old enough, Toby would not have given permission to apply.[1] (Regardless of Toby's reluctance, it is possible that Ken's lack of Intermediate science and mathematics qualifications would have counted against him.) Not to worry. The air force was not the only way to satisfy an interest in aviation.

In 1934, Nevil Shute Norway, author, aeronautical engineer, and principal of Airspeed (1934) Ltd, had started an aeronautical college based at the Airspeed factory in Portsmouth, England's island city on the southeast coast of Hampshire. (Norway had formed the company in 1931 and the factory moved to the airport in 1933.) After its public listing, in 1934, Airspeed grew to such an extent that it needed to ensure a steady supply of engineers and, more importantly, recruits for the sales and design aspects of the industry. The cream of the college's graduates would be absorbed into the company and others could find places in the ever-expanding aeronautical industry. The college offered two courses. One, open to those who were 18, was for budding ground engineers. The other, offered to those who were at least 17 and could give evidence of a good general education and sound common sense, was for those who wanted to specialise in aeronautical engineering.

Courses, which started in April and September, had limited places and were advertised in enthusiast magazines such as *Flight*. Ken sent away for a prospectus. Aeronautical engineering caught his eye, and he was just the right age. Maths wasn't stipulated as a prerequisite, so perhaps it wouldn't matter too much that it wasn't his academic strong point, especially as he'd passed his other Intermediate subjects. The course was non-residential and of three years' duration and cost 250 guineas. Students were given comprehensive practical experience in all branches of aircraft manufacture – the company produced a number of types, including the Courier, Envoy, Viceroy and Oxford – with theoretical training in aeronautics. The school encompassed a fitting section, machine shop, drawing office, lecture room, and instructors' and administrative offices. Students were offered experience in all departments, from factory to office, and attended lectures at Portsmouth's technical college. The course did not offer flying tuition, but if the opportunity arose, students could fly as a passenger in one of Airspeed's aircraft. If they wanted to take the controls themselves arrangements could be made for lessons with the nearby Portsmouth Aero Club.[2]

Ken was keen but there was one snag. Toby's allowance was good but it would not stretch to Airspeed's fees. Happily, Toby liked what the college offered so agreed to pay for Ken's studies and to subsidise board and allowance for the duration. Ken sent off his application form, was accepted, and enrolled in the aeronautical engineering stream in April 1937.

He moved to Portsmouth and boarded close to Airspeed. He was cheerful and outgoing and soon acquired a large circle of friends, including fellow boarder and aeronautical student John 'Paddy' Lindsay and Philip 'Pip' de Lacey Markham, who was two years older than Ken. Ken and Pip shared an exuberant sense of humour and on one occasion amused everyone in the engine shop when they broke out into an impromptu ballet.[3] Ken's sunny nature, however, was counterbalanced by a darker side. Pip recalled that Ken had quiet and reflective moments, and displayed the odd flash of temper. He also discovered that Ken had a tendency towards stubbornness, but his friend's usual joie de vivre would quickly reassert itself.[4]

Toby bought Ken an Imperial 250 c.c. motorbike, and he often took it for a spin to the Hampshire Downs and occasionally arranged a combined walk and reliability trial with other motorbike enthusiasts. His passion for all things aviation grew. He was around the Airspeed types every day. He regularly worked on them and enjoyed seeing them put through their paces. With camera in hand, he attended nearby flying events, and where there was some 'good flying', he 'took flicks of [the] latest aircraft. Verboten really. Super display by … a Belgian Firefly'. Ken was always on the go but also enjoyed the times when he 'lazed about and wrote poetry'. On one occasion he 'rode up Southwick and read Scott's "Lay" by the setting sun' and copied lines from Tennyson's 'In Memoriam' into his diary.

Ken worked hard at Airspeed but managed to find time for a full social calendar. There was one glitch in his happy, carefree life: Toby still withheld permission for his ward to join the air force. Even when he turned 18, on 29 January 1938, Ken still deferred to his guardian's wishes. Toby did, however, allow Ken to join the Civil Air Guard.[5] Created in 1938, the government-sponsored scheme operated in conjunction with flying clubs to provide pilots to assist the RAF in times of emergency.

In August 1938 Toby sailed to Sydney, planning to be away for the better part of a year. Even though he had signed up for the Civil Air Guard, Ken still wanted to join the Royal Air Force Volunteer Reserve. He missed Toby and looked forward to his letters but also hoped that his airmailed entreaties to join the reserve would elicit a favourable response. On 27 February 1939, after a day spent at the Airspeed factory dismantling and cleaning valve-holding gear and later attending a Moth lecture, he opened a foreign-stamped 'cheery letter' from Toby. He was over the moon when he read the happy news that his guardian had finally relented and granted him 'permish to join RAFVR', with the qualifier that he would 'prefer that I should wait until summer'.

'I'm not going to wait until I'm 21'

Back in Australia, John Crossman was waiting to hear the outcome of his second application for a short service commission in the RAF. Spurred on by the RAF's August 1938 advertisements in the Australian newspapers, he had braved his father's ire and bluntly told him, 'I'm going to see if I can get in. I'm not going to wait until I'm 21. I'm 20. I'll be 21 in a few months' time'. Ted relented and gave his permission. John wasted no time in sending off the signed papers. He was shortlisted and interviewed by the RAAF, acting on the RAF's behalf. He was recovering from a serious bout of influenza but said nothing of it, as he didn't want to spoil his chances. When the letter from Air Board arrived, however, it advised that the medical had revealed his level of fitness was below the physical standards. The doctor had detected the lingering effects of the flu and so he was rejected. Undeterred, John decided to go to England and apply directly to the RAF, but Air Board suggested he would be disappointed and advised him to reapply in 12 months.[6] He took their advice for the time being, but when a new round of RAF advertisements appeared in the papers in January 1939, he reapplied.

On 30 March, before his next selection interview, he joined the Hamilton branch of the Australian Air League and proved a 'very keen and active member'. Who knows if this further proof of John's keenness impressed his second selection board, but he passed his medical and, on 5 June, was advised by Air Board that he was 'to proceed to England to undergo flying training with a view to a subsequent appointment to a short service commission in the RAF'.[7] He was on the cusp of realising his flying dreams.

'No bloody good'

Ten days after John Crossman received the news he had been so desperate to hear, Bill Millington arrived at Tilbury docks, in London. He had enjoyed his return voyage to his homeland and reported to his sister Eileen that the 'trip over was jolly good'.[8] It was almost 13 years since he had left his homeland. He cleared customs and caught the train to St Pancras. He booked into the Museum Hotel, in Bloomsbury Street, and went straight to the Admiralty. Dick Glyde and the Point Cook boys were already perfecting their flying skills, but Bill's immediate hopes of joining the Fleet Air Arm were dashed: he was told he could not start training until November. This was 'no bloody good'.[9] Bill had not come all this way to wait months to enlist. Besides, funds were limited and, at 25s per week for bed and breakfast, would soon run out. He arranged to meet a Lieutenant Commander Webler, who suggested that his best option would be to join the RAF and organised an interview with the Air Ministry at Adastral House. In the interim, Bill decided to visit his mother's brother and sister-in-law, Alec and Florrie Reid, who lived in Banstead, a village located near the Surrey border, about 13 miles south of London. It was a 'pleasant family day'. He enjoyed his time catching up so much that he 'unfortunately missed the last bus and stayed the night'.

He travelled up to London on the morning of the 19th with his cousin Sylvia for his 11 a.m. appointment at Adastral House. There, he 'filled in [the] necessary forms and now have to wait for a few days for a reply re interview'. He visited the British Museum and on the 20th went to Banstead again. The Reids invited him to stay, so he gave up his room at the Museum Hotel. The next day he explored the village. Then, 'after tea, uncle, aunt and I walked over the Epsom Downs ... Very nice walk through country lanes. Fine avenue of silver birches. Race course looked very picturesque'.

His interview with the RAF board on 23 June went well, so he was sent to Astor House, where the medical examination was conducted. 'Eye tests, heaving lungs, nervous reflexes, general physical fitness. Passed OK.' He was granted a short service commission and allocated service number 42720. He was only one of two that day to be accepted for pilot training. Bill later told his sister Eileen that 'after 12 months I'll probably be transferred to the Fleet Air Arm'. Until then, he would 'have to do the flying training on land. I go down to Reading, Berkshire, on 24 July for two months'. He put the long wait down to receiving his vaccinations, but it wouldn't be without diversion.[10] Soon after arriving in London, Bill had heard from Miss Celia Macdonald of the Isles, who, along with Lady Frances Ryder, ran the Dominion and Allied Services Hospitality Scheme. She welcomed him to

England and advised that they would be pleased to arrange visits to hostesses in the country as well as outings with new friends in London. They also invited him to come along 'to have tea with us' any time he wanted, 'as you will always find somebody here'.[11]

Bill initially thought 'London was rather depressing', but after his first visit to the hospitality scheme's headquarters, at 21B Cadogan Gardens, in Sloane Square, on 24 June, he was caught up in a social whirl and found he was 'rapidly becoming accustomed to it'. He was drawn to Miss Macdonald, a woman of great warmth. She held a deep faith in both God and humanity and adopted a maternal role to the many young people she met through the scheme. She developed a reputation as a wise, caring and knowledgeable counsellor. Perhaps Miss Macdonald's warm demeanour reminded Bill of his mother. Perhaps he delighted in accounts of her stay in Adelaide during her world tour in 1936–37 or was swayed by her charm and ability to put everyone at ease within minutes. Or perhaps he was simply drawn to a fellow adherent of Scout Law, as he listened to stories of her time spent running the scout troop in the village of Rudston, located close to her family's estate in East Yorkshire. Whatever the basis, Bill and Miss Macdonald developed a fond empathy and she became 'a particularly good friend' to the young Australian.[12]

Under Miss Macdonald's wing, sociable Bill had a ball in the happy, crowded rooms of 21B Cadogan Gardens, where guests shared the fun of preparing their own tea. He received 'numerous invitations to dinners etc.' and joined 'a party to the open air theatre in Regent's Park. Shakespeare's play *A Midsummer Night's Dream* was presented and I thoroughly enjoyed it'. He arranged to go to a garden party in early July. 'These affairs don't cost a bean', he told his sister, 'and there are usually a few other RAF chaps present, so happy days'.[13]

'Attestation VR'

A continuing peace seemed far from viable as Hitler made obvious his intentions towards Poland and the Free City of Danzig, the semi-autonomous city-state created by the Treaty of Versailles (which had ended the state of war between the Allies and Germany at the conclusion of the Great War). Hitler occupied the Czech provinces of Moravia and Bohemia ten days before Stuart Walch's promotion to flying officer, on 26 March 1939. Believing Poland would be next, Chamberlain advised his cabinet that he would be prepared to offer Britain's assurance in guaranteeing her independence. On the home front, the Territorial Army was doubled, and plans to evacuate two and a half million children in the event of war were drawn up. Ken Holland counted the days until Toby Ripley returned to Cornwall, and Chamberlain pressed for conscription.[14]

During his free time from the aeronautical engineering course at Airspeed College, Ken followed the news reports and worried about how a forced call-up would affect his plans to join the air force. Chamberlain persuaded his cabinet to agree to conscription, and on 26 May the *Military Training Act 1939*, which covered single men aged between 20 and 22 years, was passed. Ken had turned 19 in January, and although he was still a few months short of being covered by the act, he didn't want to risk being compelled to army service. He would not do anything until Toby returned, but he grew impatient.[15]

Ken waited for his guardian, and the RAF's squadrons continued to convert to modern fighter aircraft. Jack Kennedy watched as 65 Squadron's first Spitfire arrived. He and his fellow pilots were excited and keen to test the new arrivals. Conversion was completed by 19 April, and as they became more familiar with the Spitfires, some started to show off.[16] A favourite stunt was to retract the undercarriage on take-off while the Spitfire was still only a few inches above the ground. It was an impressive trick but it required dexterity. Usually, the right hand was on the control stick and the left held the throttle forward. But the undercarriage pump was on the cockpit's starboard side, and while the pilot pumped up the undercarriage with his right hand, he had to take his left from the throttle and clutch the stick. The nose invariably dipped during the hand shuffle, so the real trick was to maintain level height and pump at the same time.

Jack was perhaps the first of his group to master the new technique. But he had a rival in A Flight. Pilot Officer John Nicholas's motto was anything Jack could do, he could do better. 65 Squadron's pilots had been joined by most of those from 54 and 74 squadrons, also based at Hornchurch, when Nicholas climbed into his Spitfire. He was a competent pilot and confident of his superiority, but something went wrong. As the wheels retracted, the Spit's nose dropped. The propeller blades hacked into the grass, gouging out divots. Just as it seemed that the Spit would burrow prop first into the ground, Nicholas forced her into a climb. He circuited the airfield, landed with the curled propeller blades and climbed from the cockpit with a beetroot face. Jack laughed loudly for at least a month. Less than three years earlier, his Point Cook instructor had considered he wouldn't make the grade if his flying didn't improve.[17] Now *The* Kennedy was the squadron's best.

Not far behind 65 Squadron in acquiring new aircraft was 72 Squadron, and their complement of Spitfires began to arrive in April. They too were eager to try out the sleek new fighter, and Des Sheen had his turn on 14 April when he took a 35-minute flight in Spitfire K9926 (RN-B), which had arrived only that day. He found it 'marvellous ... a delight to fly'. It was 'quite exciting' and 'rather like flying a new racehorse'. The Spitfire was 'very light, it was very manoeuvrable and it had a lot of power'. Des recalled that 'everybody loved it. I can't think of anybody who has ever had a harsh word to say about it … It seemed to just fit round you'. Above all, 'it just felt right'. As he had done with his favourite Gladiator, Desmond commissioned a watercolour of Spitfire K9941 in flight.[18]

While Des admired his new Spitfire, Toby Ripley was on his way back to England. He arrived on 24 May and confirmed his permission for his young ward to join the air force. Ken sent off his application. He received word on 29 June that on 5 July he was to report to Portsmouth's recently opened volunteer reserve centre at Northleigh House for his medical and selection boards. On 1 July he took delivery of Toby's latest gift, a new Ariel 350 c.c. Red Hunter motorbike. He thought it 'wizard – like riding an armchair', but it would not start on the morning of his all-important appointment. He managed to arrive in time but only after hitching a 'hair-raising ride'. After a 'very searching medical' he passed his boards. He wrote to Toby that night to tell him of his success, and on 12 July he proudly headed his diary page 'ATTESTATION VR' and noted that he 'was sworn in as Sergeant RAFVR', service number 754503.[19]

'You must have caught me in your spell'

One of Jack Kennedy's friends had been invited to lunch on 13 June at Whitstable, a seaside town in Kent 50 miles or so from Hornchurch. His hosts were William and Doris Jourd, who enjoyed entertaining and frequently invited RAF officers to share their table. The friend had been ill so asked if Jack would drive him there. Jack, who had been promoted to flying officer on 26 May, three days before his 22nd birthday, agreed. He was always happy to act as chauffeur to his friends. The Jourds' 18-year-old daughter, Christine, who was working in London, decided to visit that day. She had left school at 12 because her father, a headmaster whom she termed an 'eccentric scholar', believed that girls did not need an education. She was intelligent, however, and would often debate subjects in which she was interested. She was a beautiful young woman, slim, fair and of medium height, with elegant, patrician features that were perfect for modelling. She applied for a job as a mannequin with an exclusive Mayfair court couturier and was successful. Her family had travelled about when her father was in the army, including to South Africa, but despite the broad horizons Christine had had a sheltered life. Although she was working, she lived with her aunt and cousin in Beckenham, Kent, and caught the train to the couturier's.[20]

When Christine arrived, she met a young man at the garden gate. Jack Kennedy was heavily tanned and appeared to her as the archetypal tall, dark and handsome. He did not speak much, and the young woman thought him a 'very quiet young man'. After lunch, they went to the beach for a swim. Everyone raced to the water and splashed about, but Jack just lay down on the beach. 'Suddenly, Jack got up, walked into the sea and swam straight out … like a torpedo and out of sight.' He returned to the shore and flopped down without saying anything to anyone. Christine found out later that he was a champion swimmer.

The Jourds' guests returned for tea. Later, they decided to go to the pub, but Christine had to return to London so pleaded her excuses. Everyone left, so she sat in the garden until it was time to catch her train. Then Jack appeared. He asked if she would like to come to the pub after all. She was already starting to succumb to the charm of the silent young man, so after only a little persuasion, she agreed. Jack found his tongue and they talked all evening.

A few days later, Jack phoned Christine at the salon and asked if he could drive her home. He pulled up in the Lagonda and instead of going to her aunt's they met a group of friends. After dinner, he drove to Beckenham, about 16 miles from Hornchurch, almost in silence. He walked her to the door and asked to kiss her.

Christine was not impressed by her escort's forwardness on such a short acquaintance so slapped his face. She regretted it instantly but strode inside without speaking. Jack was not deterred. He had fallen in love, almost from the first moment, and so was on the phone the next morning apologising and asking if he could come over. All was forgiven.

Christine fitted well into Jack's group, and she encouraged her beau to bring his pilot friends on their outings. Soon, Jack baulked at the crowd. One day, at Christine's behest, he brought his friends to Beckenham to see her. When they arrived he told her he wouldn't come again as he believed she wanted him around only because of his friends. Christine was dumbfounded that he could think such a thing, and the threat that she would not see him again jolted her into the realisation that she was in love and could not bear to lose him. From then on they spent as much time alone together as possible.

Jack might have been hard pressed to write to his family, but he wrote frequently and passionately to Christine. 'Christine my love, I hope you're missing me just a little. It fills me with a sort of pleasant warmth to think you care … I do love you so.' He was often silent in Christine's presence, but, he explained, 'it's not really speechlessness, darling … there's no necessity for talk, everything is complete enough as it is'. He was smitten. 'My dear I find it's sort of a sweet ache loving you as much as I do. I can't stop thinking about you.' He confessed that 'you must have caught me in your spell. I feel as though I go on loving you all the time. I won't be happy until I have you in my clutches again'.[21]

Jack spoke little of his squadron life beyond the cheerful friendships kindled among men with a shared passion for flying. Nor did he mention that the squadron had dubbed him *The* Kennedy. Christine soon found it out, however, and at the same time discovered how much Jack cared for her: when she was first introduced to Flying Officer Robert Tuck – known to all as Bob – he said to her, 'You must be *The* Christine'. Jack didn't even speak about his love of flying or what he felt when putting his Spitfire through its paces, but she saw for herself why he was known as *The* Kennedy. One time, when visiting her parents, she was sitting on the beach and saw a Spitfire approaching from over the sea. It came in low then circled before waggling its wings goodbye. Her heart leaped when she realised it was Jack. She recognised his skill with the Spitfire; it was as if he and his Spitfire were one. 'What a wonderful pilot he was.'

Low flying became Jack's 'signature' and it seemed as if no matter where Christine was he would be there in his Spitfire keeping an eye on her and showing her he was thinking of her. Once, while at the beach, she watched as he skimmed above the heads of a group of nuns and young children, who huddled together in fear. During one aerial visit 'we all rushed out when we heard the drone of the aircraft'. They watched as it 'flew round the house so low'. That evening, Jack phoned and laughingly told her he had seen 'Weaver (my father's batman) with a blue hot water bottle in his hand – he had obviously been making the beds!'

Another time, Jack and Christine were staying with friends whose house was on a poplar-lined road. He returned the next day to execute the RAF's traditional hospitality thank-you and beat up to the house, taking the tops off the trees. That day's news included a report of a lone Spitfire flying low over London. Jack later told Christine he was keeping quiet about the incident as someone was on the warpath. Christine smiled at his flying antics and recalled that 'life was hectic and lots of fun, with many phone calls and brief visits from Jack. There was talk of war but we were young and a lot of it went over our heads'.

'The more I see of flying, the better I like it'

Jack and Christine may have been barely aware that war was imminent, but the RAF had no doubts. More and more young men were accepted for aircrew training, and Bill Millington was just one of many who made their way to training stations, arriving at 8 Elementary and Reserve Flying Training School, Reading, about 40 miles west of London, on 24 July 1939. After dropping his bags at the officers' quarters at Hawkhurst, an old, rambling English manor, he was issued with flying kit. Before the day was out, his eight-week course had begun, with 36 minutes in the two-seater Miles Hawk low-wing monoplane. He found the Hawk 'rather strange after Moths ... Not so sensitive on controls'. The next day he flew another 80 minutes and practised take-offs, landings and circuits, and attended his first lectures.[22]

'The more I see of flying, the better I like it', he told his sister Eileen. He soloed in early August and set about 'chasing the hours, having to complete 25 hours dual and 25 hours solo before leaving here'. At the end of the month he would take 'the 5-hour test by the commanding officer. This is given after 5 hours solo flying, and includes take-offs, circuits and landings and spinning'.[23]

As Bill chased the hours, Ken Holland was studying. He had sat for his exams in July and was not too confident of his results. He 'made a balls as usual' of mathematics and thought the engine shop exam was 'lousy'. Even so, his marks, while not outstanding, were better than expected and his report was 'not too bad'. He had done well in materials, passed engines and just failed metallurgy. He received only 40 per cent in drawing and 20 per cent in mathematics, proving this was a continuing weakness. Even though Ken received an average mark of 52.2 per cent, one instructor was happy with his improvements and hoped they would continue. His engine shop instructor, however, considered him 'too knowy'. Happily, the chief instructor thought Ken's results 'quite good', and, most importantly, Toby Ripley was 'pleased with [the] report'.[24]

War Week exercises

As August began, the RAF geared up for War Week, during which squadrons carried out war simulation exercises. Pat Hughes and 64 Squadron moved from Church Fenton to Duxford, Cambridgeshire, on 8 August, and as well as practising night flying they worked the patrol lines. They also successfully carried out mock interception exercises. A large part of eastern England was blacked out on 11 August, and Jack Kennedy and 65 Squadron took the opportunity to practise flying in blackout conditions. The weather was bad. There was no moon and limited natural light to guide the pilots. Their only landing guides were two low-wattage lights on the aerodrome. Safely on the ground, Jack and his friends reported on the effectiveness of the blackout. Overall it had been successful, but some larger towns had had a few lights showing and the Thames was visible in their reflection. They were recalled from the exercises on the 24th because of the increasingly threatening international situation.[25]

At Debden, Dick Glyde and 87 Squadron flew day and night. It was a punishing regime. Dick's fellow countryman John Cock – known as Johnny to his squadron friends – for example worked 17 hours a day, from 4 a.m. to 9 p.m., and managed only a handful of hours' sleep. Looking back over the War Week activities, 87 Squadron's earliest historian was doubtful whether any squadron could have conceived that they would be at war within a month. Perhaps if they had had time to read the papers they might have had more of a clue, as the press was constantly reporting an expected conflict – *Picture Post*, for one, had even commenced its 'Britain Prepares' series, featuring the Territorial Army, in May.[26]

August also saw the passing of the *Emergency Powers (Defence) Act 1939*. The Imperial War Museum evacuated the first of its paintings, and the Tate and National galleries started preparations to safeguard their own. In spite of these clear signs, many hoped war would be averted. 87 Squadron even assumed that 1939 would see its own version of the Munich Agreement. Their false sense of security, however, did not stop them following the lead of the major museums and galleries. As August closed, they prudently deposited the squadron crest, Great War diary and mess silver in Barclay's Bank at Saffron Walden, near to their base.[27]

'Today I sever connections with Australia'

'Today was the day', John Crossman noted in his diary on 12 August. 'I really did sail for England. It was almost too good to be true.' After wanting it for so long, 'my feelings were awfully mixed and I didn't feel so good after I said goodbye to everyone'. After a grand farewell from his fiancée, Pat Foley, his parents and other family and friends, John had boarded the RMS *Orama* – namesake of the vessel that had carried Ted Crossman to Australia in 1913. As he stood at the rails, he kept his eyes on 'Pat's pink feather in her hat' and his mother's yellow jumper, which 'showed out'. He watched his father waving furiously until he'd disappeared from sight, and as the RMS *Orama* passed through Sydney Heads he realised that 'the great adventure has started and we are well on our way'. But excitement turned to bitter sadness as he left Australian waters for the last time, on 13 August, after a stopover at Fremantle: 'Today I sever connections with Australia and I don't feel so good about it'; he missed Pat and his family 'like the devil'. Behind his sadness was an element of fatalism. He believed he 'probably won't see them again'.[28]

John may have been clear headed about his desire to fly, and everything he did was geared towards the moment when he would gain his wings, but he did not close his heart to the other important things in life. He was in love. Patricia Foley, known to all as Pat, was 16 when she met John in 1935; he was her first boyfriend. She worked in the Newcastle tourist bureau and, like John, loved the theatre. Pat and her Johnny, as she called him, made a handsome couple – her dark-haired attractiveness complemented his good looks, and they made the most of any opportunity to put on their dancing shoes or go out into the countryside on romantic picnics.

Pat's family were Catholic and John's Anglican, but the religious differences meant little to them and both families approved of their relationship. The Crossmans loved Pat as another daughter and John was welcomed into the Foley family. Pat and John had recently become engaged, but while John was assured of a future flying for the RAF, there was less certainty about when they would embark on their life together. Pat dreamed of marriage and children, but John was committed to a short service commission of four years after he graduated from flying training.[29] Pat's dreams would have to be put on hold just as her fiancé's were coming true.

John took part in all the shipboard activities. He joined in the daily callisthenics to keep in shape and made new friends, including Jack Burraston. John thought Jack, who was born on 21 July 1917 in Glen Innes, New South Wales, 'a fine fellow'. They soon discovered they had much in common and became firm friends. 'Both Jack and I want to go to the same flying school if we can', he declared in his diary. They studied together every day, as they were keen to get as much of the theoretical component of their training under their belts before arriving in England.[30]

'It seems unlikely that I'll ever see home again'

As John steamed towards England and RAF service, Stuart Walch, at North Weald, was constantly in the air as 151 Squadron ramped up its training by focusing on interceptions, mock attacks and gunnery skills. Stuart was promoted to A Flight's sub-flight leader, the flight commander's deputy, and appointed signals officer. Pat Hughes was also elevated. He became sub-flight leader in 64 Squadron's A Flight. At Hornchurch, Gordon Olive was promoted to flight commander of A Flight. If war was declared, he would lead Jack Kennedy into battle.

Like all squadrons, 65 Squadron usually shut down in summer and personnel took a month's leave. Not so in 1939. All leave was cancelled, and squadrons adopted a war footing. On 22 August, Jack watched as 65 Squadron's Spitfires were spread out around the perimeter of the airfield. Two days later, at Church Fenton, Des Sheen learned that 72 Squadron had received a top secret signal advising that orders would be issued to disperse their Spitfires as well. Both of 87 Squadron's flights were put on readiness, and Dick Glyde and his fellow pilots slept in one of Debden's camouflaged hangars.[31] Throughout Fighter Command, night patrols increased. During the day, brush and paint were taken to aircraft, and wartime identification codes replaced the peacetime codes.

The world crisis also intruded on shipboard life. As August drew to a close, John Crossman listened to the news from London every night. Neither Ted nor his son had paid much attention to growing European tension. They ignored regular reports from Ted's sister, Ann Brawn, in Chalfont St Giles, Buckinghamshire, that war was brewing, so the Australian branch of the Crossman family believed John would see out his RAF career in peacetime. Ann thought the Australian connection daft for not heeding her warnings, but as the RMS *Orama* dimmed her lights at night and sailed under the escort of a destroyer, 'purposely off course [over] the last two days', John finally realised that the 'war scare is very bad now'.[32]

Bill Millington also understood that Britain was but a hair's breadth from conflict. He could not see his homeland taking the appeasement route again. He believed 'there is a grim determination to go through with it this time, and friend Adolf will have his hands full if he knocks the chip off Britain's shoulder'.[33] Ken Holland, however, was not as perceptive. He gave little thought to the perilous state of affairs as he anticipated his first flight. At the top of his 31 August diary entry he excitedly proclaimed, 'RAFVR – FIRST DAY DUAL INSTRUCTION' and flew 35 minutes in a Tiger Moth.

Ken was at the aero club on 1 September when the BBC announced that Germany had invaded Poland. For irrepressible Ken, the news signalled more an exciting lark than potentially life-threatening times ahead. Indeed, he recorded 'great seciteMent [sic]' at the news, especially as 'the reservists had been called up'. He lost no time in reporting to Northleigh House but was told to return the next day. Back at the airfield he was disappointed there would be no flying training as the weather was 'too thick'. He returned home and 'mobilised [his] belongings completely', to be ready if he received a posting in the morning.[34]

On 2 September, Bill Millington's cousin Sylvia was getting married in Surrey before setting out to the south of France for her honeymoon. Bill had hoped to attend the wedding but was not able to obtain leave. He spent the day at the flights, and while he was in the air Ken Holland returned to the volunteer reserve centre. He had a perfunctory medical inspection and after lunch assisted with the evacuation of Portsmouth's school children, their teachers, pregnant women, blind people and mothers with young children. On the RMS *Orama*, John Crossman kept his ear to the ship's radio. 'Poland is being attacked and we expect hourly to hear that England is going to have a go at Hitler.'[35] Meanwhile, RAF squadrons all around the country closed off their pre-war operations books and made their final preparations for war.

Dick Glyde was packing. The RAF was preparing to send two air formations to the continent. The Advanced Air Striking Force was a light bomber force, consisting of Fairey Battle and Blenheim squadrons supported by the Hurricanes of 1 and 73 squadrons. 87 Squadron had been ordered to vacate Debden. They, along with 85, 607 and 615 squadrons, would form the air component of the British Expeditionary Force, charged with providing air cover to the force as it held the area between the Belgian frontier and the Maginot Line, the stretch of concrete fortifications and weapons installations intended to defend France's border with Germany. As Dick decided what to take to France, Great Britain and her ally demanded the withdrawal of German troops from Poland and gave a deadline for compliance.

At 10 a.m. on Sunday 3 September 1939, the BBC alerted its listeners to a broadcast of 'national importance'. Church services were interrupted and congregations prayed for their country and loved ones who would soon be caught up in conflict. People gathered around their radios. Squadron Leader Teddy Donaldson of 151 Squadron called his pilots to the officers' mess. At 11.15 a.m. Stuart Walch and his fellows listened to Chamberlain announce that the British ambassador in Berlin had handed a final note to the German government stating that unless Germany committed to pulling her troops out of Poland a state of war would exist between the two nations. Germany did not withdraw; nor did it undertake to do so. In a tired, sad and – to some – heartbroken voice, Chamberlain with solemn dignity then advised that 'this country is at war with Germany'. With the prime minister's final words that 'right will prevail' ringing in their ears, Donaldson, Stuart and the pilots of 151 Squadron stood at attention as the national anthem was played. The notes, however, were drowned out by the sounds of a siren. It was a false alarm but a strident signal that they were at war.[36]

At Church Fenton, 72 and 64 squadrons also gathered around the radio. Des Sheen recalled there was a sense of relief that the waiting was over. 'There'd been so much messing around' during the Munich crisis the year before. Then, it had just been a question of 'when', but 'now we can get on with it'.[37]

Like Bill Millington's cousin Sylvia, Pat Hughes had planned a holiday in France and anticipated a month's leave during which he could 'just sit and swim'. His plans were shot now, because 'old Adolf the unwashed has rather been carried away in his old-fashioned enthusiasm and now there's war in the land so to speak'. He was not surprised. 'The National Socialists in Germany have been bred and reared in a military atmosphere and war is as much in their destiny as Christmas and plum pudding is in ours.' He too was pleased that the waiting was over: 'It will be an awful crack to start with because all of our chaps here are just sort of waiting now'. He thought the squadron would stay in England for home defence, but there was a possibility it might be sent to France, so, just in case, he started sorting out his belongings and decided what to send back to Australia.

Pat did not fear for the future. He believed that 'the chances of living through it are equal anyhow and that is all one can ask'. But he didn't entirely believe in fate. He had in his pocket a silver cartwheel his brother William had given him before he left Australia. It was tarnished 'from carrying it in my pocket and spilling ale on it', but Pat believed he and his lucky charm would be 'going home in 1942' at the end of his short service commission.[38]

Dick Glyde took a break from packing and also listened to the radio. He and the other Debden pilots were 'in rather a daze' when they heard Chamberlain's broadcast; 'few had had any experience of war, except for what we had read in books', recorded the squadron's earliest historian. It was sobering, but like 64 and

72 squadrons, 87 felt a sense of relief that they were now committed.[39]

Meanwhile, at Portsmouth, Ken Holland again reported to Northleigh House. He received the news of war, as well as his £3 advance pay, with excitement – 'Up the RAF' – and later headed his diary 'War', noting, 'War declared 11 a.m. on Germany by Britain'. During the last days of peace, posters had been put up around Portsmouth urgently calling for volunteers to fill sandbags to protect public buildings and air raid shelters from bomb blasts (preferably bringing their own shovel). Ken spent the afternoon hauling sandbags to help safeguard the Airspeed works. That done, he then 'drove around in lorries' for Portsmouth's Air Raid Precautions branch and worked up a 'grand sweat'.[40]

Bill Millington, at Reading, also heard Chamberlain's announcement. Afterwards, he 'spent the day at the flying field making up for lost time'. When he was released from training he and the other officers at Hawkhurst were 'ordered to stay within call. No lights except in lounge and writing room are permitted'.[41]

At her aunt's house at Beckenham, Christine Jourd was terrified of the screaming air raid siren and hid under the stairs. She and Jack Kennedy had arranged to meet later that day, and she feared he would be killed. The alert was a mistake, but, trembling in the dark, she was not to know that – all she could do was think of Jack and pray he would be all right. Within an hour he roared up the driveway in the Lagonda. It was such a relief! Jack had come safely to her.[42] But it was not the same old Jack. She saw, for the first time, that he was in uniform. Before, he had always been wearing civilian clothes. She realised that her life had been irrevocably changed.

At 4.15 p.m. ship's time on the RMS *Orama*, John Crossman and the other RAF recruits gathered to hear the news that 'war has been declared by Great Britain on Germany'. Some cheered, and a bottle of champagne was opened to toast the moment. For the majority, however, 'there was really no great excitement as we had been expecting it for days', and 'everyone on board is very calm'. John's reaction was subdued: 'Should this last any time it seems unlikely that I'll ever see home again'.[43]

5

First wartime operations

'No place to go as yet'

Pat Hughes had a quiet time at 13 Group's Church Fenton during the opening days of the war. He had heard rumours of early raids on London: 'How true they are I don't know, but it's quite possible the fun has started in earnest at last'.[1] He wanted to turn his boundless energy and natural aggression against the Germans and 'give 'em hell'. He was not alone. 'All of our chaps here are just sort of waiting now in a period of inaction, so that when it does break they will be damned hard to stop.' But 64 Squadron had no operational work – just a 'few sort of tentative prods from either side', and Pat had had no part in them. That quiet period, experienced throughout Fighter Command, was characterised by a general lack of offensive operations from both sides of the conflict. It extended into the first half of 1940 and became known as the Phoney War.

Pat had initially believed that 64 Squadron was headed for France, but it wasn't long before he realised he had been mistaken. He didn't think home defence was too bad a deal, however, as it 'promises to be livelier than anything else'. In the meantime, he hung around 'the aerodrome with a lot of aeroplanes and guns and such with no place to go as yet'. With nothing 'much else to do except sit and wait till it breaks', he decided to catch up on his overdue correspondence. He told his brother William that he was 'hale and hearty' and committed to clearing 'these Huns from the blue skies of old England'. He had no idea how long the conflict could be expected to last and would 'hate to guess'. He was certain, however, that 'until this has been going on for a while we won't be able to judge much about [the enemy's] men or machines or whether they fight well or indifferently', and that both the Luftwaffe and the RAF would be 'out to show just how bad the other one is'.

'Confirmed victory'

On 16 and 17 October 1939, Des Sheen's squadron moved from Church Fenton to Leconfield, just north of Hull, in Yorkshire's East Riding. The squadron was under 13 Group's jurisdiction and, in addition to defending the north of England and Scotland, would be required to protect the vital coastal convoys in that area's waters. In the early afternoon of 21 October, an enemy force was detected approaching a convoy off Spurn Head, a narrow sand spit on the tip of East Riding's coast that reaches into the North Sea. 72 Squadron was alerted. A Flight scrambled at 2.15 p.m. and B Flight's Blue Section was put on readiness. Green Section, led by Des in Spitfire K9959, scrambled at 2.30 p.m. He and Flying Officer Thomas 'Jimmy' Elsdon sped to Spurn Head and soon sighted a loose formation of 12 to 14 Heinkel He115 three-seater floatplanes.

As they intercepted, three of the Heinkels 'attempted to provide covering fire and went up and astern prior to attack', but Des and Elsdon pounced on them. 'As I closed on my He115', recalled Des, 'its rear gunner attempted to put me off my aim by blazing away with his weapon, but I soon silenced him'. He thought he had killed the pilot, as the 'Heinkel started to fly very erratically'. It was obviously in trouble. It dived swiftly and was weaving, with petrol tanks leaking.

Des 'never actually claimed the floatplane as destroyed' but was 'later credited with a confirmed victory'. He was the first Australian to engage the enemy in combat during the war; it was 19 days after his 22nd birthday. He had felt no fear, later reflecting that 'one concentrates on what you … [are] doing and you ignore the other'. He described the brief battle as 'really good fun – as exciting a 5 minutes as anything you could wish for'.[2] Fun perhaps, but Des had demonstrated that he possessed the killer instinct. He was a fighter pilot.

'Had the satisfaction of using my guns'

Dick Glyde's first France-based sortie had occurred on 10 September, the day after 87 Squadron arrived at Boos, near Rouen (the historic capital of Normandy), in northwestern France. Flying Hurricane L1776, he patrolled the district for 2 hours. The squadron carried out a great deal of flying and air firing practice during the next two weeks, including a demonstration flight over Paris with 85 Squadron.

Conditions at Boos were not good. There was a grass strip, tents and little technical support. Equipment was missing, and the Hurricanes were refuelled by pouring petrol from 4-gallon cans through chamois leather funnels, which absorbed any water accumulation. There was no accommodation, so the pilots had billeted at a hotel in Rouen. They were appalled at the situation, but even so, morale was high.[3] On 29 September, they relocated 160 miles to Merville, a village near the city of Lille, a short distance from the Belgian border. Again, there was no accommodation, so the pilots commandeered nearby estaminets and houses. The plan was to remain in Merville until facilities at Lille-Seclin, one of the six airfields in the Lille area, were completed.

The squadron was tasked with patrolling the Channel to protect British troops from Luftwaffe attack as they were ferried from Dover to Boulogne. This was carried out in pairs. The vessels were never left unescorted, and Dick spent an hour over them each time. The pilots enjoyed these patrols, because they could increase their flying hours and at the same time familiarise themselves with the French countryside and significant landmarks, including fields still littered with debris from Great War battles.

The weather soon closed in. Heavy rains turned the airfield into a quagmire, making take-offs and landings difficult. The excess water proved itself a nuisance in more ways than one. On 31 October, Dick was coming in to land when his engine cut out because of water in the fuel system. He was unhurt, but Hurricane L1743, which had become 'his' aircraft, was a write-off.[4]

On 2 November, Dick and his friends were lazing about, waiting for a possible call to scramble. Some read, some wrote letters, others dozed in the late autumn sunshine, which offered little warmth. As they often had over the last weeks, eyes turned to the sky, raking it in the hope of espying an enemy aircraft. At 10.30 a.m. some He111s were spotted. The airfield defences blasted away, and 87 Squadron scrambled to intercept the enemy aircraft. Three of them chased a Heinkel to the Belgian border. They fired and watched as it appeared to shudder then put its nose down.[5]

Meanwhile, Dick's flight commander, Robert Voase Jeff, followed vapour trails for 20 minutes, with Dick fast on his heels in Hurricane L1613. At 11 a.m., Jeff climbed and spotted one of the Heinkels. The bomber spotted him too; the rear gunner opened fire when they were 600 yards away. Jeff continued to close. At 300 yards, in a position slightly beneath and behind, he opened fire until torrents of black smoke spurted from the Heinkel's engines. Dick also 'had the satisfaction of using my guns … and scoring a few hits on it'. He later told his mother that he 'had the pleasure of seeing it crash' at Stables, near Hazebrouck, in northern France.[6] Squadron records do not support Dick's assertion, but a young man would not write a blatant lie to his mother! So, we can take it from Dick that he played a part in the air component's first victory.

Conditions at Merville soon became impossible for operations, so the squadron moved to the Lille-Seclin airfield on 5 November, even though their quarters weren't ready. Laundry and bathing facilities were non-existent, and pilots had to rely on the good nature of locals for hot baths. Their sleeping huts were built on wooden piles about 18 inches off the ground, and throughout the bitter winter the cold assailed them from above, below and all sides. There was only a small solid-fuel stove in the centre of each hut for warmth. At least one pilot went to bed in fur-lined jacket, thick socks and flying gauntlets with all sorts of clothing oddments piled on top. In fact, it was so cold that when one of the men poured stove-warmed water into a glass to take a dose of Eno's Salts, the water froze instantly.[7]

As well as the move to Lille-Seclin, 5 November was a red letter day for Dick: it was the day Hurricane L1813 arrived to replace L1743. Four days later, he, Jeff and Pilot Officer Horatio 'Jimmy' Dunn pursued a reported enemy aircraft over Calais that turned out to be a French Amiot. He flew three patrols the next day to Dunkirk, but visibility was bad and he saw nothing. L1813 was proving to be a 'beauty', and Dick soon had it 'tuned to perfection'.[8]

'Everything is perfectly under control'

Hornchurch was under 11 Group's purview, and Jack Kennedy – like every other pilot in the London-based squadrons – expected to be called to the city's defence at any moment. He and Christine Jourd rarely spoke of the possibility of enemy invasion or Jack's death in combat. He did not fear death – it appeared 'a little thing to him' – but when Christine knew he was flying, she fretted for his safety.[9] Jack tried to console her. 'My darling', he wrote. 'Don't worry yourself, everything is perfectly under control.' He begged her not to 'worry much about this war business … I'm hoping that as soon as we get cracking properly, we should finish it off pretty conclusively'.

Despite his optimism, there was little operational flying in the early weeks of the war. Even so, he was still tied to the station and had little free time. A new pattern of life began for him and Christine: a whirlwind of stolen moments, rushing to meet briefly, parting tearfully, then expectantly awaiting the next hurried encounter, phone call or hours together snatched from full duty rosters. There was a strong sense of 'hallo–goodbye', and if Jack missed Christine's call his frustration and emotion boiled up. He vented it in a dashed-off note: 'I felt pretty low, for I had been looking forward to speaking to you and hearing your voice again. Darling, I did so want to tell you how enormously I love you'.

'The last will and testament'

News travelled quickly in the RAF, and perhaps Stuart Walch heard of Des Sheen's and Dick Glyde's successes, confirming what some in his squadron already believed – that enemy air activity would increase in the near future. Accepting the inevitable, Stuart decided to be prepared and, on 15 November, walked into a solicitor's office at Epping. He sat down and dictated 'the last will and testament of me Stuart Crosby Walch'. To one friend, and co-executor, he bequeathed his gold watch. To another, he left his gold cigarette case that bore the Hutchins School crest. One-half of his estate was to be divided equally between his parents and the other was to go to his sisters and niece. To his mother he bequeathed his RAAF tunic, showing clearly the central importance of flying in his life.[10]

Legal affairs out of the way, Stuart focused on his flying duties. On 2 December, he was appointed officer in charge of Link training. The Link Trainer was a special flight simulation apparatus in which pilots learned to fly by instruments or honed their skills once they had mastered the basics. Stuart issued an order for all pilots to notch up at least 2 hours per month in the Link to ensure they could successfully operate at night or in cloud.[11] Before the year was out, Stuart was on the night flying roster and during the day carried out standing patrols, sector reconnaissances and convoy protection duties. But there were no enemy sightings.

'One feels most frightfully useless'

At 1.30 p.m. on 14 November, 87 Squadron's commanding officer, Squadron Leader William Coope, Pilot Officer Frank 'Dimmy' Joyce and Dick Glyde were ordered to intercept an enemy reconnaissance aircraft heading towards Boulogne. They patrolled above the clouds but did not encounter the intruder. On their return, fuel was running low so they came down to pinpoint their location. They did not recognise anything. As Dick put it, Coope 'was unlucky enough to lose us after a long patrol above the clouds'.[12] They had overshot the airfield and crossed into Belgian air space, which, given Lille-Seclin's proximity to the border, was not hard to do.

Belgium had announced its neutrality when war was declared. The military strictly observed a status of armed peace, and the air force was tasked with guarding the borders. As Coope passed over Ostend, still trying to locate a familiar landmark, the Belgian anti-aircraft batteries opened fire. All three Hurricanes were damaged, though not seriously. Coope traced the coastline towards France with Dick and Joyce behind. By 3.30 p.m. they were about 50 miles from Lille-Seclin, and Coope's tanks were almost empty. He put down on a beach, hoping they were safely in France. Joyce continued to base, while Dick landed a short distance from his squadron leader.[13] But they weren't in France. They were in Belgium, less than 2 miles from the border.

Realising their mistake, both tried to take off, but Coope's tanks ran dry as soon as he opened up the throttle, and one of the wheels of L1813 sank into a patch of soft sand. It would not budge. 'If only I'd been able to get off', Dick later bemoaned, 'I could have landed a bit further up the beach in France as I had a few gallons left'. He was just climbing out of his Hurricane 'to see what a bit of digging would do' when some gendarmes approached. 'And that was that.'

Belgium may have been neutral, but the people on the beach indicated their support of the Allied pilots with shouts of '*Vive la Grande Bretagne*' and '*Vive la France*'. Dick realised they were trying to cheer them up, but he did not feel too clever facing an indefinite internment in a neutral country when the war was little more than two months old. He hoped that 'it won't be too long before Belgium comes into the war as one feels most frightfully useless and foolish in a situation like this'.

The authorities arrived to take them and their Hurricanes away. Dick was the first Australian internee of the war. It was an ignominious moment: 'You can imagine how we felt to be led off in captivity leaving two perfectly good aeroplanes behind and almost within a stone's throw of France'. That evening, Dick and Coope were driven in a 'very nice' staff car to Ghent, located about 35 miles west of Brussels, Belgium's capital, where they were 'received by a very kind old general'. Indicating his sympathies, the general 'said how sorry he was that they couldn't let us go' and 'gave us an excellent dinner'.

Next stop was Brussels, where they stayed a few days at the gendarmerie's barracks. The Belgians treated them well, and Dick and Coope were even allowed to 'ride their horses in an indoor riding school'. The next day 'we saw the Royal escort, which is formed by the gendarmerie, ride out of the barracks'. With so much freedom, a British agent was able to approach them in a cafe and they planned their escape.[14]

On about 17 November, Dick and Coope were driven 30 miles or so to Borsbeek, a Flemish village close to Antwerp, and interned in Fort Two, which had been built at the end of the 19th century for the defence of the city. To his dismay, Dick saw that the fort was 'completely surrounded by a moat about 50 yards across'. Inside the moat, the fort was 'entirely surrounded by earthen ramparts about 30 feet in height'. The walls were of an 'impenetrable thickness', and it was 'altogether a pretty tough sort of place'.

Dick and Coope weren't the only internees at Borsbeek. A number of Allied airmen had been installed there since their capture during the first days of the war, including Jimmy Dunn, with whom Dick had chased the supposed enemy plane over Calais. He had been captured and interned on 10 November, the day after the Calais flight, when, as Dick put it, he 'chased a German a bit too far into Belgium before turning back and ran out of petrol on the wrong side of the border'.

The officer pilots 'lived quite comfortably'. Dick and Dunn shared a room, and, incarceration aside, the Allied airmen were all treated well. They had access to pen, ink and paper, and Dick made good use of his by writing to his mother. He knew she would be worried, so he played up the good points of internment. 'We are allowed quite a bit of liberty inside the ramparts and are soon to be allowed out for a few hours two days per week on parole.' But they were forbidden to venture into Antwerp or any other big town. They were 'comfortable in [the] mess and quarters, which are in the same building ... even have a small rose garden'. They had sporting equipment, access to a billiards table and tobacco rations, but although they were treated well, Dick, Coope and Dunn weren't ideal guests. Coope and Dunn shattered a glass, and the three of them had a hand in breaking a billiard-ball.[15]

It wasn't long before Dick and his commanding officer put their escape plan into effect. They took Dunn into their confidence and worked out the finer details. First, they acquired shorts, gym shoes, a skipping rope and a medicine ball. Then, tossing the ball, skipping rope and running 'around the fort every afternoon', they ensured their guards were well used 'to seeing us doing unusual things'. It worked: they were soon known as 'the mad English boys'.[16] Athletic pursuits over, Dick, Coope and Dunn would rush to the showers in the main part of the fort, where they would stay until just on dark. They were 'never allowed outside the ramparts, and had at all times to be within sight of the sentries, and we had to be in the mess, or in the quarters before it got dark'. Even so, they made their return from the shower later and later each day. Then, when 24 November, 'the appointed day', arrived, 'instead of going back to the mess we took advantage of a place where we were out of sight of the sentries for a few yards to scramble up onto one of the parapets'. They were protected from anyone looking up because of a 'slight depression running along the top'. They 'crawled along this for about 250 yards, at the rate of about 20 yards a minute', and passed 'right over the main gate' and outside 'the window of the Belgian major who commanded the camp'. When they reached 'the point where the parapet turned at right angles we slid down to the moat'. They took off their clothes 'and tied them round our heads'.

Darkness descended. It was raining and misty, and the ambient temperature was mild. Not so the moat. Coope led the way. He stepped into the reed-filled water, which reached to his knees. 'He murmured something about it being rather cold, took another step and disappeared beneath the surface.' His clothes fell into the water, and Dick and Dunn tried to restrain themselves 'as best we could' from laughing out loud. Halfway across, 'Dunn's clothes came unstuck', and, 'blowing like a grampus and swimming as well as he could with a pair of trousers in one hand, and a jersey in the other', he made it to the other side. Dick was luckier. He suffered no mishaps and was able to don dry clothes before they trudged through the fields 'to the rendezvous about a mile away'.

They had arranged to meet the British agent at 6 p.m. but made better progress than anticipated and had to wait 25 minutes until their 'outside helpers' arrived. Dick was still dry so found the wait no great hardship – other than anticipating that they might be located by their former captors – but Coope and Dunn were wet through and 'rather cold'. When their contacts arrived, the escapees were driven to Brussels by a circuitous route and kept in various apartments within the city until they could be taken to France. Their helpers 'were marvellously kind, and had things organised beautifully'.

Dick, Coope and Dunn did not have to hide for long. Coope passed into France on 26 November, and the others followed the next day, dressed 'in the most fantastic clothes'.[17] They were taken to the RAF's headquarters in France, where Coope awaited them. They were greeted by the Advanced Air Striking Force's commanding officer, who 'seemed very glad to see us back', and were then taken to see Lord Gort, the commander-in-chief of the British forces in France, who 'handed us a pat on the back'.

That night they returned to the squadron, where, no doubt, they received more than just a pat on the back. Dick would have heard the happy news that on 24 November, while they had been preparing for their last stint with the skipping rope and medicine ball, his promotion to flying officer had been confirmed.

The three airmen were then whisked to England to report to the Air Ministry, where 'we were congratulated by the Air member for personnel and his senior satellites, and given a week's leave in England and some money to replace the stuff we had to leave behind'. Dick also received a high commendation for his part in the escape. He remained convinced he had eluded a wide-spread search, but it appears that neither the Borsbeek guards nor the Belgian authorities made any effort to recapture the absconders. There has been speculation of a silent agreement between the British and Belgians to turn a blind eye to Allied escape attempts. Certainly, a French pilot escaped on 24 November, followed by two RAF airmen on 2 December. Belgian archives indicate that although Dick failed to mention it in his account, he, Coope and Dunn were accompanied by some French internees.[18] Quite a large group to slink past the prison commandant's window unnoticed.

'A thump in the backside'

A week after Des Sheen's first victory, 72 Squadron's A Flight relocated to Drem, in East Lothian, Scotland, with B Flight and the rest of the squadron following in December. Looking back over the Phoney War period, there were only 20 minutes Des never forgot. Five related to his first combat, on 21 October. The other 15 occurred just after noon on 7 December.

Des and B Flight were ordered to patrol over Montrose, a coastal town about 40 miles north of Dundee. It wasn't long before they spotted a formation of seven twin-engine Heinkel He111 fast medium bombers. B Flight split into two. Des, again flying K9959, led Blue Section into an attack on the Heinkels' rear formation. He zoomed past a lighthouse in pursuit of a fleeing bomber. (He later joked that the lighthouse keeper would have had a grandstand view of the fight.) He opened fire but the return barrage was heavy. He continued his attack, and the Heinkel 'dropped his undercarriage, a sure sign of distress'. As the enemy machine lost height, Blue Section turned its attention to the other three at the rear. 'We circled to come at them again … We finished the turn and attacked … [I] went for the Heinkel on the extreme right.' Even as the enemy pilot 'had ceased firing, and was losing formation', the 'other three turned their guns' on the

Australian and, as Des later recalled, K9959 'stopped a couple of bullets'.[19]

As well as 'a thump in the backside' from one of them, Des copped 'a bloody great bang in the ear' from another, which smashed into the earphone cover attached to his flying helmet. It thwacked the Bakelite cup containing the radio telephone receiver and ripped through the leather on the other side. The young pilot had been an inch from death. Then K9959 'took a pasting' as a third bullet ruptured its fuel tank. 'Petrol began to stream into the cockpit, and I couldn't see very clearly. I went in again to attack but I was dizzy now and I decided to turn for home.'

Des had been lucky twice, but still fortune favoured him. He wasn't able to make it to Drem so limped into RAF Leuchars. When he landed, 'there was terrific excitement … The whole station was running around in circles trying to decide what to do with the casualty!' While the medical officer tended his wounds, the ground crew patched up K9959. They found an incendiary in the petrol tank. Three times lucky. No wonder Des dubbed this 'the most hectic 15 minutes of my life', adding, 'in fact they nearly put an end to it'.

Des recorded 'two Heinkels shot down', but when the combat reports were analysed he was credited with only a one-third share. He wasn't able to celebrate with his squadron friends: he was whisked away to the military hospital that had been established at Edinburgh Castle, where he spent 'a very pleasant Christmas'.

6

Training for war

'Enjoying every minute'

There were so few ab initio schools in the early stages of the war that something had to be done with the new recruits. Accordingly, initial training wings were set up as holding units, in which little work actually took place. While Dick Glyde was embarking on his first France-based sorties, Bill Millington was in the final throes of his elementary flying training. He completed it on 16 September, and after a brief visit to relations he started packing for 3 Initial Training Wing, Hastings, in East Sussex. His diary suggests that he was exposed to precious little learning there.[1]

By the end of the month he was on leave, catching up with Lady Frances Ryder and Miss Celia Macdonald at the Dominion and Allied Services Hospitality Scheme and enjoying suppers and teas with London hostesses. He visited more relations, received another raft of inoculations and then started packing for 10 Flying Training School, Tern Hill, Shropshire. He arrived on 7 October. Lectures started the next day, and the chief flying instructor allotted trainees to either bombers or fighters. On 10 October, Bill had his first 'dual instruction on Harvards'. Compared to the Tiger Moth, the monoplane trainer was a giant, with much more power generated by its 600-horsepower radial engine. Bill had no problems with them though. 'Extra good show. Spinning, low flying etc.'

Bill could not have been happier. He was 'enjoying every minute' of his training and was 'keeping fit'. He was so busy he could pen only a brief postcard to the folks at home. 'Regret have very little news to offer as several matters cannot be communicated on account of some war or other over in Europe.'

'Fed up'

After the declaration of that 'war or other', the RMS *Orama* acquired escorts, changed her route and went around Africa. John Crossman and his friend Jack Burraston realised how much their plans would be affected by war. No longer would they be flying for the sheer joy of it. They talked it over and made an important decision. 'Now that war is declared and it looks as though we will see service, we both will try to get into fighters instead of bombers as we had intended at first.'[2]

The voyage to England took longer than originally scheduled as the ship zigzagged to elude enemy submarines. Anxious to start his flying training, John became impatient with his confinement and the lengthy delay. On the day Bill Millington arrived at Tern Hill, John recorded the rumour 'that we may make port next Thursday or Friday. I hope so as we are all most sick of this old tub and dead keen to get ashore and start flying'. Six days later, after two months and two days at sea, 'England today'.

John reported to the Air Ministry on 14 October and received his first training posting. There was just enough time before he was due at 1 Initial Training Wing, at Jesus College, Cambridge University, for a quick visit to his father's sisters, Ann Brawn and Mabel Crossman, at Chalfont St Giles. As he told them excitedly about his dreams of flying, they judged him to be 'full of promise' and 'a typical Englishman and quite proud of ... being British'.[3]

John and Jack Burraston were billeted together at Cambridge. John was impressed by the size and quality of their accommodation after the long weeks on board the RMS *Orama* – rather than a room, which he had expected, he and Jack shared a comfortable flat – but he was less enamoured with the training program. 'After breakfast we parade at about nine and then march off to one of the other colleges (generally to Downing or Emmanuel)' for what 'are supposed to be lectures'. As far as he was concerned, it was 'an absolute farce as the stuff we get is usually about first year high school standard and more often than not there is no lecture'. He was frustrated. 'We are all pretty fed up.'

On 28 October, John was advised that in two days' time he and Jack – whom John had affectionately dubbed Burry – would leave for 9 Elementary Flying Training School, Ansty, in Warwickshire. 'We ... are very glad to be going.'

'Posted at last'

The day after war was declared Ken Holland revved up the motorbike and drove to Melorne. 'Weren't we glad to see each other', he happily recorded, but 'good old T. a bit het up'.[4] It was no wonder. Toby had seen war before and knew the cost. As much as possible, though, he put his fears of a bleak future aside and hid his feelings. He gave Ken 'a super watch' and they spent the next few days talking, swimming and enjoying the Cornish summer. 'How far away the war seems just now', Ken mused. His joy was complete when, on 8 September, he recorded that Toby 'is going to leave Melorne to me. Also ... my name may be changed to Ripley, but difficulties abound'.

He returned to Portsmouth, and as he waited to hear of his posting to a training station he read and reread Toby's letters and those from Seina Haydon, the elder daughter – and second of six children – of Dr William and Mrs Mary Haydon, who lived at Garmoe House in Camelford, a short stroll from Melorne.

Eight months older than Ken, Jean Marguaretta Haydon, known since childhood as Seina (pronounced Sheena), was born in Glasgow. Her mother was Scottish but as the family had lived for many years in England Seina had none of her accent. She would, however, assume one when regaling her friends with riotous anecdotes. She loved classical music, was intelligent and well read, and could converse knowledgeably on a great range of subjects. She had dark hair with a light wave, a long face with broad forehead and pointed chin, and greenish brown eyes. She was vibrant, had a keen sense of humour and loved to laugh. Her smile was one of her most striking features, and her face lit up when she was happy. Healthy and active, she loved rambling in the countryside. Of slim build and flawless complexion, the attractive 20-year-old, at 5 feet 4 inches, was shorter than her Australian beau.

The two had met in the summer of 1937. Although Seina's parents were key figures in the local community, their paths had not previously crossed, because soon after completing her education at her Norfolk boarding school, Seina had started training as a radiographer at Torbay Hospital, in Torquay, Devon.[5] The pair hit it off, and Seina asked Ken to come and play tennis at Garmoe House. He soon became a regular visitor, enjoying the company of his young hostess as well as that of her siblings, particularly Seina's brother Francis – known as Ian – who had joined the RAF in 1936.

Ken was keen on Seina from the start, but her heart had been won by her father's new assistant, Alex Hutchison. They were head over heels in love and became engaged, much to the fury of Dr Haydon. In the end, because of her father's opposition to the match, Seina reluctantly broke off the attachment. 'Ken came back into my life again in the summer of '39.'[6] He was besotted. 'Seina?!?! I almost k[issed] her but didn't dare. She is my reason [sic] d'être.'

His love grew and he excitedly made plans: 'This war is going to bring Garmoe and Melorne together more which is a good thing'. For the time being, however, they wrote to each other and Ken pounced on Seina's 'glorious letters' and rhapsodised in his diary. 'To Seina. I love you three bags brimming.' Even so, there were times when he could not 'quite get how the land lies'.

Ken's confusion over the depth of Seina's feelings was not helped by the lack of training news: 'Paraded, no postings!' There was still no word by 15 September and he was 'fed up'. Frustratingly, still 'no orders, no drill on the 21st'. On 27 September, Ken finally received good news. 'Posted at last! Hastings. At last! To an initial training wing – on Monday. YIPPEE!'

Like Bill Millington, Ken was off to 3 Initial Training Wing. He caught the train to Hastings on 2 October. Next morning, 'allotted to C Flight No. 3 Squadron. Drilled solidly. Filthy good'.

'What he could do with a plane!'

Early in November, Pat Hughes was again packing his bags. He had been posted from 64 Squadron and Church Fenton, though he did not have far to travel. He was following Des Sheen to Leconfield, to join the newly reformed 234 Squadron.

Squadron Leader William Satchell had taken command on 30 October, and the next day his flight commanders, flying officers John Theilmann and Howard Blatchford, arrived from 41 Squadron, followed by pilots, administrative staff and airmen. Satchell was injured in a motor car accident on 2 November and hospitalised, and two days later Blatchford returned to 41 Squadron, 'thus terminating', as the squadron historian put it, 'what must have been two of the shortest command appointments ever'.[7] Within days, Squadron Leader Richard 'Dicky' Barnett had arrived to replace Satchell, followed by Pat on 8 November to replace Blatchford as B Flight's commander.

The majority of 234 Squadron's pilots had only just completed flying training. Pat was responsible for preparing his flight's new boys for operations. He had proven himself capable of such responsibility on the occasions when he'd stepped into the shoes of his flight commander at 64 Squadron. He had matured after more than two years' experience in the RAF and took his role seriously, soon gaining respect as the squadron's 'Australian mentor'. Even so, according to Pilot Officer Robert 'Bob' Doe – a man of few words who had been born in Reigate, Surrey – Pat was still 'one of the lads', and 'not a remote figure'. More importantly, he was a 'cracking good pilot', recalled New Zealander Pilot Officer Keith Lawrence. 'What he could do with a plane!'[8]

But what sort of aircraft was the squadron to fly? And, for that matter, what sort of squadron was it to be? Bomber or fighter? It was a mystery. Barnett was in the dark, and the only aircraft in the new squadron's charge were two Miles Magisters. By 11 November, the complement of Magisters had increased to three, and the pilots took it in turns to clock up 2 hours 30 minutes' local flying in them and 40 minutes in the Link Trainer.[9] It wasn't a good start.

Confusion reigned. On 16 November, one Fairey Battle – a single-engine light bomber – arrived along with three obsolete Gauntlets on loan from 616 Squadron, which was also located at Leconfield. What would Pat have felt at the thought of ending up as a bomber pilot after disputing his initial categorisation at Digby? Still, nothing was certain. Rumours started flying – and were reinforced by the arrival of wireless operator / air gunners – that perhaps they might be destined for Bristol Blenheim 1F fighters.

By the end of the month, the rumours were confirmed. Eight Blenheim 1Fs arrived on 28 November, and another three were collected from a maintenance unit on the 30th.[10] They were a fighter squadron, or at least they would be when they became accustomed to the new machines. It did not take them long: 15 pilots had soloed on the new machine by 22 December.

Pat had mastered the Blenheim at 64 Squadron and, like his former squadron leader, was an advocate of tight flying discipline. He was in his element, and whenever the miserable winter weather allowed he schooled his boys in the RAF's rigid fighter attack patterns. They perfected wingtip-to-wingtip formation, practising so often that Bob Doe recalled in understated fashion that they were 'good at formation'. On one occasion, however, the Australian flight commander was accused of taking things too far.

Pat was leading and called his pilots to formate on him. Tight flying in a Blenheim was dicey, as the engines obscured the pilot's view of the wingtips. Even so, his men flew closer and closer. But it was not good enough. Pat kept signalling Keith Lawrence to move in, and the inevitable happened. Lawrence's wing touched Pat's. The Australian ordered his wireless operator to bale out while he fought for control. He landed safely, but it taught him there was such a thing as flying too close.[11]

'A fine old English house'

Bill Millington was going from strength to strength at Tern Hill. Two days after his first flight in a Harvard under dual instruction, with only 3 hours' dual to his credit, he soloed. During a height test on 21 October, he broke his training squadron's record, taking his machine to 18 000 feet.[12] In her most recent letter, his sister Eileen had asked if he went out at night. He cheekily replied, 'Quite a bit – out into the blue'. He found night flying 'rather tricky at first but becoming more enjoyable every flight, depending mainly on the weather'.

Bill progressed well except for a mishap with Harvard N7030 on 25 November, when he landed with the undercarriage retracted. 'Rather bad show.' But fortunately there was 'little damage except to airscrew'. He received mixed results in the exams which marked the conclusion of his intermediate training: 86 per cent in armament and 90 per cent in signals, but his airmanship results of 57 per cent let him down. Overall, he was ranked 22nd out of the 29 officers on the course, with an average of 71 per cent, just below the officers' average of 73.5 per cent.[13] Results in hand, he was off. He had been invited to join the Reid Walker family at Ruckley Grange, 'a fine old English house', located 20 miles or so from the training school. That was followed by a trip to London to visit his relatives and Lady Frances Ryder, and to catch up with Captain Reid Walker at the Café Anglais and Boodle's, a gentlemen's club in St James's Street.

If anything outstanding happened in training during the last weeks of 1939, Bill didn't record it. His last diary entries for the year were devoted to his Christmas leave. At midday on 22 December, Captain Reid Walker picked him up from the mess and drove back to Ruckley Grange. Almost immediately, Bill rolled up his sleeves and attacked the rhododendrons. Over the next few days he worked in the pine plantation and the sycamores and spent more time pruning the rhododendrons.

Bill liked nothing better than being with family and friends, and with the Reid Walkers he had both. He was embraced by a large, welcoming family who did not stand on ceremony, and his first Christmas in England since he was a lad was a warm, happy affair. He was pleased to see Glen Grindlay, a Canadian he had met through the Dominion and Allied Services Hospitality Scheme, join the house party and had 'a very enjoyable time' full of 'hunting, felling trees, shooting, skating and tobogganing'. He particularly took to ice skating, which he thought 'a lot of fun and I was duly initiated into the art, taking a number of falls in the process. Actually I find it much easier than roller skating, but have to glide into somebody or something to stop'.

Bill and Grindlay leaped out of bed at one o'clock on

Christmas morning and crept downstairs. They quietly let them-selves out of the house and, securing axe and rope, dashed through the snow-encrusted grounds to a stand of trees from which they selected a well-shaped Christmas fir and chopped it down. Alter-nately dragging and pushing, they returned at half past two and managed to erect it in the 'large room set aside for the festivi-ties'. As silently as possible, Santa's most recently employed helper elves then set about decorating it. With the last fragile bauble trembling at the end of a branch, they scooted upstairs to sleep the sleep of the not-so-innocent.

When everyone awoke and gathered by the tree, Bill was 'given the job of Father Christmas' to hand out the parcels, and 'things went off exceptionally well'. The party then settled down to 'ten courses, followed by crackers etc. We finished off the evening with dancing in the ballroom'. It was a happy day and riotous evening. In contrast, the final day of 1939 was a quiet one. Bill arrived at Tern Hill just before midnight on the 30th and on New Year's Eve 'wrote letters most of [the] time'. He did not celebrate the waning of 1939 and the dawn of 1940, but 'retired 10.30'.

'I'd hate like hell to go back a failure'

Every service pilot dreaded being scrubbed from his training course, and John Crossman was no different. When he arrived at Ansty on 30 October, he felt the pressure to fly quickly and well. He was in the air that afternoon and took over the controls of the Tiger Moth almost as soon as his instructor, Sergeant Webb, cleared the aerodrome. He then flew '35 minutes straight and level. At least I tried hard to do that. It was great'.[14]

Next morning, he was in the front seat of Tiger Moth N5472. Under Webb's careful guidance he taxied into position to take off. When they were airborne, Webb said, 'You've got it'. John 'took over and flew it straight and level for a while and then the instructor brought it down and I taxied back to the tarmac'. It was a grand moment. Webb was pleased with John's progress after 65 minutes' dual, and the young Australian hoped to advance to turns the next day. As it happened, he had two training sessions on 2 November, again practising straight and level flying as well as climbing, gliding and stalling, and, finally, medium turns. He was quietly pleased that his 'climbing and gliding [are] quite good now and also my turns'.

John progressed satisfactorily in his first flying week. Webb told him he was 'doing quite well and wants me to do some more landings and a few spins and then go solo'. Even with this vote of confidence and the fact that 'I have had no trouble flying up to date', John was a perfectionist and wanted more dual hours under his belt. 'I feel I'd like to do a few more landings myself ... and get fairly proficient at it before I do go solo'. But as the Point Cook boys had found, the pressure was on to solo as quickly as possible, and as Pat Hughes in particular had discovered, flying lessons were often a case of one step forward and four backward. After 10 hours 50 minutes' dual, John carried out a solo test on 15 November. It did not go well. 'Landed all over the place again. In the air I fly well but am gone 30 feet from the ground.' Flight Lieutenant Williams, who took the test, put John's poor performance down to a problem with his eyesight, but a check-up revealed nothing wrong. Perhaps John would benefit from another instructor? And so, under the guidance of Pilot Officer Underhill, John continued dual instruction until 20 November, when, with 14 hours 35 minutes notched up, he retook the solo test. This time he was successful and was allowed a 10-minute solo flight. 'It is absolutely marvellous to think that at last I've flown a plane on my own as I've wanted to do for a very long time now.'

There was no time to rest on his solo laurels, as the progress of trainee pilots was carefully scrutinised. John was lucky that Williams had given him a second chance, as three days later two young men 'failed their flying tests and will be leaving for Australia soon'. And the reason? 'They were both taking too much time to go solo and after being taken up for tests were told they were not fit for flying.' Although John was 'awfully sorry' for the 'poor beggars' who had to pack their bags, it was hard to put aside his own dread: 'Hope I'm never passed out. I'd hate like hell to go back a failure'.

With the ejection of the two Australians, 'not a few of us feel very apprehensive about it as the course is very rigorous'. John did not often dwell on the past, and he would never have dared, under normal circumstances, to criticise his father, but he was uneasy and in a letter home admitted that 'I have never regretted anything more in my life than not learning to fly before I came here'.

If the trainee pilot could not change the past, he could at least exert some control over the present, and John and Jack Burraston determined that they would not return home with their tails between their legs. They had again arranged to share quarters. 'I am lucky in having such a decent chap as Jack with me and each night we go over the day's work and test each other on what we've had.'

One more trainee was scrubbed from the course. Again, John was 'awfully sorry about it' and rationalised that 'it wasn't his fault, he just could not fly well enough', but his own place was now secure. 'We all feel very relieved … as we hear that there won't be any more [discharged] as the weeding out is now finished.'

The flying days sped by. 'We haven't been allowed to do much slacking as the Air Ministry is rushing us all through at a great pace.' John 'thought we'd have to work over Christmas and now we find we have a week off'. After his warm welcome by Ann and William Brawn shortly after he arrived in England, he had initially planned to spend the holidays at Chalfont St Giles if he had time off. But, not realising the young Australian had family he could go to – and without John disabusing him of this belief –

the training school's commanding officer organised for John and Jack to stay with the Parkes family at Stratford-on-Avon, about 25 miles from the training station.

Like Bill Millington, John happily fitted in to his hosts' Christmas festivities. Mrs Parkes, known to all as Granny Mary, was 'a wonderful woman and awfully kind'. The family was well off, with 'a big Buick and three Standards and a staff of servants. It must cost 40 pounds a week to run that house'. He enthusiastically embraced the comforts of his affluent Christmas billet and was in danger of letting them go to his head. 'We sit at dinner and drink champagne and look absolutely it. There's no doubt how these people do live well.'

Despite the excitement of his first English Christmas, at which he and Jack sat 'down to Christmas dinner with a terrific array of knives and forks on each side of us and being asked by the butler what we'd have from champagne downwards', and the kindness of the Parkes family, John felt 'awfully homesick for Australia and the folks and Pat'.

Two days later, he was at Chalfont St Giles for a belated family Christmas. Knowing her brother would want a full report of how his son was faring, Ann Brawn turned a critical gaze towards John. She noticed that he was 'the picture of health. If anything not quite so thin'. She judged erroneously that he was not pining for his life back in Australia. 'Don't get any idea into your minds that he is homesick. He is not.'[15]

Ann also saw that John was developing spendthrift ways but realised much of it had to do with 'meeting a class of people whom even the regular English would not'. She was astounded at 'what he spent on smokes. Approximately what I have kept the home on (not counting Mabe) for the last four months'. Even so, she did not think he was 'fooling away his money'. But he was. Like his friends, he purchased decorative wings for his mother, bought lavish Christmas presents for the Parkes family, his aunts and Uncle Will, and spent freely when on leave. Notwithstanding her mild criticism, Ann saw only the good in the nephew she had already come to love. 'He has a GOOD heart', 'never speaks an ill word' and 'has no vices'. Above all, 'he will be all right. Neither of you need worry. His head is screwed on just where he wants it'.

Before he left, Ann wanted to assure herself and her brother that John was indeed happy with his new flying life. 'He said it was the thing. The one thing he has always wanted.'[16]

'Oh my diary who records my hopes and fears'

'Life very dull', recorded Ken Holland in late November.[17] 'Routine drill', 'routine lectures' and 'rugger'. There was so little excitement on offer that Ken took to documenting the war news in his diary to fill the pages. To relieve his boredom he joined in with the 'very objectionable scrum in our part of the room' and made friends. One was George Charles Palliser, from West Hartlepool, in County Durham.

Palliser, who was known as Charles, or more commonly Tich (he was 5 feet 6 inches), was almost exactly a year older than Ken. They bumped into each other in the mess one day and started chatting. Palliser talked of his childhood and Ken told him about Australia. He thought Ken a nice boy and particularly knowledgeable about aeroplanes generally as well as the aircraft industry.[18]

Ken enjoyed Hastings but occasionally suffered from feelings of isolation. In spite of the circumstances of his home life in Australia he dutifully wrote to his parents. He had not heard from his mother and perhaps thought she welcomed the lengthy separation from the son she had not wanted. His loneliness at times became so intense that it crowded out the feelings of rejection he harboured, and he was delighted to receive a long-overdue letter from Ina which revealed that none of his correspondence had reached Sydney. Always welcome were letters from Toby and

Seina Haydon, and Ken fretted if he didn't receive any. 'No word from Seina … God forbid she has met someone else as I believe she is the girl for me for always now … T. is dear to me as always and his letters help a lot but if my darling leaves me …'

On 3 December, Ken was posted to 11 Elementary Flying Training School, located at Scone, near Perth, in Scotland, over 550 miles from Camelford and Toby. He arrived the next day, ready to start elementary training. The following day, Ken was introduced to his flying instructor, Flight Lieutenant Holmes. A calm, serious but pleasant man, Holmes was ever tolerant of his pupils and paced them carefully. As far as Ken was concerned, at least, he was also long suffering, with the patience of Job.

Holmes took his new pupil up for 25 minutes in a Tiger Moth to develop a sense of the effects of the controls and become familiar with the cockpit layout. Over the next few days, Ken practised taxiing and flying straight and level, medium turns and navigating through mist. He moved on to gliding, climbing and stalling. He blitzed his first navigation test, scoring 14 out of 15.

After his earlier success in the air Ken encountered some failures. He attempted his first landing, but it was 'v. bad indeed. Got a ticking off'. He received almost full marks in the next navigation test but 'made a hell of a mess' of his spinning and circuits lesson. He kept 'making silly mistakes', and after an entire day's attempt to perfect circuits and bumps, he managed to leave the patient Holmes 'hairless'. There was no improvement on the 17th – 'absolutely hopeless' – and Holmes threatened to ground him. Ken didn't record his feelings in his diary that night, but it would not be surprising if he felt worried. Tich Palliser had soloed the day before, the first on their course to do so, after 6 hours 35 minutes. Others were also champing at the bit and perfectly capable of taking the controls on their own. Palliser recalled that the 'atmosphere on the course was really exciting'.[19] For everyone but Ken, perhaps, with the threat of expulsion hanging over him.

But Holmes didn't ground Ken. Just as Flight Lieutenant Williams had given John Crossman a second chance, Holmes must have seen something in his bright young pupil who diligently went back to his billet most evenings to study. On 18 December, Ken took his solo test with Flying Officer Sayers. He practised spinning and circuits, and when they landed Sayers sent Ken up on his own. It was 'a great day' for the young Australian. 'FIRST SOLO.'

Unlike Pat Hughes, Jack Kennedy and John Crossman, who all seemed to regress after soloing, Ken gained confidence. With Holmes back in the instructor's seat he carried out sideslips, circuits and bumps, and medium turns. Holmes came out of it 'in good nick', and Ken was allowed to solo for 45 minutes. On the next lone effort, he carried out 'a lovely left hand [turn] from 4000 to 1000 [feet], not easily pulled out of'. He passed more tests and on 21 December had a 'grand' dual session of low flying and map reading. To top it off he received the happy news that he had eight days' leave over Christmas. This was a privilege, as some trainees were not permitted any. After notching up another 25 minutes' dual flying and map reading on the morning of the 22nd, he caught the train – final destination Melorne. 'What a joy to be going home.'

Ken had a blissful Christmas. He and Toby Ripley exchanged gifts and then shared a festive dinner at the Elliott Arms. They went to Garmoe House for a party that evening, and Ken did the honours as Santa Claus. Seina gave him socks, perhaps not the most romantic gift, but they would come in handy in the worsening Scottish weather, as would the furry slippers and scarf from his guardian.

Boxing Day was even more joyful. After a morning spent chatting and sipping sherry with Toby's brother, Guy, who had come to visit, Ken went on an afternoon shoot. He hadn't lost his eye and was pleased to bag a snipe. It was all 'good fun'. He then took Seina, who 'looked stunning', out to dinner and a dance. Afterwards, they returned to Melorne to discover that Seina's parents had stopped in for a few drinks. While Toby entertained the Haydons, Seina quietly told Ken that her mother had asked if she were fond of Ken. Seina confessed to the young man that she had initially hedged before answering truthfully that she was. She did not, however, admit the cause of her hesitation. Ken had earlier visited her at Torquay and had proposed. She admitted, 'I wasn't very sure about it'. As the war had progressed, however, and 'as life was becoming so uncertain, I felt that perhaps it was the right thing to do'. After gentle probing from her mother regarding her feelings and apparent closeness to Ken, Seina decided she should marry the young Australian because it would give him 'something to hold on to in a very uncertain world'.[20] And so, for perhaps the wrong reasons, she told Ken she accepted his proposal.

Ken was jubilant. 'S. said yes!' And even better, the Haydons 'were pleased!!!!' No matter Ken's humble origins; it seems that Toby's guardianship had given him a social cachet above that of poor Alex Hutchison, who had been deemed such an unsuitable match. Ken knew nothing of that sad affair and was delighted to record that 'tonight they (*mère et père*) came into Melorne and asked T. if he approved and T. said yes in an indefinite sort of way and vaguely said 25! i.e. my minimum age on marriage'.

Ken did not explain why he had to wait until he was 25, but whatever the reason, it would be a long engagement. Seina would not turn 21 until 20 May 1940, and her fiancé was still a few weeks shy of 20. Perhaps Seina knew this when she accepted Ken's proposal. Waiting aside, Ken was happy. He believed Seina loved him, and her parents were delighted with the match. Most importantly, the only child who was not wanted by his own parents was being welcomed into a large family with the approval – of sorts – of the man he looked upon as his father.

Despite his elation, Ken had a small niggle of apprehension

that his dreams for the future might not eventuate. 'Oh my diary who records my hopes and fears', he confided. 'I wonder will you see me a pilot officer RAF – married happily to S. and living at Melorne with T. smiling benignly at us and still retaining his love. Pray God this last and most important will ever last.'

7

The Phoney War continues

'All but essential flights were discontinued'

Like many aerodromes and stations throughout the country, Tern Hill was blanketed in snow, and Bill Millington was one of the volunteers wielding shovels to dig out their stranded Harvards in early 1940. Little flying training was carried out during January and February, as 'the severe winter' took its toll and 'all but essential flights were discontinued'. To make up for the lack of flying, 'much ground work, such as checking the accuracy of flying instruments, and the swinging of compass, has been done of late'.[1] The switch to ground work was all well and good on a training station, but when Des Sheen, fully recovered from his encounter with the enemy Heinkel He111s over the Scottish coast, rejoined 72 Squadron at Drem there was little to do. And when the squadron returned to Church Fenton, in January, the Yorkshire weather was just as bad. The situation didn't improve on 2 March, when they relocated to Acklington, just north of Newcastle, in Northumberland.

As Des flew 'boring' coastal patrols which were 'just a question of going round and round over the shipping and never seeing anything but water', he bemoaned the fact that 'I've not had a scrap' since December. 'Other Fighter Command squadrons seem to have had all the luck.'[2]

Perhaps, but Stuart Walch's 151 Squadron was not one of them. Like 72 Squadron, they were consigned to convoy protection duty spiced up with the occasional non-result interception. They put a brave face on things and flew whenever the weather permitted, often quipping that it was 'only unfit to fly when the birds were walking'. Even so, they were as disconcerted as Des with the lack of activity.

Flight Lieutenant John Thompson took command of the squadron on 24 January, and Stuart's patient training work was recognised – as was his three-day stint relieving Thompson in October 1939 – when he was promoted to the acting rank of flight lieutenant and commander of A Flight on 3 February, less than two weeks before his 23rd birthday. The weather improved, a raft of new pilots arrived, and Stuart and the other experienced pilots were constantly in the air training the new boys. The Tasmanian relinquished A Flight's command on 1 April, when the new flight commander arrived, but he was just as active throughout that month and the opening days of May, as the training program was revised to include high-altitude as well as low-level combat.[3]

'I thought he was conceited'

At Leconfield, Pat Hughes daily risked getting his feet wet as he tried to navigate a weather-ravaged aerodrome. For most of January and into February it had been unserviceable for 234 Squadron's Blenheims, as fog, frost, snow and ice prevented flying training. The situation was so bad – for a squadron that had yet to attain operational status – that they managed a combined total of only 25 flying hours during January. Yet again, Pat shivered through a Yorkshire winter, and instead of basking in the Australian sun he warmed himself in front of a well-stoked fire at the Beverley Arms, a short stroll from the station.

One evening he walked into the pub carrying an Airedale

puppy known as Flying Officer Butch.[4] Looking back, Keith Lawrence could not remember if the mini scruff bucket had arrived at Leconfield with Pat or if Pat had acquired him afterwards. Obscure origins aside, Butch was a popular member of the squadron and it seemed as if he was always running around the mess chasing after Pat, or up in the air as an unofficial (and forbidden) passenger while his master carried out training exercises.[5] 'We all admired [Pat] and his constant companion', recalled Bob Doe.

Pushing through the crowded room towards his friends, Pat saw an attractive, well-dressed young woman chatting and laughing with them. She was Kathleen Agnes Brodrick, known as Kay. She lived with her widowed mother in nearby Hull – her father, Percy, a consulting engineer and surveyor, had succumbed to tetanus in early 1935. She was the second daughter; her younger brother, William, had died as an infant.

Born on 2 July 1916, Kay was a few months older than Pat. At 5 feet 6 or 7 inches, auburn haired, with 'kind of brown' eyes and a flawless fair complexion, she was decidedly attractive. She was spoiled by her doting mother, Theresa, had her own car and loved pretty clothes. A stereotypical redhead, she had a temper that could blaze from nowhere, but people usually saw only her happy, bubbly personality.

Kay held court in the front bar of the Beverley Arms, and, as she later told it to her son, the 'Brylcreem boys' were like bees to honey. For her part, she liked being seen with the best looking men. Kay was never short of boyfriends, but from the moment she saw the Australian pilot muscling to the front of the pack at the bar, she was captivated. She wasn't put off by his fierce moustache. 'With his good looks, moustache and smart uniform' he reminded her of Errol Flynn. Pat did indeed look handsome and dashing in the uniform, according to Bob Doe. 'When he wore his best uniform – it was Royal Blue with gold rank badges', Doe

reminisced, 'he looked fantastic'. Even so, Kay was not an immediate conquest.

Pat assumed she would fall for his charm, but as she felt the
full blast of his personality and swagger, the young woman initially reacted against his brash self-confidence. 'I thought he
was conceited', she admitted. 'He asked me to telephone him. I
didn't.' Pat, however, was instantly smitten. His favourite song
was 'Where or When', which had been written by Richard Rodg-
ers and Lorenz Hart and featured in the 1937 musical and 1939
movie *Babes in Arms*. In it, a young couple who meet for the first
time are instantly struck by the feeling that they have been in love
before, but they can't work out where they met, or how long ago.
Their strong impression of déjà vu, along with their immediate
attraction, create the sense that they belong together, and so it was
for Pat. Assured of their shared future, Pat telephoned Kay three
days later and invited her out.

Kay was swept off her feet. 'He was a smashing bloke.'
Romance blossomed, and they started courting.[6] It was not all
bliss, however. Pat had a temper to match Kay's, and, combined
with Kay's almost wilful sense of freedom and Pat's tendency to
wild boisterousness with a touch of cruelty, it led to inevitable
clashes. But if anyone could tame the auburn-haired beauty it was
Pat, and if anyone could rein in the Australian it was Kay. For so
long Pat had resisted forming any relationships with women as
he focused on flying. The love of his close-knit though far-flung
family had been enough. Within weeks, Kay discovered that 'he
loved flying – and Britain', he loved 'flying – and his family', he
loved 'flying – and her!'

On 14 March, Pat and his fellow pilots farewelled their Blenheims and former crew members and welcomed the arrival of the
Spitfire. They walked around the first one, sat in it, stroked it. 'It
was so beautiful', thought Bob Doe. 'We all fell a little in love
with it.' Even the ground crew were taken with the impressive

new machines. 'Everyone was over the moon', remembered Joe Roddis, one of the fitters. 'Everyone wanted to work on the Spit-fires.' As far as Keith Lawrence was concerned, they could not believe their eyes or luck. 'They were to fly the best fighter air-craft in the RAF. It was something pilots only dreamed of.' And perhaps Airedales. Doe recalled that Flying Officer Butch 'had more flying hours in Spitfires than some pilots'. As more Spits arrived, Doe and his friends felt 'for the first time, we were a real squadron' – not a bomber squadron, not a Blenheim squadron, but a proper fighter squadron flying the RAF's best. Pat claimed Spitfire AZ-Q as his own.[7]

'The only person I shall ever want'

Jack Kennedy also flew the RAF's best fighting machine – when he had the chance, that is. Like Des Sheen, he was frustrated by the lack of enemy action as the Phoney War drifted on. Des at least had tasted battle and scored early success, but for 65 Squad-ron – which had relocated to Northolt in October – there was next to no meaningful activity. Compounding Jack's dissatisfac-tion was the enforced separation from Christine Jourd. 'You are in my mind all the time', he wrote. 'I try to imagine you in my arms.'[8]

To him, 'this bloody war business is rapidly becoming some-thing of a farce'. He was 'absolutely bored to tears by the whole affair' and annoyed at how difficult it was to 'promise some defi-nite time to see you'. The best he could do was hope that 'as soon as I get half a chance I'll dash over to you'. It would not be easy. 'Even if I did get the time off, on account of the blackout and car lights it would simply take hours.' Christine was more philosoph-ical about their situation and told Jack that at least 'we have each other, and can think about one another, and our few moments together'. But Jack was not as accepting. 'It makes me mad when

I think how this bloody business has come along just as I realised how much you really mean.' As far as he was concerned, 'the sooner we give old Hitler a good kick in the bottom the better, and every kick I give him will have so much extra personal venom behind it'. But there was little hope of that at the moment, so Jack chafed at their separation. He found the situation 'so futile and exasperating that both of us are doing practically nothing all day and yet we can't get together. I feel cooped up and helpless. I'd like to pull somebody's nose'.[9] Happily, for the sake of someone's nose, Jack became involved in useful work.

Jack, Gordon Olive and Flying Officer John Welford joined a course at Fighter Command's tactics training school, which was also located at Northolt. They analysed reports from France and carried out a number of experiments to determine whether Hurricanes and Spitfires would be able to successfully dogfight with German fighters. There had been ongoing doubt and debate over this, as Royal Flying Corps veterans believed dogfighting wouldn't be possible because of the excessive gravitational forces involved at turning speeds in the 400 miles per hour range. After ten weeks or so, Jack, Olive and Welford proved that the British planes were more than capable. All too soon the trials were over, and 65 Squadron was ordered back to Hornchurch on 28 March, tasked with convoy patrols. There were precious few of those, and Jack flew only three, in late March and early April, while the squadron diarist recorded two solid months of 'nothing to report'.[10]

With little to occupy himself, Jack wrangled two days' leave. 'Petrol was so difficult to get', Christine recalled, so 'he filled his car up with high octane which was used for the aeroplanes'. They set off and the war was forgotten. Jack found 'a lovely old inn' at Edenbridge, in Kent, about 30 miles from the station.[11]

Both revelled in the bliss of their seclusion. Jack had 'never been so perfectly and gloriously happy'. As he gazed into

Christine's eyes, with 'that marvellous sort of misty look', a 'yearning power [drew] me to you'. He felt a 'choking in my throat as a message in my eyes seemed to go out to yours, and get that wonderful answer there – that you love me too'. By now Jack was 'absolutely certain that you are the only one I could love and the only person I shall ever want'. Within hours, their private moments were no more. Jack received word to return to Hornchurch. Even the excitement of a police escort could not dispel Christine's bitter disappointment, but she knew Jack's duty had priority.[12]

Kay Brodrick's relationship with her Spitfire pilot was also progressing in leaps and bounds, and Pat Hughes slipped a diamond ring on her finger. They planned to marry after the war. Like Christine Jourd, Kay found herself almost a Spitfire widow as Pat devoted his time to training his men – and himself – on the RAF's classy fighter. But Pat wasn't responsible only for B Flight. About this time, according to Bob Doe, the pilots noticed the commanding officer and other flight commander weren't doing much flying, and it fell to Pat to supervise the squadron's conversion. By the end of March they had accrued 185 hours on Spitfires, and Pat's men saw that 'he was a good leader'.[13]

As 234 Squadron fast approached operational status, Bill Millington also came closer to participating in the war, which, he hoped, when won, would result in 'a greater freedom, democracy and peace among nations'. On 10 April, his advanced training concluded. Improving on his intermediate course results, he passed out 14th of the 29 officers, with an average of 75 per cent, just above the officers' course average of 74 per cent. His final assessment for qualities of an officer was 78 per cent, which was above the course average of 75 per cent, and his 74 per cent for qualities of a pilot was right on average.[14]

Ten days later, Bill was confirmed as a pilot officer on probation and posted to 17 Operational Training Unit, at RAF

Upwood, in Cambridgeshire. Equipped with Blenheims and Ansons, the unit was a bomber training school, yet Bill had completed advanced fighter training. What had gone wrong? Perhaps his low intermediate course ranking indicated he was less suited as a fighter pilot than other trainees. Perhaps, with the expected increase in RAF activity after Germany's invasion of Denmark and Norway on 9 April, there was a more immediate need for bomber pilots for mine-laying sorties and operations against enemy shipping. Whatever the RAF's rationale for not sending Bill to a fighter unit, Bill offered little explanation. 'We must leave these details until after the scrap. Sufficient to say that we're on the job seven days a week. Leave is a myth, but nevertheless, the indomitable British spirit prevails.' He was supremely confident that the RAF would triumph. 'After all, if we don't lick 'em today, we'll lick 'em tomorrow.'[15]

On 17 April, 234 Squadron returned to Church Fenton for intensive training. They had been joined on 10 April by Durham-born and Australian-raised Pilot Officer Vincent 'Bush' Parker. They expected to pass out as operational at the end of the week – even Parker, who had had less than 12 months' flying experience – but it was decided they should carry out more testing at Leconfield. During this period Pat Hughes consolidated his position, and as Nigel Walpole, the squadron historian, put it, 'despite its paucity of experience', the squadron 'began to become a viable force'. Pat had come a long way from his final cadet assessment of having 'no outstanding qualities'. Now, according to Bob Doe, 'we respected him, listened to him'. Certainly, 'he was the real power behind the squadron'. In going to Britain, he had indeed done 'something special'.[16]

After days of formation flying and interception and attack exercises with a Hurricane unit that had seen action in France, 13 Group declared 234 Squadron 'operational by day'.[17]

'Flying is in my blood'

John Crossman's end-of-year break concluded all too soon and he was back in the air again on 1 January 1940. 'I thought I'd have lost touch, but apparently not as I'm flying just the same as ever.'[18] The next day, Ansty was officially designated an RAF station 'in every sense of the word and now we have to wear uniform all the time … [and] go round saluting and being saluted and my hand seems always to be at my forehead'. But the added work of saluting left, right and centre was overshadowed by the unwelcome news that, instead of Ansty continuing as a training school, 'this aerodrome and all other training schools are to be taken over as either bomber or fighter units'. John would remain at Ansty until 7 March, at which point he expected to go to Canada for advanced training.

John was not impressed with this turn of events, as he had already completed over 40 of the allotted 50 hours' flying practice and, instead of going on to advanced types, would 'have to do a lot more flying on elementary types than we had first imagined'. Within a week, the mandatory flying hours had been extended to 90. John's natural impatience again reared its head but for once was replaced by insight: 'In spite of the 50 hours flying I've had I realise … just how much we don't know. I'll admit it isn't so very hard to fly a plane but it is very hard indeed to do it really well'.

As it happened, John failed to achieve the 90 hours. He 'succumbed finally to the English climate and caught myself a beautiful chill'. He was confined to bed for six days. Fully recovered, he enjoyed 'an organised brawl in the snow when two of the chaps … charged me and we all fell over with yours truly underneath'. The result? 'One broken collar bone.'

John stoically accepted that he would not be able to fly for some time but did not welcome the news that 'once again our departure is to be postponed … we are to stay here now until

10 April. We are all very disgusted indeed'. He was fit to fly on 4 March and 'was very glad to get in the air again'. Four days later the flight commander told him his flying was good and his blind flying was even better, then 'asked me what I wanted to fly. I said fighters and he is going to recommend me for them. I'm very pleased'.

That same day, 'we had our first decent crash'. A hapless trainee and his instructor 'were doing night flying and came in too low. They carried away a high hedge and an iron fence ... The only part of the machine intact is where the cockpits are'. The rest of the aircraft was a mess. 'God knows', John wondered, 'how they got out with only one broken nose between the two of them'. He rushed out the next morning and snapped the crumpled aircraft but could not add the photos to his collection as they were confiscated. As Pat Hughes had discovered at Point Cook, and Bill Millington at Tern Hill, training accidents and deaths were a sad reality. Bill had shrugged off his 'bad show' and crumpled airscrew as he focused on exams. He and his friends were 'quite hardened' to their school's training losses.[19] John, too, thought little of the crash other than as a photo opportunity, but a funeral following a fatal test flight sparked a significant realisation about his own potential fate.

John heard on 7 March that one of his former instructors, who had left Ansty to work as a test pilot, had been killed. Edward 'Dan' Godfray had been testing an Armstrong-Whitworth Whitley 'when it dived, crashed into the deck and burst into flames'. John had always been aware that he might not survive the war, and Godfray's death brought this home. 'He was a man of 9000 hours and yet he was killed. It shows how safe any of us are when anything goes wrong.' He thought Godfray's funeral on 9 March was an 'awful affair and very depressing, weeping women etc. We all saluted the grave one at a time from Squadron Leader Pope downwards'. The scene affected John deeply. 'When I go out I pray God it will be in the air.' A quick bullet in combat would be a much cleaner way to die.

John's 22nd birthday, on 20 March, was quiet. 'No one even knew about it', he told his family, 'but I knew you'd all be remembering even though you were a long way away'. The rest of the month was uneventful, with leave and study for final exams. He didn't feel confident about them and failed signals. 'I have been gated along with others to ensure that I would stay here and get ... up to date'. His restriction to the training station didn't last long, as he went to town to visit the dentist on Friday 5 April. When he returned, one of his friends told him he had been suspended, and his flight commander unofficially confirmed the distressing news. John was devastated. 'It may mean that I will have to go back to Australia if I can't fix it up', he confided to his diary. 'I simply can't do that as I'd hate to go back home a failure.'

He was confused, as he had been told his flying was good. He agonised all weekend. The commanding officer 'refuses to give anything definite as yet and I don't know just where I stand'. He clung to the possibility that 'some mistake must have been made'. In case there was no error, he 'decided that should I be kicked out I will go to China and join their air force if it is humanly possible. I could never stay on the ground now; flying is in my blood and I couldn't go home and face my people after that'. Plans for China aside, 'one thing is certain – I won't leave the service without a fight. I like it too much'.

It was an agonising weekend but then, 'Everything is OK'. John heard on 8 April that 'it was all rubbish', a terrible mistake. 'I will go on to Cranwell with the rest of the crowd ... thank goodness.'

With 45 hours 5 minutes' dual flying and 34 hours 55 minutes' solo under his belt, and a proficiency rating of average as a pilot, he arrived at RAF Cranwell, in Lincolnshire, on 10 April with a recommendation for fighter training.[20] John took his first flight in a Hart on 11 April. He was nervous at first about trying out the more advanced trainer, as 'I thought it was going to be a case of learning to fly all over again but it was only a matter of getting the feel of them, and that didn't take long'. He found the Hart 'surprisingly easy to fly', though 'hard to control on the ground'. He thought it 'handles very well and is about twice as fast as a Tiger [Moth]'. In fact, he discovered that 'Harts have tons of power and climb like rockets'.

John's first Hart solo, on 17 April, 'went swimmingly'. The next morning he tried aerobatics, afterwards declaring that 'these Harts handle very well', and generally feeling 'quite pleased with life'. However, on 25 April he 'crashed Hart today' while practising forced landings, which involved simulating engine failure and gliding in to land. As he approached the Welbourn landing ground near Cranwell in K5801, John flared the aircraft too high and lost airspeed. At that point, he should have opened the throttle, climbed away and tried to land again. He didn't. The Hart's nose was too high and its speed too low. It lost momentum and stalled. To get out of the stall – and thus avoid a crash – John had to push the nose down and apply full power. If he regained flying speed, he could pull smoothly back on the control stick. But if he couldn't get enough height, he would crash. And that is exactly what happened.

K5801 landed on its nose with its tail in the air.[21] The propeller broke, the struts on the starboard bottom wing collapsed, and the wing itself bent upward. John was uninjured but was so shattered by the crash and the ensuing court of inquiry that he couldn't tell his family about it. He did not even enter the details in his diary but slipped an account into the cover. It later disappeared, and whether he decided to remove it or it was lost is unknown. His confidence was shaken, and 'I don't feel so awfully cocksure now as I did'. John was lucky that K5801 had a sturdy nose, as it meant his cockpit had not crumpled on impact. He walked away with more than his life; he had learned an important lesson. 'My crash has in a way been a good thing as I'm almost too careful now.'

'Pass – in, fail – out'

Ken Holland had been back in Scotland with a cold and mild depression after saying goodbye to Toby and Seina following their Christmas festivities. The new year opened with a change of instructor, an engine lecture, a game of squash and a hot whisky. If the whisky did nothing for his health, at least it would warm him up a little. It was '10 degrees below – how I do dislike this cold'.[22]

Like their colleagues at Tern Hill, Ken's instructors took advantage of the foul weather to focus on ground subjects. He may have had some early success in navigation, but it was now proving to be his bane. Sound mathematical skills were vital for aero-navigation. For example, with dead, or deduced, reckoning, the pilot had to calculate his current location by fixing an earlier position then advancing that position based on known or estimated speeds over elapsed time and course. There were many elements to this, and the pilot had to determine climb, cruise and descent speeds and allow for wind drift and head or tail wind. Once airborne, he had to read his map to ensure he was on course, and if not, adjust his heading. On top of all that, he had to apply magnetic variation to the aircraft heading and take into account compass deviation, which was peculiar to each aircraft. Accuracy was all. Even a small miscalculation could send the pilot miles off course. Exams started on 16 January, and, having failed Intermediate maths at school, Ken was struggling. He was happy with the engines and airmanship papers, but the navigation one was 'not so good'. He was worried. 'Have I passed in nav? I doubt it.'

Ken had good cause to worry. As at Ansty, some trainees had already been ejected because of weaknesses in flying and ground subjects.[23] When the results came in, he found that he had performed as suspected, receiving 93 per cent in engines and 79 per cent in airmanship but only 41 per cent in navigation. The course average for navigation was 71 per cent. He was called before the chief ground instructor and trembled as he awaited the verdict. Incredibly, he was not turfed out or even suspended. The instructor told him he had to resit the exam and issued a stern warning as he left the room: 'Pass – in. Fail – out'.

Ken passed his flying test on 22 January and prepared for navigation on the 26th by carrying out a number of instrument flying and navigation exercises. He crammed hard, and it paid off. 'Nice paper but made some stupid slips so got 62 per cent. Just through.' For now. He realised he was 'not safe by any means', as he still had to get through the end-of-course exams. In the interim, he enjoyed 'quite a good binge' at the pub 'with the crowd' and the next day 'rushed to Station Hotel to see Toby', who had come to visit bearing gifts to celebrate Ken's success. 'Made me so happy to see him.' They were at the Station Hotel again on the 29th to toast Ken's 20th birthday, but it was an early night and he was back at his billet by 7 p.m. to write up his notes.

And so the weeks passed. Lectures, flying, ground work, letters in and out, news from Toby and Seina and the inexorable progress of the war. Before Ken knew it he was on leave. His excitement at being with Toby again was dulled by the disappointment of not seeing Seina when he returned to Camelford, as she was on duty at Torbay Hospital. At his first chance, he was off to visit '*Sister Haydon!* Who seems now to hold a v. responsible position – darling Seina has grown up and is now a most self-possessed young lady'. Ken said nothing more of their reunion, and his diary pages from 25 March to 5 April remained untouched. He returned to Scone and within days was 'out of love with Seina and in love with Jae'. He penned no details about his new amour, but it seems their relationship did not get off to a good start: Jae was in quarantine with German measles, and Ken embarked on an 'intensive swat' as he worked towards his final course exams on 12 April.

As with his half-term exams, he wrote, 'all good papers except nav. I made a mess of the problem – probably failed it'. But he didn't. With 58 per cent he had again scraped through. He did well on most of the other papers, including 84 per cent in airmanship and 88 per cent in engines, but his 62 per cent for armament combined with the navigation mark brought his average down to 77 per cent, which was below the school average of 80.5 per cent. But that didn't matter. He had passed and could progress to intermediate and advanced training. Within days he was posted to 6 Flying Training School, Little Rissington, Gloucestershire.

Shortly after arriving, 19 Course's trainees were divided into fighter and bomber streams. Ken was allocated to fighter training and, like Bill Millington, was introduced to the Harvard. He carried out cockpit drill on 30 April, which was initially 'very complicated' but 'gradually became clearer'. His first flight was the next day, but he did not take to it as quickly as some. By 5 May, 'everyone else solo but me'. On the 7th, a 'glorious day', he spent 4 hours flying mainly circuits then took his 'solo test with chief flying instructor. OK and went off solo'.

Ken flung himself into mastering the Harvard, relishing the freedom of the more powerful aircraft, but there was a cloud on his horizon. A board comprising senior RAF officers had interviewed Ken and his course mates about their backgrounds, what work they had done before joining the air force, and their academic qualifications, sporting interests and general knowledge. From the answers they would determine those who were officer material and those who would continue to wear sergeant's stripes. Ken had hoped for a commission, but soon after arriving at Little Rissington he 'moved to meals in airmen's mess'. He was 'bitterly disappointed but managed to conceal it – for it may mean *no* commission'.[24]

'Life was rosy'

Dick Glyde's new year had started with a detachment to Le Touquet, a smart coastal resort in northern France more than 100 miles from Lille-Seclin. There, he carried out his first post-internment sortie: an interception of an aircraft that proved friendly. A number of convoy patrols followed, but he saw nothing. B Flight returned to Lille-Seclin on 10 January. Four days later, the squadron received a signal cancelling all leave until further notice because of the possibility of a German invasion of Belgium and Holland. The new commanding officer, Squadron Leader John Dewar, who had replaced Coope on his posting to 52 Wing, gathered his pilots to go over tactics and methods of attack. Three days later, Dewar and Robert Voase Jeff went to the French air force's air base at Orleans-Bricy, about 65 miles southwest of Paris, to fly a captured Messerschmitt Me109, but it proved unserviceable. Dewar returned to Seclin, but Jeff stayed behind. Dick temporarily assumed command of B Flight.

The invasion scare was short lived, which was a good thing, as France was gripped by the same foul weather that had disrupted operations and flying training in Britain. While Ken Holland enjoyed his 20th birthday with Toby Ripley in the warmth of the Station Hotel, Dick shivered through his 26th birthday, on the same day, as snow and frost turned 87 Squadron's landing area into a hard, bumpy field and later a quagmire, when it started to thaw out in mid-February. They resumed their operational routine in March, and Dick flew patrols over Lille, Amiens, Douai and Arras – the northern cities closest to France's border with Belgium – and on 21 March he was night flying over Dunkirk.

Towards the end of the month, rumours of attacks resulted in trench digging, a gas attack rehearsal and a practice evacuation of an aerodrome rendered unserviceable through bombardment. Morale was high, and warmer weather was approaching, which, according to the waggish squadron diarist, marked 'the end of the months of appalling cold, described rather aptly by the *Paris Soir* as "unbearable as Nazi-ism"'.[25]

For the most part, 87 Squadron's French sojourn was an interlude of calm before the storm. They worked hard, but it was spiced with good fun. Soon after Squadron Leader Dewar arrived, 87 and a nearby French squadron swapped aircraft and had 'a grand dogfight'. Work over, 'there were some terrific parties in the evening'. Dick gained renown as one of the 'mad English boys' who had evaded the Belgians. His fellow Australian Flying Officer Johnny Cock overshot the landing strip on one occasion and ended up in a reservoir. On another, Flying Officer Roderick 'Roddy' Rayner landed with his wheels still retracted. His excuse? 'Just forgot them, old boy.' As Flight Lieutenant Ian 'Widge' Gleed recalled it, 'life was rosy' during the Phoney War.[26]

The squadron's 1940 account opened on 10 April, when Johnny Cock opened fire on a Heinkel 15 miles northeast of Cap Gris Nez. (It was the closest he had come to England for some months: the cape's cliffs are 21 miles from Dover.) The Heinkel managed to escape into cloud, but as far as the squadron was concerned it was a confirmed victory. It may not have been Dick's, but at least an Australian had claimed the first for 1940, and Dick joined the crowd in the local bar knocking back cocktails on Cock's tab.[27]

At the beginning of May, the squadron moved over 220 miles east to Senon, close to Metz and the Great War battlefields of Verdun. The pilots camped out in tents set up in the woods bordering the airfield. During time off, Dick helped repair muddy tracks and built seats and washstands, and went boar hunting. In the air, 87 Squadron escorted photographic reconnaissance Lysanders over France's Maginot Line and Germany's Siegfried Line, the latter a series of defensive fortifications extending over 390 miles from the Dutch to the Swiss border with Germany.

Patrols – sometimes two or three – were carried out daily, and there were never fewer than nine aircraft in the air at a time.

On 9 May, all Allied units in France were put on full alert and immediate readiness. An enemy advance was expected. Dick and his friends were ordered on dawn readiness. They weren't concerned, however. They had heard before that a German offensive was imminent and had grown sceptical of such warnings.[28]

8

The Battle of France

'War really starts'

Nine Dornier Do17s sailed over 87 Squadron's aerodrome as dawn broke on 10 May 1940. The anti-aircraft defences went into action and the deafening noise woke the slumbering pilots. Johnny Cock exclaimed, 'Ack-ack Hell!' and they hurled themselves out of the tent as more explosions set a suspended lamp swaying vigorously. He joined the group of pyjama-clad pilots standing in a clearing watching the approach of an enemy formation, their excited conversation punctuated by machine gun fire. Roland Beamont had a bad case of dysentery so returned to bed groaning and clutching his stomach, but Dick Glyde and the other able-bodied pilots pulled flying gear over pyjamas as they dashed to their Hurricanes.[1]

The mighty Blitzkrieg, Germany's three-pronged attack on France, the Netherlands, Luxembourg and Belgium, had begun. Operating in relays throughout the day, 87 Squadron met the Luftwaffe's onslaught. Combat over, pilots returned to Senon so their aircraft could be refuelled and rearmed or repaired in the shortest possible time. And then they were in the air again and again. No one sat down afterwards to count the individual sorties (one operational sortie equated to one man in the air), but Pilot Officer Dennis David, for instance, flew six that day – 7 hours in his Hurricane – and those others who were fit would have had similar tallies. They were worn out at the end of it, but the results spoke for themselves: 22 enemy aircraft destroyed, five probably destroyed and five damaged. It was an impressive tally for little cost. No personnel were injured, and only two Hurricanes were damaged with another two rendered temporarily unserviceable. Senon airfield, however, was out of commission and the squadron moved back to Lille-Seclin.

The first 24 hours of the Battle of France concluded with a night interrupted by air raid sirens, anti-aircraft fire and the rumble of bombs exploding over the Belgian border. Sleep was restless and dreams were few. And then Dick and his exhausted friends had to rise to face the relentless Luftwaffe again. And then again. When things settled down a little, Dennis David added a notation to his flying log for 10 May 1940: 'WAR REALLY STARTS'.[2]

'To meet and repel any invaders'

As Britain awoke to the news that the Phoney War had ended Neville Chamberlain was still prime minister, but by day's end Winston Churchill had agreed to lead the nation to victory. The RAF immediately reacted to the German Blitzkrieg. At North Weald, 151 Squadron was on dawn readiness. Red Section's first base patrol was cancelled before the pilots took off. Later that morning, A Flight was ordered up but then told to land before reaching the patrol line. Blue Section left for Martlesham Heath to carry out operations from there, and at 4.15 p.m. Stuart Walch, leading Green Section, followed.

At Leconfield, Pat Hughes continued his training program and, on 13 May, led Red Section on their first operational flight. No contact was made, and he then settled into a period of night flying training. At Cranwell, John Crossman had his leave cancelled – as did all RAF personnel – and he watched as the training aircraft were picketed around the aerodrome in case of an air raid. He fully expected Cranwell to be bombed, 'as it is a definite objective', and it seemed to him that everyone was 'expecting parachute troops'. At Little Rissington, Ken Holland worked on navigation, maps, guns, signals and airframes. In the evening, the training school enforced a total blackout. Like Cranwell, it was considered a prime Luftwaffe target, so, Ken noted, 'all aircraft at dispersal points ready for anything here'.[3]

As soon as he arrived at Hornchurch, Jack Kennedy realised why his romantic interlude with Christine had been so abruptly curtailed. He had been promoted to flight lieutenant and was off 'to teach young pilots to fight'. He phoned Christine to tell her the news. It was clear to them now that 'the great battle was about to begin'. Jack was one of only two of 65 Squadron's pilots to be rated 'exceptional'. His skills would be recognised as he assumed the role of flight commander in the newly formed 238 Squadron at RAF Tangmere, an important 11 Group sector airfield in West Sussex. When he arrived on 15 May, he discovered that his old Point Cook course mate Stuart Walch had also been promoted and would be 238's other flight commander. Jack was pleased with the promotion. He did not regret leaving his friends at 65 Squadron; he was excited that the war was hotting up. He considered it a challenge to train the new squadron's green pilots to operational standard in preparation for the expected invasion. He realised it was a great responsibility but was more than prepared to accept it.[4]

Stuart was in charge of B Flight, and Jack commanded A Flight. On 16 May, the squadron diarist declared that 'the squadron is considered to have come into being on this day'. Two days later, 238's commanding officer, Squadron Leader Cyril Baines, arrived.[5]

While Jack and Stuart initiated their training programs, Bill Millington wrote to his sister in Adelaide and told of Britain's preparations 'to meet and repel any invaders', which included 'air raid precautions, such as anti-aircraft batteries, trenches, air raid shelters, gas masks etc.' and which were 'taken by John Citizen as a matter of course'. Knowing that all at home would be concerned about their London-based family, Bill related how sandbags were stacked up to protect buildings and important monuments, glass had been removed from shops and 'air raid shelters abound in the streets and parks'. Civilian service personnel such as 'air raid wardens, casualty station attendants, auxiliary fire service ... are on duty day and night'. Petrol rationing and high car taxes had reduced road traffic to a minimum, and 'all cars must travel with masked lights at night. Blackout restrictions are in force throughout the country. No visible light being permitted after sunset'. He became almost poetic as he recorded the nightly sweep of 'the silvery fingers of the searchlights' as they sought 'the ever elusive marauder, beckoning him on into range of the anti-aircraft fire'.[6]

'I then got on his tail'

The Germans progressed swiftly and implacably. In an attempt to stem the advance, the RAF was tasked with destroying two of the Albert Canal bridges southwest of the Dutch city of Maastricht. On 12 May, a section of three France-based Fairey Battles from 12 Squadron joined 24 Blenheims from 15 and 107 squadrons from Bomber Command's 2 Group. The Advanced Air Striking Force's Hurricanes, along with 85 and 87 squadrons, were their escort. The Luftwaffe threw a mighty force at the RAF, whose fighters were kept furiously busy. 87 and 85 squadrons encountered the enemy at 9 a.m., and among a number of successes Dick Glyde claimed a Heinkel destroyed. It was his first victory in the Battle of France. But the operation was a disaster for the RAF, with many deaths, including one from 87 Squadron.

The 13th was a quiet day for 87, with only Johnny Cock report-ing contact with the enemy, when he intercepted ten Me109s over Louvain and shot one down.[7] The following day was much more active. While the Advanced Air Striking Force's bombers attacked pontoon bridges over the Meuse and Chiers rivers near Sedan, the air component Hurricanes concentrated on intercept-ing Luftwaffe formations. At 9 a.m., a large mass of Henschel Hs123s and Heinkel He111s escorted by Me109s was reported approaching the Louvain area. 85, 87 and 607 squadrons were ordered to intercept: 607 attacked the Henschels while 85 and 87 targeted the Heinkels. Dick and his confreres were forced back by what appeared to be 100 Me109s and lost two men, includ-ing 20-year-old Pilot Officer Paul Jarvis, who had been flying in Dick's section and was last seen attacking a bomber.

The Dutch capitulated on 15 May. It seemed Belgium and northern France would fall as well. Indeed, the French prime minister, Paul Reynaud, telephoned Churchill declaring that France was defeated. He then asked for ten more squadrons. With the backing of the chief of air staff, Air Chief Marshal Cyril Newall, Air Chief Marshal Sir Hugh Dowding, the head of Fighter Command, refused, but he agreed to send reinforce-ments, and 87 Squadron moved to Lille-Marcq, another of the six airfields in the Lille area, to make room for the new arrivals. They were hardly secure there, as it was crowded with aircraft and presented a ripe target for the Luftwaffe.

The battle score increased, as did 87 Squadron's own death count, and on 17 May, German troops entered Brussels. The German army was advancing so rapidly towards the Channel it seemed likely the British, French and Belgian armies would be encircled. Dick was on duty at dawn on 19 May, and, as it hap-pens, the Antipodes were well represented in the first patrol of the day: Dick and fellow Australian Johnny Cock united with two New Zealanders, flying officers Derek Ward and James 'Buzz'

Allen, for a patrol to Le Cateau-Cambrésis, in the far north of France, quite close to the Belgian border.[8] Dick was leading. It wasn't long before they encountered a reconnaissance Henschel Hs126.

Dick dived to one side of the enemy aircraft. He and his number two carried out a stern attack, with apparently little damage. Ward then fired, silencing the Henschel's rear gunner. Dick and number four followed through with short bursts. Smoke poured from the stricken aircraft as its pilot took vigorous evasive action. He failed to elude Ward's persistent fire.[9] The Henschel crashed in flames, exploding as it hit the ground. Dick gave credit to the team effort: each 'had an equal share in shooting it down'.

At 10 a.m., two Lysanders from 4 Squadron were practising landings at Lille-Seclin when without warning a pair of Me109s hammered onto their tails. Both Lysanders plunged into the ground. 85 Squadron, which had been patrolling the airfield, engaged the Me109s and 87 Squadron scrambled to assist. Dick was in the air again – they took off in a 'panic climb'.

Dick was south of Lille at 8000 feet when he 'saw a 109 at a lower level being attacked by two other Hurricanes'. The 109 tried to evade Widge Gleed's and Derek Ward's guns, so Dick 'decided to join in'. At this point Ward broke off, as he mistook Dick, who was coming up from behind, for a 109.[10] The Australian got into position and 'took several deflection shots'. He manoeuvred onto his foe's tail and continued to take 'vigorous action'. He 'fired several short bursts without success' but finally found his target. 'Vapour began to stream from [the Me109's] engine, which then lost power considerably.' Even so, the Messerschmitt maintained its 'determined evasive action' and Dick failed to 'get in a conclusive burst'. Then the Me 'banked over the vertical at about 500 feet, and disappeared'. Dick thought it had crashed so 'flew round looking for the wreckage'. He couldn't find it and decided 'he must have got away, though I don't think his engine could have taken him far'. Dick could not confirm the 109's demise, so the squadron credited Dick, Gleed and Ward with its probable destruction.

Dick returned from battle uninjured, but his Hurricane was not so lucky; it was pocked with bullet holes. At least one other Hurricane was holed as well: such was the confusion in the air Dick had mistaken Sergeant Ivor Badger's Hurricane for an enemy aircraft. With a broad grin, Badger later declared to Dick, 'You *are* a rotten shot, sir!'[11]

There was little time to cast aspersions on Dick's shooting skills, as the Luftwaffe continued to attack the Lille airfields. All aircraft were ordered off the ground in the early afternoon, but Dick was late in taking off and followed the others on his own. He climbed to 13 000 feet and found himself in the middle of a whirling air battle. He saw a Hurricane assailed by two Me109s. He had a 'slight advantage of height' so joined in, aiming for one of the 109s. It dodged Dick then climbed to meet him. 'We came at each other head-on, both firing, but without any apparent effect', because Dick was too far away: the Hurricane's eight machine guns used .303 bullets, which didn't carry much of a punch unless fired close enough to a crucial point in the target.

The Messerschmitt 'passed a few feet below'. The Hurricane may have been no match for it in speed, but it had a tighter turning circle, so although the 109 twisted and turned to evade Dick's machine guns, the Australian clung to 'his tail, and fought him down to about 2000 feet'.

Fully aware of the Hurricane's limited ammunition, Dick took 'short bursts at him, as he kept turning at right angles across my sights'. The violent evasive moves failed to shake the Australian. Taking advantage of an aircraft that handled well and was a rock-steady firing platform, he used the most complex of shots, the one that required judgement, awareness and steely-eyed skill. He 'finally got his engine with a full deflection shot'. It was well judged and timed, proving again that Dick had the killer instinct.

The pilot – Hans-Christian Schäfer – was wounded. He baled out, and Dick offered the courtesy of not shooting at the descending German. It was a chivalrous action and appropriate for the circumstances, as the battle had been conducted over Allied territory. Schäfer was captured by French troops and imprisoned.

After his third successful sortie for the day, Dick returned to dispersal, where the pilots sat awaiting orders to evacuate. The call came through at 6 p.m. They were to leave for Merville. Dick and the rest of the air party took 15 minutes or so to fly the 40 miles to their old stomping ground. The road was chock-full of fleeing refugees and retreating army personnel. There was no accommodation, so Dick and his companions had to fend for themselves. Such were the conditions that some were grateful to sleep in a pig sty. When they arrived, the officers had to organise their billets. At about 11.30 p.m., while Roland Beamont helped Squadron Leader Dewar load his gear into the billet he was sharing with Dick, searchlights coned a circling He111. Like the crowded Lille airfields, Merville offered easy pickings. Both of 87 Squadron's flights were dispersed along the roadside. Opposite was 85 Squadron, and a little further on were 17 and 32 squadrons, recent reinforcements from England. Sleep was impossible during the airfield defence's noisy and bright display.[12]

Despite the ramshackle accommodations, 20 May saw 87 Squadron again on dawn alert. After the nocturnal activity, a large raid was expected. They flew two early morning patrols and then, at 10 a.m., the airfield was attacked. A salvo of bombs landed on one side; some fell at 87 Squadron's end.[13] Dick sprinted to his Hurricane and joined his comrades in their pursuit of the intruders. They recorded no victories, but one was wounded and later died.

Another evacuation order came through: all Merville-based squadrons were to return to England. Before they could leave,

87 Squadron had to carry out a strafing run on a Panzer division on the Arras road.[14] Dick and Roddy Rayner returned late from the operation to discover that after all the confusion of the retreat from Lille-Seclin the night before no one knew what had happened to their kit. The pilots' batmen were nowhere to be seen, so nearby houses and barns were searched. Eventually, they found most of it dumped in a large barn.

Several squadrons had already departed, but 87 hadn't received its final orders. There were no messing arrangements, and the boys had eaten nothing other than a rushed sandwich lunch. It was nearly 6 p.m. and they were famished. Widge Gleed and Rayner decided to drive into the village and rustle up something. They forced their way into a bar and waved a 100-franc note. Soon a plate of thick omelette sandwiches was handed to them, and armed with those and a few bottles of beer, they returned. Gleed recalled that 'the boys were overjoyed to see us. The sandwiches were damned good and cheered us up quite a lot'.[15]

And then it was time to leave. Everyone arrived safely in England; the only casualty was the bulk of the squadron's records, which was destroyed on the quay at Boulogne.[16] It was good to be back on British soil, but in the rush to evacuate Dick had abandoned most of the items he had accumulated since arriving in England three years earlier: letters from family and friends, books, gifts and other tokens of remembrance of his life in the RAF. He carried only what could be crammed into his cockpit.

Post-war research indicates that Dick and his fellow pilots of 87 Squadron were responsible for 55½ confirmed and 12 probable victories in France. What records remain show that Dick's total score for the Battle of France was two and a quarter destroyed and one-third probably destroyed, but as far as his squadron friends were concerned he had notched up four victories. Notwithstanding the odds against them, overall, the Hurricane pilots in France – which included those of the air component, the Advanced Air

Striking Force and Dowding's reinforcements – claimed at least 499 victories and 123 probables between 10 and 21 May against an assessed Luftwaffe loss of 299 aircraft destroyed and perhaps 65 seriously damaged. The price was high. The RAF sent 452 Hurricanes to France; only 66 returned to England. Sixteen of the lost Hurricanes were from 87 Squadron. The total combined pilot loss of the Advanced Air Striking Force, air component and 11 Group reinforcements between 10 and 21 May was 56 killed, 18 taken prisoner of war and 36 wounded. Six of those killed and four wounded were from 87 Squadron.[17] Dick had been fortunate to survive his first experience of sustained combat. But it wasn't all luck. He was a skilled fighter pilot.

'It was something new'

While Dick fought tirelessly for France, Des Sheen carried out reconnaissance flights with a photographic unit established by Australian-born Sidney Cotton. Before the outbreak of war, Cotton had used his private Lockheed 12A, under the auspices of promoting his film business, to gather photographic evidence of a German military build-up for MI6, Britain's Secret Intelligence Service. On the strength of that, the RAF had invited him to take over their fledgling photographic unit. Cotton was given the honorary rank of wing commander and took command of 1 Photographic Development Unit, based at Heston, a civil aerodrome about 15 miles west of London. Although his methods were unorthodox and strictly non-service, he built up a successful outfit which kept expanding. 72 Squadron was asked to provide a fully operational pilot for the unit. Des later recalled that he selected 'the short straw'.[18]

Des's friends were sorry to lose one of their most popular and accomplished pilots, with Squadron Leader Ronald Lees rating him exceptional as a fighter pilot and above average as a pilot navigator.[19] Just as he would have accepted a posting to Bomber Command when he first joined the RAF, Des was pragmatic about his new job. 'It was something new.' And of course, it might provide a bit of excitement, as nothing had been in the offing since December. Even so, Des 'didn't know quite what to expect'. But then, 'Why not?' he thought. 'It's flying Spitfires. Be something different.'

Different indeed. The reconnaissance Spitfires, with cameras fitted into their wings, were unlike those Des had flown into battle. Sidney Cotton had had them painted duck-egg blue to reduce the likelihood of detection. He removed the armament as well as the armour plating behind the pilot's seat to reduce weight. To diminish drag, he fitted metal blanking plates to the gun ports and sealed all gaps between panels with plaster of Paris. External surfaces were polished to a hard, sleek gloss.[20]

Des took his first flight with the unit on 23 April and carried out a number of training flights over the next two weeks. He discovered that getting into position over the target was not as easy as it seemed, but once there, photographing it was a snap, so to speak. To operate the camera, he recalled that 'we had a little control panel where the gunsight used to be on the Spitfire. We pressed the buttons at the appropriate time to start them and stop them'. He told his parents that 'the job is going OK and I'm trained now and expect to go to France any day. It is a safe job though so keep cool'.

On 8 May, one of his colleagues came to him in the mess and offered his congratulations on the award of the DFC, which recognised his successes in October and December 1939 and praised him as 'a keen and courageous officer'.[21] 'I discovered the DFC had been dished out … It was a complete surprise and put me quite off my breakfast.' The commanding officer gave him a day's leave, and he 'went up to town and had the ribbon put on. I must say it feels darn queer and will take some getting used to … I've only worn the darn thing a day but most people know the ribbon and it is rather embarrassing at times!'

Congratulations and embarrassment were put aside on 10 May, when the Germans launched their Blitzkrieg offensive. The photographic development unit covered the advance, and Des flew to France twice in Cotton's Lockheed. They overnighted there, and as it appeared likely that Italy would enter the war if France fell, Cotton sent a party, including three Spitfire pilots – Flight Lieutenant Eric le Mesurier, the officer in charge of the detachment, Des, and Canadian-born Flying Officer George Christie – to Le Luc, near Toulon, in the south of France. (Second in charge, Wing Commander Geoffrey Tuttle, remained at Heston to supervise the rest of the unit.) They were supplemented by Blenheim and Hudson pilots. Soon after they arrived on the 11th, Des and Cotton were off to look for an airfield closer to Italian bases. When they landed at Bastia, in Corsica, they were met by Frenchmen wielding bayonet-fitted rifles who thought they were Italians.[22]

Des's first France-based photo reconnaissance flight was on 18 May, when he flew to Emden, in Germany's northwest, and the Dutch cities of Groningen and Amsterdam. It was followed by a dozen over Italian bases. Routine photographic work may have been boring after the excitement of fighter operations, but Des enjoyed his new duties. 'Oh yes, I loved it. Very good. One was on one's own … it was good fun really.'

There was one occasion when he felt frustrated at the lack of armament in the stripped-down Spitfire. He had been flying over a naval air base in the south of Sardinia and 'was very disappointed because on the water were about a dozen sea planes which were just sitting quietly there and I was thinking that if only I had some guns and ammunition perhaps I could have some sport'. Des was not alone in his desire to take a shot at the enemy. His colleague George Christie didn't let a lack of ammunition deter him from making three dummy attacks on an Italian bomber, forcing it to ditch.

Allied soldiers who had been isolated in Dunkirk by the Battle of France were evacuated between 26 May and 4 June. Cotton had been ordered to withdraw his unit, but he believed France could be saved, so the unit stayed. He stopped off at Le Luc and assured Des and his fellows that everything would be all right. So they continued their work.

But France was on the verge of collapse. The French government left Paris, and Italy declared war on France and Great Britain on 10 June, threatening, among other things, British military bases in the Mediterranean. The Germans entered Paris on 14 June, but still Des took intelligence photos. On 15 June, he flew from Le Luc to the northern Italian cities of La Spezia, Genoa, Savona and Mondovi, and Hyères, in the southeast of France; this was his last photographic trip. The unit's position was soon untenable. 'We were right in the thick of things.' They 'watched a couple of big raids … [and] caught a packet!!' Des 'spent half an hour in a ditch 18 inches deep and boy, rabbits have nothing on me when it comes to burrowing a hole'.

Soon they were 'in a fair amount of trouble'. One of the unit's Blenheims came and collected their photographs, but before taking them back to Britain the pilot stopped off at Seclin. 'Things were in a pretty bad way. So they [came] back and warned us.' Des then took a Tiger Moth to Seclin and saw 'a lot of Wellingtons which were all revved up to bomb the attackers but they'd been forbidden by the French who'd covered the whole airfield with vehicles to stop them taking off'. It seemed as if the 'French have packed up'. Des realised things were 'getting pretty dicey'.

Cotton had only 'visited us once on the way when we were in Le Luc' and had 'said it would be all right'. It wasn't. Des 'never saw him again'. Without Cotton, Des and his colleagues 'decided to evacuate ourselves'. Cotton, however, remembered it differently. He recalled that he arranged the unit's evacuation and made his own way back to England.[23] Regardless of who organised it, 'we only had one serviceable aircraft, a Spitfire', Des recalled. 'The rest had been destroyed on the ground by the Italians.' As George Christie had an important date in London, he took the Spitfire. Des, Le Mesurier and the ground crew made their way to Hyères. 'Things [there] got very tricky', and on 17 June, the day before the last RAF squadron based in France withdrew, they joined a small party of naval officers and their wives and 'beat it on a special boat'.

9

Action at last

'Let's not waste any more time, darling'

On 25 May 1940, as Lord Gort, the commander-in-chief of the British forces in France, concluded that he could save the British Expeditionary Force only by conducting a fighting retreat to the French coast and creating a bridge-head at Dunkirk from which to evacuate troops, Pat Hughes and the boys received orders that they were moving back to their old quarters at Church Fenton, where they would join the newly arrived Dick Glyde and 87 Squadron. Did the two Australians meet? Did Pat offer his congratulations to the combat-weary pilots as they received much well-deserved recognition, including Dick, who was awarded the DFC on 4 June for his 'great dash and offensive spirit', which had 'accounted for four enemy aircraft' in France? It is likely, but unknowable.

While 87 Squadron focused on rebuilding and retraining – they would be fully operational by 21 June – 234 was on readiness, and on the afternoon of 28 May, Pat led Blue Section to intercept an unidentified aircraft which turned out to be a Whitley bomber. He was in the air again later that day but was recalled after 10 minutes. Following that small flurry of activity all was quiet, and 234's dearth of action continued into June with nothing until a scramble on the 6th.[1]

The young Australian continued to train his men for the inevitable battle. As Keith Lawrence recalled, they were dependent on him and looked to him rather than to their squadron leader for guidance.[2] Pat snatched what free time he could and spent it with his fiancée. Kay Brodrick picked him up in her little car and they tooled along country roads. If they returned after dark, she dimmed her headlights by fitting Fuller's cake boxes pierced with small holes over them. This had its hazards, and one night they pranged the car and Pat was late back.[3] On 9 June, they escaped the war and picnicked at a quiet, grassy spot a short distance from the station. Pat tried to relax: shirt sleeves rolled up, papers strewn about, thermos at the ready and Flying Officer Butch checking out the rabbit situation. Despite the joy of sharing precious time with the woman who wore his ring, the grind of constant training and long hours waiting for a call to scramble that only rarely came had taken their toll. Pat looked care worn and older than his 22 years as he tried to smile for Kay's camera.

Ten days later, 234 Squadron transferred to RAF St Eval, Cornwall, to protect westward convoys and the naval base at Plymouth. It was important work, but St Eval was more than half a country away. How could Pat bear to be so far from Kay? The simple answer was he couldn't. He phoned her and pleaded, 'Let's not waste any more time, darling; we can get married at Bodmin Register Office', 20 or so miles from St Eval. Kay spoke to her mother about it. Although the sensible thing would be to wait until after the war, as they had originally planned, 'my mother said I should grab whatever happiness I could as no one knew what was going to happen'.[4] The next time they spoke, she agreed to marry him. All they needed now was for Kay to drive down to Cornwall – not an easy endeavour with travel restrictions and petrol rationing – and Pat to wangle a leave chit.

'The privilege of being killed'

As the tired and battered RAF contingent arrived back in England after evacuating from France, John Crossman realised that 'this war is really getting serious'.[5] The RAF thought so too, and John and his Cranwell class mates were advised that their course was to be shortened, and they would go on to the advanced training school (also located at Cranwell) before the end of May. John concluded that this second cut was because they had lost so many pilots during the Battle of France. He was weeks away from his wings examinations but had been told 'exams are now of only minor importance' given the need to replace pilots quickly. Even so, he worked hard and was in 'a bad state of nerves just now and I don't get too much sleep; find my face twitching on left side at times'. The irony of being trained for an eventual death was not lost on him. 'It's damn funny. We fellows work like blazes to pass exams just for the privilege of being killed. It will be a pleasure though if I only get two – one to equal me and one to justify myself.'

Cranwell was bombed on the night of 6–7 June, and John sat the last of his exams after spending most of the night in the shelter. The results came through on the 12th. He passed with an average of 75 per cent, but perfectionist John's thrill of finally donning his wings was tempered by the fact that he had expected higher marks in armament and airmanship. Within days, he was flying Hinds. 'They are quite a bit faster than Harts and much nicer to fly. We are going on to really advanced stuff now such as machine gunning … good fun and quite a change.'[6]

'Wings exam passed'

Ken Holland was in a mess. It was less than a month until his wings exams, but although he had accrued 150 flying hours his performance in the air was less than satisfactory.[7] The root of his trouble was a woman – or, more to the point, three women. As well as his budding romance with Jae, who was keen on him and bombarded him with letters, he still had feelings for Seina Haydon. He felt like a 'swine' for making love to Jae, as it was not likely he would have a chance to see her again. 'It is rather a hopeless show for I don't see how I can get there again.' To make matters worse, he had also met Evelyn. 'Jae, Seina, Evelyn – I don't know what to do about them all. I think I really love Seina, yet I think I love each one when I am with them.' The 20-year-old was far from his usual happy-go-lucky self. He was confused and guilty, and considered that 'I deserve to be punished for my sins and am, I guess, by my bad flying'.

His mood did not improve. As well as hearing that Flying Officer Ian Haydon, Seina's 23-year-old brother, and his Handley Page Hampden crew had failed to return from a bombing operation on 4 June, Ken had to accept that he would not receive a commission. As his course mates took their seats in the officers' mess, he spoke to the chief ground instructor about his chances of joining them, but he was no help at all. 'Rather disappointed', he commented in his diary on 11 June.

As the Germans advanced towards an undefended Paris, Ken knuckled down to pre-exam revision. He tried to absorb a constant barrage of information from the ground lecturers. Paris fell, and he 'made rather a balls' of a flying test. On the 17th, he was in the air practising low-level bombing. On 20 June, his wings exams began. For once his navigation skills did not fail him, and on 28 June he recorded in screaming capitals, '*WINGS EXAM PASSED*'. With the elation of officially becoming a pilot, he pushed his problems with the women in his life from his mind and diary and concentrated on his advanced training.

'The possibility of a hasty departure'

The RAF had lost many Hurricane pilots during the Battle of France and, as John Crossman correctly surmised, needed to replace them. Whatever the reason for Bill Millington's posting to 17 Operational Training Unit for bomber training, on 1 June he packed up his brand-new mulga-wood map of Australia and other 'souvenirs from down under', his growing photo collection and the rest of his kit and made his way to 6 Operational Training Unit, Sutton Bridge, in the southeast of Lincolnshire, for conversion to Hurricanes. Sixteen days later, he was posted to 79 Squadron at RAF Biggin Hill, an important 11 Group sector station near London.[8] He was a replacement for one of their pilots who had been lost in France. He was now a fighter pilot.

Bill spent his first few days at Biggin Hill familiarising himself with the local area and building up hours in the Hurricane. During a quiet moment, anticipating that he would soon scramble with his new friends, he wrote a letter to his family. It is undated (other than June 1940) and was perhaps inspired by the recent publication in *The Times* of a letter from 'An Airman to His Mother', which spoke of a willing 'fight with evil', and the fulfilment of the young RAF pilot's 'earthly mission'. Like the anonymous airman, Bill knew that what he wrote, should it ever be read by his family, would be treasured as his last words. His favourite hymn had always been 'Fight the Good Fight', and his 'last letter' explained how he would willingly 'go forth into battle … determined to do my bit for the noble cause for which my country is fighting'.[9] He shared the joy he felt when he was flying, the happiness of service friendships and the pride he experienced in upholding his and his parents' principles, 'dictated by honour and chivalry'. He apologised 'for any sorrow or suffering I may have caused' and begged them not to 'grieve over my passing'. He had no regrets. He would have no regrets. He gave the letter for safekeeping to Miss Celia Macdonald, 'who has been a particularly good friend to me'.

There was little time to contemplate an uncertain future. At 8.35 a.m. on 27 June, 79 Squadron took off for RAF Manston, in Kent. From there, along with 32 Squadron, they escorted six Blenheims to Saint-Valery-sur-Somme and Berck-sur-Mer, in northern France, on a photographic reconnaissance. It was Bill's first operational sortie. The outward flight was incident free, but when they left the French coast Pilot Officer Thomas Parker, a veteran of France with two victories and a probable to his credit, observed three Me109s on their tails. He tried to warn the rest of the formation but was not heard over the radio telephone. The 109s struck. Bill survived his first battle, but Flight Lieutenant James Davies plunged into the water about 10 miles off Le Touquet, and Sergeant Ronald McQueen, who baled out of a burning Hurricane, was dead when a lifeboat picked him up. With his first experience of battle and the deaths of two new friends, Bill realised that 'the possibility of a hasty departure from this life is ever present'.[10]

'How did we know it was all so precious?'

With three Hurricanes on charge, Jack Kennedy and Stuart Walch would have been under the impression they had been posted to a Hurricane squadron, but before they knew it the Hurricanes were sent away. Four Spits arrived on 18 May, with 12 more following the next day. Jack was the only pilot in the squadron who had flown Spitfires.[11] *The* Kennedy was in his element, but Stuart had to master them even as he trained his B Flight charges.

In the normal course of events, when new pilots came to established squadrons, there was time to train them up individually; they learned to fit in to the routine and friendships as best they could. But now everyone was new, and 238 Squadron's two

Australian flight commanders had to create a unit from a collection of disparate men of varying degrees of experience and flying ability. Most were fresh from training school, and this was obvious. Jack 'hoped that we [do] not encounter the enemy as the young pilots could hardly fly fighter aircraft let alone fight'.[12]

Sergeant Leslie Gordon Batt joined 238 Squadron on 21 May. He wasn't quite out of training when he was allocated to Jack's flight – he had come via a four-day stopover at 253 Squadron – but as far as he was concerned, none of the pilots, from the commanding officer down, had had any operational experience. He felt it was a case of the blind leading the blind.[13] Neither Jack nor Stuart allowed this attitude to deter them. They made their charges examine the Spitfire's pilot notes then quizzed them as to where everything was located. Only then would they let them take the controls.

By 25 May, four days before Jack's 23rd birthday, the total squadron flying time on Spitfires was 71 hours 30 minutes. It was not all smooth flying, however. There were a number of crashes in those first few weeks at Tangmere, and even Jack forced the maintenance boys to work overtime when he crashed.

In less than three weeks, ten Hurricanes arrived and the Spitfires were dispatched elsewhere. After 439 hours' total flying time on Spitfires and increasing pressure to become operational, 238 was again a Hurricane squadron. As Gordon Batt recalled, it was back to the pilot handbooks. And perhaps Jack consulted his as well. His reacquaintance with the Hurricane proved less than auspicious: on 16 June he ran out of petrol and had to force-land. He damaged the undercarriage, airscrew and starboard mainplane.[14]

Jack did not feel frustrated at the chopping and changing – Hurricane to Spitfire and back to Hurricane. He was more concerned about the time taken up with squadron work which kept him from Christine Jourd.

Christine's employer had closed her couturier salon after

war was declared, so as soon as he arrived at Tangmere Jack had arranged for Christine to stay in nearby Chichester. 'It was so wonderful to be together every evening and really to have more time to get to know each other', she recalled. The only cloud was her fear that Jack would die in battle. She worried constantly, and, as he had done before, Jack tried to reassure her. He told her 'not to worry'. It was 'all under control'. After a rushed weekend together he dashed off another note. 'The whole thing was simply heaven from start to finish. I remember vividly every moment.' He ached for the day 'we shall be together again and relive it all'.[15]

Jack and Christine talked little of the future. The Australian was not sure if he would stay in the air force after the war and had no concrete plans. He toyed with the idea of medicine, or even the secret service, but his main thought at this stage was of Christine – 'the grand times together are ahead of us'. One thing was certain: he would continue to live in England. Christine did not want to leave, and nor did he. And if their plans were loose, what did it matter? Christine never had a sense that time was running out. She felt that 'in those days life as it was, was going on forever. How did we know it was all so precious?'[16]

Their first anniversary approached. On 7 June, Christine's 19th birthday, Jack took her for dinner. It was a perfect summer evening. He ordered champagne and proposed. He was over the moon when Christine accepted. He missed the formal announcement in the *Telegraph*, but Stuart Walch told him about it later. He sent his fiancée a telegram and scribbled a brief note: 'Darling, I'm very happy. I hope you are too … I'm very much in love'.[17]

On 15 June, Jack flew to Middle Wallop, Hampshire: the squadron had been transferred and Jack was in the advance party. (Although in 10 Group, the new station was still under the operational control of 11 Group; it and its Warmwell satellite, which was located between Weymouth and Dorchester in the heart of the Dorset countryside, would not come under 10 Group's jurisdiction until the second week of August.) Stuart and the rest of the squadron followed five days later. Christine stayed in Chichester, but the couple exchanged telegrams and telephoned when they could.

Middle Wallop was operational but still under construction. Only one hangar had been completed, there were a number of open trenches, and three mobile kitchens provided cooking facilities for 238 and the other units located there. The pilots slept in tents and wrapped themselves in blankets. Jack was furious. 'This Middle Wallop dump is bloody – there's nothing here at all. Miles and miles of f— all.' Even so, their new station offered Stuart at least one attraction: there was an Australian camp nearby, and he met up with a few Tasmanians, including 'all the chaps who were in the 40th [Battalion] with me'.[18]

There was little rest for Jack and Stuart as they drilled their green pilots. Jack hadn't seen Christine since their engagement dinner, and 'it seems much longer'. He was even overdue in scrawling one of his missives, 'but honestly I've been so busy and I've hardly had time to wash and eat. When I'm not flying, I'm sleeping. I find I need just about all the sleep I can get and we are on duty from dawn to dusk'. He was 'absolutely dying to see you but just can't imagine how it can be done at the moment. The mere thought of leave is ridiculous'.[19]

'The war has woken up'

On 18 June, Winston Churchill announced in the House of Commons, and then broadcast to the nation, that 'the Battle of France is over, I expect that the Battle of Britain is about to begin … Hitler knows that he will have to break us in this island or lose the war'.

There was a general sentiment that Britain was well shot of France. Des Sheen, still on his way back to England, via Algiers,

Casablanca and Gibraltar, believed 'France was sold out by the men on top and treachery everywhere' and was much happier at the prospect of 'fighting on our own ground'. Bill Millington, who experienced combat for the first time nine days after the prime minister's speech, considered that 'things have improved a great deal recently as we are now fighting over our own territory or close to it'.[20]

German troops jackbooted over British soil on 30 June, occupying the Channel Islands within 24 hours. With (erroneous) reports on 1 July, particularly in the Birmingham area, of enemy parachutists landing, invasion seemed inevitable and imminent. Britain determined to 'fight to the finish'. Following the rapid demise of Poland, the Netherlands, Belgium and France, and Denmark's capitulation in the face of a prospective blitzkrieg, Germany was all set to do it again if only the Luftwaffe could annihilate the RAF before the autumn gales.[21]

Bomber Command was on the offensive targeting enemy aerodromes and other important military installations, while Fighter Command focused on protecting the essential convoys that plied the coastal sea routes. Bill Millington and 79 Squadron moved to RAF Hawkinge, Kent, the airfield closest to the French coast, and on 2 July, 238 Squadron was declared operational. Even though he was rostered off, Jack Kennedy welcomed the move: 'We've been damn busy lately and at last we've become operational'.[22]

B Flight scrambled for the squadron's first 15 uneventful sorties. Stuart Walch led three of them. Jack was in the air again on 3 July and carried out another three. The first two were uneventful – not so the third. At 4.26 p.m., Red Section was ordered to patrol Middle Wallop and environs. Squadron Leader Cyril Baines was Red One, and Jack, flying P3700, was Red Two. They detected a group of Junkers Ju88 fast bombers and Baines led the chase out to sea. The Ju88s opened fire at about 1000 yards' range. P3700 was hit. Bullets penetrated near to Jack's seat and struck the radiator system below the centre section. He was unhurt but was ready for revenge. He positioned for attack and 'shot one of the buggers'. He had at last given Hitler, or at least one of his minions, 'a kick in the bottom'. Although his 'kick' was not acknowledged by the squadron, post-war research ascertained that Jack had indeed damaged one of the bombers. 'Thank heavens the war has woken up a bit now', Jack told Christine. 'We are getting a bit of action at last.'[23]

The war may have woken up for Jack, but it was still sleeping as far as Pat Hughes and 234 Squadron were concerned. Interceptions were few and far between at St Eval. By the end of June, Pat had carried out only four, with three of them on the same day.

Pilot Officer Kenneth 'Ken' Dewhurst damaged a Ju88 over Plymouth on 7 July. 234 was again detailed for convoy duty on the 8th.[24] Blue Section – Pat, in P9320, Keith Lawrence and Sergeant George Bailey – set off for their turn at shipping protection at 4.35 p.m. All was quiet as they circled the vessels. At 6.15 p.m., while Pat was above a cloud layer and his confreres were maintaining their guard at 1000 feet, Lawrence espied a Ju88 diving steeply. He turned towards the convoy to intercept just as Bailey sighted it. The Junkers then climbed through the clouds to escape, coming into Pat's range.

Lawrence carried out a dead astern attack. The Ju88 veered to port, and, closing from 150 to 50 yards, the Australian used a slight deflection, expending all his ammunition. As the Junkers emerged from the cloud, Pat broke away to port and downward as Bailey attacked from dead astern. 'The enemy aircraft gradually lost height in a slow left hand turn, attempted to climb but finally landed on the water. It floated for about 20 minutes and then sank, leaving the men on the surface.' Pat, Lawrence and Bailey speculated that the 'apparent cause of destruction was engine failure as the aircraft appeared to be under control until it hit the water'. Whatever the reason, it was a combined effort and 'this aircraft is claimed by this section'.[25]

The Junkers was the squadron's 'first confirmed enemy casualty', with a one-third credit to each pilot. It was also Pat Hughes's first combat victory and the first indication to Keith Lawrence of what would make his flight commander such a successful fighter pilot: his ability to shoot and hit a moving target; he was a 'natural born good shot'. It was also the genesis of Pat's personal preference for getting in close before firing. Lawrence recalled that as they had turned in to the Ju88 he and Bailey had found themselves in front of Pat and were opening fire at the enemy aircraft from 600 yards. When they landed, Pat asked why they had wasted their ammunition: they had been too far away to hit anything![26]

'Cold matter of business routine'

Bill Millington carried out a number of sorties in the first week of July. He hadn't encountered the enemy but was looking forward to meeting 'Jerry', especially as 'in the last few days [he] has been getting quite cheeky and sending aircraft over to our side of the Ditch'.[27] He might not have drawn German blood but his friends had, and he revelled in their success. 'Black crosses and swastikas make us see red and we welcome the opportunity to line a Hun plane up in the sight.' And they had good cause: Squadron Leader John Joslin had been shot down while on patrol on 7 July. Bill and his friends were 'absolutely fighting mad ... Apart from being an ace pilot he was a personal friend of each of the pilots and just one of the boys'. In this instance Bill's fury was misplaced, as the 24-year-old Canadian had been downed by Spitfires. The shock of losing a beloved leader was followed on 8 July by the deaths of Pilot Officer John Wood and Flying Officer Edward Mitchell. Wood was picked up by a naval patrol boat before he died of burns. Mitchell's death was particularly horrific and the nightmare of any pilot. His Hurricane crashed in flames and burned for over an hour. He could be identified only by his guns' serial numbers.[28]

Bill had flown on the same sortie but had come to no harm. Even so, the war had suddenly taken on a new perspective. He realised 'we can't expect to get away scot free'. Indeed, 'when comrades go the will to win gets stronger, and we will go down fighting'.

And there was much fighting. The Luftwaffe's major effort against shipping in the Channel and the south coast ports – the Kanalkampf – engaged considerable Fighter Command resources in its opening week, and those resources were becoming stretched. During the week of 2–9 July, Falmouth, Plymouth, Weymouth and Dover were bombed. Channel convoys were harried seven times. Three of the attacks, on Dover and the Isle of Portland, the latter an important Royal Navy base, as well as three on the convoys, had been carried out by formations of 15 to 20 bombers accompanied by a similar number of fighter escorts. To meet these raids, Fighter Command's daylight sorties jumped from 91 on 2 July to 282 the following day, and on 8 July sector controllers dispatched 339 fighters. They claimed 11 enemy bombers and 13 fighters but lost 15 aircraft and 12 pilots, including Bill Millington's friends. Neither Portland nor Dover harbour was closed, but Fighter Command's losses proved they could not assume an easy victory and should expect high casualty rates while protecting Channel convoys.

Bill was in the air again on 9 July. At 3.05 p.m., A Flight embarked on a patrol over Dover. Bill was Red Two. Thirty minutes later, the Hurricanes spotted a formation of nine Me109s. Yellow Section and Red Three climbed to intercept and were lost in the clouds. When Bill and Red One reached 20 000 feet, they orbited to maintain height until they were within range. It wasn't long before they were 'milling around in a terrific dogfight'. Bill 'climbed up behind two Me109s who ventured from the base of thick cloud'. He 'carried out an astern attack on the rear enemy aircraft' and opened fire at 300 yards with a 3-second burst. His aim was sound, and he watched the bullets hit the cockpit; a piece flew off. A plume of thick black smoke streamed from the engine as the 109 hurtled into the water a few miles from the French coast. And then another enemy aircraft came down in a diving turn, and Yellow One, who had emerged from the cloud and found his bearings, joined Bill in a chase towards France. Yellow One was closer and his aim was true. Black smoke poured from the Messerschmitt as it rapidly lost height.[29]

Bill was modest about his first victory: 'I was fortunate to get on the tail of a Hun and he was soon diving for the sea in flames'. He had 'avenged the loss of one of my comrades', but there was more to his good marksmanship than just revenge. Regardless of his honourable aims, the 22-year-old had discovered there was nothing chivalrous about battle. He accepted 'that fighting in the air has to be a cold matter of business routine, no longer sportive'. He was 'sorry in a way' but acknowledged that 'the war has to be won and how!' For the time being, however, that war would have to be won without Bill. Exhausted, suffering too many losses in too few days, with only seven of their pre-war pilots left, 79 Squadron was ordered north just as Churchill's predicted Battle of Britain was about to begin.[30]

10

10 July – 7 August

Defining the Battle of Britain

Despite the increase in enemy activity over Britain and her home waters in July 1940, some later believed the Battle of Britain began on 8 August, and this date was promulgated by the Air Ministry's account of the Battle, first published in 1941. Air Chief Marshal Sir Hugh Dowding disagreed. He acknowledged that it was difficult to determine an exact beginning, as many different types of operations had 'merged into one another almost insensibly', but suggested 10 July because on that day Germany had sent over its first large formation, 'intended primarily to bring our fighter defence to battle on a large scale'. He conceded that there were grounds for accepting 8 August but ultimately rejected it. The Air Ministry eventually settled on 10 July.[1]

According to the RAF's Air Historical Branch, the first phase of the Battle – 10 July to 7 August – consisted of attacks on Channel convoys and south coast ports. The second, from 8 to 18 August, marked the beginning of the Luftwaffe's intensive day operations and the heavier attacks on coastal airfields. The third, from 24 August to 6 September, saw concentrated strikes on fighter airfields near London and wide-ranging night attacks. (Enemy activity abated during the five days between the second and third stages, and the Air Historical Branch excluded this interlude.) The fourth phase, from 7 to 30 September, marked the first heavy daylight onslaught on London and the beginning of the Blitz. The fifth, which commenced on 1 October and concluded on the 31st, saw the gradual decline of the Battle. Australians died or were wounded in every phase.[2]

Awaiting 'the blitzkrieg on England'

On 10 July, Des Sheen was enjoying the last days of his sea voyage while Ken Holland did an hour of formation flying in 'filthy weather' and 'was told off for not returning'.[3] Pat Hughes was up at dawn for convoy duty and was in the air again at 6.25 p.m. leading Blue Section on a scramble. It was a non-event. Bill Millington, still flushed with the success of his first victory, was in transit. Bad weather had impeded the squadron's move north, and on the 10th Bill and his friends spent the night at Biggin Hill. At RAF Exeter, in Devon, Dick Glyde and 87 Squadron were on readiness. They had moved from Church Fenton on 4 July and were one of seven fighter squadrons tasked with protecting shipping in the western half of the Channel. At 2.50 p.m., Dick led a patrol which, along with a handful of others, was a nil-report outing. Stuart Walch and Jack Kennedy woke to an overcast day at Middle Wallop. Stuart, who had carried out eight sorties between 4 and 9 July – a mixture of base, local and convoy patrols – was off duty. It was Jack's turn, as part of A Flight, to wait at dispersal. All was quiet until 7.45 p.m., when they were called out to Portland Bill, the rocky promontory at the southern end of the Isle of Portland. It was another anticlimax. There was no enemy encounter, so after landing Jack returned to his shabby quarters to await 'the blitzkrieg on England'.[4]

'We all miss Burry very much'

At Cranwell on 10 July, a stunned John Crossman was in the escort party for a funeral. His friendship with Jack Burraston had grown. They had continued to share a billet and study together, and both had expected to be posted to a fighter squadron, hopefully the same one. But on 6 July, shortly before they were due to leave the RAF college, John, who was on leave and enjoying a night out at the Nottingham Palais de Danse, was told by 'a girl friend of Burry's' that 'he had been killed in a crash'. He rushed back to his hotel and phoned Cranwell. 'It is true. [Burry] and Parker were killed in a crash this morning at 10.00. It is unbelievable.' Details were scanty, but 'I think I know what has happened'. John assumed that 19-year-old Leading Aircraftman Ronald Parker had taken Burry 'for a joyride and as usual has been showing off and flying too low and crashed. This is only supposition but if I know Parker is probably true'. Having someone to blame was the only consolation John had at this point. 'I simply can't realise it, surely they could have got anyone but Burry. He wasn't the sort to be killed … I do feel rotten.'

He had 'an awful night' with 'little sleep. I kept seeing old Burry'. John later confided to his Aunt Ann that Burry was the finest man he had ever met, and perhaps the hardest part of all, as he looked forward to an operational posting, was that Jack Burraston had not even had his chance to fight for England.

When John returned, on 8 July, he discovered that 'Burry luckily was killed instantaneously and had his neck broken'. Parker, however, 'lingered on for an hour afterwards'. He also found out that, 'as I thought, Parker was showing off too close to the ground and tried to do a stall turn too low and never pulled out'.[5]

In his grief, it seems John may have wrongly accused Parker of larking about. John 'Tim' Elkington and Parker were old friends. Elkington noted in his diary that 'Ronnie Parker, with

Jack Burraston in the back, stalled off a stall turn at 800 feet in a dogfight'. There was no aerial tomfoolery as far as Elkington was concerned. It was a run-of-the-mill aerobatic session in a Hind. Jack's death was difficult for John to accept, but at least he had not seen it. Parker's was harder for Elkington. 'When they were hauled out of the [River] Trent (where they ended up) Ron was alive but unconscious (thank God) and body smashed. He died soon, being half drowned.' Both men grieved the loss of their friends. And, indeed, there was a pall over the entire school. 'All our chaps are in a very gloomy mood', wrote John. 'We all miss Burry very much.'[6]

'The squadron's first confirmed scalp'

On 11 July, the Luftwaffe sent a number of reconnaissance aircraft over the British coast throughout the morning and attacked a convoy moving eastward across Lyme Bay, away from Portland to the west.[7] Between 10.30 and 11 a.m., a large formation of 30 to 40 Messerschmitt Me110 twin-engine fighters, escorting 15 Junkers Ju87 Stuka dive bombers, set off from the Cherbourg Peninsula, on France's northwest coast, towards Portland tasked with carrying out a follow-up raid on the convoy. Six Hurricanes from 601 Squadron, based at Tangmere, already in the air to intercept a reconnaissance aircraft, were vectored onto the raid at 11 a.m. Shortly afterwards, when the exact location of the raid was determined, more aircraft were ordered up, including 87 Squadron's Blue Section: Squadron Leader John Dewar, Dick Glyde, who was Blue Two and flying Hurricane P3387, and Pilot Officer Dudley Trevor Jay (known as Trevor).

The Ju87s dropped their bombs at 11.53 a.m. unhindered by the RAF aircraft, which had not had enough time to intercept. At noon, Blue Section was west of Weymouth at 5000 feet. Dewar sighted a group of Me110s escorting Ju87s and a smaller

169

group of Messerschmitts approaching Portland from the south at 15 000 feet. They had not seen the Hurricanes.

Dewar ordered Blue Section to climb, veering south, so they could get in between the enemy aircraft and the sun. He watched as Stukas harried a convoy below, then saw another squadron's Hurricanes attacking the Me110s, which had started to form a defensive circle.[8] This tactic was known in the Luftwaffe as a death circle. Following the aircraft immediately in front, thus protecting their tails and giving the rear gunners the best chance of providing defensive fire-power, the aeroplanes rotated over a fixed point.

When Dewar, Dick and Jay were positioned with the sun behind them and thus were invisible to the rotating Me110s, Dewar called the attack and dived. Dick fired two deflection bursts at the nearest Messerschmitt then firmly positioned himself on its tail. As it turned slightly, he fired again, closing from 200 to 80 yards. 'My bullets appeared to be hitting him, and both engines began to stream white vapour thickly.' The Messerschmitt lost power and Dick overshot 'but got in another burst as I closed in'. The Australian veered away sharply so he could turn back onto the Me110's tail but was attacked from behind. Three bullets ripped through P3387's starboard wing tip, and another tore a large hole in the rear panel of his cockpit canopy. He executed a half-roll then dived steeply to evade further fire; it was 'a near escape'.[9]

His adversary had disappeared. Dick scanned the sky and saw a Hurricane engaging an Me110 at 6000 feet. He attacked as well, firing several deflection shots, but with no apparent effect. Another Hurricane joined in. The Me110 descended to 3000 feet and tried to escape seaward. Dick was slightly above and, using the boost cut-out, caught up. As he closed from 250 to 100 yards, he 'got in a burst which produced white vapour from his engine'. Most of the rear gunner's answering 'bursts went wide, but one bullet made a long hole in the central panel of the hood and struck the armour plating close to my head'.

The Western Australian had had another close shave. Not so his target. 'He dived to sea level and I fired again from behind and slightly to one side.' Dick watched the Me110 make a 'controlled landing not far from a lightship, east of Portland Bill, and near to a smaller boat, which moved towards him'. He had not seen his first Messerschmitt crash but was 'convinced that he was badly damaged and probably disabled'. He watched as the second 'aircraft sank within 30 seconds … I did not see anyone get out of it'. When the victories for the day were tallied – both Dewar and Jay were also successful – Dick was credited with one destroyed and 'probably another'.[10]

While Dick twisted, veered and jinked, Stuart Walch entered the fray. At 11.55 a.m., just after the enemy bombers had dropped their load and about the same time that Dick was ordered to intercept, the Tasmanian and B Flight, who had been patrolling Warmwell, were directed to Portland.

They arrived over the naval base at 10 000 feet. The enemy aircraft were at 12 000 feet, so Stuart, who was Blue Leader and flying Hurricane P3124, 'ordered aircraft line astern' and 'climbed towards combat'. When they were roughly 3 miles southeast of the base, Stuart saw one Me110 diving towards a ship off Portland Bill. He 'ordered Green Section to stay above in case of escort fighters'. Then, just on noon, he and pilot officers John 'Jackie' Urwin-Mann and Brian Considine fired. The twin-engine fighter turned towards Stuart, who cut loose 'two 3-second bursts' closing from 'about 300–200 yards'. While they were still in line astern formation, Urwin-Mann made a beam attack, firing into the side of the Messerschmitt. Stuart fired at it again, this time from 250 yards closing to 50. As the Me110 straightened out, white and black smoke gushed from its engine, which then caught alight. The Messerschmitt plummeted. Stuart followed and 'saw it crash into [the] sea'. Urwin-Mann and Considine confirmed the destruction, and although Stuart's combat report states that 'Blue One, Two and Three attacked in order', he was the only one credited with 'the squadron's first confirmed scalp'. At least one post-war researcher, however, correctly attributed the Tasmanian with a one-third share of the downed Me110.[11] It was his first victory.

Both Dick Glyde and Stuart Walch opened their Battle of Britain account on the 11th. But who was the first Australian to claim victory in the world's first great air battle? Their combat reports record encounters at noon, but is it likely that both looked at their watches just as they fired and noticed it was exactly midday? Such was the nature of battle they probably didn't look at their watches at all. Combat times were based on information from operations controllers, eye-witness accounts both in the air and on the ground, and post-battle debriefs that took into account take-off and landing times. At best, they were only informed guesses. All that can be said is that Stuart's destruction and Dick's probable (followed by a confirmed victory within 5 minutes) occurred – officially – simultaneously. They thus share the honour of being the first Australians to draw blood during the Battle of Britain.

'A blinding flash and a column of smoke'

Jack Kennedy was back in the air the day after his compatriot claimed 238 Squadron's first victory, leading Red Section on an early morning sortie and a base patrol just after noon. No enemy aircraft were sighted on either occasion. Flying duties over, he wrote a quick note to Christine Jourd. 'It's just about a month I think since I saw you; it seems much longer … I am frantic with love.'[12] He stamped the letter and sent it on its way, knowing it would soon be in his fiancée's hands.

Jack and Stuart Walch awoke early on 13 July to fly to Warm-well, about 50 miles away. The squadron had been ordered to use it as its daytime forward base, returning to Middle Wallop at night.[13] The weather was cold for the time of year and overcast with gusty rain showers. The Australians shivered as they waited in dispersal.

The weather improved, and convoys plying the southern waters attracted the Luftwaffe's attention. One neared Lyme Bay in the early afternoon. This area, west of Portland, was considered dangerous, with vessels vulnerable to enemy attack. At 2.45 p.m., three Spitfires from 609 Squadron, which was also using Warm-well as a forward base because of its proximity to the naval base at Portland, along with 12 Hurricanes from 238 Squadron, were dispatched to intercept a raid of 20 to 30 Me110s near Portland. Jack was leading A Flight in Hurricane P2950, and Stuart, flying P3124, led B Flight.

A Flight was 12 000 feet over Portland Harbour when they spotted a Dornier Do17 heading towards the coast in a shallow dive. Stuart and B Flight joined 609 Squadron to deal with the Messerschmitts, while Jack ordered Red Section into line astern to follow the Dornier. The anti-aircraft guns were blazing. Ignoring the ack-ack, Red Section pursued the enemy bomber across the Dorset coast's Chesil Beach towards some oil tanks. It released a bomb, which fell near a gun position.[14]

Jack called the attack. According to Red Two, Pilot Officer Charles Davis, Jack flew 'right in close' and 'succeeded in disabling one motor with his first burst'. Davis thought Jack had probably killed the rear gunner. Then, 'the Hun turned back towards the shore', and Davis and Sergeant Cecil Parkinson, who was Red Three, 'closed in' and fired. They watched it plunge into the sea off Chesil Beach.

While Davis and Parkinson finished off the Dornier, Jack proceeded 'to look for more Huns'. According to Davis, 'eye-witness accounts state that a Hurricane attacked and shot down an Me110 fighter'. P2950 'was then attacked and disabled by three others'.[15] Jack lost height and struggled to maintain control as he approached Weymouth. To Private Acutt and his colleagues at the Cranford depot of Weymouth's St John Ambulance Brigade, it appeared that he was trying to find a suitable place to land. Jack skimmed 'over the tops of the houses ... barely missing the chimney pots'. Then, 'a second later', Acutt and his friends saw a second aircraft, following Jack, 'as though in pursuit'. He wondered if 'this [was] a dogfight and were we in at the kill?' Jack was roughly 2 miles from Warmwell. He 'just cleared a hedge, swerved', then a 'wing seemed to touch something, a telegraph pole or something of that nature'.

P2950 nosedived into a hillside at Southdown Farm, near Littlemoor Road, north of Lodmoor, just outside Weymouth. 'A crash!' exclaimed Acutt. 'A blinding flash and a column of smoke.' The Hurricane's engine exploded. The 23-year-old was the first Allied airman to be shot down in the Weymouth area and the first Australian to die in the Battle of Britain.[16]

'Highly esteemed'

Jack Kennedy, Charles Davis and Cecil Parkinson were each credited with a one-third share in the Dornier. Davis felt some responsibility for the squadron's first death in combat. 'I do wish Jack had waited for the other two of us as I feel we might have been able to do something to help.' He believed his Australian flight commander was the Hurricane pilot witnesses had seen bringing down the Me110. 'The times given and the subsequent happenings coincide very closely with what we know about Jack's death and I think it is very probable that it was indeed he who shot down the 110.'[17] Even so, neither the Me110 nor the Ju88 that Jack had kicked on 3 July were recognised by the squadron.

Jack's one-third share in the Dornier was his only officially acknowledged combat victory.

Stuart Walch had lost a friend. Sergeant Henry 'Tony' Marsh of A Flight marked the passing of 'a damned fine bloke'. Jack's death was a shock to Gordon Batt, who had been in Yellow Section and embroiled in his own battle when Jack fell. He had revised his original low opinion of his flight commander. He now considered him one of the 'damn nice blokes' who were lost during his time with the squadron. Charles Davis and his comrades were 'terribly sorry to lose him – he was a grand chap to have in the squadron either as a flight commander or friend'. Father Arthur Kavanagh, who had only recently arrived at Middle Wallop, 'heard of him from all sides' and discovered the young Australian 'was highly esteemed and deservedly popular'. More than that, the squadron had lost 'an officer of high calibre' and of 'great promise'.[18]

'Go on loving me more and more'

Later that day, Christine Jourd, who was staying with her grandmother in Somerset, phoned the squadron and asked to speak to Jack. There was a pause. She was told to ring back. She enquired why, and then the phone went dead. Later, she heard on the news that one of the squadron's aircraft was missing. Despite the mystery of the phone call, she did not think anything had happened to her fiancé. After all, he had told her often enough that everything was under control. But as time passed and she heard nothing, doubts set in. She told her grandmother that if Jack *had* gone down in the sea, he would have survived as he was such a good swimmer. Out of the corner of her eye, she saw her mother (who was also visiting) shake her head. Slowly, she realised the truth. She fainted, and a doctor was called. When she recovered, she refused to believe that Jack was dead, so her father contacted the

Australian high commissioner, who sent a telegram confirming that Jack had 'lost his life as a result of air operations'.[19]

Christine was stunned. The last telegram she had received was from Jack, telling her how happy he was at the formal announcement of their engagement. Now, she held one advising his death. Much of their time had been spent apart, but Jack's fervent letters, scribbled in the mess or as he waited in dispersal, had made separation bearable.[20]

His final letter – written the day before he died – arrived. In it, he exhorted her to 'go on loving me more and more and do love me fiercely. I think of you all the time and love you so much'.[21] How could someone who expressed such depth of feeling be gone forever? How could someone so vibrant, so full of love, so passionate, be dead? But he was. They had had just 13 months together – they had met on 13 June 1939, and he had died on 13 July 1940. They hadn't planned anything concrete beyond the moment of their love and would never have the chance. Jack *was* dead. Christine was desolate.

No one from 238 Squadron visited the grieving woman; nor did any of Jack's friends from 65 Squadron. They were too busy. But 238 Squadron's new commanding officer, Squadron Leader Harold 'Jim' Fenton, sent her Jack's cigarette case. She turned it over in her hands. It had been bent and looked as if someone had attempted to straighten it out. Christine opened it, hoping to see the small photo she had sent Jack. She recalled how much the portrait had meant to him: 'The snap of you was a marvellous idea. I'm carrying it around with me'. It became his talisman, and 'every time I feel browned off I dig it out and have another look'.[22] But the photo was not there. Christine assumed it had been destroyed in the crash.

Jack was buried with full military honours on 19 July at Holy Trinity, Warmwell, a small church close to the airfield. Christine didn't know he was a Catholic, but one of her friends did and ensured he received a Catholic funeral, although Holy Trinity was an Anglican church. A priest officiated, and Jack was accorded 'all the services of the church'. Christine was too grief stricken to attend, so her friend went in her stead but also to carry out an important task. She knew that, although 238 Squadron's adjutant had formally identified Jack's body, his young fiancée still believed he would turn up. So she insisted the coffin be opened before burial.[23]

She had to steel herself. Crashed Hurricane pilots usually suffered severe burns. If they could not get out, they would die in rapidly engulfing flames. Christine's friend did not expect to see the Australian's handsome features; she was looking for the gold tooth that would prove it was Jack. There was no doubt.

'One day it'll always be like this'

After his first victory, on 8 July, Pat Hughes and 234 Squadron had been occupied with interception scrambles, local patrols and convoy protection. Pat was often in the air three times a day, but there was little result.

The southwest region had been assailed by raids, and Home Intelligence reports indicated public consternation about local defences, which in some areas had proven inadequate. On 13 July, Pat and 234 Squadron's Blue Section were detached and sent to Roborough, located 50 miles or so from St Eval, to help provide better air coverage to Plymouth. They stayed a week carrying out patrols but returned to St Eval on the 20th because the small airfield was unsuitable for Spitfires. Their work for the important naval city continued, however, with night patrols over the naval base and surrounding areas. Not all of 234's pilots were operational at night, and the burden fell to a handful, including Pat and Bob Doe. It soon became obvious that the Spitfire was unsuitable for night flying. Pilot Officer Geoffrey Gout crashed on the night of 25 July, and Sergeant Tommy Thompson was so badly injured after crashing in the early hours of 31 July that he never flew again.[24]

A number of factors relating to defensive operations over the Channel became apparent at about this time. One was that RAF pilots rarely intercepted before the enemy dropped their bombs. Another was that the Luftwaffe bombers were so well protected that the defenders were overwhelmed by the escorts and suffered inevitable fatalities and near misses. A third factor was that when they were directed to the high-flying Messerschmitts, Fighter Command's pilots often found themselves far below the attackers and at a tactical disadvantage. (It was not the radio direction finder operator's fault. In hindsight it was accepted that lower height registers came about perhaps because of 'a bias that way in the equipment'.)[25] Pat Hughes and Blue Section were misdirected on 27 July and found themselves below a raider. Pat, in Spitfire N3280, Flying Officer Francis Connor, who was Pat's number two, and George Bailey as Blue Three were ordered to patrol Land's End, the westernmost point of mainland Britain. They took off at 2.45 p.m., and 15 minutes later, when they were 25 miles southeast of Land's End, Pat was ordered to take his section to 23 000 feet. They saw a lone Ju88 directly above, just as its pilot saw them. The German carried out an aileron turn then dived and veered towards the sea.

Pat may not have had the tactical advantage but he had lightning reactions. As the Junkers careered down at an estimated speed of 300 miles per hour, Pat followed, with Connor and Bailey right behind. Pat caught up to the Junkers, closing to 200 yards. As the Ju88's rear gunner fired, the Australian attacked 'from astern, using deflection'. N3280 was struck by a bullet in the mainplane as Pat followed the enemy aircraft down to the water. He fired three bursts at the Junker's tail, putting 'both rear guns ... out of action'. With no more rear fire to contend with, he was in the clear. His bullets smashed into the Perspex in the Ju88's cockpit,

Left 'How did we know it was all so precious?' A poor copy of a copy. One of the few photos of Jack Kennedy that Christine Jourd possessed. Courtesy of Christine Stanley-Hughes

Below Nineteen-year-old Christine Jourd with a family friend, 1939. She was looking grumpy at the time because Jack Kennedy 'was flying overhead. I was so anxious'. Courtesy of William Stanley Hughes

Below left 'Darling, I did so want to tell you how enormously I love you.' The RAF wings brooch Jack Kennedy gave to Christine Jourd. Author's photo

Above The Hutchins School's football and tennis students on their 1933 Melbourne tour. Stuart Walch, with scarf, is behind the microphone, to the rear. Courtesy of The Hutchins Archives and Heritage Collection, The Hutchins School

Right Stuart Walch proudly displaying his wings on graduating from 20 Course, 1 Flying Training School, Point Cook, June 1937. Courtesy of The Hutchins Archives and Heritage Collection, The Hutchins School

Far right Stuart Walch in front of one of 151 Squadron's Hurricanes. Courtesy of John Walch

Above Young Dick Glyde. Courtesy of Robert Glyde

Above right 87 Squadron scrambling at a French
aerodrome, 1939. Courtesy of Andrew Rennie

Below right Trophy from the Heinkel He111 which Dick
Glyde 'had the satisfaction of using my guns ... and
scoring a few hits on'. Author's collection

Langham   Perth.

Above Despite the relaxed setting, Pat Hughes looked careworn and older than his 22 years as he tried to smile for Kay Brodrick's camera, 9 June 1940. Courtesy of *After the Battle*

Right The 'Brylcreem boys' were like bees to the honey. And it is no wonder. Kay Brodrick, the woman who stole Pat Hughes's heart, 1940. Courtesy of David Moor

Far right 'No one who saw the mask of age which mantled the faces of these young men ... is likely to forget it.' This photo of Pat Hughes was taken shortly before his death. It is hard to believe he was just a few days short of his 23rd birthday. Courtesy of Nigel Walpole

Above A happy Ken Holland with furry friend, May 1939. Courtesy of Jonathan Falconer

Left 'I believe she is the girl for me for always now.' Ken Holland's fiancée, Seina Haydon, in 1953 when she was about 34 years old. Courtesy of Carolyn Evans

Right John Crossman and Pat Foley made the most of any opportunity to go out into the countryside on romantic picnics. Courtesy of the Bowden family

Above John Crossman and his mother, Mick, before he boarded the RMS *Orama* on 12 August 1939. Courtesy of the Bowden family

Right Studio portrait of John Crossman, with wings, taken in Newcastle-upon-Tyne during 32 Squadron's Acklington exile, August/ September 1940. This was one of the photos treasured by Pat Foley. Courtesy of the Bowden family

Above Rabbit shooting in the
Adelaide Hills, January 1939. Bill
Millington never lost his 'eye'.
Courtesy of Simon Robinson

Above right Bill Millington with
Pipsqueak, 'a little black and
white terrier of indeterminate
ancestry'. 249 Squadron, 1940.
Courtesy of Simon Robinson

Right Bill Millington with
Wilfred the duck and Tom Neil
with Pipsqueak. 249 Squadron,
1940. Tom Neil recalled that Bill
'appeared to enjoy flying as my
partner ... and often told me so'.
Courtesy of Simon Robinson

Far right Desmond Sheen
DFC and bar, with Australia
shoulder flash. Courtesy of
Diane Foster-Williams

Above This photo of Des Sheen wearing his flying helmet with leather-covered earphone gives a sense of how close he came to death on 7 December 1939 when it was pierced by a bullet in combat. Courtesy of Erik Mannings, 72 Squadron historian

Left Des, Rusty and the soon-to-arrive Des Jr, who, like his father, would become a pilot. September 1941. Courtesy of Diane Foster-Williams

Far left Des Sheen receiving the DFC from King George VI, 16 July 1940. Courtesy of Diana Foster-Williams

Above William and Elizabeth Millington showing Group Captain Carr the brochure of the Battle of Britain Memorial window in Westminster Abbey, London, at the Cross of Sacrifice, Adelaide, on 15 September 1947. Courtesy of Bruce Robinson

Right Those who fought and died in the Battle of Britain were considered to have made the supreme sacrifice. Scroll issued to next of kin in 1947. Courtesy of Robert Glyde

Far right Battle of Britain Memorial window in honour of 'The Few', Westminster Abbey. Courtesy of Beryl Kennedy

GVI RI

This scroll commemorates

Flying Officer R. L. Glyde. D.F.C.
Royal Air Force

held in honour as one who
served King and Country in
the world war of 1939-1945
and gave his life to save
mankind from tyranny. May
his sacrifice help to bring
the peace and freedom for
which he died.

THIS PANEL IS DEDICATED
TO THE MEMORY OF
FLT. LT. P. C. HUGHES. D.F.C.
KILLED IN ACTION
BATTLE OF BRITAIN 7TH SEPT. 1940
AGED 23

Above William Hughes's visit to this memorial plaque at Christ Church, Kiama, led to the serendipitous discovery of his brother Pat's missing medals. Courtesy of Michael Molkentin

Right John Crossman's grave at Chalfont St Giles (before its regular spruce-up by the parishioners). John continues to be remembered. Each year, a floral tribute is laid by his headstone. This, in 2012, was 'To John, one of "The Few" from the people of Forest Row and the Wheeler Family'. Courtesy of Ian Johnson

and as he fired he saw 'parts of aircraft [fall] from both engines'. Ammunition spent, he 'broke away to port'. Connor and Bailey emptied their guns at the failing Junkers. It seemed certain that it would drop into the waves, but it pulled up twice to a height of 300 feet or so before they lost sight of it. Each man was credited with a one-third share of the damaged Ju88.[26]

The Australian flight commander was hard at it again on the 28th. He was on dawn readiness, and shortly after 5 a.m. he, Ken Dewhurst and Pilot Officer Patrick Horton – a one-time student at The Hutchins School about three years behind Stuart Walch – were ordered to investigate an enemy aircraft over Plymouth. As they approached the port city, shell bursts from the anti-aircraft guns illuminated a lone Ju88 'diving steeply towards some objective on the land'. This time flying Spitfire N3239, Pat followed the Junkers down but waited until it 'pulled up' and then 'opened fire at 100 yards closing to 50 yards'. He held this position and blasted off a number of 2-second bursts, continuing as the enemy aircraft began to turn. The German rear gunner kept up a constant barrage, and Pat's Spitfire was hit by a solitary bullet in the radiator. N3239 was fine, but smoke began to trail from the Ju88's starboard engine and a 'red hot object' broke off. The Junkers began to lose height. Dewhurst and Horton fired. The damaged engine burst into flames and the German bomber slowly turned to starboard and hit the water. It disappeared within seconds; there were no survivors. There was no doubt about this one. Blue Section claimed a destroyed and each was credited with a one-third share.[27]

Three successful battles in three weeks, and in each Pat had demonstrated a trade-mark combat style: get in close and keep firing. Indeed, his mantra to his pilots became 'get in close and you can't miss'. It was risky but effective; as he had found on 27 and 28 July, he was likely to be hit as well. Pat, however, ignored the enemy fire. In favouring a 'close quarter' combat style, he proved himself a 'fearless and determined fighter pilot' who 'commanded the greatest respect from his pilots' and set them an example they – like Francis Connor on 27 July – were willing to follow.[28] If Pat displayed a touch of ruthlessness in ensuring he maximised his chances of destroying enemy intruders, it was simply an extension of his lively aggression at Point Cook and nothing more than any skilled pilot exhibited.

On 31 July, Pat was reassigned to night flying duties, but he was up early on 1 August. He had a special licence and 24 hours' leave, and Kay Brodrick had driven down from Hull. With strangers as witnesses, he and Kay exchanged vows at Bodmin Register Office. She had come alone, and, other than Flying Officer Butch, no one from 234 Squadron could be spared to attend. But that did not matter. They had each other.[29]

They revelled in a brief solitude at The Buck, their newly rented cottage at Treyarnon Bay, in North Cornwall, about 3 miles from St Eval. With sea views from the house and garden it would have reminded Pat of his joyous holidays at his sister Midge's home at Kiama. Even though they both 'knew of the dangers facing Pat he never spoke about what he was doing and was always cheerful', Kay recalled. 'We were so marvellously happy.' Pat risked a thought for the future. 'One day it'll always be like this' – just 'you, me and another Flying Officer Butch … I mean if we ever have a son'.[30]

'It was a question of being patient'

After Dick Glyde's success of 11 July, he laughed his way through many 'good natured comments about his similarities to a cat' and shrugged off the admiration of his fellows for not turning a hair when the enemy bullets struck his Hurricane in battle.[31] As Dick and his friends celebrated their victories, they also toasted Squadron Leader Dewar, who had been promoted to command RAF

Exeter. His place was taken by New Zealander Squadron Leader Terence Lovell-Gregg.

No doubt their great success of 11 July would have given Dick and 87 Squadron a taste for more, but initially it appeared to be a one-off. They continued their convoy work but soon became bored.[32] A change of scenery was in order. Like their colleagues at 234 Squadron, they were off for a bit of night flying. Not quite what they had been hoping for, perhaps. A Flight had already had a stint at Hullavington, in Wiltshire, carrying out night patrols against German raiders who had been attacking Bath, Bristol and surrounding areas. B Flight replaced them on 24 July.

Like Spitfires, Hurricanes weren't designed for night operations. For one thing, the pilots were blinded by the glare from the exhausts of those in front. For another, it was impossible to see the enemy (unless it was a moonlit night), so pilots had to rely on ground control. Very few victories were notched up after sunset, and Dick's four night flights from Hullavington proved fruitless. One pilot, however, achieved success. On 26 July, 5 minutes before Dick took off, Johnny Cock saw an He111 lit up by searchlights. He shot it down moments later. He was the first from 87 Squadron to account for a night intruder and the first Australian to claim a night-time victory in the Second World War.

The day after Dick had claimed his first victory in the Battle of Britain, Des Sheen finally reached Liverpool following his long sea voyage from France and received a welcome similar to the one that had greeted his arrival in England in February 1937: 'thick fog and pouring rain'. By the time he returned to Heston, Sidney Cotton had been relieved of command and his outfit renamed the Photographic Reconnaissance Unit. Des flew some recce flights over Germany and the Netherlands but decided he 'wanted to get back to fighters now'.[33] He asked to rejoin his old squadron. Fighter Command still needed to swell its ranks to make up for continuing losses, so Des's request was granted.

He returned to 72 Squadron at Acklington on 29 July to find that Squadron Leader Ronald Lees had relinquished command and taken up duties at 13 Group's headquarters. He had been replaced by Squadron Leader Anthony Collins.

During Des's absence there had been little other than training flights, routine readiness and convoy patrols, and his old friends were good-naturedly envious of his experiences in the south of France. Bill Millington and 79 Squadron, who had joined 72 Squadron at Acklington on the same day that Des had arrived back in Britain, were also having an uneventful time. Now under the command of Squadron Leader John Heyworth, whose remit was to bring the squadron back to operational status as soon as possible, Bill and his friends were restricted to training flights. Working with experienced pre-war veterans such as Flying Officer Edward 'Teddy' Morris, Heyworth constantly drilled his squadron into operational readiness. In the process, according to Pilot Officer George 'Neddy' Nelson-Edwards, he 'proved himself to be a brave and inspired leader'. Morris thought 'the reforming period at Acklington could not have been better'.

Bill's RAF appointment was confirmed on 20 July, and 79 Squadron was granted operational status on the 31st. Bill and his fellow pilots celebrated by carrying out practice attacks and formation flying. But although they were now officially on readiness, nothing changed. They waited for the ops phone to ring, drank cups of tea, chatted, wrote letters home and on 11 August perhaps raised a jar in honour of Bill's 23rd birthday. There was no action to be had. Nelson-Edwards recalled, 'Sadly the Luftwaffe ignored our sector, except for an occasional lone intruder to break the monotony'. Perhaps they commiserated with 72 Squadron's pilots, who were also kicking their heels in the north. As Des put it, 'Everybody was anxious to get down south and where the combat was getting much more violent. It was a question of being patient'.[34]

'A helluva nuisance'

As Dick Glyde and Stuart Walch awaited the call to battle on 11 July, John Crossman heard that those trained on 'single-engine aircraft were posted … the twins are left'.[35] He was going to '32 Squadron at Biggin Hill, Kent, just south of London. Whoopee'. He was thrilled to be posted to a Hurricane squadron. 'Now I have all I want from the RAF.'

Four days later, John unpacked his gear from the second-hand Austin he had just bought and rushed to dispersal. 'We have Hurricanes here and they look damned nice too. With a little luck I may fly one tomorrow.'[36] Just as Dick Glyde had not been allowed near the Hurricane until he was totally familiar with the Gladiator, John too was forbidden to fly the sleek fighter. He reluctantly accepted the situation, as 'I have lots to learn'. It wasn't until 25 July that he had his chance. Although he had hoped for an earlier try-out, 'there always seems to be a hitch in the proceedings'. Perhaps it was for the best that he acquired some experience on the Magister beforehand 'to give me an idea of what a monoplane is like'. Whereas the Magister was 'a very easy kite to fly and particularly responsive to controls', the Hurricane was 'an aeroplane and a half and its power and speed scares me almost. It is very easy indeed to black out in a tight turn as I found out'.

Life was looking brighter. John flew as often as he could, and his confidence in the Hurricane increased. 'They sure are swell planes.' An old friend from the RMS *Orama* and his Cambridge and Ansty days, Scottish-born, Queensland-raised John 'Tiger' Pain, joined the squadron from 7 Operational Training Unit, Hawarden, in Wales. John thought it 'rather good as I have one of the original Aussies with me now and that is something'. As he contemplated selling his Austin and purchasing 'a Ford which belonged to one of the pilot officers who was killed in action', he learned that 'I am to go away for five weeks to an operational training unit'. He wasn't impressed, 'as I am just nicely settled here now'. Before John could pack, however, he was told he would not have to go after all, 'which is a relief indeed'. But his reprieve from operational training was short lived. He was told on 2 August that 'I will have to go to No. 6 Operational Training Unit at Sutton Bridge for five weeks and when I get back will be operational. It's a helluva nuisance but orders is orders'.

'You have got to work hard for a few hectic minutes'

There was no time to grieve during the Battle of Britain. When Jack Kennedy died, on 13 July, for instance, 238 Squadron flew 38 sorties. The next day, eight sorties were mounted.[37] How could they mourn when the enemy was on the doorstep and replacement pilots were already dropping their kit in dispersal? An operational squadron could not afford to be down one flight commander, so one of the replacements was Flight Lieutenant Donald Eric Turner. Squadron Leader Jim Fenton, who had arrived on the 13th, replaced Cyril Baines, who had been posted to the Middle East. At Middle Wallop, Fenton met 'a potentially excellent bunch', but 'the snag was that we were at once placed on readiness. We badly needed even a few days to get to know each other and work out tactics'. In his opinion, 'just a week would have made a great difference'.[38]

Following a two-day hiatus in operations because of bad weather, Stuart Walch was in the air again at 1.45 p.m. on 17 July, when the squadron scrambled to intercept a raid off Portland. His new mount was Hurricane P3618, which he had taken charge of on 15 July.

After a series of uneventful patrols, Red, Blue and Green sections were on convoy protection on 20 July. Blue Section had a new member that day, Sergeant Leslie Pidd, who had recently arrived from 6 Operational Training Unit, Sutton Bridge. Stuart was introducing him to operations as his number two. Flying at 8000 feet, Blue Section arrived at the convoy, which was 15 miles southeast of Portland, at 12.20 p.m. They encountered the enemy 'in force' and 'the sections broke for individual combat'.

Stuart 'twice investigated aircraft which turned out to be Hurricanes'. By 1 p.m., he had lost sight of Pidd and Blue Three, Sergeant Eric Seabourne. His main petrol tank was empty, so he switched to the reserve and decided to return to base. Approaching Swanage, a coastal town about 60 miles from Middle Wallop, he climbed from 6000 to 8000 feet and 'observed 15 aircraft flying in formation towards the convoy on [a northerly] course at approx. 12 000 feet'. He was too far away to identify the aircraft, but given the direction they were taking he concluded 'they were hostile'.

Stuart tried to contact control to see if the relief section was on its way but could not raise them. He then 'turned and headed for convoy climbing to get into sun'. When he was 5 miles from the vessels, he saw bombs exploding around the escorting destroyer. Despite being alone, he 'pulled the plug and went after the enemy aircraft which had turned southwards'. When he was southeast of the convoy, at 10 000 feet, he saw 'three Me109s flying in wide vic at about 9000 feet'. He dived and attacked the machine on the left, opening fire at 200 yards and firing two rapid 2-second bursts as he closed to astern at approximately 50 yards. He watched as 'black smoke poured from under the engine of the enemy aircraft'. It 'turned right and made vertical dive towards sea'. He did not follow it down to confirm its destruction, 'as the other aircraft were trying to get astern of me'. His tanks were almost empty, so he 'pulled up in a steep stall turn and made for home'. Stuart did not mention it in his report, but as he had 'fired a burst causing the Me109 to catch fire' he had been assisted by another friendly aircraft and was accordingly credited with a one-half share of the 109.

At 3.35 p.m. the next day, 43 Squadron was finishing a stint on protection duties just off The Needles, Isle of Wight, when a formation of Do17s and Me110s escorted by Me109s attacked. 43 Squadron's relief, Stuart and Blue Section, arrived while the Me110s were 'dive-bombing' the ships 'from the northern side'. Stuart ordered his section 'in line astern and gave the order to Blue Two and Three to select a target each and to attack independently'. Brian Considine and Sergeant Ronald Little carried out their own battles as Stuart dived to 8000 feet, following the last aircraft in the formation as it headed back to France. He closed to 500 yards. The Messerschmitts caught sight of him and went into a right-hand turn. The Australian followed and narrowed the distance between them. 'The aircraft I was following swung out on the turn and was on the outside' of a defensive circle. Opening fire at 250 yards and closing to 50, Blue Two attacked the Me110 on Stuart's right while Stuart's target 'tightened his turn and dived towards the sea'. The Tasmanian broke off, as 'the starboard engine of the enemy aircraft was emitting black and white smoke'. He 'pulled away in a left-hand turn' and lost sight of the stricken machine.

A few seconds later, he saw a low-flying Messerschmitt. 'It went straight for about a mile then dived straight into the sea. I cannot say whether this was the enemy aircraft which I attacked or the one which Blue Two attacked.' He then saw 'three Me109s in line astern formation coming towards me on the beam at about 10 000 feet'. They ignored Stuart but turned to the southeast. Stuart 'started to follow but saw an aircraft I thought to be an Me109 flying at sea level towards the convoy. I broke off following the three Me109s and dived to attack the aircraft which I had just seen'. He recognised Blue Two just as he drew into range, and stayed his guns. 'By the time I had climbed up to 10 000 feet again all hostile aircraft had disappeared.' Like Pat Hughes, Stuart had fired from as close as he could get, and this dangerous strategy had paid off for him as well. He was credited with one destroyed Me110 and one damaged.

Stuart did not encounter the enemy again until his second sortie on 26 July. At 11.42 a.m., the squadron took off to patrol Swanage at 10 000 feet. Stuart was Blue Leader. Ground control advised that 'bandits' were southwest of Portland at 12 000 feet, but, as so frequently happened at this time, the controller had miscalculated the height. South of Portland, Stuart caught sight of three Me109s flying at 14 000 feet. He ordered Blue Section into line astern and climbed behind the enemy fighters, which had by then attained 18 000 feet. Stuart later reported that two of the Me109s were 'in vic formation and one loose on right'. (German fighters usually flew in two pairs, called a finger four formation. Perhaps the third Me109 pilot had already lost his partner in battle.) They were almost to the French coast when Stuart lined up the straggler and 'fired one short burst (1 second) from a shallow quarter deflection'. The Messerschmitt 'half rolled then dived vertically down, then went into spin and broke up, the wings dropping off and fuselage going into sea'.[39] Stuart was credited with destroying the Me109.

Stuart flew nine more sorties as July drew to a close. He was constantly busy, constantly tired, but he managed to find time to write home. He did not go into too many details of his flying adventures and played down the danger so his parents would not worry. 'Some of the combats I have been in have been rather wild while they lasted', he told them. 'So far I seem to have been in the show with my section only.' As he had done with Leslie Pidd, it was his practice to take operationally inexperienced pilots under his wing. Despite his good intentions in developing their skills he conceded that his two offsiders were 'not a terrific support against the odds we have met from time to time'. Even so, 'my boys are damn good and have proved themselves very reliable supporters, as you can imagine'. Then he told his mother and father of how 'we (the three of us) met 30 and got a couple. Once my flight (six of us), which I was leading, met 80 and again when I was on my own I got mixed up with 15'. Just as his terse combat reports belied the sweat, adrenalin and frenetic movement of battle, so too did his letter as he modestly asserted to his parents that 'you have got to work hard for a few hectic minutes on those occasions'.[40]

11

8–18 August

'Dauntless in the face of danger'

Hitler's Directive 16, issued on 16 July 1940, authorised preparations for Operation Sea Lion (Unternehmen Seelöwe), the invasion of Britain. It laid out his plans 'to eliminate the English motherland as a base from which war against Germany can be continued', and the Luftwaffe was placed at full readiness.[1]

Hitler reinforced his plans in Directive 17, released on 1 August, the same day that Pilot Officer Bryan McDonough of 236 Squadron and his gunner, Sergeant Frederick Head, were reported missing. Tasmanian-born McDonough was the second Australian to die in the Battle of Britain. The new directive listed operations to bring about 'the final conquest of England'. In it, Hitler ordered the Luftwaffe to 'overpower the English Air Force with all the forces at its command, in the shortest time possible'. The Luftwaffe's wide-ranging campaign against the RAF would target 'flying units, their ground installations, and their supply organisations ... the aircraft industry, including that manufacturing anti-aircraft equipment'. The Fuehrer did not set a date for the beginning of the campaign but indicated it should be on or after 5 August, the day Dick Glyde attended an investiture at Buckingham Palace to receive his DFC. The final decision regarding the beginning of 'the intensification of the air war' as a prelude to invasion, declared Hitler, would lie with the Luftwaffe.[2]

Reichsmarschall Hermann Goering started implementing Hitler's directive on 2 August. He intended to throw all his resources at the RAF in an operation dubbed Adlerangriff, the Attack of the Eagle. He named the opening day Adlertag. Eagle Day was originally set for 10 August then deferred to 13 August. In the interim, the Luftwaffe continued its relentless air war over the Channel.

Stuart Walch and 238 Squadron carried out convoy duties during the first week of August. Just after noon on the 8th, Stuart led the squadron into action a few miles south of the Isle of Wight. They intercepted a large formation over the 'Peewit' convoy, which had been under attack for a number of hours. With their sirens wailing, Stukas dive-bombed the ships. There were aeroplanes all over the sky, and Stuart and his men flung themselves into the swirling mass. A 'confused dogfight occurred'. The squadron claimed 'nine enemy aircraft falling to 238's guns', but the cost was high. Eric Turner was lost, as was one of Stuart's B Flight charges, 24-year-old Flying Officer Derek MacCaw. Making things worse, Squadron Leader Jim Fenton was attacked while looking for Turner and baled out. He banged his head as he exited his Hurricane and bobbed in the water dazed, until a trawler fished him out. He required 17 stitches in his forehead and three weeks' sick leave.[3]

After non-event patrols on the 9th and 10th, Stuart was at dispersal again on the morning of 11 August, and Hurricane R4097, which he had been flying since the beginning of the month, was primed for battle. Since 2 July, Stuart had notched up 54 operational sorties, more than anyone else on the squadron, and had taken on 'all the most dangerous jobs himself'.[4] Operationally speaking, he was 238's senior man.

While Green Section carried out a base patrol to investigate an unidentified aircraft at 5.20 a.m. which turned out to be a Whitley, Stuart and Blue Section remained at dispersal, as did A Flight, now led by Flight Lieutenant David Hughes, who had arrived at Middle Wallop the week before, after Hurricane conversion at Sutton Bridge. Over at Exeter, Dick Glyde was also waiting to scramble. Back on duty after his investiture and a short period of leave, he had not flown ops since his last night patrol at Hullavington, on 30–31 July. Like Stuart Walch, he and 87 Squadron had had no part in the early morning patrols and interceptions.

Formations were detected off the Normandy coast in the Baie de la Seine and east of Dover. A number of squadrons were ordered to the Dover raid, which, although it was not realised at the time, was intended to distract attention from the forces assembling in the Baie. Between 10.05 and 10.09 a.m., the plotters tracked three formations. It seemed that the Baie de la Seine formation was 30 or so strong. Another formation, of perhaps 50 or more, was spotted north, and a smaller group northwest, of Cherbourg.

As there were no convoys in the area at the time, it seemed the enemy was aiming for a coastal target, probably Portland. If the Germans launched their expected invasion, operations against German sea communications could be mounted from the naval base. Portland had to be protected, so 1, 145 and 609 squadrons, which were already in the air, were directed there at 10 a.m. They were followed by 601 Squadron from Tangmere and Warmwell's 152 Squadron. At 10.09 a.m., they were joined by Exeter's 213 Squadron. Within minutes, Stuart Walch, on his 55th operational sortie, and 238 Squadron were in the air, as were Dick Glyde, in Hurricane P3387, and 87 Squadron's B Flight.

The enemy was met by 609 Squadron, which made little impact. They were followed by 601 and 145 squadrons, which were overwhelmed and couldn't break up the formation. At 10.30 a.m., Robert Voase Jeff, who was leading 87 Squadron's

B Flight, caught sight of retreating German bombers. He ushered his pilots into a line astern position to face the enormous formation, which straggled from 10 000 up to 15 000 feet. It was a daunting sight. Dennis David recalled that 'there were six of us and it looked like hundreds of them'.[5]

Jeff called the attack. Before they could strike at the Ju88s, the Hurricanes were scattered by Me109s diving through them, a ploy to keep them occupied while the bombers continued unhindered on their homeward journey. Jeff was hit. As he tumbled into Portland Harbour, Dick and his friends turned, dived and fired on the 109s.

There is no combat report for Dick, and his name is not included in the squadron 'bag' listed in the operations record book, but it can be assumed that his battle was as intense and dangerous as those of his confreres. Ivor Badger damaged one 109 but was himself struck. He then shot down the one that had attacked him. Pilot Officer Andrew McLure, who managed to out-turn one of the 109s and send it spiralling into the sea, was also attacked. He was wounded and his Hurricane damaged, but the Messerschmitts continued to chase him until he force-landed near Warmwell. Johnny Cock destroyed two and probably took another two out of the battle before his Hurricane was damaged so severely that he had to bale out. Slowly descending in the midst of the aerial mêlée, he was a plumb target; indeed, a Messerschmitt shot at him as he dangled from his harness, cutting through some of the parachute cords. Dennis David chased the German then returned and circled over Cock until he landed, in the sea off Chesil Beach.[6]

While Cock swam to shore under David's protection, Stuart Walch and 238 Squadron were homing in on the enemy force. After take-off, A and B flights had followed different tracks. David Hughes and A Flight were sent east of Weymouth. Stuart, leading B Flight, was vectored 5 miles south of Swanage; they crossed the coast east of Portland at 16 000 feet, arriving at almost the same time that Dick Glyde saw 100 or so enemy aircraft directly in front and about 5000 feet above.

Stuart ordered B Flight to climb into the sun. Jackie Urwin-Mann took Green Section to the left and above Stuart, Flying Officer Michal Steborowski and Sergeant Geoffrey Gledhill. Before they could get into position, however, B Flight was 'caught between two waves of a very big raid and so were heavily outnumbered'. They 'put up a really good show'. Pilot Officer Frederick Cawse's Hurricane splashed into the water, and Leslie Pidd sustained heavy damage. Urwin-Mann broke downwards to evade attack. He managed to deliver his own blows and brought down an Me109. While Urwin-Mann and Pidd struggled, Stuart tried 'to rescue two boys from a hopeless position'. But he failed. The 'vastly superior numbers told in the end'. 'The whole of Blue Section was lost.' No glimpse of parachute, no wreckage. Stuart, Steborowski and Gledhill disappeared.[7]

To some, Stuart Walch 'had the reputation of being the father of his squadron'. To others, he seemed 'like a brother to the younger men, many of whom never realised how his superior skills saved them'. Father or brother, he was loved and respected for being 'completely careless of his own welfare or success' and for shepherding the 'inexperienced boys' into battle.[8] He was the third Australian to die in the Battle of Britain.

A Flight fared much better. All pilots returned. David Hughes and Sergeant Marian Domagala each claimed a 109, and Sergeant Eric Bann and Tony Marsh shared an He111. Together with Urwin-Mann's 109, the squadron recorded four confirmed victories. But the success did little to overcome the shock at the deaths of Cawse, Steborowski, 19-year-old Gledhill, on his first sortie, and Stuart Walch, the squadron's third flight commander lost in less than a month.

Stuart's official tally for the Battle of Britain was two destroyed enemy aircraft, two shared destroyed, one unconfirmed shared destroyed and one damaged. Given his demonstrated prowess in the month since his first victory, it is likely it would have been higher if he had survived. The squadron's praise for this skilled pilot – and indeed for all their companions – was heartfelt and genuine. The diarist recorded a personal tribute to the dead which would become part of the official record. Steborowski 'was of a cheerful nature – his rugged face and gentle smile are greatly missed'. Cawse was 'a man of quiet manner and a happy disposition', and although 'Gledhill had been in the squadron barely a weekend [and] had hardly time to get to know his comrades or they to know him', his new friends had met 'a gentle boy, ruddy of countenance'. Stuart was lauded as 'dauntless in the face of danger, careless of his own personal safety and comfort, thoughtful for all who came in contact with him'. In addition to his sterling personal qualities, he 'had an innate gift for administrative duty which should have taken him high in his country's service'.

For the squadron diarist, 'the only reflection of good there is in a gloomy day is the thought that these gentlemen of England have exacted a toll which will go far to wear down the German beast'.[9] It did not matter that Stuart had been born in Australia or that Steborowski hailed from Poland. They had given their lives for Britain's defence. But more battles would need to be fought to quash the beast. 238 Squadron was in combat again the next day, and the next. Tony Marsh's death, on 13 August, was the eighth since Jack Kennedy's. The tired, tattered, shell-shocked remnants of the valiant squadron were sent to St Eval to rest and rebuild.

'Down somewhere in the sea'

The 11 August assault had demonstrated the Battle's growing intensity. Including the deaths of Stuart Walch, his 238 Squadron charges and Dick Glyde's one-time roommate Robert Voase Jeff,

Fighter Command lost 25 pilots killed or missing. There would be no respite.

The following day heralded the beginning of heavy attacks against the RAF's coastal airfields and radar defences, but Dick Glyde, who flew two nil-report patrols, saw none of the furious action that resulted in 31 German aircraft being shot down. The RAF's infrastructure took a hammering, but important facilities were either not seriously damaged or off line for only a short time. Losses, however, were heavy. Twenty-two aircraft were destroyed and 11 airmen were listed as either killed or missing in action, including 29-year-old Flight Lieutenant Latham Carr Withall (known as Carr), an Australian with 152 Squadron, who faced a mighty force south of the Isle of Wight. He was the fourth Australian to fall in the Battle of Britain.

As 13 August dawned, the Luftwaffe's forces were poised to attack. It was Adlertag. The early morning was foggy, and thick cloud covered the English Channel. The meteorologists, however, predicted it would clear by the afternoon. Goering decided to postpone operations until 2 p.m., but the order to defer take-off did not reach all his forces.

Once again, 87 Squadron was on duty. Dick Glyde had been woken for dawn readiness by his batman and, like his fellows, drank the obligatory morning cup of tea while lounging around until the call to the cockpit.

Fighter Command picked up only a few early morning plots, and it was not until they detected two large formations in the Amiens area, in northeastern France, between 5.30 and 5.40 a.m. that they felt any concern. At almost the same time, the plotters detected another sizeable cluster on the coast at Dieppe and a smaller but still significant group over the Channel north of Cherbourg. By 6.15 a.m., three full squadrons and sections from three more were in the air.

One enemy formation powered towards Littlehampton, on the

coast east of the Isle of Wight, so between 6.30 and 6.40 a.m., 601 and 213 squadrons scrambled to reinforce the defences between that point and Portland, to the west. A panic call also came through to 87 Squadron. Dick and B Flight took off at 6.40 a.m. They were to assist 601 and 213 squadrons.

Dewar led. Dick, flying P3387, was Blue Two, and Trevor Jay was Blue Three. Roland Beamont, Sergeant Sidney Wakeling and Ivor Badger were Green Section. They were vectored to Selsey Bill, 25 miles east of Portsmouth, but Blue and Green sections became separated; Green did not encounter the enemy.

Blue Section had been in the air for 50 minutes before they sighted a lone Ju88 south of Selsey Bill. Dewar ordered Dick and Jay into line astern. The Ju88 climbed into the cloud, and Dewar, Dick and Jay followed. They saw it dive so roared down too. When the Junkers tore out of the cloud, Dewar was so close he had to break away. Dick veered to the right and Jay to the left. They turned back on the Junkers, closing from 100 to 50 yards, and were almost on top of it as the rear gunner tried to protect its tail. P3387's glycol tank was hit. That did not deter Dick. He and his confreres positioned themselves with the target in their gun-sights. It was an ambush; Dick and Jay fired from astern and Dewar from quarter and above. The Ju88's starboard engine stopped. They watched it pitch into the sea.

The three formed up to return to base. Dick was trailing. Jay glanced behind and noticed white vapour streaming from P3387. When Jay and Dewar looked again, Dick had gone.[10]

Back at Exeter, A Flight was at readiness. Widge Gleed was keen to find out how B Flight was going so phoned the ops room for details and heard they had sighted a Ju88. When he checked again he was told that Dick was 'down somewhere in the sea'. Gleed confidently told his boys that Dick had had 'showers of near escapes. I expect he'll come smiling out of the drink'. He reminded them of the day just a little over a month ago 'when his glasshouse got shot off' and he had not even 'turned a hair'. He believed Dick would be picked up. 'One thing, it is a damned nice day for a bathe', he joked to relieve the tension.

Speculation about when Dick would reappear had to be put aside. The weather improved, and Goering launched Adlerangriff. The squadron was called to action. During a quiet moment later in the afternoon, Gleed asked Derek Ward if he had heard anything of Dick. 'Not a thing, old boy', said the New Zealander. Still they hoped he would be pulled from the water.[11] But he wasn't.

Dewar and Jay submitted their combat reports. Each claimed the Ju88, but it was a shared victory, so the squadron's diarist recorded that Blue Section had brought down the enemy aircraft. As far as the squadron was concerned, Dick had accumulated 'nine confirmed victories and had destroyed at least five other enemy aircraft' in the battles of France and Britain. For them, he was almost a triple ace, but with lack of supporting evidence from France, his final score sat at three and a quarter destroyed plus this one-third shared destroyed, one-third probably destroyed and one damaged.

No one had known it at the time, but when the bullets missed Dick on 11 July he had used the last of his nine lives. They sincerely regretted 'the loss of Dickie, who fought so well and hard, of whom we all retain such happy memories'. Roland Beamont spoke for all when he later wrote that Dick 'deserved a better end' than the silent plunge into the waters off Selsey Bill.[12] The fifth Australian to die in the Battle of Britain had proven to be much more than just 'a good average pilot'.

'A successful day out'

Pat Hughes spent only a little time with his bride. 247 Squadron had recently reformed at Roborough and was declared operational on Pat's wedding day. Armed with the outmoded Gladiator, the squadron was given a fortnight to familiarise themselves with the sector and patrol lines around Plymouth. Almost as soon as he and Kay exchanged vows, Pat was seconded to the new squadron to help with operational training. While Pat and his fellow pilots and ground crew were billeted locally, Kay awaited her husband's return to their lonely seaside cottage.[13]

It wasn't long before Pat was packing his bags again. When the enemy-ravaged 238 Squadron was sent to St Eval to recover from their heavy losses after the hectic fighting of 11 and 12 August, 234 Squadron was ordered to relieve them at Middle Wallop. Squadron Leader Dicky Barnett relinquished his command following the departure of John Theilmann, who was posted out on 7 August as 'non-effective sick' because of asthma. It was a popular decision. The intelligence officer, Pilot Officer Gregory 'Krikey' Krikorian, observed that 'Barnett couldn't and wouldn't lead the squadron into battle'.[14]

Bob Doe recalled that 'it was left to Pat to create a squadron'. According to Keith Lawrence, 'Being the natural leader he was, he stepped straight into the command'. Pat made the transition to leader well. In some ways, remembered Joe Roddis, he was distant towards the ground crew. Part of that was the acknowledged gulf of rank, but Pat would 'listen to what you had to say and make you feel like you were doing an important job, even if you felt you weren't doing anything special'. He was 'well liked, respected' and 'a wonderful, wonderful man' to whom the less experienced pilots readily turned for inspiration and guidance. Sergeant Jozef Szlagowski, for example, remembered how Pat had offered reassurance, telling him to keep calm, over the radio telephone when he ran out of fuel on a patrol in thick fog.[15]

As well as the squadron's de facto leader, Pat was also a young husband who had to tell his bride that, after a few precious days together, he was off to Hampshire. But he had a plan. When he phoned Kay about the surprise move, he told her to 'lock up the house and get to the White Hart. *Be* there, now'. As he prepared to fly to Middle Wallop, Kay packed, loaded her car and drove to the pub in Andover, which was conveniently located 5 miles from Pat's new quarters.[16]

Although 234 Squadron had bridled at the lack of action at St Eval, as soon as they arrived at Middle Wallop they knew they had finally joined the war. The aerodrome had been bombed the day before by a lone Ju88, the only one of its unit to locate the RAF station. Bombs had also fallen near the village of Nether Wallop and 238 Squadron's soon-to-be-vacated dispersal with, according to 238's diarist, 'no damage caused'. The other Ju88s had dropped their bombs on Andover. Shortly after Pat arrived on 14 August, Middle Wallop was targeted again. Bob Doe recalled that 'we landed on the grass airfield, were put into a lorry and, halfway up to the mess, they bombed the airfield'. One of the hangars was hit, and a member of the Women's Auxiliary Air Force (commonly referred to as a WAAF) was 'killed in a trench'. An airman was wounded and three were killed, as were some civilians working on the station. Three Blenheims and several Spitfires were destroyed, but 234 Squadron had landed away from the hangars so their Spits were safe.[17] The Luftwaffe paid a return visit the next day.

As Pat and the boys became familiar with the slit trenches, it was still quiet in the north. At Acklington, 79 Squadron had carried out convoy protection, night flying and routine patrols over the last few weeks. Other than an He111 shot down into the sea by Neddy Nelson-Edwards, Flight Lieutenant Rupert Clerke and Sergeant John Wright on 9 August, there had been little action. Des Sheen took to the air with 72 Squadron's Green Section on 14 August for his first patrol since returning to Acklington from the reconnaissance unit. It was uneventful, but that situation soon changed.

On 15 August, the Luftwaffe launched a series of attacks designed to overwhelm RAF defences. Almost the entire British

Isles was within range. Kent's forward airfields were targeted between 10.45 and 11.30 a.m., and four squadrons were dispatched to counter the intruders. For the main part, the enemy fighter escorts either refused to engage or circled over their charges so tightly that the defenders had difficulty breaking through to the bombers. Dover, Hythe and Folkestone were bombarded, but Lympne suffered the most damage and was unserviceable for two days. The next 2 hours brought more flurries of activity in the Dover area, but it was nothing compared to what was happening up north.

At about 9.30 a.m., a large formation of He115 floatplanes took off from Stavanger, in Norway, on course for Dundee, Scotland, tasked with attracting the fighter squadrons based around Edinburgh. They were followed half an hour later by 72 He111s, each loaded with high-explosive bombs, with their escort of 21 Me110s fitted with long-range belly tanks. (Some of the bombers later turned back, and only 63 reached their destination.) The floatplanes and the main force were supposed to follow separate tracks, but a navigational error by the Heinkels resulted in them flying along almost identical courses. The 115s turned back about 40 miles from the Scottish coast.

Fighter Command's plotters initially thought just three aircraft were on their way. This was soon amended to over 30. The Acklington squadrons were on readiness. At noon, an order to take off was blasted over the tannoy. 72 Squadron was in the air within 20 minutes, and 79 Squadron followed at 12.42 p.m., with three other squadrons not far behind.

Flight Lieutenant Edward 'Ted' Graham was leading 72 Squadron on a base patrol. Des Sheen, in Spitfire X4109, was Green Leader. When the He111s swung south to correct their navigational error, the squadron was ordered north to the Farne Islands, off the Northumberland coast, to intercept.

Just before 12.45 p.m., they encountered the enemy formation

30 miles east of the islands. Des thought the German onslaught looked like 'a large swarm of bees'; as he headed towards it, all he saw 'was line after line of bombers'. The pilots passed sighting reports to Graham, but he didn't acknowledge them. 'Can't you see the buggers yet?' Des asked over the radio telephone. Graham replied, 'Of course I can see the bastards – I'm just trying to work out what to do!' Within an instant he ordered Des's Green Section to patrol both flanks of the bombers at 21 000 feet as rear-guard. Coming from the seaward side, with the sun shielding his attack, Graham led Blue and Red sections through a gap between the lines of bombers and their escort. As the Heinkels dropped their bombs the enemy formation broke up. Some aircraft left the scene, and others followed the leader into a defensive circle. Des ordered Green Section to carry out individual attacks.[18]

Des eased into a circle of Me110s and closed on one, which, with its belly tank, looked like it was carrying a 'bloody great bomb'. He was fleetingly mesmerised but shook away his surprise and opened fire from 200 yards' range dead astern and slightly below. His second burst hit the aircraft. It exploded into a mass of debris. Flying through it was 'a frightening experience'. As he dodged the wreckage, 'the rest of the [enemy] squadron … took advantage of my temporary preoccupation by diving at high speed towards sea level and home'. Unscathed, Des climbed and spotted another circle of Me110s and attempted to 'pick one out', but 'another showed signs of attacking me'. He took 'a deflection shot approaching head-on' but missed. 'Another enemy aircraft appeared in the sights head-on and a no-deflection shot was made.' Better luck this time: 'Immediately flame and smoke appeared near the inside of the port engine'. Des then became the target, as 'the enemy aircraft either with the pilot shot or in a deliberate attempt to ram me approached head-on left wing low'. He took 'violent evasive action' and ducked away. 'The aircraft disappeared over my head with the flame and smoke greatly increasing in volume ... The remaining enemy aircraft were then lost in cloud and attempts to locate the main body failed.'[19] The Australian returned to base and refuelled after the furious battle, which had lasted all of 5 minutes.

After its clash with 72 Squadron, the enemy formation had split; part of it progressed in a northwesterly direction, and the other followed a southwesterly track. While Des was delivering his blow to the enemy, Bill Millington and 79 Squadron had been in the air for 3 minutes, on their way to the Farne Islands. Shortly afterwards, the controller reported a large raid approaching Acklington. Bill and his friends changed course. Squadron newcomers had been excited about their first opportunity for combat, but as Neddy Nelson-Edwards later recalled, they were 'clearly ill prepared' for the 100 or so enemy aircraft, comprising 60 to 80 bombers escorted by Me110s, that they encountered at 1 p.m.[20]

Squadron Leader John Heyworth ploughed his men into the bomber stream, breaking it up. It was utter confusion and every man for himself as the sky filled with twisting and turning dogfighting aircraft. They accounted for two Me110s shot down and one probable. It wasn't long before they encountered another seemingly overwhelming enemy formation. Again, 79 Squadron pounded into the mass of He111s. Bill found himself alone with a target in his sights. He fired. After trailing black smoke, the Heinkel exploded into flames, but Bill's attention was already focused on another. He fired again and the squadron's third confirmed fell to his guns.

Bill returned to Acklington; he and his fellows landed safely, with only one badly shot-up Hurricane to their debit.[21] But the battle still raged. Next to face the raiders were 41, 607 and 605 squadrons. The Yorkshire squadrons – 616, 73 and 219 – joined with north Lincolnshire's 264 Squadron to engage a force as it approached the Yorkshire coast. The last of the north's invaders were on their way home by 2.30 p.m., and Fighter Command's attention turned to new battles over Dover and the Thames Estuary.

Eleven squadrons were deployed to meet the next wave of intruders in a series of combats which lasted about an hour and a half. The skies above the Strait of Dover were all but empty by 4 p.m., but Fighter Command could not rest. Within an hour, Portland and Portsmouth were on the alert as between 200 and 300 enemy aircraft approached. Half were on track for Portland, and the rest were powering towards the Portsmouth and Isle of Wight area. Warmwell's 152 Squadron was the first in the air, at 5 p.m., followed 5 minutes later by 234 Squadron, led by Pat Hughes. Both squadrons were part of the largest force to date – approximately 150 Fighter Command aircraft – to encounter a single enemy formation.

Pat patrolled his men up and down in sections line astern. As the controller directed him to the best height to engage the enemy, the other pilots concentrated on formating on him while keeping their own positions. Pat was the only pilot able to keep an eye out for enemy fighters. By rigidly clinging to him, his men were vulnerable to attack from above by an enemy hidden by the sun. Those in the rear were defenceless.

They continued on duty for about an hour. Red Section was straggling, and just as they were on the turn over the Isle of Wight, someone realised that Pilot Officer Richard Hardy and Bush Parker were missing. They had disappeared, along with Yellow Section's Pilot Officer Cecil Hight. Then, as Bob Doe recalled, almost before they fully registered their loss, 'we found ourselves in the middle of a gaggle of Me110s and 109s. God knows how we got there; we just landed in the middle of them'. Following Pat's lead, they ploughed into a confusing mêlée. Now on their homeward journey, a formation of 50 Me109s and a bomber version of the Me110 – referred to as Jaguars by the squadron – was upon them. Pat fired at a Jaguar then broke away. Doe, who was

Blue Two, followed Pat, firing until it hit the water. Meanwhile, Pat had claimed one of his own. After the demise of his 110, Doe chased three more diving through the haze. He expended the rest of his ammunition at the nearest. As he broke away to avoid debris, he watched Pat finish it off. The enemy aircraft caught fire and plummeted into the water.[22] Guns exhausted, battle over, Pat and his men returned to base.

The fighting continued until after 7 p.m. The Luftwaffe left considerable damage in its wake that day, but Britain would recover. Fighter Command sustained losses: 34 aircraft destroyed and 17 killed, including the sixth Australian to die in the Battle of Britain, 25-year-old Western Australian Pilot Officer Frank Cale of 266 Squadron, who had attended the same school as Dick Glyde. Losses aside, Fighter Command had more than held its own in what was by far the largest air battle in which it had engaged. For the Germans, Black Thursday resulted in 76 aircraft shot down.

The Australians acquitted themselves well. Pat Hughes was credited with a destroyed Me110 and another shared destroyed, and Bill Millington destroyed all three of his He111s. Des Sheen recorded his two Me110s and a 'squadron bag' of 11 in his flying log and recalled that the atmosphere at Acklington at the end of the day was 'very elated ... because it was the first action for some of them and it was a successful day out. Very good'. There was mixed joy, however, at Middle Wallop. As well as Pat's and Bob Doe's victories, pilot officers Edward 'Morty' Mortimer-Rose and Janusz 'Jan' Zurakowski also claimed destroyed aircraft, and Ken Dewhurst damaged an Me109. But the squadron also mourned Cecil Hight, who had been killed in action over Bournemouth, and awaited reports about the whereabouts of Richard Hardy and Bush Parker. It was some time before they discovered that Parker had baled out at 900 feet over the Channel after his engine 'gave up' following 'two combats with Me110 which I shot down'. After almost 4 hours in the water, he was picked up by a German launch. He, like Richard Hardy, who had been forced by Me109s to land at Cherbourg, was imprisoned.[23]

'It'll never happen to me'

Before the close of day, Goering's commanders were obliged to digest the Reichsmarshall's latest directive. It was essentially an appraisal of the effectiveness of Luftwaffe activity in light of Fighter Command's stern resistance. Changes were needed. Among other things, Goering called for more fighters to escort the Stuka formations. Three fighter groups were needed for each bomber group: one to cling to the Stukas, one to fly ahead over the target at a medium height to engage the RAF defenders, and one to protect the whole attack from above. He also ordered that 'operations are to be directed exclusively against the enemy air force, including the targets of the enemy aircraft industry'. Convoys were to be attacked only where conditions were favourable, and Goering conceded that there was little point in maintaining the assault on radar sites, 'in view of the fact that not one of those attacked has so far been put out of operation'.[24]

Pat Hughes was also taking stock and faced a sad realisation that precision flying had resulted in the loss of three men. He had to bear that responsibility. With the clear vision of hindsight, Bob Doe recognised that their patrol formation that day was 'the stupidest ... you could possibly fly in ... We patrolled up and down the sun ... a stupid way of flying'. At the time, however, they were, as Doe acknowledged, 'a very green bunch of pilots, still believing in the laid down fighter tactics'. Despite the weakness of the tactics employed by Pat, his esteem in the squadron did not fall. Yet again, he had contributed to an increase in the victory tally. Keith Lawrence believed Pat had 'the tactical skill needed for a good leader of a fighter squadron in the air'; he was able to swiftly assess 'the direction of the sun and the likely sudden appearance of escorting enemy fighters [and] know just where to position the squadron for an effective attack on the bomber formation ... and lead the squadron into the fray'.[25] Pat's men had no doubts about him. They would continue to follow him into battle.

Pat spent the evening with Kay. She was distressed at the death of Cecil Hight and the loss of two others and feared what might happen to her husband of just two weeks. Pat tried to comfort her. 'Don't be so upset', he pleaded. 'It'll never happen to me.'[26]

'Good show, Pat!'

After their hectic sessions in the air on 15 August, Bill Milling-ton and Des Sheen settled down to await the next clang of the scramble bell. But the main action was still in the south, and the following days offered little more than uneventful patrols for the Acklington boys. Pat Hughes and the Middle Wallop squad-rons, however, were still in the thick of it when the Luftwaffe returned on 16 August.

From 11.45 a.m. it was obvious the German air force was again on the attack, and until 2 p.m., when the last of the enemy aircraft had crossed the Hampshire coast on their way back to France, Fighter Command allocated its resources to face large and aggressive formations targeting the Portsmouth anti-aircraft battery as well as airfields at Hornchurch, Tangmere, Kenley, Biggin Hill, Manston, West Malling and North Weald. Con-trary to Goering's most recent directive, the Ventnor radar sta-tion on the Isle of Wight took a hit. Bombs landed in London suburbs and on the railway station at Malden, in Surrey, killing staff and passengers and closing the lines. There was a brief hiatus until 4 p.m., when large formations were detected near St Omer, Boulogne and Dunkirk. At the same time as one force powered towards northern Kent, Essex and Suffolk, another was detected off the Normandy coast.

Eight squadrons were dispatched to cover the area between Portland and Worthing, but only one enemy formation was intercepted on the inward journey. In the Solent, the strait separating the Isle of Wight from the English mainland, 234 Squadron caught them on a homeward track. At 6.15 p.m. they were 5 miles south of the Isle of Wight, at 16 000 feet, when Pat, who was leading in Spitfire R6896, saw '109s circling 4000 feet above'. There were so many it was difficult to estimate the exact number. Pat thought there were 50, while Bob Doe, Yellow Two, counted 40.

The rigid strike formation may have failed the day before, but once again Pat's 'sections immediately formed line astern and climbed'. The enemy aircraft closed into a defensive circle but scattered in the face of Pat's attack. Three Messerschmitts lunged behind them, and as Doe climbed to 21 000 feet he came across another seven flying in line astern. He glanced behind and saw three more. He dodged away and found himself on the tail of another. He gave it two bursts. Smoke poured from the stricken Me109's engine. It turned on its back and crashed into the water, with Doe following it down. He was vulnerable, and a vigilant 109 took the advantage and closed on him. Pat saw what was happening and dashed to cover his charge. He 'took a deflection shot', and 'after a short burst it caught fire and blew up in front of Yellow Two'. But, just as he saved Doe from enemy fire, Pat's Spitfire was hit. The young Australian 'felt a jolt'. He 'turned sharply and found another 109 on my tail'. Messerschmitt and Spitfire twisted and turned in an energetic life-and-death dogfight, but Pat outmanoeuvred his foe. The 109 'climbed away and pulled up in front of me'. He could not miss. 'I shot him behind the cockpit and he caught fire and crashed into the sea.'

Pat didn't make Doe's mistake of following the diving Messerschmitt. He saw four Ju87s heading south and closed on them, but 'as I fired my first burst my tailplane was shot through by a 109'. The unbalanced R6896 dropped; the trim tabs – vital for aircraft stability – had been shot away. Pat still had control, however, and as he dived the 109 overshot. He turned onto the Messerschmitt but had only a quarter of a second's worth of ammunition left. When that was exhausted, he had to break off. The adrenalin had been flowing for just 15 minutes from when he first saw the enemy aircraft to the moment he turned back towards Middle Wallop.[27]

During a day and night in which the Luftwaffe put up 1715 sorties, Fighter Command again had its successes. At the time, it was believed 100 enemy aircraft had succumbed to Fighter Command guns, but the true total was less than half that number. Even so, it was a good start, and 234 Squadron had contributed to it. Pat may have missed out on a third Me109, but Doe, totally oblivious to his leader's protective fire, had gone on to claim a Dornier Do18 flying boat.[28] Patrick Horton had shot down one, and Sergeant Zygmunt 'Ziggy' Klein had claimed his first victory in the Battle of Britain.

As usual, there was a cost. Six men of Fighter Command had been killed in action – another would die from his injuries the next day – and two had failed to return; they would later be declared presumed dead. 234 Squadron's Ken Dewhurst safely baled out over land, and Francis Connor parted company with his Spitfire over water and was later picked up, wounded, by a naval launch. He was out of commission for two months. Aircraft were rendered temporarily unserviceable, such as R6896, which, as a Category One damaged, could be repaired by the squadron's ground crew. Others were good only for parts or were at the bottom of the Channel. Cloud cover had ensured many bombs missed their marks, but Brize Norton, Harwell and Farnborough airfields had been hit. (None were Fighter Command facilities. Farnborough received only minimal damage, but Brize Norton lost 46 aircraft, including a number of Hurricanes awaiting repair.)

At the end of another long day during which many pilots had

been in the air two, three and even four times, Winston Churchill was thinking. He and his chief staff officer and military advisor, General Hastings Lionel 'Pug' Ismay, had followed the action at 11 Group's headquarters at Uxbridge. Churchill was impressed by the cool way in which the battle had been handled but unnerved by the apparent paucity of resources in reserve. (He had not seen those of 10 and 12 groups.) When they left, Churchill told Ismay not to speak to him. 'I have never been so moved.' Five minutes later, he uttered the words that would, within days, be broadcast and immortalised: 'Never in the field of human conflict has so much been owed by so many to so few'.[29]

At about the same time, Pat Hughes and the boys, accompanied by Kay and Flying Officer Butch, were in the White Hart's bar. They put aside the previous day's losses and celebrated the results of their latest aerial battle. The old tactics might not be the best, but they worked. The boys had not lost faith in their leader. 'Good show, Pat!' they exclaimed, as they slapped his back and stood him a beer. 'How many did you get today?' they laughed, as if they didn't already know. Yet again, the Australian had proven to be a 'natural born good shot'.

As they laughed and congratulated each other, Kay watched. She could see they were tired, but exhaustion was kept at bay by sheer exhilaration. She realised how the pilots with whom she had so happily chatted at the Beverley Arms earlier that year had grown up. No longer boys, they were men. She may not have known it, but the one who had matured the most was her 22-year-old husband. He looked older than his years as he accepted the responsibility of his pilots' lives as well as the duty of defending Kay's homeland from invasion.

Pat Hughes had come a long way from the larrikin who had erected a toilet outside the pub at Digby, and much of the brashness had worn off. He had had a near miss. His confidence that 'it'll never happen to me' was shaken. He hid his new fear from the boys and joked with Kay, telling her, 'In case of accidents make sure you marry again'.[30]

'Large raid approaching'

Although 234 Squadron needed new men, they had to wait. Fighter Command's squadrons were short by 350 pilots; its establishment was only 900 to 1000 instead of 1300 to 1400, and some of those counted in squadron totals, like John Crossman until he was packed off to Sutton Bridge, were still under training. The operational training units could not keep up with the rate of attrition, even with course lengths slashed. 234 Squadron was also short by one leader, so Pat Hughes continued as de facto commanding officer. But not for long. Although Keith Lawrence believed Pat's recent combat experience and natural leadership tendencies qualified him for promotion, 10 Group had other ideas, and on 17 August, Squadron Leader Joseph 'Spike' O'Brien took command.[31]

The Luftwaffe reconnaissance spies were out and about shortly after dawn on 18 August checking weather conditions and shipping activity. By lunch-time, aircraft were massing in the Channel. Radar plots indicated it was the largest build-up of enemy aircraft so far, and 11 Group's squadrons were on readiness. The first formation crossed the coast at 12.49 p.m., followed closely by the second, powering onward in another all-out effort on the RAF's coastal airfields. One squadron was already in the air to greet the German bombers and their escorts. The rest of the 11 Group resources weren't far behind. Even so, the Me110s and 109s successfully distracted them, and Kenley, Croydon, Biggin Hill and West Malling were bombed. Both Biggin Hill and Kenley continued to operate despite some damage.

Even as the airfield attacks were underway, three more formations were detected over the central Channel. By 2 p.m. it was obvious they were heading towards the Solent. Most of the squadrons from Exeter to Tangmere were already on alert. 601 was patrolling Tangmere, and 213, 152, 43 and 602 had scrambled from 2.05 p.m. to defend the areas around St Catherine's Point, Portsmouth, Thorney Island and Westhampnett. At 2.15 p.m., following Squadron Leader O'Brien on his first sortie with the squadron, 234's pilots were on their way to the Isle of Wight to intercept a 'large raid approaching'.[32]

Pat Hughes had already gained his reputation as an aggressive and competent fighter pilot. It was reinforced just after 3 p.m., when about 20 Me109s 'appeared above me in the sun'. As usual the squadron was outnumbered, but with 12 Spitfires facing 20, the odds weren't so bad. O'Brien called for a battle climb and ordered individual attacks. Pat, who was Blue Leader, 'climbed towards them' in Spitfire X4036. Then they were 'broken up in dogfights', with each man picking out his own target and engaging separately. Pat fired his first burst at 150 yards but with no results. 'Then I found myself attacked by two Me109s.' One took aim 'at extreme range. [I] turned and set this aircraft on fire but was immediately attacked by the second one so could not follow it down'. After discharging his guns, the second 109 climbed away then dived. Pat followed, getting closer, 'until he started to pull up'. The Australian 'shot him with two bursts of 2 secs each' and watched the pilot bale out and his aircraft crash a few seconds later. Within a blink, he 'saw a second cloud of smoke and fire just off the Isle of Wight which appeared to be the first 109'.[33]

Pat was not alone in his success. O'Brien's call for individual attacks had paid dividends. The squadron's new commanding officer accounted for a probable 109, and Bob Doe, Morty Mortimer-Rose, Sergeant Alan 'Budge' Harker, Pilot Officer William 'Scotty' Gordon and George Bailey also contributed to 234 Squadron's destroyed, damaged and probables, all adding to Fighter Command's tally for the day.

The RAF and Luftwaffe each lost more aircraft on 18 August than on any other day of the Battle of Britain. In hindsight, it proved to be almost as decisive as Black Thursday. A turning point had been reached. Previously, the Luftwaffe's forces had all but overwhelmed Fighter Command on every encounter, and there were insufficient reserves. On the 18th, however, Fighter Command had deployed enough Hurricanes and Spitfires to make the combat ratio almost one to one, and its best pilots had accomplished a kill ratio of two to one. More importantly, the Luftwaffe still had not achieved air supremacy and, other than in a few isolated instances, would not send Stukas over Britain again. In the words of Battle of Britain historian Alfred Price, who dubbed 18 August 1940 'the Hardest Day', the 'laurels for the day's action went to the defenders'.[34]

12

19–31 August

'150 yards, closing to 30'

With no flying duties on offer at Acklington, Des Sheen had plenty of time to pen a long-overdue letter to his parents. He was concerned they were worrying unduly about him and their British relatives, so he tried to allay their fears. He assured them that 'things really aren't too bad' and apprised them of an exaggerated Luftwaffe loss of 'nearly 400 aircraft, probably more'. He was pleased to relate that 'the public laugh at the invasion. Not that they don't expect it but they are determined to make it fail. The confidence is incredible'.

Des also reported that the 'RAF is quite popular'.[1] Even so, Britain's aerial champions still had a long way to go before they could claim their final triumph against the Nazis. Until the next crop of operational training unit graduates came on line, Fighter Command, particularly 11 Group, had to husband its resources. On 19 August, Air Vice-Marshal Keith Park, the air officer commanding 11 Group, issued an instruction to his controllers which stressed that they could not afford to lose pilots through forced landings in the sea. (At that point, few RAF pilots downed in the Channel were rescued; the British had no dedicated air-sea rescue units or aircraft and only a few crash boats.) Controllers were to avoid sending fighters to deal with reconnaissance

213

aircraft or small formations over the sea. Their priorities were large enemy formations that were already over land or within easy gliding distance of the coast. When resources were directed to contend with mass attacks, the minimum possible number of squadrons was to be allocated to deal with the enemy escorts. Park also advised that when it was obvious an enemy formation was heading towards an aerodrome, one squadron or even the sector training flight should be ordered to patrol under the clouds.

On the other side of the English Channel, recognising that 'we have reached the decisive period of the air war against England', Reichsmarschall Goering also took the opportunity to bring about changes. He was not impressed with the way things were going so relocated one unit equipped with Me109s closer to the Channel and detailed it to bomber escort duties. He brought in aggressive young fighters such as Adolf Galland, who had earned his first combat honours during the Spanish Civil War.

Goering laid down his own new strategy. He declared that if the Luftwaffe could not force the RAF's fighters into the air they would attack them on the ground or bomb significant inland targets such as aircraft factories and bomber squadron infrastructure. Airfields would be a priority. Although his bombers usually succeeded in divesting their loads, Goering decided his fighter aircraft had to cling more tightly to their charges, even if it meant more German escorts would fall to the defenders.

Enemy incursions dwindled over the next five days, and Fighter Command's battle-weary pilots rested. The RAF speculated that the intensity of the Luftwaffe's recent activity had overstretched its resources, but with clouds and occasional showers in the east on 19 August, low clouds, wind and rain on the 20th, continuing clouds and rainy patches on the 21st, squalls on the 22nd and more showers and clouds down south on the 23rd before a return to sunshine on the 24th, it seems the weather had much to do with it. In the north, Des Sheen and Bill Millington had no operational work whatsoever.

It was a welcome lull for Fighter Command but especially for 10 and 11 groups, which had borne the brunt of defensive operations over the past ten days. 234 Squadron, for example, had flown 136 sorties and engaged the enemy five times. Since 15 August, Pat Hughes had accounted for five and a half destroyed and one shared. He continued to prove his steely determination to bring down the Germans, and his aggression was increasing. On 8 July he had closed from 150 to 50 yards to fire on the Ju88 in his gun-sight. Now he delivered his final bursts at 30 yards. 90 feet. Roughly the length of three Spitfires, nose to tail. It was, according to Keith Lawrence, 'dangerous, risky' and meant that 'he himself was vulnerable to attack'. As Pat drew closer 'his guns were more effective and he was more likely to hit something'. And he did. He overcame the weakness of a squadron locked into a rigid formation by instituting a head-on attack. Enemies scattered, he picked his target, manoeuvring into a better position, and then started firing at '150 yards, closing to 30'.[2]

'Terrifying experience'

John Crossman was well advanced with his training. After hearing the less than delightful news that he was being sent to 6 Operational Training Unit, Sutton Bridge, he had sold his Austin, bought a second-hand Ford, which he dubbed his 'auto', and set off first thing on 3 August. Judging by the almost continuous absence of entries in his diary during his first two weeks at Sutton Bridge, John's operational training went well, apart from the fact he hadn't 'had a great deal of sleep lately'. But on 18 August, the day Pat Hughes notched up another two victories against the Luftwaffe, John discovered a new terror that had him once again confiding in his diary. 'Was up doing strenuous aerobatics this morning and blacked out and then fainted at 7000 feet.' When he came round, he had just enough height 'to pull out few hundred feet up. Terrifying experience. Must have been doing over 500 [miles per hour] in dive … [I] was going straight for ground at helluva bat'.[3]

John had succumbed to the forces of gravity. As blood was pulled from his head, his brain was starved of oxygen. He lost vision at 4 *g*, when he 'blacked out', but was still conscious. As the pressure increased to between 4.5 and 6 *g*, he lost consciousness or, as he put it, 'fainted'. Once the pressure was relieved, he recovered but would have experienced confusion for 20 to 30 seconds. 'One experience like that's enough. Was too close to ground for my liking when I came out.' But this wasn't the first time John had blacked out. It seems he had forgotten about passing out while practising a tight turn during his first Hurricane flight in late July. John did not realise that he had been overwhelmed by gravitational forces. He thought he was just overtired. 'I'll see I get plenty of sleep in future.'

A good night's rest would have helped John stay fit and healthy, but it would not necessarily have prevented him from yielding to the effects of gravity. Tall, slim men were particularly susceptible, and at 6 feet and weighing 10 stone 10 pounds, John was more slender than most. Other factors could impact on a pilot's ability to withstand the pressure, including emotional state, alcohol intake, cardiac efficiency, hunger levels, general health and fitness and amount of sleep.[4]

'I am head over heels in love with her'

On the same day that John Crossman pulled up the auto at Sutton Bridge, Ken Holland arrived at 5 Operational Training Unit, Aston Down. Located on the Welsh border, it was close to RAF Gloucester, where Toby Ripley had been posted after being appointed a pilot officer on probation on 14 July. Ken had his first taste of more advanced aircraft on 5 August. '*MASTERS!!* Did three circuits in a Harvard and then 2 hours on a Master. Very nice but too light to land.' The next day, '*SPITFIRES!!* Rushed to flights and was sent off on a Spitfire and did 2 hours this day getting the feel thereof'. A few sessions later, he was almost an old hand. 'I like these Spitfires.'[5]

Ken progressed well, benefiting from the experiences of a cadre of skilled instructors. Aston Down, for instance, had provided a respite for conflict-hardened but weary 1 Squadron pilots such as Flying Officer John Kilmartin, who had survived France. The instructors prepared a clutch of keen pupils for their own future battles by describing how Luftwaffe fighters escorted the bombers in a stepped-up layer effect. They told them that the Germans were adept at carrying out set manoeuvres but had an inherent weakness: if disturbed from their preordained path, the enemy pilots became confused. They stressed the advantage of height – always attack from out of the sun – and reminded them that the Germans would jockey for that position as well, but if they could not fight with advantage they were disinclined to engage. They emphasised that the Me109 was vulnerable to a rear attack, and if chased the pilot favoured a half-roll then a vertical dive to evade Spitfire or Hurricane fire. Most importantly, they were taught never to follow a stricken enemy aircraft down, as they would open themselves up to attack, either from a rear gunner making a last-ditch effort to knock out his assailant or from another enemy fighter firing on his tail.[6] The lesson was easy to remember. Fire, get out, survive.

Unlike John Crossman, Ken still found time to write in his diary, and it is sprinkled with training notes along with details of his after-flying jaunts to Gloucester to visit Toby and to the pub and 'flicks'. He wasn't always alone or with fellow trainees. He met a 'nice girl' named only as Bobbie. 'This child Bobbie', he wrote, 'is rather a nice child in many ways'. Seina Haydon was all but forgotten.

On 10 August, Ken's natural vibrancy took a blow. 'Spitfire and Blenheim collided. Both up in flames. Three dead – horrible show. Bit shaken.' As almost every trainee pilot before him had discovered, accidents were an inevitable part of flying training. A young man could not think of his own mortality if he wanted to be a successful fighter pilot. He had to distract himself. Ken dashed into Gloucester the next day to see Toby and later went for a drive with Bobbie in his recently acquired Morris 8 saloon. It looks like he had upgraded the motorbike to something more practical for courting young ladies. You can't blame a 20-year-old for allowing his head to be turned by another pretty girl and forgetting a fiancée on duty in a Torquay hospital.

As Fighter Command retaliated against Goering's Adlertag, Ken went into Gloucester to celebrate Toby's birthday. 'Dear old T. another birthday of his together – hope we see lots more.' On 14 August, he was back in the air for a dogfighting session, but not in the Spitfire. He had 'changed over to Hurricanes which are heavier and rather lumbering after Spitfires'. As he became more familiar with the sturdy fighter, he concluded, 'Don't like H. as well as the Spits'. He didn't fly the Spitfire again and did not put in too many hours on the Hurricane either before leaving Aston Down. Formation practice, dogfighting, 'some bomber attacks on other Hurricanes' on Black Thursday and then, on the last day of his course, there were 'no Hurricanes available. Had a Master and played about above a thick mist. Force-landed at a new 'drome about 30 miles from Bristol and also at Rissington and low flew [*sic*] up the Severn. Good fun'. After chasing his clearance chits he left Aston Down at lunch-time on 17 August. He farewelled Toby in Gloucester then 'pushed off to Warmwell', arriving late that night. On reporting to the orderly room, he found there was 'nothing doing'.

He didn't hang around but drove to Weymouth. There, he met up with Seina, who, she recalled, had 'managed to get leave …

(I also had to get police permission as it was a restricted area)'.[7] Ken fell in love with Seina 'all over again', and Bobbie was ancient history. They 'put up at Albany Hotel' but, for the sake of propriety, 'in *separate* rooms'. After breakfast, they were off for a paddle. 'I am head over heels in love with her.'

After waking and breakfasting at the Albany on 19 August, Ken returned to Warmwell. He exuberantly noted in his diary, 'No. 152 (F) SQUADRON' and was introduced to Squadron Leader Peter Devitt, 152's commanding officer. Happily, given his preference for the Spitfire, he would soon be a Spitfire pilot.

Shortly after the opening of the Battle of Britain, Ken's new squadron had moved to Warmwell. Along with 238 Squadron, its key task was to protect the naval base at Portland – which was approximately 3 miles northeast of Warmwell – as well as important West Country cities such as Bristol and Exeter. The squadron had lost three men during the intensive fighting of 11–12 August, including their Australian flight commander Carr Withall, but had suffered no losses since.

Ken was not the only Australian at Warmwell. Pilot Officer Ian Bayles, of A Flight, had been posted to the squadron on 20 April 1940. Even with a shared nationality, it is unlikely that Pilot Officer Bayles and Sergeant Ken Holland would have had much to do with each other. Pilot Officer Roger Hall's reminiscences of his time with 152 Squadron imply a clear separation of officers and sergeants – he describes 'only some of the pilots in the squadron for I didn't know them all', but those he did know were all officers and he rarely named the sergeants. The silvertails of Toorak and old boys of Winchester College like Bayles rarely mingled with the boys from Bondi, even if they had had their rough edges smoothed off by the likes of Toby Ripley at Melorne.

Initially allocated to A Flight, Ken was 'changed later to B' with Canadian-born Flight Lieutenant Peter O'Brian. Squadrons were divided into two flights, but 152 had its own take on the disposition of its sections. Rather than two sections of three men per flight, it had three of two, although a new pilot like Ken might be attached as a third man. A Flight comprised Red, Yellow and White sections, and Blue, Green and Black sections made up B Flight, but the squadron exercised some flexibility when allocating men to sections.[8] For example, Ken would fly with Blue, Green and White sections, and Bayles would on occasion be attached to Black.

Despite the weather, Ken had high hopes that he would be in the air on 20 August and was excited to hear there was a 'flap on. O'Brian, [Sergeant Leslie] Reddington and self to fly if any machines left'. But then the flap was off. He did, however, make it into the air. 'Formation practice.' Ken was disappointed, but given his lack of solid Spitfire training at Aston Down, the extra experience wouldn't have gone amiss.

In the quiet days that followed, he carried out more formation practice, including one session in which the 'commanding officer led us an awful dance in line ahead', and he had plenty of time to write up his log book – 'an awful bore'. At least there was Seina waiting at the Albany. She 'stayed the week', and Ken 'came over from Warmwell every evening'. The blissful week was marred a little for Ken: 'She let me love her to the full but won't let me sleep with her'. His passion had been rekindled, but common sense quelled his ardour. 'I love her terribly but not enough to rush off and get married without T.'s consent.' Even though Toby wanted them to wait until Ken was 25 before marrying, Ken 'gave her a fraternity ring – what will happen when T. finds out?' Then he put aside his worries about Toby's reactions and speculated about their future. 'Query: would she be content to live happily at Melorne?' They parted on 24 August. Seina recalled little of Ken's pressure to take their relationship to a more physical level. She remembered only that 'the weather was glorious and we enjoyed the time we spent together'.[9]

'All quiet on Dorset Front'

Fighter Command's respite from heavy action ended on 24 August, when its pilots contended with six intense attacks in the space of 10 hours. In hindsight, it was apparent that this was the start of a new offensive, hallmarked by two weeks of large-scale aerial bombardment. 152 Squadron, however, was not immediately called to battle. After farewelling Seina, Ken carried out formation practice. He was tired from dancing with his fiancée until 3 a.m. so turned in early, but many others did not have a peaceful slumber, as Luftwaffe night bombers ranged across Kent, Sussex and Surrey. Hitler had specifically instructed that London was not to be attacked, and the RAF, too, had eschewed civil objectives, concentrating on infrastructure related to the war effort, such as ports. But something went wrong that night. Bombs meant for an oil storage depot at Thames Haven and the Short aircraft factory at Rochester were instead released 30 miles or so off target on the City of London. Fires raged at Bethnal Green, and shops were damaged in Oxford Street. Nine people were killed and 58 injured. At that stage, Bomber Command had refrained from attacking Germany's capital, but now the flying gauntlets were off and Berlin was targeted the next night.

As Bomber Command planned its first assault on Berlin, 152 Squadron's brief lull ceased. Ken 'faffed' until 5.30 p.m. on 25 August and 'then a RED'. They were off. A large formation of more than 300 German aircraft had split into three on reaching the British coast, and each section sought out Dorset targets. Hornchurch, North Weald and Manston had been bombed the day before. It was now Warmwell's turn, while the other formation offshoots attacked Portland and Weymouth.

The squadron scrambled to meet the enemy force, but without Ken. He rushed to the 'shelter trench with the commanding officer and troops' as '40 Dornier 17s and Ju88s and 50+ Me110s and 109s stepped above them came over at 8000 [feet] and dropped about ten eggs'. The sick quarters were destroyed, both hangars were hit, and telephone lines and the teleprinter were put out of commission. Ken was far from frightened and was generally impressed by the airfield defence. 'Light Bofors on the 'drome were super and kept popping away – got one.'

Ken emerged from the shelter to count exploding 'eggs' and noted the locations of 'some time bombs' – delayed action bombs. Meanwhile, the squadron engaged the enemy west of Portland. The pilots broke formation, and it was every man for himself in a series of dogfights. As instructed by Goering, the Me109s clung to their charges and the squadron couldn't penetrate to the bombers.[10] Even so, their bag was respectable, with claims for two destroyed Me109s, one destroyed Me110 and one probable Ju88. But as far as Ken was concerned, '152 Squadron boobed'. Apart from what he considered a low tally, 'we lost Pilot Officer Wildblood, Pilot Officer Hogg shot down'.

Ken carried out his first operational patrol the next day, as Yellow Two. But they met nothing. The squadron appears to have thought little of this non-encounter, as it is not recorded in the operations record book, but Ken headed his diary entry, 'X RAID PATROL FIRST'. (An X raid is one of unknown derivation. More often than not they turned out to be friendly aircraft.) This was followed up by a 'Big Flap in evening' during which '234 Wallop had a dogfight with six 109s'.

At about 5 p.m., a few miles south of the Isle of Wight, 234 Squadron, led by Ken's fellow Australian Pat Hughes, 'intercepted eight Me109s at 16000 feet followed by 30 Me109s 2000 feet above and 3 miles behind'. Flying Spitfire X4009, which had become 'his' aircraft, Pat ordered his section into line astern and 'attacked the leading eight, who immediately split up into sections of two aircraft each'. As Pat closed he fired a 5-second burst. The closest Messerschmitt 'caught fire and dropped vertically'. The other climbed away and 'was shooting from above'. Pat was in pursuit. As the Me109 dived, Pat caught it with 'a long burst from dead astern'. It burst into flames. Within minutes, the pilot baled out, splashing into the water near what appeared to Pat 'to be an ordinary auxiliary launch painted dark grey and blue'. The vessel opened fire on X4009, and Pat climbed away towards the coast. As he evaded the launch's guns, he encountered three more Me109s. One 'shot at me from about 1000 yards, but I had no ammunition'.[11]

Pat landed safely at Middle Wallop to toast his two successes, as well as those claimed by Bob Doe, Pat Horton, Morty Mortimer-Rose and Sergeant William Hornby. It was a good result, and as the squadron historian put it, they 'brought the memorable month of August to a fitting end'.[12] It was a significant month for Pat as well. In addition to destroying outright or sharing in the destruction of nine enemy aircraft, he had scored double victories in his last three combats. His preference for close-range attacks – he had again fired at 50 yards – continued to bring results.

Other than one interception scramble by three aircraft on 27 August – later recognised as one of the month's quietest days – and three security patrols, Pat and his friends had little to distract themselves, and Squadron Leader Spike O'Brien settled down to write out a DFC recommendation for Pat, lauding the Australian's battle prowess and courage, and praising 'his example, leadership and control', which had 'in all respects been exemplary'.[13]

Ken Holland's Battle of Britain was also on pause, as the only action on offer was a couple of 'flaps' in which the 'bandits' either turned back or weren't there. He was more than ready to test his courage in battle, but as 152 Squadron's Pilot Officer Eric 'Boy' Marrs recorded, 'we have been having a very slack time here … The Hun has been concentrating entirely on the southeast and the London area and doesn't seem to be bothering about Southampton and Portsmouth any more'.[14]

'Lots of incendiaries' had been dropped in the area, resulting in 'heath fires raging all around N and NE of Warmwell', and on 28 August, in between breathing the smoke-laden air and hanging around dispersal 'to relieve others at meals' and 'at readiness' from 1 to 8 p.m., Ken wrote his will. Unlike Stuart Walch, who had consulted a local solicitor, Ken prepared his 'under the provisions of pages 147–148 of manual of Air Force Law'. There is no hint in his diary as to why he decided to do this when he did. Perhaps seeing Pilot Officer Walter Beaumont returning from an action-induced bale-out two days after the deaths of pilot officers Wildblood and Hogg, following closely on the heels of the fatal Spitfire-Blenheim collision at Aston Down, had affected him more than he'd let on. He and Timothy Wildblood had been the same age – only five days separated their birthdays – and Richard Hogg had been six months older. Perhaps the deaths of two contemporaries, coming less than three months after that of Seina's brother Ian, who had been shot down in flames, made carefree Ken realise that war was not just about flying. It was about death. And that death could be his own.

To Seina, he willed his new Morris 8. Given he had fallen in love with her all over again, it is interesting he left her nothing more intimate. However, the Morris, which if new would have cost £120 or so, depending on the inclusions, would give Seina independence, an important gift for a young woman. He did not forget his friend Pip Markham, who had recently become engaged. He left the pair, 'jointly, the sum of £70 in defence bonds as an aid to furthering their marriage'. Finally, to Toby, 'I do hereby leave all my remaining property to be *solely his property*'. As well as his diary and personal effects, this would include a residual estate of £195.[15]

Ken's last testament reveals much. For one, it shows how generous he was to his friends. It also demonstrates the extent of Toby's generosity to his ward. In the space of four years, he had funded a car (not to mention two motorbikes), a good watch and an estate of £265. In leaving his guardian his personal possessions and strongly emphasising that he was the main beneficiary by underlining his direction, Ken highlighted the central importance of Toby in his life. Finally, Ken's bequests demonstrate how affected he had been by the knowledge that he was an unwanted child. He left nothing to his parents. Toby had replaced them totally in his affections. Ken had led his new acquaintances to believe that he was an orphan, and his will reinforced the impression. It seems the emotional detachment that had commenced before his birth, and which had been extended to a physical separation with his departure from Australia, was now complete in Ken's mind.

As August drew to a close, Ken had plenty of free time on his hands. He went drinking every night and, perhaps missing the surf of Bondi, was tempted to 'a swim at Lulworth Cove'. It was a 'lovely swim but stay too short'. For Ken, it was 'all quiet on Dorset Front' – that is, until 31 August, when, during a night out in Weymouth that included 'some drinks and a dance at the Regent – fun', he left early and 'went for a ride with Mrs Kay Muir. *Très Passione* [*sic*]'. Ken was in love again. Not only was Kay a married woman, but she had two children.

'We'll never see any action here'

It may have been all quiet on the Dorset front during the last days of August, but it was all go at Biggin Hill. While carrying out his operational training at Sutton Bridge, John Crossman had followed the activities of his squadron companions and proudly told his parents in his regular missives home that 'when you hear of all the Jerries being shot down in the southeast of England you'll know my squadron is there. It has more victories to its credit than any other'.[16] Indeed, 32 Squadron had become

Fighter Command's top-scoring unit, but its pilots were weary.

They were ordered north for a rest, and John, who had returned to Biggin Hill on 26 August thoroughly fed up with training, was not impressed. Unlike Ken Holland at Aston Down, who had flown Harvards, Hurricanes and Spitfires, John had drilled almost exclusively in the Hurricane and had acquired 30 hours 55 minutes on the hardy fighter over 38 sessions.[17] He had had enough practice and was now keen to see action.

He had to leave his car behind, as the squadron 'flew up to Acklington in formation' on the afternoon of 28 August. A raid came over 'and the last thing I heard before we left was from the loud speakers round the camp: "All personnel not actively engaged in getting aircraft off the ground take cover"'.

The squadron arrived at Acklington late in the afternoon. 'It's a lousy place', thought John. 'Miles from anywhere and fearfully quiet. We'll never see any action here.' The Germans had given Acklington a wide berth. Des Sheen, for instance, had not flown a patrol since 24 August, and 72 and 79 squadrons had been almost idle since their activities of the 15th had sent the enemy packing. As John wryly commented, '32 Squadron will now read the news instead of making it'.[18]

'Holed in 30 places'

Bill Millington and 79 Squadron had arrived at Biggin Hill the day before John Crossman flew to Acklington: they had been ordered back to their old stomping ground to relieve 32 Squadron. Although John did not mention it in his diary, his and Bill's paths may have briefly crossed during the change-over. Teddy Morris recalled that it was 'good meeting good friends' and 'more importantly getting their views on the best tactics to attack large bomber formations escorted by shoals of fighters' as well as their opinions on the strengths and weaknesses of the Me109s and 110s.[19]

Bill's squadron also received an official briefing on how to deal with the enemy. The pilots were given strict orders to break off any engagements at the Channel mid-point, as RAF losses were higher closer to France. They were called for dawn readiness on 28 August, and Bill was just one of those who slept in armchairs scattered about the dispersal hut until they were relieved for breakfast. They had just returned at 8.25 a.m. and started climbing into their flying kit when the ops phone rang. Two of the three small enemy formations that had been detected earlier and crossed the coast at separate points had joined up and were on their way towards RAF Eastchurch, located on Kent's Isle of Sheppey.

With Teddy Morris leading, they reported seeing 18 He111s and several Me109 escorts. They were well below the enemy formation, which was so large the aircraft appeared to Morris 'to stretch from horizon to horizon with the sun glinting on their canopies'. The Hurricanes climbed to engage, and just as they struck the rear of the bombers they were overwhelmed by enemy fighters. According to Morris, 'They had the advantage of height and speed'. Even so, he led his men into the attack, 'which became a dogfight with every man for himself'.

As Bill, Morris and company battled with the Me109s, the enemy bombers continued on their path and dropped their load on Eastchurch. They blasted the landing ground, destroyed two aircraft and damaged two more. 79 Squadron may have been distracted from the enemy bombers, but they had some success nonetheless. Rupert Clerke accounted for one Me109 probably destroyed, and Neddy Nelson-Edwards probably downed one of the Heinkels.

There was no operational flying for 79 Squadron on the 29th, but 30 August saw the Luftwaffe return in force, with a total of 1345 sorties in a series of large-scale attacks launched, for the first time, exclusively against southeast targets. At about 10.30 a.m., a large formation was plotted off France. As it moved closer to British waters it became apparent that Fighter Command would have to deal with three separate formations of He111s and their escorts. In addition to squadrons already patrolling the coastal airfields, nine more were dispatched to aerodromes and key areas such as Maidstone, in Kent, 32 miles southeast of London, and Dover. By 11.20 a.m. Biggin Hill and Kenley were identified as the main targets.

Within 10 minutes, eight aircraft from 79 Squadron, again led by Teddy Morris, were patrolling Biggin Hill. It wasn't long before they encountered 18 He111s and 30 Me110s and 109s. For once, recalled Morris, they were at the same height as the enemy, so he ordered Blue Section to attack the bombers while Green would deal with the fighters.

Morris led Blue Section, including Bill, past the Heinkels. When he thought they were far enough ahead he directed them into a 180-degree turn. They attacked head-on and scattered the bombers. Pilot Officer Paul Mayhew claimed one Heinkel destroyed, as did Pilot Officer Owen Tracey. (There was a suggestion that this Heinkel had been attacked by Spitfires, but Tracey was confident of his victory.) Morris chased the leader of the bomber formation, and Bill watched as he 'collided with a Heinkel 111 and both machines crashed but ... [he] baled out and reached home safely'. Morris was later humorously credited by the squadron diarist with one 'He111 destroyed by collision'. Bill claimed one Heinkel and another probably destroyed by the more conventional method of turning his guns on them.

While Morris slowly descended, unhurt, to land safely, Bill flung himself into a frenzied dogfight with an Me110. He damaged it, then, ammunition exhausted, he executed what was later termed a 'hair-breadth escape' when he retreated while under attack by 109s. Bill had again proven he was a fighter pilot of high calibre. When he had gone on readiness that morning, he'd had a personal bag of one destroyed Me109 and three destroyed He111s. He was almost an ace. By the time he 'limped back home with my machine badly shot up' at about 12.15 p.m., he was an ace.[20]

Later that day, just as the airmen had finished their evening meal, enemy aircraft were spotted over Biggin Hill. They were part of a force that had been clocked over the Strait of Dover at 5.50 p.m. Five minutes later, a smaller formation speared off to the west, crossed the coast near Dover and headed towards the Isle of Sheppey. Squadrons had already been dispatched but did not intercept as the Junkers came in low towards the station and bombed it. 610 Squadron was already airborne but too far away to come to Biggin Hill's defence. 79 Squadron's B Flight scrambled at 6.05 p.m. as 15 to 20 Ju88 bombers, 30 Me109s and 30 Me110s or Jaguars passed overhead. The Hurricanes hadn't even completed their first circuit before the bombs dropped. They tried to stop the enemy force but it was too late. Bill didn't add to his tally, but Flight Lieutenant Geoffrey 'David' Haysom and Sergeant Henry Bolton each claimed probable Me109s. Paul Mayhew's Hurricane was deemed unserviceable thanks to a shot-up rudder. That was the least of the damage done to Biggin Hill assets that evening.

As the bombs fell, the airmen on the ground rushed to their shelter. It was too small to accommodate all of them, and some hurried off elsewhere. Five minutes later the shelter took a direct hit, leaving nothing but rubble and a huge, gaping crater. Meanwhile, the station's only medical orderly, Tasmanian-born Aircraftwoman 1st Class Edna Lenna Button, evacuated patients from the sick quarters. Patients safe, the popular Button joined the other WAAFs in the airwomen's shelter. Within moments, the entrance was blown in. Then the concrete walls collapsed.

When Bill and B Flight landed at 6.30 p.m., the aerodrome was littered with bomb craters. As they climbed from their

Hurricanes, they surveyed the scene. Fewer than 20 bombs had dropped, but they had left a wreck of a station, in perhaps the Luftwaffe's most successful airfield raid so far. Workshops, cookhouses, the meteorological office, stores and armoury were all out of commission. The sergeants' mess, the 'WAAFery' and the airmen's barracks were uninhabitable. One of the hangars had taken a direct hit. Most of the station vehicles had been struck, and two aircraft on the ground were burned out. On top of the visible damage, water, gas and electricity had been cut off, and the ops room had lost contact with 11 Group headquarters.

As the drone of bombers subsided, everyone pitched in to restore the station to order. Airmen and pilots pulled bodies and limbs from the airmen's shelter and scrabbled and dug through rubble to rescue the WAAFs. Bill's part in the rescue efforts is not recorded, and he failed to mention it when he next wrote home, but the young man who fought bushfires, raised money, pitched in with the Ruckley Grange rhododendrons and adhered to the tenets of Scout Law would have been there with the diggers and scrabblers as, one by one, the airwomen were pulled from the earth. Perhaps the Australian was there when they dragged the body of 39-year-old Edna Button from the shelter.[21]

By the end of that long night the bodies of the 39 dead had been laid out and the 26 injured personnel tended. Somehow, the WAAFs put together a welcome meal of bangers and mash. Phone links were re-established, and the ops room came again on line. Those who could, slept, but not for long. Bill Millington and 79 Squadron were on dawn readiness.

'August 30–31 were rather epic days'

The last day of summer was shaping up to be fine, clear and hot: a perfect day for the Luftwaffe to leave its explosive calling cards, and so it did, launching a massive offensive lasting from 8 a.m.

to 7 p.m. As before, the southeast and eastern airfields were the main targets. As Bill waited at dispersal, 13 Group headquarters rang through to Acklington: Des Sheen and 72 Squadron were to transfer to Biggin Hill. Just as 79 Squadron had relieved 32 Squadron, 72 was to trade places with battle-wearied 610.

The ops phone rang at Biggin Hill. A raid was on its way and 79 Squadron was ordered to protect the station. Bill and his friends ran to their Hurricanes. The repair squadrons had done much to restore the pockmarked airfield, but it was hazardous. As Neddy Nelson-Edwards recalled, there were 'craters everywhere, not to mention unexploded bombs'. Successfully navigating the ene-my-created obstacle course, the pilots climbed into their cockpits but were too late; bombs tumbled from the sky before they could take off. Some managed to dodge the explosives as their Hurricanes roared away, at 8.40 a.m., and gave chase to the Messerschmitts, with David Haysom claiming one destroyed and Squadron Leader John Heyworth probably accounting for a Ju88. Nelson-Edwards came under attack. As his engine seized, he switched everything off and made for a patch of green. He crashed into a 12-foot-high brick wall and was out cold. Meanwhile, the rest of the squadron landed at Croydon, because Biggin Hill was again unserviceable and the repair crews needed time to finish filling the fresh craters.[22]

At 12.30 p.m., just as Des Sheen and 72 Squadron farewelled Acklington, Bill and 79 Squadron were in the air again. Another formation of about 40 Ju88s and escorts had crossed the coast near Folkestone and was heading for Croydon. Before the bombers had a chance to drop their load, the defenders attacked. Heeding Goering's recent directions, the escorts clung tightly to the Jun-kers, hampering the Hurricanes' efforts to strike at them. Accord-ingly, the squadron 'engaged about 20 Messerschmitt 109s'.[23] Yet again, the enemy had the upper hand. Diving from out of the sun, the 109s surprised Bill and Blue Section. Within an instant, Hur-ricanes and Messerschmitts were dogfighting furiously, ranging from 15 000 down to 3000 feet. Bill twisted, turned, ducked and dived until he gained a clear line of sight on his target and shot it down. Regardless of the greater odds and height disadvantage, 79 Squadron 'slapped quite a few'. In addition to Bill's destroyed Me109, Pilot Officer Leofric Bryant-Fenn claimed one Me109 probable, and Pilot Officer Brian Noble recorded another Me109 probable and one damaged. The Junkers powered towards their target and bombed RAF Croydon at 1 p.m. Despite this, the station was still in better condition than Biggin Hill, and all but Bill landed there. The young Australian was 'again badly shot up'. With his hydraulic system on the fritz, he 'made a forced landing near Folkestone and returned to my station per police car'.[24]

While Bill made his way to Croydon courtesy of the local constabulary, Des Sheen and 72 Squadron were on their way to their new quarters. They refuelled at Bicester, receiving a civilised welcome which included soft drinks, fruit and food served by the squadron wives. This pleasant interlude was soon a dim memory; chaos awaited them at Biggin Hill.

Within hours of their arrival, the alert sounded again. At 5.45 p.m., 72 Squadron was ordered to Dungeness, 79 Squadron's A Flight was sent to the Strait of Dover, and B Flight was tasked with aerodrome guard duties, as another powerful enemy force streamed towards Biggin Hill. Spitfire X4109 would not start, so Des Sheen sat and watched as Spitfires and Hurricanes, including Bill Millington in P3050, took off. They soon sighted 15 Dornier Do215s escorted by large numbers of Me109s and 110s. 72 Squadron intercepted near Dungeness, and 79 Squadron plunged into battle as the enemy force approached Biggin Hill.

Bill 'attacked a large formation of Dornier 215s which were protected by large numbers of enemy fighters' with little regard for risk. 'What is one fighter compared with a German bomber?' he later remarked. He lined up a Dornier and fired, setting alight the port engine. He followed it down, and while he was distracted by bits of the Dornier shedding over Biggin Hill aerodrome, he was in turn pounced on by three Me109s. He eluded them then took the offensive. He 'shot down a Messerschmitt 109 after a dogfight with three of them' – well, damaged it, anyway – then shook off the other two. By then Bill was alone; his squadron companions were engaged in their own battles. Close to the coast, he pursued the bombers on their homeward track but was beset by more Me109s. He dodged one and pumped the last of his ammunition into another. It caught alight and ploughed into the military firing range south of Lydd, in Kent. His attention was again diverted as he watched the pilot climb out of the crashed Messerschmitt. Another mistake: he was caught by an Me109 over Romney Marsh. A cannon shell exploded on the left side of his cockpit.[25] P3050's engine and radiator were hit, and, Bill told his sister a few weeks later, 'I was shot up badly by cannon fire and wounded in the thigh'.

The engine started to burn and flames licked his skin. The cockpit filled with heavy black smoke. Bill struggled to open the hood. As the flames took hold, he prepared to bale out. But he looked down and caught sight of Tenterden, in Kent, nestled on the edge of the Weald. Although he knew full well the horror of a death in flames, he hesitated. The memory of Edward Mitchell, who had burned for an hour on 8 July before his unrecognisable body could be retrieved from his Hurricane, would not have been far from his mind. But Scout Law was at the heart of his existence: he always put others first, and he did again. 'I considered it unwise to bale out', he later explained, 'as my machine would probably have crashed into a small village'. Bill stayed at P3050's controls and 'crash-landed in flames' at Conghurst Farm, Hawkhurst. Onlookers rushed to his assistance, and one of the local lads watched as Bill was dragged from his Hurricane.[26] Seconds later, 'the machine exploded'.

In attempting a controlled landing of his burning Hurricane,

Bill had lived up to 'those standards dictated by honour and chivalry' that he held dear. He had also demonstrated a courteousness embraced by airmen since the Great War, during which enemy pilots had waved and smiled at each other from their aircraft. Lauded by newsmen, the newly dubbed 'knights of the air' saw themselves as members of an international aerial brotherhood, with both sides in the Great War observing a 'special chivalry'.

There is no place for such good-naturedness in warfare. Offering courtesy to one's foe could result in him re-entering the conflict at a later date. For example, after Dick Glyde refrained from hindering Hans-Christian Schäfer's descent on 19 May 1940, the enemy pilot did not languish as a prisoner of war for the duration. After France capitulated, all German prisoners were released, including 400 pilots. Schäfer returned to operations and before his death, on 12 May 1943, accounted for a number of Allied airmen.[27] But Bill Millington's consideration was not to the enemy. He was fighting over his homeland and he had to defend his own people. Outside battle, and regardless of risks to themselves, Bill and his aerial colleagues willingly offered their lives to protect innocent civilians. Just weeks before, Flying Officer Dennis Grice of 600 Squadron had given 'his life to save [a] town'.[28]

Bill was a true knight of the air. Although 'covered in blood and grease' and wounded, he walked with assistance towards a nearby farmhouse 'to clean up and [drink] the inevitable cup of tea'. Then, 'the typical village police constable turned up, pulled out a note book and said "name and address please". He wouldn't believe I was the Prince of Wales!!' Not surprising, given there wasn't one at the time.

It had been a big day. Des Sheen's squadron contributed four damaged bombers to Fighter Command's victory count. Bill's squadron too had inflated the bag. In addition to Bill's Dornier, plus two destroyed and one damaged Me109, they recorded a downed bomber by Owen Tracey and a Do17 destroyed and another probable by Pilot Officer Donald 'Dimsie' Stones. Yet again, however, success came at a cost. Bill was out of commission, and 21-year-old Henry Bolton, who had joined the squadron less than a month earlier, did not survive his forced landing. 72 Squadron sustained its own losses. Squadron Leader Anthony Collins crashed, Flight Lieutenant 'Hiram' Smith was wounded, and 23-year-old Flying Officer Edgar Wilcox was shot down near Dungeness and later found riddled with bullets.[29] Fourteen of Fighter Command's pilots were killed and 39 Hurricanes and Spitfires either written off or lost at sea as the Luftwaffe pounded the RAF airfields, especially the key ones near London. But Fighter Command had almost achieved parity with the German air force, which lost 41 aircraft during the 24-hour period. As Bill later summed it up, 'August 30–31 were rather epic days'.

'Well worthy of reward'

The last day of summer was also epic for Squadron Leader Peter Townsend, 85 Squadron's commanding officer. After destroying one Me109 and probably destroying another, he was attacked by a 110 and wounded in the foot. He parachuted out and landed at Hawkhurst. He was taken initially to the local cottage hospital, but the resident doctor thought the foot required more attention than he could give. Before he was transferred to an establishment with surgical facilities, Townsend recalled, 'Tradition required that I be conducted to the Royal Oak. We raised our tankards to the damnation of our enemies'. Toast over, he was joined by other pilots who had parted ways with their aircraft mid-air, including his 85 Squadron charge 19-year-old Pilot Officer Pyers Worrall, who 'had been shot up from behind and collected some splinters in his thigh' before baling out over Tunbridge Wells. Then, 'in came a chubby little Australian … "Bill Millington" he said, and a pint was thrust into his hand'.

The liberal dosing of liquid analgesia was fast wearing off, so a Bedford truck arrived to take the pilots to Croydon General Hospital. Townsend recalled that as they left they were surrounded by a group of people asking for autographs. They 'made us feel like champions of the home team'. They were cheered off by their fans, who cried out, 'Go it, RAF' while 'Pyers, Bill and myself lay on the floor ... wrapped up in our parachutes, shivering as the pain of our wounds became more insistent'.[30]

Within hours, they were in surgery. 'Most of the shrapnel in my thigh was removed', Bill later reported to his sister. 'The few pieces remaining will probably eventually work out causing no inconvenience.'

The squadron totted up Bill's victories, noting that he had accounted for six enemy aircraft, two probables and one damaged. The Australian had taken part in nearly every patrol since joining 79 Squadron in June, and his reputation of displaying 'great courage in attacking superior numbers of enemy aircraft' had been cemented. Squadron Leader Heyworth recognised that bravery as well as Bill's chivalry in choosing 'to make a crash-landing rather than abandon his aircraft and let it fall in flames into a village' and recommended him for a DFC. Attached to the recommendation were Keith Park's additional remarks: 'I consider he is well worthy of reward and strongly recommend him for the Immediate Award of the Distinguished Flying Cross'.[31]

13

1–6 September

'A grandstand view of the scraps'

As Bill Millington recovered from 'wounds received in the course of two days of violent fighting' during which his Hurricane 'was twice riddled with bullets', Des Sheen was caught up in the aftermath of Biggin Hill's most recent raid.[1] His Spitfire had finally made it into the air, but he had not been able to catch up with his squadron so conducted a lone patrol over Kent. He returned to an airfield that had received another pasting: the Dorniers had dropped their bombs almost on his heels.

Biggin Hill was 'a mess', Des recalled. 'There were quite a few fires and many holes in the airfield.' The few undamaged buildings from the previous raid had been hit, the armoury was on fire, four Spits on the ground had been burned out, and the good work to restore the ops room the night before had been undone when a bomb severed all communications but the direct line to 11 Group headquarters. The road through the station was again full of craters, and when Des climbed out of the cockpit his WAAF driver skilfully negotiated her way through 'with a nonchalant disregard of the many unexploded bombs'. The officers' mess had been hit, and Des remembered 'eating supper by candlelight' with the station commander, Group Captain Richard Grice, who had been 'walking around heavily bandaged' after being wounded by glass shards when the operations block took a direct hit. That evening, Des slept in a mess that had four delayed action bombs in the kitchen. He laughed it off when he reported it to his parents: 'When one is tired it's easy to sleep!'[2]

After a week of intensive effort by the Luftwaffe, Manston had been abandoned as a forward aerodrome, and Kenley was far from full strength. Although the repair crews were working overtime, Biggin Hill was again declared unserviceable, so at 6 a.m. on 1 September, 72 Squadron moved to Croydon. It had limited facilities but was better than Biggin. The Airport Hotel was taken over for the officers' mess, and a makeshift field kitchen was set up. But every time the pilots scrambled, dust and grass were blown into their food.[3]

At Croydon, they met Ronald Lees. Des had been flying photo reconnaissance operations when his fellow Australian had destroyed a Ju87 over Dunkirk on 2 June, but since Lees's promotion to wing commander and a stint in the ops room at Newcastle, he and Des had often come into contact when the squadron was at Acklington. When his former charges were posted south, Lees resolved to take a week's leave, and he had every intention of spending part of his break in the air with them. With Anthony Collins's crash the day before, he had assumed command of the squadron.[4]

At 10.54 a.m., the squadron was once again airborne, tasked with searching out 'bandits over Tunbridge Wells'.[5] This time, Des took off behind Ted Graham, who was leading, and was soon embroiled in his first Biggin Hill battle.

As they approached Tunbridge Wells, at about 30000 feet, the squadron saw 30 to 40 Do17s escorted by about the same number of Me109s. The chase was on over a wide front between Maidstone and Beachy Head, about 40 miles away, on the East Sussex coastline. In Spitfire X4109, Des lined up a bomber but 'glanced behind and found six Me109s bearing down on me'. He 'mixed for quite a time' with them. As he frantically twisted and turned, he 'collected a shell in the engine. After I had disengaged I was climbing to re-engage … when the Spitfire started to burn'. He 'was left with no option'. He unstrapped, pushed back the canopy, rolled X4109 onto its back and pushed the stick forward. The aircraft bunted, and 'I went out clean as a whistle'. He somersaulted, straightened out and counted to ten before pulling the ripcord. 'The parachute opened smoothly and there was a reassuring jolt, as it took effect.' While he gently swayed beneath the ballooned silk, he surveyed the battle, noting the incongruity of 'bombs bursting in the Dover area and the answering fire of the anti-aircraft defences' during a 'clear cloudless day … a beautiful Sunday morning'. Drifting down, he watched 'a series of running fights'. His descent, 'which took some time, was very pleasant' but not without a sense of danger. 'Quite close to me an Me109 went down vertically in flames', and 'another Me109 turned towards me but a Spitfire turned onto his tail and both disappeared'.[6]

Des was lucky the Me109's attention was deflected from him. 'The Jerries shoot us coming down now and as I was surrounded didn't feel too happy.' Air Chief Marshal Sir Hugh Dowding believed that 'British pilots descending over England are still potential combatants', and as such the Luftwaffe was 'perfectly entitled' to fire on parachutists. The practice may have been condoned, but Des did not have to like it. As it happened, 'quite a few Jerries were shot down so I was lucky and got away with it'. He 'had a grandstand view of the scraps … Six aircraft crashed within 2 miles of where I landed and the countryside is absolutely littered with them. Kent is just one large scrap heap at the moment'.[7]

Spitfire X4109 crashed at Court Lodge Farm, but Des landed safely in a field at Ashford 'with nothing but a slight jar'. He picked himself up, climbed out of the harness and rolled his parachute. Moments later, an army lieutenant appeared, waving a revolver. 'There was no doubt that he was wondering whether I was a German.'

Australians weren't common in the RAF, and the lieutenant did not recognise the dark blue uniform as belonging to an ally. Des ignored the revolver, continued to pack up his life-saving silk and started to chat with his doubting assailant. All was soon sorted out, and his army escort took him back to his mess for a welcome meal and shave.[8]

Des found 1 September 1940 memorable for more than just a bale-out and a good meal. That was the day he 'scrapped my dark blue uniform for fighting' and donned the lighter coloured RAF kit. He would not be mistaken for the enemy again. Pat Hughes, who had clung to his Australian uniform for as long as he could, had also recently adopted the RAF's. He had started to grow 'quite fat each year and eating even more if that is possible'.[9] Perhaps his ever-expanding girth had made the original too tight a fit!

'Flying darn nearly all day every day'

The weather continued glorious, hot and cloudless – perfect raiding conditions – and the Luftwaffe again took advantage of it. Biggin Hill was bombed twice on 1 September, as were Debden and Kenley. Detling was struck twice and Eastchurch once. Biggin Hill received another visit on the 2nd, as did Hornchurch, Gravesend, Lympne and Detling, and Eastchurch was struck twice. On 3 September, Biggin Hill was blasted twice, and North Weald received its first blows since the end of August. The repair crews did what they could, and Fighter Command squadrons maintained their defence. 72 Squadron flew a number of frenetic sorties with some success, but the constant readiness, many sorties and nuisance of shifting base – as the squadron relocated from Croydon to Hawkinge and back to Croydon – took their toll.

One of the casualties was accurate record-keeping, and there are a number of discrepancies between Des Sheen's flying log and later accounts and the squadron's operations record book. For example, Des told his parents that after baling out on 1 September, he was 'up flying again the next day and a couple of days later after a couple more scraps'. He next appears in the record book's 'Detail of Work Carried Out' sheet on 5 September, yet his flying log records an interception and a patrol on the 3rd and two patrols on the 4th. The squadron later realised that errors had been made, as the pages have a number of 'incomplete' and 'incorrect' annotations as well as amended totals of aircraft taking off. The pilot lists, however, have not been corrected. With all the turmoil of those early September days, it is not surprising record-keeping was a low priority.

According to Des, he was next in the air on 3 September, when 'we attacked about 20 Me110s and 20 bombers trying a low level penetration near Dungeness … I was flying top cover at the time but went down to attack an Me110 which was supposed to be escorting the bombers. I clobbered the port engine and this aircraft turned inland. This was quite a good party'. But most of the pilots had been stood down on 3 September, and the operations record book states no activity. Des's recollection, however, does accord with the squadron's 2 September report of a patrol during which Do17s and Me110s were sighted 5 miles south of Dungeness. 'The enemy was attacked first from astern and later a beam attack was made. Four Me110s were damaged.' If Des's clobbered Messerschmitt was included in this total, it was not acknowledged in the post-war tally sheets. Des later admitted that the details of this period were sketchy. 'So much has happened the last week … It seems ages since we came south but actually it's only about five or six days ago … [We] have been ever since flying darn nearly all day every day.'[10]

Des was not the only one with a skewed sense of timing. Wing Commander Lees was 'shot up' during his first encounter with the enemy. One bullet sheared through the hydraulics and another bent the canopy rail. The engine seized and spurted glycol. Lees was trapped and could not bale out. He force-landed, wheels up, on a clear patch of grass, and recalled that 'the worst moment of the war was seeing a burly sergeant with a fire axe raised above his head about to crash it down through the canopy'. He returned to Croydon with his head intact, if not his Spitfire. He saw nothing on his next sortie but was attacked again during the following show. His leg was riddled with shrapnel, and his Spitfire was seriously knocked about. The reunion with his old squadron was brief, as he was whisked off to hospital. His flying log states that these sorties all occurred on 1 September, but squadron records indicate they took place on 2 September. Lees had a good excuse for muddling his dates. He almost lost his leg to gangrene, but it was saved by a combination of an experimental drug technique and penicillin.[11]

On 4 September, nine units were dispatched to intercept a 300-aircraft formation comprising Ju88s and their Me110 escorts. 72 Squadron scrambled at 12.55 p.m. Jimmy Elsdon led the squadron: six Spitfires were in his main formation, and three, including Des, were in the rearguard. Elsdon ordered Red and Yellow sections into line astern for the attack. As he did so, the enemy formation broke up and attempted to form defensive circles, but before they could, Elsdon led his six Spitfires into the first six of the enemy aircraft, shooting down their leader. The other rearguard converged to assist Elsdon and his dogfighting confreres. Des dived in and 'carried out a quick attack' on an Me110 as it tried to join a protective circle. 'White smoke immediately began to come from the port engine.' He 'broke off' and 'climbed up to keep a further look out for escort fighters', but the sky had cleared.[12]

The squadron had a good day, claiming six Me110s and three Ju88s destroyed, three 110 probables and one 110 damaged.

On the debit side, the squadron lost another Spitfire when Pilot Officer Ernest Males was shot down, but he baled out and returned uninjured. One of the probables was Des's: he had seen his 110 head inland in what seemed like a shallow dive. It was his last victory of the Battle of Britain.[13] His total claim to date was three and one-third destroyed and one probable.

Since leaving Acklington, the squadron had had little free time. Des recalled that after dark they usually lounged in the mess, had a few beers and that was about it, as they were up at dawn the next morning. On the night of the 4th, the pilots were given a rare night off to go up to London. They had much to celebrate – their victories over the last few days, a wire from Air Vice-Marshal Keith Park congratulating them on their good work, safe bale-outs and Des's promotion to flight lieutenant, effective from 3 September. But the evening was a fizzer. They were exhausted, so they returned early to their billets and tumbled into bed.[14]

'Shot up twice in five days'

The Luftwaffe launched two major attacks on 5 September. In the morning, Biggin Hill was bombed for the tenth time since 30 August, and at about 2 p.m. more enemy activity was detected in the Strait of Dover. Fighter Command dispatched its squadrons, and 72 was ordered from Croydon to patrol Hawkinge. Ranks were depleted, so only eight Spits were airborne, with Des leading in X4034.[15] They were flying at 25 000 feet when they encountered two formations of Me109s at 2.25 p.m. 'We were surprised from above.' There was 'no warning', and before Des knew it the 'aircraft shuddered'. He felt 'the familiar bang in the leg and found all my controls had been shot away. I collected some shrapnel in about the usual place and a few in the left hand with odd spots on the nose'. His oxygen bottle exploded. He 'passed out, and came semi-conscious God knows how much later with my machine doing about 600 miles per hour in a vertical dive completely out of control'.[16] He released his harness 'and was sucked out onto the top of the fuselage with my feet jammed in the windscreen'. It was a terrifying moment. 'There I was in a flat out dive, lying along the top of the cockpit with my feet fastened. I had given up hope.' Des struggled as the Spitfire plummeted. 'Finally, for no apparent reason I came free.' He was about 800 feet from the ground. 'By pure instinct [I] pulled the ripcord.' His speed of descent was such that 'the parachute should have been torn to shreds but it held and opened about 50 feet over a wood which slowed me up and I landed as soft as a feather' near Canterbury. 'It was pure and simply a miracle.' He commented later that 'by the law of averages I should have been killed'. For the second time, Des's parachute had saved his life.

Within minutes, half a dozen land girls were dashing towards him brandishing 'sticks, a spade, a hoe and a pitchfork'. Des called out, 'Hallo girls! Help me out of my brolly, will you?' His accent revealed that he was not a German parachutist, so they dropped their makeshift weapons and asked if they could call a car for him. Before the Australian had time to reply, 'the women suddenly dived for their sticks again, yelling "Hold off!"' Des 'looked round to see them running at a Home Guard who was stalking me 200 yards away with his rifle to his shoulder'. A crowd gathered as 'they persuaded him I was harmless'. Then, a uniformed officer approached on a bicycle – not, this time, a soldier wielding a revolver but a policeman who pulled a welcome flask from his pocket. The policeman quipped that Des had been a bit late in pulling the ripcord. The Australian agreed, but said, 'It was certainly not by choice!'

Despite the soft landing, he had hurt his legs and back. When an ambulance came to take him to hospital, he thought his 'adventures were over'. But he was wrong. 'The ambulance took a bend too fast and turned over. I was picked up by a fire engine dashing to the spot where my Spitfire was blazing furiously.'[17] With aching back and leg and 'full of very tiny pieces of shrapnel', he eventually made it to a 'wizard hospital', a converted private mansion. With a total of just over 750 flying hours to his credit and all the experience that had afforded him, Des was grounded. He wasn't happy, and he felt 'very fed up at being shot up twice in five days'.

'I shall probably never see my people and friends again'

Given the number of raids Fighter Command had to contend with in the southeast, it was almost impossible to believe that some pilots were getting restless because they had nothing to do. It seemed to John Crossman that, during 32 Squadron's three-week northern sojourn, they were spending most of the time 'in dispersal hut all ready with flying clothes and the old Mae West but nothing ever happens here'.[18] With plenty of time on his hands, he determined to catch up on his correspondence. Dorothy Foley, his fiancée's mother, had sent a number of 'most welcome letters', and he owed her one.

Dorothy's mother lived in the Croydon area, and he knew Dorothy would be concerned, 'especially as Croydon aerodrome has been bombed'. He would not have known the exact numbers, but 62 people had been killed during the 15 August raid. He told her she 'shouldn't worry too much as Jerry doesn't have too much time to attack non military objectives' and 'our chaps keep him much too busy'. Even as he assured her, he was anxious. He hoped they would not bomb Biggin Hill again, 'as all my bags are down there and I'd hate to lose them', as well as his books, letters from home, photos and keepsakes from Pat. He had sent her a cable for her birthday, on 24 August, but did not mention her again in his diary. She was never far from his mind, however. Her photo was tucked into the diary, and during his Acklington exile he visited a photographer and sat for a series of formal portraits in his RAF uniform which would be treasured by Pat and by Mick Crossman. His fiancée appeared between the lines in the letter to her mother, as John confessed that 'Newcastle seems a long way off these days and I assure you I still miss everyone a great deal'. In particular, he longed for someone he could confide in. 'I have to unburden myself sometimes and it's hard not to be able to tell my folks.'

He had not admitted to crashing the Hart back in April, and there were other things 'I've never told Mum, and just can't, but they'll learn them all from my diary'. He was desperate to get into action but was aware of the likely outcome when he did. It worried him, so he entrusted his deepest fears to his fiancée's mother. 'A pilot's life in the air force in wartime isn't worth sixpence', he wrote. 'I've seen too many good fellows who didn't come back', and even though he was yet to encounter the enemy, 'we never know which day will be our last'. He confessed that 'it's very hard to have to go on knowing that I shall probably never see my people and friends again. It isn't that I'm afraid, but I've seen what this war's like and if it goes on long enough, well, I guess I'll go the way of the rest'.

'Like a cat after a rat'

While John lounged around the dispersal room 'looking for something to do and hoping a Jerry will venture over', Pat Hughes was busy. After a quiet conclusion to August from an operational perspective, he flew two patrols on 1 September and two more the next day. There was no aerial activity for 234 Squadron on 3 September. But the brief respite did not last. At almost the same time that Des Sheen and 72 Squadron scrambled on 4 September, Pat and 234 Squadron were on their way to Tangmere: both squadrons were part of the 11 and 10 group resources dispatched to counter a formation of more than 50 aircraft on its way to north Kent. At about 1.10 p.m., near Littlehampton, Pat spotted '50 110s approaching coast with about 15 110s circling' about 20 miles away, 'south of Haslemere'. Ten minutes later, the Australian effected his trade-mark head-on attack against the 15 Me110s, followed closely by Blue Section, while Flight Lieutenant Cyril Page, who had been with the squadron at St Eval before transferring to 145 Squadron on 16 July, and who returned on 19 August to replace John Theilmann as the A Flight commander, led Red, Yellow and Green sections towards the larger mass of Messerschmitts to the rear.[19]

As Pat rammed Spitfire X4009 into the 110s, they 'immediately formed a circle'. He 'fired two short bursts and the leading aircraft pulled up', then he fired another short burst into the fuselage. 'This aircraft caught fire and crashed.' While his confreres whirled in their own dogfights, the Australian pursued another 110, attacking 'from dead astern'. Two short bursts later and 'this aircraft rolled on its back and dived vertically to the ground and blew up, 10 miles northeast of Tangmere'. There was no time to savour victory. He was 'attacked by three 110s in a circle whilst another circled round behind'. He fired three short bursts to break them up then dived away. He chased one and exhausted his ammunition. 'One engine appeared to catch fire and the aircraft turned slowly towards the coast heading inland.' Within a blink, 'both engines appeared to be on fire'.[20]

Pat had scored a hat trick: three enemy aircraft downed in the space of 15 minutes. And he was not alone in his success. The squadron claimed 14 Me110s and one Do17 destroyed, and seven Me110s damaged, 'making a record bag for the squadron'. And there were no casualties.[21]

Pat's combat report indicates his cool-headed aggression. Yet again, he got in close; he fired from 100 to 25 yards. He chased his prey, as aviation historian Norman Franks put it, 'like a cat after a rat'.[22] But unlike a cat, when Pat pounced he finished his victims off quickly.

On 5 September, 234 Squadron was hard at it again. They were ordered to patrol Kenley, taking off at 2.45 p.m. They saw anti-aircraft fire and went to investigate. As they approached Gravesend, in northwest Kent, Blue Section, led by Pat in Spitfire X4009, was attacked out of the sun by three Me109s. Pat dodged the enemy bounce and positioned himself to attack. But instead of the three, he saw 12 Me109s coming up the Thames Estuary. He turned and dived and was joined by two Hurricanes. A roiling dogfight ensued over Eastchurch. Pat fired a full deflection shot – a 4-second burst – at one of the Me109s and hit its ammunition bays. The enemy aircraft blew up and spun down. He then faced a vic of three Me109s. He selected one, chased it and, attacking from dead astern, directed a long, 6-second burst into the Messerschmitt's fuel tank. He was so close that oil splashed over X4009's wings. Another 109 was out of commission – it force-landed in a field 15 miles south of Manston. With four kills over the last two days added to his previous tally, Pat was now more than a double ace.[23]

While Des Sheen settled into the 'wizard hospital' that Thursday evening, his former Point Cook course mate stole precious moments with his wife in the White Hart. But the joy Pat and Kay felt at being together was overshadowed. Although Andover had not been bombed since 13 August and Middle Wallop and Warmwell had been ignored as the Luftwaffe blitzed London's airfields, there was no knowing if they would be targeted again as Warmwell had been on 25 August. Pat had been in the air six times since the beginning of the month and in furious close-contact combat twice. He was tired and worried. 'We're getting so much trade that I want you to go home to Hull for a while', he told Kay. They had spent little time together since their subdued registry office wedding – Pat had not even slept one night under the roof of their secluded seaside house at Treyarnon Bay, though he had enjoyed some respite there – and yet he wanted to send his wife away. Kay did not immediately acquiesce. 'I'll fetch our things from Cornwall, first, and stay at the White Hart on Saturday', she decided.[24] Pat was all too ready to agree. They would have one more night together before she returned to her mother's house.

'It was already too late'

Kay drove to Cornwall to pack the remainder of their possessions. It would be a long, tiring trip. Treyarnon Bay was 158 miles from Andover, but she had to contend with road blocks and detours. Meanwhile, her husband was facing another in a string of exhausting days of dawn readiness. A succession of raids crossed the Kent coast, ranging over Hythe, Dover and New Romney just after 8.30 a.m. At the first hint of enemy action 11 Group had responded, and 234 Squadron was called on to supplement the defenders, embarking on a 2-hour patrol of the Brooklands area, over 100 miles from Warmwell, at 8.40 a.m. B Flight, led by Pat in Spitfire X4009, had been in the air for about 50 minutes when Pat 'saw enemy fighters below'. The cluster of 25 Me109s was at 24 000 feet, but for once Pat was higher and had the advantage. Diving thousands of feet, he 'attacked with section astern'. Closing from 150 to 50 yards, he 'fired a long burst into one Me109'. He watched it crash-land then 'climbed back to 10 000 feet and intercepted five Me109s escorting an Me110 across Dover'. The Me110 had already been damaged. 'One engine was on fire and just after passing Dover the crew baled out and the 110 crashed into the sea.' Pat then turned his attention to the stricken aircraft's escorts. He 'attacked the rear 109 and had to fire a long burst into it as three 109s dived at me from the beam. I emptied all my ammunition into this 109 and the oil tanks burst, and my own aircraft's windscreen and mainplane were covered in oil'. The 109 was losing height and smoking badly, but Pat did not follow. Vision obscured, he 'broke away and attacked the three 109s', even though his guns were empty.[25]

As usual, Pat had gone in close and hard, and his innate aggression was again apparent: he had attacked despite his lack of ammunition. A brave man and a skilled shot, he was credited with one Me109 destroyed and one probable. The squadron also added to its combined victory count, but William Hornby was injured when he crash-landed, and for the first time in three weeks, one of their own was killed in action: 20-year-old Scotty Gordon of A Flight had crashed and burned out.

After debriefing, Pat went back to dispersal and waited. His day was not yet over. His second sortie, beginning at 12.25 p.m., was 1½ hours' patrol of Warmwell. The third, commencing at 5.35 and concluding at 6.50 p.m., was another patrol of Brooklands. It was his twelfth operation in a week; that day's three sorties had him in the air for almost 5½ hours. In a photograph taken at about this time, he looked tense, almost diminished. There was nothing of the single-minded, aggressive pilot as he sat slightly hunched forward with hands resting in lap. His forehead was creased. He could barely muster a smile for the camera. David Stafford-Clark, a medical officer attached to Bomber Command, who, after the war, wrote extensively about his experiences treating combat stress in over 4000 operational aircrew, could have had that photo in his hand when he stated that 'no one who saw the mask of age which mantled the faces of these young men … is likely to forget it. Their pallor, the hollows in their cheeks and beneath their eyes, and the utter fatigue'.

It was no wonder Pat was tired. Multiple combats were physically stressful. The rise and ebb of adrenalin during and after battle were wearing. High speeds and positive g forces experienced in aerobatic manoeuvres induced muscle fatigue and pulled blood from the head, resulting, as John Crossman had discovered, in lack of oxygen to the brain and varying degrees of vision impairment. Rapid changes of altitude contributed to ear problems.[26]

There was little opportunity to relieve the physical exhaustion of combat. The days were long – typically beginning at 3 a.m. and ending at 7 p.m. unless they were holed up with the intelligence officer for a debriefing session – punctuated by lengthy periods waiting for something to happen. But there was more to Pat's enervating and visible tiredness than long days and too many combat hours. Spots kept appearing in front of his eyes when he was flying, indicating that he was suffering the physiological strains of combat. On top of that, he felt depressed and unsettled.[27] Like his Great War hero Mick Mannock, an aggressive, high-scoring pilot who later suffered from nervous tension, Pat had begun to exhibit signs of battle fatigue.

Battle fatigue, or flying stress, was a reaction to fear. Most pilots experienced some anxiety before going into battle. It was a perfectly natural response. Pierre Clostermann, who joined the Free French Air Force in Britain in March 1942 and was posted to an RAF squadron in January 1943, spoke of fear in the 2004 introduction to his memoir, *The Big Show*. He acknowledged that fear during combat was a constant and could not be ignored. For some, he conceded, it could paralyse the reflexes, but for him and many others – including, it seems, Pat Hughes – fear released an energising burst of aggression after which he lost all sense of caution and discipline.[28]

Clostermann, who became a high-scoring ace, admitted his reaction to combat fear towards the end of a long life. Few wartime pilots spoke openly of it because of perceptions of cowardice. Some even denied it. Des Sheen, for example, claimed to feel no fear during his first combat and later looked on it as an exciting experience. Others succumbed and assumed they would be killed. (John Crossman's statement that 'I'll go the way of the rest' was an acceptance that he might not survive.) Most, however, believed they would not fall in battle. Importantly, they thought they were in control of their fate: they were in tune with their machines, they could pounce, they could fire, and they could outmanoeuvre their foe in a dogfight. They would prevail because of their skill.

Pilots tried to deal with their apprehension. Alcohol, riotous parties, writing up flying accidents in their diaries, light-hearted banter, and underplaying the tragedy of death – he 'went for a Burton', he's 'gone west', drawing lots for an abandoned car – were all ways to deal with it. Some pilots hedged their bets and doffed their flight caps to superstition, performing pre-flight rituals or clinging to lucky charms. Pat, who fingered the silver cartwheel his brother had given him and perhaps attempted to double the luck when he gave Kay a gold charm bracelet, was one of them. But the pressures of constant battle, little rest, seeing close friends die, even grief, exacerbated their unease, and there came a point at which anxiety couldn't be managed.

The symptoms of battle fatigue fell into two categories: behavioural changes and physical ailments. The former included inability to concentrate, excitability and irritability and, in Pat's case, depression and restlessness. Some pilots exhibited an almost obsessive interest in their aircraft by supervising repair work and inspecting it carefully before take-off. Obvious social signs were quietness before an operation or conversely a false over-exuberance, increased smoking and drinking too much. Physical symptoms included tiredness, insomnia, headaches, backache, weight loss, tics, sinus trouble, stomach upsets ranging from mild dyspepsia to vomiting, grumbly bowels (or worse) and eye strain.[29]

As Pat's third combat day in a row drew to a close, he was drained. But his men had no idea that something was wrong. He 'just got on with it', Keith Lawrence recalled. 'As a good leader [and] flight commander Pat continued to lead, as was his job ... He would not have said anything to his junior officers, particularly those who relied on him in battle. If he were tired, Pat would simply press on. He would have felt it was his duty.' And indeed it was. Good leadership was, after all, vital for morale, and none knew this better than 234 Squadron, which had already suffered from a commanding officer who appeared to shirk his flying responsibilities. Pat had always led by example and could not let any of his charges see him waver from his usual combat aggression.[30] Perhaps so, but when fitness broke down and exhaustion intruded it was harder to keep anxiety at bay, whether it was related to the natural surge of combat-related fear or concerns for a loved one's safety.

It was widely accepted that married men or those with sweethearts were more susceptible to anxiety than their unattached brethren, and within two days in mid-August Pat had ranged from the supreme assurance to his wife that 'it'll never happen to me' to the joking acceptance of his possible future death with the exhortation 'in case of accidents make sure you marry again'.[31] Just shy of his 23rd birthday, the pressure of responsibility combined with a breaking down of his fitness was becoming too much.

He went to see the squadron's intelligence officer. Krikey Krikorian recognised that Pat was suffering from tension, but he didn't know the extent of the Australian's emotional turmoil. If he had, there wasn't much he could do; even the medical officer would have been able to do little other than suggest a good night's sleep and offer a sleeping tablet followed by a stimulant to spark him awake the next morning. There was no psychological treatment of anxiety during the Battle of Britain. There was no time to send a pilot off for a few days' rest. There was no counselling. The emphasis was on keeping the airman in the air, and to do that the medical officer would usually tell him he was not alone and reassure him that all would be well. The pilot may have felt able to carry on, but how successful was this approach in the long run? Reflecting on those hectic September days, Bob Doe wondered how many of those 'RAF fighter pilots who survived the onslaught and became mentally and physically worn down ... were killed and betrayed by their tiredness?'[32]

Krikorian reassured the younger man that everything was all right. He took it further and pretended Pat's symptoms had arisen from drinking too much. Most of the pilots drank to relax, but not to excess; no one over-imbibed, and certainly not a flight commander responsible for leading his section, flight or squadron into battle. Indeed, as far as Keith Lawrence remembered, Pat was not drinking to excess. But for Pat to be comforted there must have been an element of truth behind Krikorian's suggestion. Regardless of how Pat felt after their talk, the intelligence officer knew he had given bad advice. 'It was already too late.'[33]

14

7–13 September

'We will raze their cities to the ground'

Ever since the Luftwaffe's accidental bombing of London, the RAF had raided Berlin. Little damage had ensued but that did not matter. The Fatherland had been breached. Even worse, Germany had not yet gained air supremacy and invasion couldn't go ahead.[1] On 3 September – the first anniversary of the war's commencement – Goering met with his commanders General-feldmarschalls Albert Kesselring and Hugo Sperrle. They had to decide what to do next.

Goering supported a full-scale blitz on London with a total destruction of morale in its wake, such as that which had occurred after the decisive air strikes on Warsaw and Rotterdam. Accordingly, he proposed a maximum attack on London, arguing (with little evidence) that the RAF was weakened to such an extent that it would offer little resistance. Kesselring, a determined proponent of terror bombing, supported the Reichsmarschall. He was of the opinion that a crippled London would be the death blow for the RAF, and Britain would reel from the destruction of docks, factories and civilian morale. Like his leader, Kesselring underestimated RAF strength; he believed Britain's air force was finished. Sperrle did not agree. He thought that Fighter Command was more than strong enough to continue a vital defence;

he even overestimated its numbers. He was outvoted, and 7 September was settled upon as the date to strike, assuming Hitler gave his permission.

On 4 September, the Fuehrer gave a speech. Conveniently overlooking Luftwaffe responsibility for the London bombs that had precipitated the recent raids on Berlin, he denounced the latter as Churchill's 'brainchild' and proclaimed that Germany would, in turn, 'raze their cities to the ground'. Daylight raids would continue, but the major bombing emphasis would be an intensive nightly blitz. This declaration of retaliation was all for show, however; the reprisals were just an excuse. Two days earlier Hitler had given his approval to shift Luftwaffe attacks from the airfields near London to the capital itself.[2]

'Passed from sight – over the skyline'

On 7 September, the Air Ministry issued an 'attack imminent' alert. The conditions that day, however, belied the urgency of the statement. There was some early activity, including a few reconnaissance flights and smaller formations, but little else. The light morning haze near the Channel areas burned off, and the day was fine and hot with little cloud. It was perfect weather for picnics and afternoon tea on the lawn or, in Kay Hughes's case, for battling road blocks and navigating without signposts as she drove from Treyarnon Bay to Andover, where the White Hart's landlord had promised her a double room if he could manage it.[3]

As Kay drove, fighter squadrons took advantage of the welcome lull in enemy activity and relaxed. Her husband and fellow pilots at Middle Wallop lounged in the hot sun, resting and simply enjoying the pleasant day and unexpected respite.[4] At Tangmere, 43 Squadron's pilots arranged deck-chairs in front of the officers' mess and casually stood and sat about for a group photo: Squadron Leader Caesar Hull reclined backwards with hands behind head, and Flight Lieutenant Richard 'Dickie' Reynell, an Australian Hawker test pilot recently attached to the squadron for operational experience, who had notched up his first success five days earlier, sat at ease with legs crossed.

The peaceful day continued. It was so quiet that Ellen Geal, known as Nell, who lived in Sundridge, Kent, 6 or 7 miles from Biggin Hill, was convinced that 'they are not coming today'. Even as she laid out her favourite tea of toasted cheese and tripe and onions for her ten-year-old grandson, Desmond Hall, and Tony, his four-year-old brother, Goering, who had travelled with his entourage from Berlin to Cap Gris Nez, in the Pas-de-Calais, was broadcasting on German radio that 'as a result of the provocative British attacks on Berlin on recent nights, the Fuehrer has decided to order a mighty blow to be struck in revenge against the capital of the British Empire'.[5]

From 3.45 p.m., enemy aircraft massed on a wide front stretching 86 miles, from Beachy Head to Kent's North Foreland, on the eastern end of the Isle of Thanet. Small groups of bombers and their escorts seemingly just sat there, waiting for more and more to join them. Soon, over 300 Do17s, He111s and Ju88s, and 600 Me109 and 110 escorts, stepped up in dense layers ranging from 14 000 to 23 000 feet, droned inland. The 'aerial armada' comprised the greatest bomber force ever convened accompanied by every available German fighter. Believing the Luftwaffe would continue as before, Air Vice-Marshal Keith Park dispatched defending squadrons to key airfields and industrial targets, ordering them to patrol away from the coast. The first was in the air by 4.20 p.m. Within 10 minutes, all of the 21 squadrons within a 70-mile radius of London were on readiness, including 12 Group's Fowlmere and Duxford squadrons. They were supplemented by 10 Group's 609 and 234 squadrons. With the clanging of the scramble bell, Pat Hughes and his friends roused themselves from the somnolent sunshine and rushed to their waiting

Spitfires. But instead of splitting up and proceeding to separate targets as Fighter Command had anticipated, the massive formation crossed the coast in two waves; the first headed towards the Thames Estuary, and the second, an hour later, 'ploughed on', as historian Stephen Bungay put it, 'like a battering ram', towards Central London and the East End docks.[6]

Desmond Hall heard the sirens from his grandmother's garden. He recalled that 'people thought it won't be much, and carried on with afternoon tea'. Their village had never been a target, and in Desmond's self-confessed 'youthful innocence' they 'felt immune and secure in the knowledge that our airmen would *always* win'.[7]

The first bombs were dropped on the Ford factory at Dagenham and were followed by high explosives and incendiaries on the Beckton gasworks. Fighter Command's squadrons could do little but pick at the seemingly impenetrable Luftwaffe hide. Nine Hurricanes from 43 Squadron were among the first to face the onslaught. Three climbed to engage the fighters; six targeted bombers. The defenders were engulfed, and the first of many RAF deaths in combat that day – Caesar Hull and Dickie Reynell – occurred at 4.45 p.m. Reynell was wounded in combat with an Me109 over South London. His parachute failed to open when he baled out of Hurricane V7257. He plummeted to his death, landing in Dartmouth Row, near Greyladies Gardens, in Blackheath. V7257 crashed about 165 yards away, and its engine smashed through one of the buildings at St Ursula's Catholic School.[8] Dickie Reynell was the seventh Australian to die in the Battle of Britain.

Still the enemy force powered on. At 5 p.m. Desmond Hall listened as the 'distant hum of aircraft engines grew louder and nearer, the planes lower. There were bursts of machine gun fire which grew more intense than we had ever heard before, spent bullets and cartridges falling like hail'.[9]

Brave men fought valiantly during the day that would soon

be known as Black Saturday. Enemy fighters fell, but the defenders could neither down nor deflect the Luftwaffe bombers. 303 (Polish) Squadron alone attacked with little interference from the escorts, but only because 603 and 1 squadrons had drawn them off. 234 Squadron was ordered to patrol Kenley and Biggin Hill at 5.35 p.m., 10 minutes before the last of the bombs were dropped and the raiders were on their return track to France. By 6 p.m. London's sky was 'orange and pink'. According to 14-year-old Olive McNeil of the East End district of Poplar, who had just climbed out of her family's Anderson shelter, 'it glowed making everything look like fairyland', but the lights were from blazing, all-destructive fires. The docks, the Royal Arsenal at Woolwich, the oil tanks at Cliffe and Thames Haven, the Beckton gasworks: all raging infernos. East End streets were in rubble; houses were burning. Ash was carried on the breeze.

The all-clear sounded at 6.10 p.m. The mighty enemy raid was officially over. Olive McNeil gazed at the sky.[10] Red and orange flames vied with black engulfing smoke to obscure them, but somewhere between London and Brighton 234 Squadron had no trouble making out a large number of enemy aircraft at heights ranging from 16 000 to 22 000 feet. Twenty-five minutes after the all-clear, when they were southeast of Folkestone, Squadron Leader Spike O'Brien ordered Pat Hughes – Blue One – and Blue Section to attack the bombers; he and the rest of the squadron would cover them.

No one knows how Pat was feeling as he faced the enemy. Had he had a good night's sleep? Did he still have spots in front of his eyes? Was he still out of sorts? Was he worried about Kay as she drove to Andover? It did not matter. He may have been depressed and unsettled the night before, but now he had to fight.

Pat thrust Spitfire X4009 towards a formation of Do17s and picked out a straggler, a photo reconnaissance machine. Tasked with photographing the London docks, it had already sustained damage from attacks by 602 Squadron's Spitfires and 79 Squadron's Hurricanes. Keith Lawrence followed Pat and watched him make a quarter attack on the Dornier. The Australian's machine gunnery was so concentrated that Keith 'saw a large piece fly off the enemy aircraft'. Next, one of the Dornier's wings crumpled. The stricken aircraft plunged into a fatal spin. 'Immediately after I saw a Spitfire which I assumed to be Blue One spinning down with about third of wing broken.' Minutes later, the Dornier crashed into the River Darent; witnesses saw it turn 'like a leaf falling … in a nose first spin'. Black smoke could be seen for miles as the machine burned. X4009 crashed in a meadow belonging to Dark's Farm, on the border of Sundridge and Bessels Green. 'Two men took to parachutes', recalled Desmond Hall, 'one of which failed to operate and the wearer, the Spitfire pilot, died among the flowers in the garden of a bungalow'. Ironically, Pat had once contemplated the exhilarating prospect of wings breaking off a screaming Moth. Now he lay dead in William Norman's garden at 16 Main Road, a short distance from his broken-winged Spitfire.[11]

There has been much conjecture about Pat's last action. There is a gap in Keith Lawrence's combat report; he did not see what ensued in between the break-up of the Dornier and Pat's out-of-control dive. Nor did anyone else from 234 Squadron. Like Bob Doe, who had climbed to 30 000 feet so he could pounce on the Me109 escorts, they were fighting their own battles. Did Pat take his trade-mark get-in-close tactic to the extreme with his Spit, flying so near to the Dornier that he could not dodge the debris? Did he then lose control, striking the Dornier in mid-air? Or did the stricken Dornier veer into X4009? Had Pat's exhaustion caught up with him, meaning he misjudged his attack, overshot and accidentally struck the Dornier? Had the spots before his eyes returned, meaning he didn't see the deadly fragment? Any one of these scenarios is plausible.

There has even been speculation that Pat was felled by friendly fire. On the face of it, this is credible. Doe reported chasing a Hurricane which, when he dived past it and looped, followed him, 'firing all the time'. Budge Harker 'saw what I thought was an Me109 attack a Spitfire, as I was about to attack I recognised it as a Hurricane, he was definitely firing' at Doe. But when X4009 was excavated, there was no sign of spent RAF ammunition in the wreck, and the speculation does not explain its broken wing.[12] There is one possibility that does.

Thousands of feet below Pat's final combat, Desmond Hall's father was watching. A coalman during the day, Charles Hall, known as Bob, was a member of the local Home Guard. He also worked in the special police on sentry duty at Fort Halstead, a secret establishment about 3 miles away, located on the crest of the Kentish North Downs. At the same time as his sons were enjoying afternoon tea with their grandmother, Bob Hall was at the family home, about a quarter of a mile away, resting before night duty at Fort Halstead. Desmond could hear the 'awesome wail of racing engines', but he couldn't see anything. Located on a hill, Bob Hall's cottage and garden, however, afforded him a clear view of Pat's final combat. 'According to my father and other witnesses', Desmond Hall wrote, years later, 'a Spitfire and a Dornier 17 appeared to collide'. Bob Hall maintained all his life that the Spitfire had deliberately rammed the Dornier. But despite his contention, Battle of Britain historian Andy Saunders considers it unlikely.[13]

Whether the collision was accidental or deliberate, Pat was the second Australian lost in combat that day and the eighth to die in the Battle of Britain. He was just 12 days short of his 23rd birthday. By tragic coincidence, like that of his compatriot Dick Reynell and like that of cadet Norman Chaplin, whose death four years earlier had so rattled him at Point Cook, his parachute had not deployed. Paterson Clarence Hughes, considered by Bob

Doe as a 'real go getter' who 'believed in getting close and doing something dangerous', was dead. The squadron had lost 'a driving light'.[14] He had displayed true courage in continuing to fight, but the luck he had invested in his tarnished talisman had run out.

Six years earlier, still a schoolboy, Pat had penned 'An Autumn Evening' for his school magazine. As an epitaph, it is strangely apt. 'The cool evening wind came whispering over the lonely land … The watcher rose slowly to his feet, and with the beauty of that autumn evening impressed on his soul, he started again on his journey. For a moment he was lost to view behind an outcrop, but then for a short time he stood, vaguely outlined against the lighter gloom of a wide-arched sky – and then he passed from sight – over the skyline.'[15]

'Felt the loss deeply'

The last of 234 Squadron's Spitfires landed at Middle Wallop at 8 p.m. One by one, as the pilots returned, Krikey Krikorian debriefed them, piecing together what had happened. But Pat Hughes did not join them; nor did Keith Lawrence. He had landed at Croydon, not returning until the next day, so was unable to tell his companions of Pat's fate. If a pilot had not returned to base, called in his position or been reported by police as having been 'brought down', he would be classed as missing 2 hours after take-off.[16] The squadron anxiously awaited news of Pat and Squadron Leader O'Brien, who was also missing.

The combat successes were tallied – three Me109s and one He111 destroyed, one Me109 probably destroyed, and one Do17 and one Me109 damaged. Pat's Dornier would later be added to the total. The Australian's personal score was ultimately assessed as 14 and three shared destroyed, one shared destroyed uncon-firmed and one probably destroyed. He had achieved the major-ity of these victories in seven encounters over three weeks, mostly

against skilled Me109 combatants.[17] The pilot who was assessed
at the end of his cadetship as having 'no outstanding qualities' and
ranked 28th in his class was, with all the part shares, a triple ace
and Australia's highest scoring Battle of Britain pilot. He was later
ranked as one of the top ten Battle pilots. Bob Doe, who survived the war, was just ahead of him. Pat was also rated in the top
three Australian aces of the Second World War and in the RAF's
top 50.[18]

Details trickled in. The squadron heard that 28-year-old Spike
O'Brien, who had done much to restore morale in the squadron
since taking command on 17 August, had been killed in combat.
They also discovered Pat's fate. Krikorian, who knew that Pat had
not been 100 per cent physically and mentally fit when he took
off that afternoon, blamed himself for the young man's death. 'In
a way, I felt responsible.' He regretted that he had failed Pat, not
even able to answer his own question of 'how could pilots cope
with tension?'[19]

Krikorian was not alone in his grief. Pat's old Point Cook
friends soon heard of his death. As he lay in his hospital bed, perhaps reflecting that 'there by the grace of God go I', Des Sheen
told his parents in his understated way that his fellow former
cadet had 'gone west'. Gordon Olive mourned the 'tragedy' of his
friend's death. He recognised that 'Pat had died at the height of
his prowess and in the full bloom of his manhood'. To him, 'there
was no more typical Australian in the fight than Pat'. He considered that 'his end was a personal loss to all who knew him'.[20]

Olive's sentiment was apparent among Pat's former charges.
There was a bad feeling when the pilots and ground crew realised
they had lost two men. Indeed, it was a 'black day', recalled Joe
Roddis. 'No one had more air sense than Pat.' Roddis considered
that 'his only problem was that he got too close but that was
his way'. As far as he was concerned, the former RAAF cadet
who (unbeknown to him) had been rated at only 60 per cent for

qualities as an officer was the 'best commanding officer we ever had', even if he had only stood in the squadron leader's stead. Most of 234 Squadron's pilots had known or flown with Pat since he had arrived at Leconfield in November 1939. They had admired him and 'felt the loss deeply'. For Keith Lawrence, who had shared in Pat's first victory – and was, in a sense, there at the beginning and the end of Pat's fighting career – 'a most skilled pilot' had fallen. He grieved for their 'born leader, a fearless and determined fighter pilot, who, by his example in engaging the enemy at such close quarters and with such success, commanded the greatest respect from his pilots'. Penned a little over a week before their deaths, Spike O'Brien's recommendation for Pat's DFC summed up the squadron's feelings about their esteemed flight commander and one-time de facto commanding officer: 'This officer's outstanding courage and leadership has inspired all those under his command with his dash and gallantry'. Air Vice-Marshal Sir Quintin Brand, air officer commanding 10 Group, concurred. He 'very strongly recommended' the award of the DFC for 'a very gallant officer'. As Keith Lawrence put it, Pat 'was in the top echelon of Battle of Britain pilots'.[21]

'I wept until I could cry no more'

Kay Hughes spent all day driving from Cornwall to Hampshire. When she was a few miles from the White Hart, she stopped off to phone Middle Wallop to let Pat know she was almost there. The adjutant, 'Bish' Owens, took the call and told her to come straight to the station. Why couldn't Pat come to the phone? She fingered her gold bracelet. Pat's gift. Then she realised. Her husband was dead.

The young widow drove to Middle Wallop in a daze; the boys met her outside. She looked for Flying Officer Butch. He was nowhere to be found. He had run out of the mess that afternoon and never returned. Kay was desolate. The little fellow's disappearance just added to her misery. Trying to console her – and perhaps themselves – Bish and the boys took her to the White Hart. The landlord welcomed her with a grin. He had kept his promise. 'I've got your double', he announced. But 'then it was a single room', she wryly recalled years later. 'Only the brandies were double.' Looking back, she admitted that she 'had never really known what true grief was. I had never cried so much in my life. I wept until I could cry no more'.[22]

Pat was buried on 13 September in the churchyard of St James's in the parish of Sutton on Hull. The rector offered a prayer of comfort for the relatives of the 'gallant airman' and his sympathy in the loss 'of such a brave and intrepid man'.[23] A week later, Kay discovered she was pregnant. She was glad. It was Pat's dream: 'you, me and another Flying Officer Butch'. But Pat would not be there.

She drove back to Treyarnon Bay, where she and Pat had been so happy. The remains of 234 Squadron also returned to Cornwall; they had been sent there to rest and recover. It was a much-changed squadron. There were, as Bob Doe recalled, only about three originals left – just three of the laughing, youthfully vibrant men Kay had flirted with in the Beverley Arms earlier that year.[24] Some had died. Others, like Keith Lawrence, had been sent to other units to inject them with experienced blood. Their places at the pub were taken by new pilots. Their presence in her Cornish retreat would have done nothing to assuage Kay's grief. She couldn't stop crying. Like Christine Jourd, her anguish was all encompassing. She remembered the six months they had had together – the honeymoon cottage where Pat had slept not one night, the 38 days of marriage.

She miscarried. It was a boy. 'After that I didn't care about anything except getting drunk and playing Pat's favourite record.' Tears streaked her face as she listened. When she received Pat's

DFC at Buckingham Palace, 'other widows were crying. I wasn't, every tear in me had poured out in 1940'.[25]

Misery aside, Kay was proud of her husband. 'Pat did his job, magnificently.' She had spent only a few months with the young man who had a swagger about him and a boyish charm – never mind his good looks – but she wouldn't have missed them 'for the world'. They had been happy.[26]

'England is unbeatable'

The next wave of London's Blitz started at 8.10 p.m. on 7 September. 'When darkness had fallen and the night bombers were droning towards London', Desmond Hall paused at the entrance of his family's shelter. He looked 'at a scene never to be forgotten. The sky to the north was alight with a warm red glow, searchlight fingers swept the heavens; sometimes they focused on one place then there were sparks of anti-aircraft fire, great pools of light were drifting down as bombers dropped flares to see their way'. It was a grim vista. 'London was on fire and the red sky was from the flames.'[27]

Church bells rang out, road blocks were put in place, and Home Guarders were on the alert. The invasion code word 'Cromwell' had been issued just before Goering's 318 bombers started pummelling London mercilessly. The burning docks provided a perfect guiding light; the fiery glow could be seen 30 miles away. Thousands of incendiaries were dropped; 300 tons of high-explosive bombs were released. Londoners, fearing the long-anticipated invasion had finally begun, hunkered in shelters until the all-clear sounded, at 4.30 a.m. on the 8th. As they emerged into the soot-laden air to survey the chaos and tally the toll – 306 civilians were dead and 1337 seriously injured – they welcomed the news that there had been no invasion. They had no idea they would have to endure 57 consecutive nights of it and spend many of the wee hours underground until 21 May 1941. But if Hitler and Goering thought a razed capital would precipitate a plea for peace from cowed Londoners, they were mistaken. Morale was not shaken, and a perception soon developed – and was fostered by propagandists – that they were 'soldiers in the front line'.[28]

There was no escape from the Luftwaffe bomber stream for Des Sheen in his hospital bed, from where he witnessed 'lots of scrapping … and to see the size of the Jerry formations from the ground even has been unbelievable … hundreds in each'.[29] He saw 'quite a few go down as some of the fighters were right over our head and one Jerry jettisoned his bombs which fell about 50 yards from our hospital'. Despite the proximity of falling projectiles, 'we were having a grand time' until, on 9 September, he was sent to an 'awful' hospital just outside London – Queen Mary's in Sidcup, Kent.

Queen Mary's had been the first London hospital struck on Black Saturday. Two nurses and six patients had been killed, and it seemed as if the Luftwaffe were still keen to make it a target. 'We get it every night now too and last night heard nothing but machines, bombers and anti-aircraft fire.' Invasion rumours abounded – particularly in the southwest – and at Warmwell, Ken Holland recorded a 'Big Invasion flap' on 8 September.[30] Des Sheen was one of many convinced that 'the invasion is about to start'.

Des settled into Queen Mary's, and the King visited the East End. He toured Shoreditch, Bethnal Green, Stepney and Poplar then crossed the river to view devastated Bermondsey, Southwark and Lambeth. Des knew his parents would be worried about how London was faring, especially Walter Sheen, who had been born in Lambeth. 'The poor old East End seems to have caught a packet', he reported the day after the King's tour. 'The amazing thing is the reaction with [*sic*] the people. It's not fear but anger and determination.' He confidently stated to his parents, 'Believe me, England is unbeatable unless we are all killed first. Every one of the 48 000 000 people [is] fighting these days'. His words were penned not just to temper his parents' fears. They reflected the general attitude. Bombs continued to fall, and most people still anticipated the invasion, but they were 'confident that it will be a failure'.

The Blitz continued. The bombs didn't fall as heavily near Croydon Hospital, recalled Bill Millington's new friend, Peter Townsend, but 'we had our share'. The nurses pulled the patients' beds into the centre of the ward, thus protecting them from glass fragments when the windows were shattered by bomb splinters. Beds safely away, the nurses, 'always superbly calm', sat by their sides and 'held our hands and told us not to be afraid'. The irony was not lost on Townsend. 'Us, who were supposed to be the aces and the heroes … Pyers Worrell, Bill Millington and I whiled away our time alone in the big ward.' When Bill was discharged after ten days, he wrote to his sister Eileen. Making light of the situation, he carefully skirted around the first nights of the Blitz and any fear he might have felt as the bombs rattled the building. 'I can recommend hospital as a very noble institution. The nurses were terrific, particularly my little Irish night nurse.' He, Worrall and Townsend 'had quite a few gay evenings together'.[31]

Like Bill and many other pilots recovering from injuries, Des Sheen thought he would return to the fray quickly. The 'chap who picked me up said "never mind. We'll get you another Spitfire"', and Des wanted to climb into it. Five days after his second bale-out, he expected to 'be back again with the boys long before this letter reaches you', but he was soon reporting that 'I'm now on sick leave for a month, which is nonsense in my opinion. I've had about a week and feel OK except for a bit of a stiff knee'.

Frustrated and impatient to get back into action, he was nonetheless under no illusions about how lucky he was to have survived his third near encounter with death. 'Despite my second jump I am well on the credit side', he joked. 'I have a knack of getting into and out of trouble.' As if to remind himself of his continuing good fortune, he had souvenired items from the three near misses: a bullet-damaged earphone from his 7 December outing and the parachute harness 'D-ring' ripcords from his 1 and 5 September bale-outs.

'Saw nowt'

It was still quiet up north and on the Dorset front on 7 September, despite it being an active day for Fighter Command in the London area. On the day London was blitzed, Ken Holland and 152 Squadron's Green Section were on patrol. Two of them chased a Do215 over Lyme Regis, but Ken, as Green Three, 'saw nowt'. John Crossman, far from the battle zone at Acklington, had leave. He appropriated the station Magister and flew to Sutton Bridge. As Kay Hughes wept for her husband, John was out dancing, and Ken Holland was again with Kay Muir in Weymouth, after spending the previous evening in her flat and not returning to Warmwell until 2.30 a.m. He confessed to his diary the next day that he 'should feel remorse about last night but don't'. He coyly recorded 'K.K.K.' (Ken Kissed Kay), but it seems that much more than kissing took place: the intimate details were later scored from the pages with black ink.

Over the next week, 152 Squadron put up a base patrol in response to an X raid and experienced a number of minor flaps in which Ken, yet again, 'saw nothing'.[32] His intense relationship with Kay Muir continued, even though he still corresponded with Seina Haydon. He went into Weymouth most nights to see Kay and returned to base in the wee hours, collapsing into one of the iron beds lined up on each side of the dispersal hut so he could sleep for as long as possible before early morning readiness.

Resource management

The intensity of daylight Luftwaffe operations waned. The turn towards London and increasing focus on the aircraft factories of the south and southwest had led to key airfields and sector facilities largely being left alone. Moreover, the nightly blitz meant that for the main part London's protection was in the hands of Anti-Aircraft Command and civilian defence units. Casualties and urban damage would be great, but the strategy shift was a boon for Fighter Command.

Air Vice-Marshal Keith Park made the most of the respite. For him, 7 September was the turning point in the Battle. It was obvious that if the Luftwaffe continued to launch mass attacks he could no longer justify section and flight defences. He needed to meet the enemy in as much force as he could muster. He devised a resource management strategy and on 9 September instructed his controllers to pair the 11 Group squadrons. The faster climbing, higher ceiling Spitfire units would engage the escorts. Hurricanes would deal with the lower flying bombers. Park refined the tactics the next day. As much as possible, squadrons from the same stations were to be paired, or at least squadrons on adjacent stations, in order to save time forming up. Controllers would advise the rendezvous point and designate the leading squadron. All orders would be provided to both squadrons so they could operate separately if necessary.

Park also issued instructions regarding fighter tactics. He had seen the foolhardiness of the close-shaped vics and prescribed fighter attack patterns. Bill Millington's squadron, for example, had lost four pilots and aircraft on 31 August, all because they had adhered to the set RAF attack formations. Park now wanted pilots to fly in loose line abreast groups of four aircraft. This was a more flexible arrangement, as they wouldn't have to concentrate on formating on the leader and could see more of the sky.

In addition, he directed, if they had to split up in battle, they should pair off; each could better keep an eye on the other's tail.[33] Park further fine-tuned his instructions on 13 September, two days after Queensland-born Flight Lieutenant Frederick Flood became the ninth Australian to die in the Battle of Britain, when he was shot down by Me109s off Calais. Whole squadrons should be dispatched, as flights and sections were too small to contend with the larger enemy formations. Pilots should not waste their efforts on stragglers and lame ducks; they had already taken a beating. They were not to follow their victims down but to rejoin battle if they still had ammunition. Importantly, fighter units were to attack head-on wherever possible. It might be dangerous, but as Pat Hughes had demonstrated, it was effective. New plans laid, it was time to implement them.

15

14–24 September

'I've never had the wind up more in my life'

John Crossman was woken up at 1 a.m. on 12 September and told to report that afternoon to 46 Squadron at North Weald, in Essex. He was a fresh, fully trained airman to supplement a squadron which had lost six pilots in action since 2 September, including two on the 11th. He left Acklington at 10 a.m. but didn't reach North Weald until just before midnight, because of road blocks and having been caught in a raid. He arrived to find that 46 Squadron was based at Stapleford Tawney, North Weald's satellite aerodrome, located 8 miles away, and he 'had an awful job getting transport'. He wasn't impressed.[1]

He 'finally arrived' at 11.30 a.m. on 13 September. While he gained his bearings, another pilot came up to him. Pilot Officer William Pattullo – known to his family as Billy but to his squadron friends as Pat – had been posted in July to train with the then non-operational 46 Squadron, located at Digby, after its return from Norway following the German invasion. He had arrived at Stapleford Tawney on 26 August and was transferred to 151 Squadron. He claimed a Dornier 17 probably destroyed on the 30th and a destroyed Dornier on the 31st. He had rejoined 46 on 1 September, when his old friends took up residence at Stapleford Tawney, and had then been posted to 249 Squadron at North

Weald on the 10th. He was in action the next day, sharing in the destruction of an He111. On the 13th he had time on his hands so was visiting his former companions. Having caught sight of the obvious newcomer he asked if he could show him round.[2]

John and Chilean-born, Scottish-raised Pat had been at 1 Initial Training Wing at the same time: Pat had arrived on 3 October 1939 and John on the 17th, six days before Pat left for elementary training. John thought him 'a nice fellow' and 'they palled up at once'.[3]

After the grand tour, John applied for 24 hours' leave to collect the luggage and car he had left at Biggin Hill during 32 Squadron's hurried evacuation to Acklington. Even after almost two weeks of repair work, he had 'never seen anything like Biggin Hill. All buildings are flat except the mess. All hangars are flat and hundreds of bombs have been dropped on it. Absolutely wrecked'.

Fortunately, his car had escaped damage, and after retrieving his possessions he drove to Chalfont St Giles to visit his aunts. 'It took me ages to go through London as it is lousy with bomb craters and had to detour all over the place.' He arrived to a warm welcome and 'a long chat until midnight'. He took the precaution of leaving behind the majority of his clothes, books, photos, letters and other odds and ends.

As he drove away the next morning, he saw his Aunt Mabel 'taking flowers down to the Harvest Festival at our church'. He pretended to run her down then jumped out of the auto to help carry the flowers. Her nephew had matured since his first visit, the previous October. 'He had grown up from what seemed to me just a boy when he arrived to a man.' Mabel's 'last picture of him' was with 'his arms so full of flowers he could not take his cap off to go into church, so he asked me to take it off and tuck it under his arm'.[4]

John's new comrades were at dispersal when he arrived at 1 p.m., but he did not join them. Newly allocated to Flying

Officer Frederick Austin's B Flight, he was told to take Hurricane V7443 up for a 40-minute sector recce to familiarise himself with the area.[5] When he landed, he decided to explore. Less than an hour later he was at dispersal and discovered that 'the squadron had just taken off. They returned soon, no luck'. They 'hadn't been back long when there was another flap'. John rushed to Hurricane V7442 – Pilot Officer Robert Reid had climbed into V7443 – and took off. A Flight was in the air at 6 p.m., and B Flight followed 5 minutes later. John was 'in action for first time'.

Implementing the new policy of flying in two squadron wings, 46 Squadron had been ordered to rendezvous with 504 Squadron over Maidstone at 15 000 feet. The wing soon encountered two separate enemy formations. Led by Flight Lieutenant Alexander 'Sandy' Rabagliati, 46 Squadron sighted 50 to 60 Me109s near Biggin Hill. They were straggling in line astern and an inverted vic formation, stepped up from 15 000 to 20 000 feet. Fighter Command had fought larger formations but this was big enough, and when John first saw the massed enemy machines he was 'scared sick and panicky'. His father had brought him up to be fearless, but this was different.[6] His anxiety did not abate as they closed onto the Messerschmitts, firing upwards into their bellies. Individual dogfights then ensued. John determinedly pushed his fear aside and 'got one decent burst into a 109 but was unable to see if I got him as had to get out of the way of a few more. Jerries turned tail and we came home'.

Rabagliati managed to fire a long burst into one Me109, setting the fuselage aflame. Reid targeted another and it was seen diving, 'obviously badly hit'. He was credited with a damaged and Rabagliati a destroyed, but if John's 'decent burst' had hit anything, it was not acknowledged. Overall, it was a good effort in a combat that, officially, was deemed to have hardly been worth it: 11 Group had had to dispatch most of its available squadrons and call upon 12 Group for assistance to meet what in hindsight was considered 'a threat which was hardly a threat at all to targets on land'.[7]

Flung suddenly into battle, John had had no time for pre-op nerves. For him, the 'worst part was just before we attacked'. He admitted that 'I can honestly say I've never had the wind up more in my life'. But he did not succumb to his fear. He lined up the enemy machine and fired. He was a fighter pilot at last, and a man of true courage.

'Entirely fearless and controlled'

Sunday 15 September saw the Luftwaffe launch a concentrated attack against London: the goal was to bring the RAF to its knees once and for all. 11 Group was totally committed, 12 Group's Duxford Wing was involved, and 10 Group's squadrons were called to protect the southwest in a series of battles and defensive actions that lasted until dusk.

From mid-morning, German forces massed near Calais. Fighter Command had had so much forewarning that 17 squadrons were airborne before three columns of bombers and their escorts crossed the coast of Kent at 11.30 a.m. en route to London. Five minutes later, John Crossman, again in Hurricane V7442, and nine others from 46 Squadron were ordered to form up with 249 Squadron over Stapleford Tawney and proceed to South London. Another four squadrons took off over the next 7 minutes.

The wing broke through the cloud cover at about 12 000 feet. Vectored south over Kent, John and his confreres climbed to 17 000 feet before catching a glimpse of the first puff of anti-aircraft fire. A little before 12.20 p.m., they encountered a 'formation of 20 Dornier 215s over South London at 18 000 feet, escorted by many Me109s 5000 feet above'. The Dorniers dispersed ahead of the approaching Hurricanes, and some Me109s dived to engage the defenders. Most, however, clung to the bombers as they had been ordered. 46 Squadron interpreted this as making 'no attempt whatsoever to assist the bombers'.[8]

To John, it appeared as if he had run into 'hundreds of Jerry kites'. Yet again, he was 'scared stiff' as 'three of us were going round to do head-on attacks on some Dorniers'. Yet again, he steeled himself for battle. He put aside his fear and carried out the dangerous tactic, but something went wrong. 'I lost speed, spun down 6000 feet, came out near 20 more escorted by about 60 Messerschmitt 109s.' His advantage was gone. Two or three 'Me109s detached themselves from the formation and dived to attack me. I turned inwards and headed for the bomber formation'. Next, he 'evaded then came round [and] did a stern attack on the Dorniers'. Closing from 350 to 300 yards, he delivered four bursts and 'put all my shots into one of them'. He 'saw black smoke pouring out from the port engine of the Do215 and the aircraft detached itself from the formation and began to lose height'. John 'saw him go down' but then 'dived away from the oncoming Me109s'. With no ammunition left, he wasn't 'going to stay round on my own with 60 Me109s' converging on him.[9]

Later, he proudly annotated his flying log, 'Shot down one Do215', but the squadron diarist simply recorded that the Dornier 'left the formation losing height' and lumped all combat successes together, stating, 'Considerable damage was inflicted upon the enemy'.[10] At best it would have been a probable, but John was not officially attributed with any part of the Dornier's demise, which, judging by the experience of Pilot Officer George Barclay of 249 Squadron, probably had many claimants. Barclay had also fired on a Dornier that day. He watched it break away from the formation, noticing that its engines were idling as it glided down; 'about eight of our fighters set on the lame duck about 3000 feet below me'. It seems that, even with Keith Park's recent orders, incapacitated Do215s were considered fair game.

'Still scared stiff in action.' Extract from John Crossman's diary, 15 September 1940. Courtesy of the Bowden family

John had no chance to rest on whatever laurels he claimed for himself. A quick lunch and he was in the air again: 46 and 249 squadrons were on their way to meet 120 to 150 intruders that would cross the coast between Dungeness and Dover in three formations 5 minutes later. The Hornchurch squadrons were the first to strike, and other squadrons attacked in succession. 249 Squadron claimed ten confirmed, the same number of probables and some damaged.[11]

The enemy eluded most of 46 Squadron, but at about 3.15 p.m., when they were over the Thames Estuary and bombs were dropping over the London metropolitan area, John 'chased a 215 into the clouds and lost him, otherwise wasn't able to get near anything. They ran too fast'. Pat Pattullo, who had returned to 46 Squadron that day and joined his friends on their second sortie, was luckier. He brought down a Do17, and Pilot Officer

Allan Johnson attacked another from the beam which was finished off by 'three other friendly fighters'.[12]

John and Pat were in the air again at 5.25 p.m. to patrol North Weald. But even though there was plenty of action elsewhere during the day's final noteworthy raid, in which the Germans failed to hit the Supermarine works at Woolston, 46 Squadron was well out of the battle area and 'enemy aircraft not sighted'. If John continued to be assailed by fear during his second and third sorties, Pattullo saw nothing of it then, or during the next two weeks. John learned to manage his panic, even as he accepted it. His friends saw only that he 'was entirely fearless and controlled'.[13]

'Claimed a third probable'

Another enemy formation was on its way to Portland. Ken Holland and 152 Squadron's B Flight scrambled from Warmwell to face it but had to contend with the He111s, without fighter escorts, on their own, as 238 – which had recently returned to Middle Wallop from St Eval – and 609 squadrons had already been directed to London's defence.[14]

Boy Marrs and another from Blue Section were patrolling Warmwell when the call came through to intercept the raid. They were joined in the air by Blue Section's third man and Green Section, comprising Peter O'Brian, Pilot Officer Arthur 'Watty' Watson and Ken Holland, who was bringing up the rear in R6764 as Green Three. Just before 3.30 p.m., B Flight was over Weymouth when Marrs sighted about 30 He111s, flying in vics of three, stepped up in an irregular line astern at about 15 000 feet, heading towards Portland from the west. With no fighter escort, which Marrs, for one, thought 'extraordinary', the Heinkels were potentially sitting ducks. Marrs climbed, hoping to come down behind them from out of the sun, but they were going too fast.

They dropped their bombs at 3.30 p.m. B Flight caught up with them within 10 minutes.[15]

Blue Section targeted a Heinkel on the extreme left of the rearmost enemy section, and Green Section homed in on a straggler. With little return fire from the Heinkel's guns, O'Brian concentrated his guns on the starboard engine. Closing from 300 to 200 yards, Ken fired off a 5-second burst from astern. The Heinkel began to lose height. Black smoke streamed from the starboard engine. Ken managed another two bursts and O'Brian fired again, followed by Watson, as it went down. Ken had 'shot all my rounds at one doing three attacks on it', but Watson had enough ammunition to attack another straggler, which blew up before plunging into the sea. When Ken returned to Warmwell, he 'claimed a third probable' and surveyed the damage to his Spitfire. 'R6764 had bullets through engine sump, tailplane, fin, one gun, oil tank! Fool's luck to get home at all.' He could not ponder his good fortune for long. There was another squadron scramble, in which he flew as White Two to Pilot Officer Graham Cox in A Flight. They 'saw a battle near Southampton but [the] commanding officer who led (for once) turned away from it'.

B Flight went off duty at 7.50 p.m., and after a celebratory drink in the mess Ken 'had an early night in dispersal hut'. His diary reflects little euphoria in scoring his first, albeit shared, victory. Perhaps there was more to his lack of underlining, exclamation points and capitals than just tiredness. Perhaps his natural ebullience had been quelled because of the hits his Spitfire had taken; that bullet to the oil tank could have been disastrous. He had indeed been lucky to get home. To make things worse, although 152 Squadron's fighter combat report noted Green Section's probable, it was not officially acknowledged. Neither Ken, nor O'Brian, nor Watson was credited with one-third shares. Watson, however, 'got one definitely' and was officially granted a destroyed Heinkel.[16]

John Crossman and Ken Holland appear to have been in the minority as far as acknowledged claims credit was concerned. When the day's figures were totted up and added to those made by the anti-aircraft gunners, apparently 185 enemy aircraft had been downed, of which 127 were bombers. It was Fighter Command's highest victory count. They had done well – except for the loss of 12 killed, one missing, one wounded who would die later, one taken prisoner of war and 26 of their own machines – but not as well as the 185 claimed, and Keith Park knew it. He thought such a high tally was ludicrous, particularly as there was little crash evidence.[17]

Even so, the Air Ministry announced the dodgy figures as fact, and the 'aerial successes ... produced enthusiastic praise for the RAF' from all sectors of the public. Even Des Sheen accepted the totals, noting to his parents four days later that 'Jerry lost another 185 machines in one day which is not exactly a promising outlook for him'.[18]

Inflated or not – post-war research indicated only 60 German aircraft – enemy losses were the worst since 18 August. The Germans had believed that the RAF was a hair's breadth from collapse and that another mighty onslaught would result in the final blow. It didn't, and Luftwaffe losses were so high they were as good as defeated. A rethink was needed. Ever since, 15 September has been celebrated as 'Battle of Britain Day', not for the real or even exaggerated RAF claims but because it marked another turning point. Five days after that failure to break the RAF and gain air supremacy, Hitler postponed his invasion plans indefinitely.

'Shot it down'

The Warmwell squadrons woke to indifferent weather on 16 September. There was little enemy activity, and Ken Holland 'did not fly all day'. He spent the evening with Kay Muir, but their relationship was proving turbulent. 'Had a long argument which ended in K.K.K. again.' There was 'nothing doing *au matin*' for 152 Squadron on the 17th; other than a few diversionary raids, most German activity was restricted to the afternoon. After lunch, Blue Section was ordered to patrol Portland Bill at 15 000 feet. Boy Marrs was leading again, with Ken as Blue Two, flying UM-J, and Peter O'Brian as Blue Three.[19] Shortly before 1.50 p.m., they were vectored onto a Ju88 at 17 000 feet which was flying north over Shepton Mallet, close to Somerset's Mendip Hills. They were about a mile away when they sighted the lone enemy aircraft.

Contrary to Keith Park's recent instructions to abandon the close-shaped vics and prescribed fighter attack patterns, they closed and carried out a number one attack. Marrs struck first, hitting his target's starboard engine's radiator. Glycol gushed out. Ken 'followed Blue One into attack from starboard beam giving bursts of 2 secs from 250–200 yards'. O'Brian was next. The Ju88 dived steeply into cloud cover at about 6000 feet to evade them. Ken, Marrs and O'Brian broke up and chased it separately. Marrs's engine seized; he had copped machine gun fire early in the attack. He retreated to find a suitable landing place, and Ken and O'Brian attacked the starboard engine 'from varying positions'. Although the Junkers was taking violent evasive action, diving, slide slipping, throttling back and doing vertical banked steep turns in alternate directions, they continued to hammer it. Taking a full deflection shot from below, O'Brian aimed at the Ju88's right wing. There was no return fire. Refusing to let the stricken aircraft go, Ken and O'Brian then directed their bullets onto the Junker's port rear quarter. It was engulfed by cloud and disappeared from sight.

Ken circled, trying to find the Ju88, but 'my engine was becoming hot' so he landed at Yatesbury aerodrome, about 75 miles from Warmwell, where he discovered that UM-J had taken

'V! *Shot it down.*' Ken Holland's diary account of his first victory, 17 September 1940. Courtesy of Sir William Ripley Bt

'bullets through glycol header, oil pipe, starboard wheel bay and tyre'. Yatesbury were 'v. kind to one and lent me a Magister – flew back to Warmwell' while the ground crew worked on Ken's Spitfire. He was in the air again later that afternoon – 'another flap Bournemouth 15 000 [feet]' – but 'saw nothing'.

All in all, Ken thought it was 'quite a good day', but the 'V!' that topped his diary page and the double underlining of *'shot it down'* belied the inherent modesty of those words. One month after arriving at Warmwell, he was credited with a one-third share of the Ju88.

The weather on 18 September still did not favour enemy action in the southwest; it was wet and windy at Warmwell, 'a v. quiet day'. With no impending action, Ken and Boy Marrs piled into Peter O'Brian's car to navigate the 2-hour journey to Warminster, Wiltshire, where 'our Ju88' had crashed. They planned to collect a few souvenirs but were disappointed to discover someone had already 'pinched things – almost everything from it'. There was a crowd surrounding the machine, which had been roped off in an attempt to keep the sightseers and souvenir hunters at bay. Ken, Marrs and O'Brian, however, were allowed to climb over the Ju88 to see where their bullets had struck. They noticed that, despite their repeated attacks, it was in surprisingly good condition. It hadn't been totally stripped, and Ken and his friends claimed an 'altimeter and petrol tank dip stick – good condition' as well as the pilot's seat.

Claiming souvenirs was not the only thing on Ken's mind as he studied the Junkers. He wanted to increase his score in future conflicts and maximise his chance of survival, so he paid careful attention to where their bullets had gone. They had penetrated the radiator, and Ken particularly noted that there were four bullet marks on the back of the pilot's armour-plated seat. It didn't take long to twig that the German had been saved because of it, so Ken concluded that next time, the way to bring down a Ju88 was 'to shoot rear gunners and then engines'.

Ken was back in action on 19 September – the day Pat Hughes would have turned 23 – when there was another 'flap after lunch'. This time, in UM-C, Ken was Green Two; Pilot Officer William Dudley Williams (known as Dudley) was Green Leader. Ken could hear the controller, but there was limited contact with Williams, so 'I took over lead as Green One'. Ken was ordered to '15 000 feet over Warmwell and was then vectored to Ju88'. There was thick cloud at 10 000 feet, so Williams flew below and Ken climbed to 11 500 feet. 'When cloud broke' he went 'to given height and sighted Ju88 ahead on the right 2 miles away'. Hoping that Williams's radio telephone was working again, Ken tried to alert him that the Junkers was in his sights. When he could not raise Williams he assumed his companion had been 'left behind below [the] cloud' and 'could not find me'. Williams, however, had returned to Warmwell as soon as they had lost each other. Ken was on his own.

Putting into practice the tactic he had determined upon the day before, he 'made alternate quarter attacks from left and right from 300 to 200 yards aiming first at the gunners' positions and then at each engine'. He saw 'smoke from both engines' and 'kept popping away'. The rear gunner did not 'return fire after my second attack'. Even so, Ken continued to blast at the Ju88, which 'dived vertically towards the sea with both engines on fire'. Ken was ultimately credited with this victory, but he was not initially certain of it and noted it in his diary as 'V!?'

Ammunition spent, he 'flew on a northerly course, and came to the Isle of Wight. My engine was missing slightly so I made for Portsmouth aerodrome, where I landed and after checking engine returned to base'. What he did not include in his combat report – and why would he? – was that before he finished checking the engine he met up with 'the old gang' at Airspeed. When his Spitfire was declared all sound – only 'one bullet through each leading edge [of the] wings' – he 'ran up engine, cleared out' and, in a final farewell, 'shot up the works'.

'A small, fair chap with a tiny moustache'

In Adelaide, Bill Millington's family had opened their local paper on 11 September and read about their only son's activities, which were touted as showing 'something of the spirit of the RAF'. The *Advertiser* had reprinted Bill's letter of 8 July in which he enthusiastically told of his earliest battles against the enemy, claiming,

'Slapping [Jerry's] ears back gives us the greatest of pleasure'. In the scouting news of the same edition, 'Scouter' noted that Bill had had his 'share of excitement in England serving with the RAF' and that 'all who knew him feel proud of his wonderful efforts, but regretted to learn that he is in hospital. We trust that he will soon be well again and back to his old form'. And indeed he was. A fully recovered Bill Millington rejoined 79 Squadron, which had recently retired to RAF Pembrey, in Wales, to rest and rebuild, on the same day he appeared in his home town press. They had lost one pilot killed and seven wounded, including Bill, and they had only a few serviceable Hurricanes left.[20] The squadron needed to recover, and Pembrey was quiet enough to get back on form.

The squadron carried out various patrols but saw no action, and on 19 September, Bill was posted to 249 Squadron at North Weald. He was a replacement pilot in a squadron that had experienced hard fighting since transferring from Boscombe Down, in Wiltshire, on 1 September to relieve 56 Squadron; it had been in action almost every day since. Notwithstanding the losses of men and machines, morale was high. New aircraft and pilots began to arrive, including Bill's fellow patient Pyers Worrall and their popular commanding officer Squadron Leader John Grandy, who, after baling out wounded on the 6th, had just returned from hospital. In addition, they enjoyed inspirational leadership from the North Weald station commander, Victor Beamish, Pat Hughes's former commanding officer at 64 Squadron, who had been promoted to wing commander in April 1940. Three days before Bill arrived, the Air Ministry had sent a signal congratulating the squadron on its 'magnificent fighting' of 15 September.[21]

Pilot Officer Thomas Francis Neil (who was known as both Tom and Ginger) recalled of that period that 'we were engaging the enemy up to four times each day … pilots arrived and left almost unnoticed. If new boys were considered experienced they were put on the state and required to muck in immediately without our paying very much attention to them'. Initially, Bill 'was one such replacement' – just 'another youthful fellow ... who had already seen combat'. Neil remembered him as 'a small, fair chap with a tiny moustache. An Australian, apparently, though he did not look or sound like one'. Bill's reputation had preceded him. He was 'pretty experienced, too'.

With his own successes, Bill would be an asset to the battle-hardened squadron. On top of that, the affable young man was readily accepted by his new comrades in the easy-going way of men who might lose a new acquaintance at any time. To Tom Neil, he 'seemed very nice'. Although Bill 'slept more or less close to me in the dispersal hut and sometimes sat next to me at meals in the officers' mess we were never especially chummy nor intimate, although we grew to be more friendly as the days went by'. Neil remembered that Bill 'was always keen to fly with me and would volunteer to do so, if given the choice'.[22]

Tich Palliser, who had arrived on 14 September, was also aware of Bill's impressive record. Palliser had come to 249 via a brief stint in 43 Squadron. There, he had been one of the butts of Dick Reynell's and Caesar Hull's shared jokes. Palliser, who was 21, looked much younger. Reynell, looking all of his 28 years, had asked him if he were only 14. Hull had taken up the joke and asked if they were being sent kids to fill the ranks. Palliser found Bill a 'damn nice lad', one of the few 'who had time for officers and NCOs'. Certainly, he was more congenial than the officers in his former squadron. The two clicked, and Palliser soon counted Bill as 'a real friend'. One of their main conversation topics – as it had been when Palliser met Ken Holland at 11 Elementary Flying Training School – was Australia.[23]

Bill was slotted into B Flight. He flew a number of patrols during his first week, but a glimpse of a vapour trail over the Thames Estuary on 24 September was the closest he came to the enemy. The major excitement was the announcement on the 25th of DFCs for Tom Neil and Pilot Officer James Bryan Meaker. Although Bill's DFC would not be gazetted until 1 October, his new friends were aware of it. 'Actually we have two other DFCs in the squadron', noted George Barclay, 'but they are replacements – Pilot Officer Millington and Pilot Officer Lewis – the former Australian, the latter South African'.[24]

'I get a very satisfied feeling'

Within days of his first combat, John Crossman was able to assure his parents that 'this air fighting is not very worrying except for the first time and one gets used to it and regards it as more or less just doing a job of work'. But John's fear was still there; he just became more adept at managing it. He diligently carried out exercises to improve his flying skills, and on sorties he scouted about for the enemy and 'went off the deep end … when he missed one'.[25]

Wartime psychological studies revealed that loss of confidence in an aircraft was a key contributor to flying stress, and some airmen were 'faddy' about their machines; if anything went wrong they became depressed and anxious.[26] Whether or not he recognised this himself, John exerted as much control over the condition of his Hurricane as he could. When V7442 was written off, on 18 September, he claimed another machine and 'had my mechanics working on my new kite all day and generally getting things ship-shape'.

After his first flight in V6748, he declared, 'It handles very well', but he then 'spent an hour checking the harmonising of the guns and sights. The sight was out and also two of the guns. The other six were OK'. It seems that his dedication was too much. 'I spend most of my spare time on my aeroplane', he told his parents. 'I absolutely mother and keep it in tip top condition.' Perhaps he realised he was obsessive, as he admitted that 'my mechanics are just beginning to get used to my ways and are keeping things clean now without being told'. But as far as he was concerned his fastidiousness was 'well worth it because now I know that everything is at its best and I can't have things better … with the result that when I go into combat I have ever so much more confidence'.[27]

Bad weather over the next few days resulted in little aerial activity for 46 Squadron. Even so, John was rostered on and still had to hang around dispersal just in case the Luftwaffe put in an appearance. Instead of waiting with his new friends, who were 'very decent and we all get on very well', John sat in the auto and caught up with his letter writing, including one to his parents in which he filled them in on his recent change of squadrons and flying activities. Much of the letter was a big whinge about conditions at Stapleford Tawney, which he considered 'an awful place'. If it weren't that 'the fellows in the squadron are so decent life would be very lousy'. Quarters were cramped. There were five men crowded into a sparsely furnished room. 'Nothing on the floors, nothing to put our clothes in or hang them from, no bathroom and no hot water laid on.' It was a far cry from the comfortable accommodation at Cambridge. 'Every five days I drive 6 miles into Epping … to have a bath at an hotel there.' On top of that, 'we are quite close to London here, so consequently the night is generally made noisy by the bombs Jerry drops and of course by our own anti-aircraft guns which are generally very active'. Despite the discomfort, John was perhaps the happiest he had ever been. 'I hope I will never have to leave the RAF. There's something about the service that gets into one's blood and these days I get a very satisfied feeling.'[28]

'High spirits'

After Ken Holland's show on 19 September, there was little aerial activity of any consequence for the Warmwell squadrons. The lull was appreciated. Boy Marrs, for instance, told his father that 'the weather has broken at last, for which I am thankful, and I expect many others are too'. Welcome as it was, the boys appear to have made their own fun. Marrs beat up the dispersal hut on the 19th after returning from a patrol in which he had chased a Ju88 for 10 miles out to sea and fired until he thought he put the rear gunner out of action. He knew it was 'strictly verboten' but he was in such 'high spirits'. He was made duty pilot and had to carry out routine administrative tasks for four days, but that punishment did not deter Ken Holland, who displayed his own share of high spirits two days later during 'a flap as Blue Two with Flight Lieutenant Thomas', in which he put up a number of 'blacks'. He flew badly then carried out a 'blitz dive' and lost UM-N's knockout patch – an oval of Perspex covering an opening in the cockpit hood which could be knocked out if the plane was hit and the pilot needed to bale out – and, if that wasn't bad enough, without a hint of enemy aircraft in the general area he fired ten rounds from each gun. He was 'ticked off' when he returned, but that didn't dampen his boyish joie de vivre. As soon as he was released, he was 'into Weymouth – saw K. and had a dance at the Regent and some drinks', turning in at the relatively early time (for Ken) of 11.30 p.m.[29]

16

25–30 September

'Nothing could be done for him'

A large formation appeared to be on course for Portland during the morning of 25 September. It was later recognised as the first occasion when the Luftwaffe sent a major force so far inland, except for attacks against southeast targets. 609 Squadron was sent to Portland, and 152 Squadron was directed to intercept the enemy aircraft flying over the aerodrome. (Red Section was already in the air and too far away to join up with the other sections.)

With little time between detection and scramble, 152 could not intercept, and such had been the mad dash to their Spitfires that they weren't able to form up. Yellow Section, under the leadership of Graham Cox, joined White Section and chased the enemy. There had been little flying for Ken Holland since his ticking off, but now he joined his fellows as Blue Two, flying Spitfire N3173. He followed closely on the tail of Blue Leader, Squadron Leader Peter Devitt. They were joined by Green Section. Black One and Two, pilot officers Ian Bayles and Boy Marrs, took off last and chased after Green Section. Red Section never caught up.[1]

The intruders powered on. One section speared off to bomb Portland, but the rest continued towards Yeovil, in Somerset, about 27 miles from Warmwell. Devitt thought they were probably targeting Bristol and led Blue and Green sections in that direction, but control advised that 'many bandits' were 15 miles north of Yeovil so he changed course. Three Hurricanes from 601 at Exeter and 238 Squadron had already been deployed towards Yeovil, along with 609 Squadron, which was diverted from its original vector when the controller determined that the enemy aircraft were making for the Westland Aircraft factory. But the controller was wrong again. The force was actually on its way to the Bristol Aeroplane works. As there were no fighter squadrons based nearby, the bombers had a clear run, and three of the four defending squadrons, including the scattered units of 152, had a 'stern chase'.[2]

Squadron Leader Devitt, who had seen over 100 bombers escorted by a sweep of 50 fighters over Bath, homed in on a vic of three Ju88s. He ordered a number one attack, but Green One, Dudley Williams, climbed towards another three Junkers that Devitt had not seen and struck almost at the same time as Devitt saw his incendiary hit the nose of his vic's centre Ju88. Williams mixed it up with his Ju88s, and Devitt fired from about 20 yards behind the machine on the left of the trio but did not see the results as he was hit in the petrol tank. He was blinded by petrol spraying into his eyes and had to retire.

Meanwhile, Black Section had caught up. As Devitt tried to find a place to force-land, Bayles and Marrs 'went head-on straight for the middle of the foremost group of bombers. Firing as we went we cut through the heart of them like a knife through cheese; but they would not break. They were good, those Jerry bombers, they stuck like glue', noted Marrs, who then ran into some Me110s and directed his attention towards them. Bayles thought one of the Ju88s had been 'destroyed by my fire'. He then saw an He111 'going down towards the clouds. I attacked from above and astern. There were also two Hurricanes and another Spitfire attacking'. The Hurricanes were those of 238 Squadron's

Ronald Little and Jackie Urwin-Mann, who had both flown with Stuart Walch's B Flight. Little gave the diving Heinkel a short burst at a range of 100 yards. He broke away, fired again and watched as black objects were blasted off the Heinkel's port engine. As the Heinkel dived, the Spitfire circled once then fired from about 400 yards. This was Ken Holland, who, after Devitt's exit from battle, had rushed up to the Heinkel.

Ken turned and fired off a second burst. He circled again; from the ground, he appeared to be executing a victory roll. As the Heinkel plunged towards Woolverton, a village about 4 miles north of Frome, in Somerset, three men baled out. Only one parachute correctly deployed.[3]

The Australian positioned himself on the Heinkel's tail, perhaps to have another shot at an obvious lame duck or perhaps to follow it down. Whatever his intention, it was a mistake, as both gunners were still on board and one continued to fire, even as the Heinkel hurtled downward. Ken was too close; he copped a burst at short range. Spitfire N3173 dropped its nose and ploughed into the ground.[4]

To Gladys Matthews of Church Farm, who witnessed Ken's apparent victory roll, it seemed as if the Heinkel 'was heading straight for the village, but all of a sudden it veered away and crashed in one of our fields'. She also saw the Spitfire fall, 'no more than a couple of hundred yards' away. It 'broke its back as it crashed'. It had all happened so quickly; Ian Bayles had not even left the scene after breaking off his attack when he saw Ken crash. Gladys told her gardener to go and see if he could help the Spitfire pilot, but 'nothing could be done for him – he had been shot right through the head'.[5]

Vibrant, happy-go-lucky Ken Holland, who lived life to the full with a girlfriend and fiancée, was dead. He was the tenth Australian to die in the Battle of Britain and, at only 20 years of age, the youngest. Since his first combat, ten days earlier, he had made a conscious effort to improve his fighting technique. But during this last action he had forgotten the fundamentals taught by Battle of France veterans at Aston Down. He had even forgotten the lesson he had learned a few days earlier: rear gunner first then engine. He had also ignored Air Vice-Marshal Keith Park's direction to leave the lame ducks alone. Forgetting any of these lessons could result in death. The irony was that nothing other than his first burst had been needed. It was discovered later from the Heinkel's pilot, Hauptmann Helmut Brandt, that 'Sergeant Holland's first burst had, in point of fact, been sufficient to put his machine completely out of action'. And if not Ken's, then perhaps Bayles's, Urwin-Mann's or Little's. Small consolation, but Ken was credited with bringing down Brandt's Heinkel. As were Bayles, Urwin-Mann and Little. It was another instance of over-claiming.[6]

The telegrams announcing Ken's death were dispatched, but Seina Haydon, Ken's recently neglected fiancée, found out in a much more bizarre way. Her mother was lunching at Garmoe House with Mrs Thomas, the mother of air gunner Sergeant David Thomas, who had gone missing with Ian Haydon on 4 June. Mrs Thomas was a psychic. As they were eating, she 'described Ken quite clearly to Mum and asked if it was a correct description of him … Mum said yes it was. So she said well, I think he has been killed because I have just seen him with my son, and your son and others'.[7]

Seina and her mother went to Warmwell for Ken's funeral, 'which was held with full military honours'. Seina may have agreed to marry him only because it was the 'right thing to do', but, nevertheless, she grieved for the faithless Ken. Toby Ripley was 'devastated by Kenneth's death'. He rushed to Warmwell to attend the funeral then arranged for his ward's body to be taken to Weymouth Crematorium on 2 October. He removed the cremated remains 'for future disposal' but did not scatter or inter them at Camelford. According to his great nephew, Toby's neighbours remembered him cradling a jar with ashes in it and weeping.[8]

Less than nine months earlier, the golden-haired boy from Bondi had written of his hopes for the future, but he was denied the fulfilment of his dearest dreams through boyish foolishness and a solitary bullet.

'I only got one burst in'

Towards the end of September, the Luftwaffe again changed their offensive strategy. As a consequence of bomber crews complaining of limited fighter protection and a realisation that the results from massed bombing raids did not justify the losses, it was decided to deploy small forces of 30 or so Ju88s accompanied by 200 to 300 fighters. The Me109F variant, with its higher ceiling, was introduced to some units. The increased altitude at which the enemy escorts could operate made it difficult for Fighter Command to detect formation size and to differentiate between fighter sweeps – which they were to avoid – and bombing raids. Accordingly, Keith Park was obliged to revert to his former practice of maintaining standing patrols. (These had been abandoned some weeks earlier because of the inherent wastefulness of keeping aircraft in the air on the off-chance the enemy would turn up. In the days when there was plenty of radar or observer corps warning of Luftwaffe encroachment, it was more efficient to order squadrons up when raids were imminent.)[9]

The more intense state of readiness was a waste of defensive resources and tiring to pilots. Park appreciated that some of his airmen weren't fit enough to fly long sorties in uncomfortable conditions. For example, despite the mild autumn weather on the ground, patrolling pilots were feeling the cold. John Crossman complained that his 'hands were frozen stiff' at 25 000 feet, and 'as we do most of our patrols in the vicinity of 20 000 feet we aren't generally too warm'. To help reduce the tension of the constant state of alert, Park made a point of ensuring pilots were released from stations whenever bad weather precluded flying. For those in the London area, he arranged for off-station billets so they could get an undisturbed sleep.[10]

John was one who benefited from the new arrangements. He and Pat Pattullo left North Weald when they could and on one occasion met up with 18-year-old Jacqueline Bush, who lived in Romford, about 6 miles from Stapleford Tawney. Jackie was a happy, uncomplicated young woman with a great sense of fun. She was not interested in romantic attachment and offered the young pilots friendship, laughter and a chance to forget the worries of war. For John, she replaced Dorothy Foley as an on-the-spot confidante.

The trio sped about in John's auto, which, Jackie recalled, was so old it was a rattling, almost ancient relic. Jackie felt 'proud as a peacock' sitting between her handsome escorts as they all squashed together in the front seat. They cracked jokes, told stories and did 'the maddest things' to forget the serious business of war. 'What fun we had', she recalled. 'We used to tear around and just shriek at the most idiotic things – just like three kids.'[11]

On 24 September, the squadron accepted an invitation to an off-station party. Fifteen or so officers went and, according to John, enjoyed the 'whisky and gin flowing freely'. One of their complement imbibed a little too heavily and was 'drunk and very funny'. After they returned to the mess, the light-hearted mood continued with 'boys squirting fire extinguishers around'. The merriment was interrupted when 'Jerry dropped a land mine at random and it fell in middle of aerodrome. Helluva row. Shook the place and broke a few windows in the mess'. Park's instructions were implemented the next day, and they were billeted out. 'I share a room at Thrift Hall with Pat. Very comfortable room.

Quite a change from the aerodrome', John wrote. On top of the improved accommodation, he had '24 hours leave from 1300 hours tomorrow. Will try to borrow a Maggie and fly up to see Granny Mary [Parkes]'.

Not all of Keith Park's new arrangements were as well received. 46 and 249 squadrons had difficulty settling into the new wing patrols. After a morning sortie on 25 September during which they 'chased round the sky' they 'saw no Jerries and came home'. John confided his annoyance to his diary: 'We are generally led by 249 Squadron from North Weald and they always seem to lead us away from any fights that there are. Our chaps think they must be yellow'. His scathing criticism was unwarranted – especially in light of 249's recent notification of a clutch of DFCs and congratulations from headquarters – and it appeared to be one sided. After one joint action, the 249 Squadron diarist applauded 46's 'very successful attack' and recorded that 'it is very much doubted whether any of [the enemy] returned at all'. John had high standards and expected others to live up to them, but it is possible his strong attitude towards his wing companions reflected his dissatisfaction at having few chances at combat.[12]

When he returned from leave on 27 September, 46 Squadron had twice been in the air with 249. Flying V6748, John joined his comrades at 2.50 p.m. on a Hornchurch patrol at 20 000 feet. Forty minutes later, the wing caught sight of 12 or 15 Ju88s flying above the Thames Estuary towards London with a large escort of Me109s. 249 led the joint attack. A 'general mêlée' resulted, followed by a running fight out to sea. A number of bombers fell within minutes, 'as they were being continuously attacked by Hurricanes', and there were only seven or eight remaining when Bill Millington, who was flying Hurricane V6614, climbed 1000 feet above them 'and made a steep dive quarter attack on the rear enemy aircraft'. His bullets found their target. His Junkers 'left formation smoking and [he] delivered a quarter attack opening fire at 100 yards, closing'. The Ju88's port engine 'exploded and enemy aircraft dived down steeply to ground in flames'. Bill glanced down and saw 'three fighters, some thousands of feet below', following the Junkers.[13]

Bill then joined Tom Neil and lined up 'the remaining Ju88 at about 4000 feet which had been attacked by numbers of our fighters'. It was 'still maintaining height and flying steadily over the coast' and could not be considered a lame duck. Accordingly, Bill 'delivered a quarter attack, opening fire from 100 yards closing and the starboard motor of enemy aircraft burst into flames'. The Junkers then 'dived steeply over the coast losing height rapidly and Pilot Officer Neil finished it off with a burst from close range'. With their ammunition expended, Bill and Neil shepherded the Junkers out to sea. It plunged into the water. They circled as a small dinghy inflated, but it and the occupants vanished within minutes. Bill realised that none of the intruders had reached the French coast.[14]

The Australian was elated. He had opened his account with his new squadron and was attributed with destroying one and a half Junkers. Later, Bill and Neil relived their joint attack 'with some glee', and Neil remembered fondly that the Australian 'appeared to enjoy flying as my partner on that and other occasions, and often told me so'.[15]

Bill's squadron claimed seven and a half Ju88s and four Me109s destroyed and one Do215 damaged, which contributed to the day's tally of 21 destroyed, six probables and three damaged. Giving fair credit for 46 Squadron's part in the battle, the squadron diarist acknowledged that their confreres from Stapleford Tawney had accounted for six destroyed, four probable and one damaged.[16] Even with the loss of 'two of our most gallant comrades' – Pilot Officer Percy Burton had been killed earlier that day, and Bryan Meaker's aircraft had been shot up in heavy crossfire during the most recent encounter – 249's diarist considered that 'today was a glorious day in the history of the squadron'.

John Crossman was again critical of 249's conduct. 'Intercepted bombers and would have got them all ourselves if 249 hadn't led us away from them. I only got one burst in.' Pat Pattullo, however, had been able to get close to the enemy. He had opened fire on a Ju88. The port engine blew up, but before he confirmed the bomber's destruction, he 'got an explosive bullet in his cockpit – just missed his head. Hit armour plate, peppered his face with pieces [of splintered glass] and he was lucky it all missed his eyes'.[17] Pat had force-landed, and although he was not seriously injured John was so shaken he annotated his flying log – usually reserved for brief comments about a pilot's own flights – 'Pat's kite shot up. Pat slightly wounded in face'.

After he was released from duty, John phoned Jackie Bush. He 'seemed to crumple up that day – he was so upset'. She didn't know what to say, other than to reassure him again and again that Pat was 'going to be all right'.[18] John had not told Jackie of his close friendship with Jack Burraston, who had died less than three months earlier, or of how deeply he had grieved. Pat was the first friend John had grown close to since losing Burry. He was rattled. Jackie could not soothe him.

Pat was taken off operational flying duties until he recovered, and John was in the air on the 28th as 46 and 249 squadrons again participated in wing patrols. John flew two, and enemy aircraft were seen on both. On the way home from his second sortie, two Me109s caught the wing by surprise. They then 'dived into clouds so we weren't able to get them. Had they not attacked from out of the sun we should have seen them'. John later noted that Pilot Officer Albert Lewis of 249 Squadron, who had been 'occupying the position in rear of squadron that I usually have', was shot down. 'Glad we were leading.' With Pat's ill-fated encounter still in mind, John realised he had had a fortunate escape.[19] In

addition, two valuable lessons from his training days were reinforced: beware of the Hun in the sun, and the tail-end Charlie is
always vulnerable.

'I have contracted a lousy cold'

John was still unsettled. What with his own near escape and his
worry over Pat Pattullo's battle injuries, he wanted to forget it all
and have a light-hearted evening. As it was Saturday, he phoned
Jackie Bush and they arranged to go to a dance at Romford. He
picked her up at her mother's house with the auto, true to form,
shuddering 'like fury' and making a 'hideous sound at the trifle
acceleration'. Jackie remembered the 'marvellous night, the sky
was simply covered with stars and we both felt very gay'.[20] After
the dance, they 'called in at two little country pubs, but the close
smoky atmosphere was too much for us, so we decided to go miles
out into the country (it was as clear as day) and walk, talk, run, or
anything that we fancied'.

They stopped a short distance from John's aerodrome and
each lit a cigarette. 'I can remember how annoyed he was because
all he could get were Player's mild. He was so indignant that I
had to laugh at him, my laughing made him laugh, so for a few
moments we both laughed at nothing.' The carefree moment
ceased when the sirens wailed. Enemy aircraft were soon overhead and the ack-ack guns 'were making the dickens of a row'.
John was angry. He told Jackie 'how he wished he could get up at
them'. Then, 'a bomb dropped very close, and he grabbed me and
thrust me down on the floor of the car'. They huddled there for a
few minutes until 'all was quiet but we could see the sky [alight]
with flashes of red and yellow'. They could still hear 'the thud and
rumble of distant bombs and guns' so decided not to go for a walk
but just sit in the auto.

The mood had soured. John's thoughts turned to Pat Pattullo

and his injuries. He couldn't shake the idea that neither he nor Pat would survive. He repeated his fears while Jackie tried to argue him out of them. She couldn't sway him; he was convinced he would not return to Australia and that Pat would die in battle as well.

Jackie calmed John down and they pushed back the seats and opened the sun roof. The moon was up and they were washed by moonlight. A bird twittered nearby. John listened. He remembered his father telling him about the beauty of the English birds, but he hadn't seen any yet. Jackie told him she would take him to find some. John then settled into reminiscence. He pulled from his wallet the photos of his mother and sister. The mood lightened again as he laughed at Jackie's large handbag, saying his mother had one just the same 'and he really couldn't imagine what we carried in them'.

They fell into silence. 'I can see now his hand, he had rather nice hands, with its gold watch with the luminous dial which showed the hands creeping yet flying round from 11 to 12 to one. It was such a beautiful night. We simply couldn't bring ourselves to go home.' But they had to.

'With much coaxing and loud spluttering' of the auto they were on their way. They stopped at an all-night cafe. As they munched on hot hamburgers and sipped coffee, they talked about Hedy Lamarr, a marvellous film star, in John's opinion. He joked that, as she was getting a divorce, perhaps she would have him! Happy and relaxed again, they made plans to hunt out some songbirds on the 30th, after John returned from a reunion at Digby with 'the few remaining Australian crowd' – he had a 24-hour pass. 'I can still see him standing there in the moonlight' just before he climbed into the auto, Jackie recalled. 'Smiling and looking really happy.'

John's light-heartedness did not last. His leave was cancelled, so the reunion was off. It was a 'very quiet day' on the 29th with little flying on offer – just a short patrol with 249 Squadron. 'Went up and saw nothing.' Although John voiced no more concerns about his wing partners on this occasion, he was no longer alone in his dissatisfaction with the joint patrols. That day's joint outing had failed, according to the 249 Squadron diarist, because of 'bad liaison between the two squadrons'.[21] John had been quick to blame the North Weald boys for leading them away from the enemy, but, as Tom Neil put it, 'there was a marked lack of flexibility and cohesion in our combined effort, more time being spent avoiding collisions than searching for the Hun'.[22] George Barclay blamed 46 Squadron for taking no avoidance action whatsoever. He believed their most recent outing had gone 'all haywire and we were really inviting the Me109s to take their pickings all the time'.[23] The situation could not continue. 249 Squadron invited 46's pilots to their mess for a conference to discuss general tactics. 'Not before time', some of them thought.

The two squadrons met after dinner. Given the strong feelings about the relative inadequacies of their cohorts, there seemed no general rancour, as 249 Squadron found their visitors 'a good crowd, though in a strange way quite unlike 249'. Did John Crossman meet Bill Millington in the North Weald mess? He didn't mention it in his diary. But how could he not have met and chatted to the gregarious young man from Adelaide, a fellow Australian with a shared passion for aviation photography and flying?

The pilots thrashed out a plan of action. According to Tom Neil, Wing Commander Victor Beamish 'had a fixation about "snakes"' and urged the 12 aircraft in each squadron to maintain a line astern formation, even on patrol. 'Dearly though I loved and admired the man,' Neil later wrote, 'on this particular issue I always felt that he was talking nonsense'. In the end, Beamish's 'snake' plan was adopted in a modified form in which one squadron would fly in section vics in line astern formation, while the other flew above, in two flights of six, weaving about to protect the

SEPTEMBER, 1940.

19th after Trinity. **Sunday 29**

Went to a dance in Romford six miles away last night. Left there at 11.30 and coming back took wrong turn and must have done a round tour of Essex. Finally got back here at 02.45 this morning. Very quiet day – went up once – saw nothing. I have contracted a lousy cold – damn nuisance.

'I have contracted a lousy cold – damn nuisance.' John Crossman's last diary entry, 29 September 1940. Courtesy of the Bowden family

lower squadron, with the last aircraft in each six weaving to protect his fellows. When the enemy was sighted, the lower squadron was to adopt a defensive snake in close line astern, and start weaving as well.[24] They agreed to try it out on their next patrol, with 46 Squadron taking the higher position.

Barclay thought, 'We'll have to see how the things agreed upon work out in practice'.[25] Neil, however, 'had visions of those at the rear of each line of six blessing the arrangement through very tight lips'. He realised they would be focused on maintaining their 'station-keeping' position and not able to keep an eye out to protect themselves. On top of that, they would use more fuel and power than even the formation leaders. It was an invidious position. Regular weaver John Crossman made no comment on the new tactics. He was tired and out of sorts. 'I have contracted a lousy cold – damn nuisance.'[26] After making a brief entry in his diary he put the ribbon marker in the next day's page and turned in.

'Stupendous courage'

The last day of the month dawned fine with only a little light cloud, and the Luftwaffe took advantage of it by launching a raft of attacks which kept Fighter Command busy. It would prove to be their heaviest operational day that month.

It was an all hands on deck – or at least at dispersal – sort of day, with 46 Squadron flying three patrols and their North Weald partners mounting four. There was no leeway for anyone not seriously injured to clutter up the sick quarters. John Crossman's cold was running its course, but even if he were the type to present himself to the medical officer – he had, after all, failed to declare a bout of influenza to his RAAF recruitment board – he would not have been spared from duty.

There are myriad physiological and psychological aspects associated with flying and combat. Pat Hughes had experienced a range of them, and John had more than once succumbed to gravitational forces. Combat or even just routine patrols at high altitude also impacted on the pilot's body. Oxygen deprivation – hypoxia – for instance, can result in light-headedness, confusion, euphoria or even hallucinations. But fighter aircraft were fitted with oxygen cylinders and pilots wore oxygen masks, so hypoxia was less of an issue under normal circumstances. Another altitude problem, which was less easy to remedy, relates to the ability of the middle ear to adapt to changes in pressure. Located on either side of the throat, the Eustachian, or auditory, tubes have the job of equalising atmospheric pressure. When a pilot rapidly ascends or descends, he has to help out by ensuring the tubes are kept clear, by talking, swallowing, yawning, chewing or blowing outwardly with mouth closed and nostrils pinched. If the Eustachian tubes are obstructed, which can occur during a common cold, middle ear pressure can't be equalised, and pilots may experience a number of effects ranging from temporary hearing loss, dizziness and ringing in the ears to unbearable pain and ruptured ear drums. Few at the time gave much thought to a cold other than the inconvenience of it, even though combat performance would be impeded.[27] And so, with a stuffy head, mucus-filled nose and potentially blocked ears, and probably still worried about Pat Pattullo, John joined his friends at dispersal.

Just before 9 a.m., a couple of enemy formations were detected a few miles east of Dungeness. They crossed the coast 5 minutes later and made their way towards Biggin Hill, just as 46 and 249 squadrons rendezvoused above Stapleford Tawney to patrol the Hornchurch line, south of the Thames Estuary, at 20 000 feet, and to carry out for the first time their newly agreed formation tactics. John saw 'a large formation [of] Me109s' pass by, but 'we did not attack – were looking for bombers'. The Messerschmitts were flying too high to engage, anyway; the 109Fs easily out-climbed the Hurricane I. The Hurricane II had been promised, and although the pilots were keen to fly the improved version, 46 Squadron never received it, and 249 had to wait until February 1941.[28]

After recording the 70-minute patrol in his log and totting up his solo flying hours – the grand total since his first 10-minute solo on 20 November 1939 was now 186 hours – John phoned Jackie Bush and confirmed their meeting that night.[29] If he could ignore his cold to fly, he wasn't going to give up an evening with someone who made him laugh so much he could forget his cares.

It wasn't long before the Luftwaffe put in another appearance, and the Biggin Hill and Hornchurch squadrons were in the air at 1 p.m. Five minutes after 150 enemy aircraft crossed the coast on a 20-mile front ranging from Rye, in east Sussex, to Folkestone, on Kent's coast, en route to London, the North Weald squadrons were vectored to the Hornchurch line. It was John's 19th operational sortie, and he was again flying Hurricane V6748. With 46 Squadron weaving above at 15 000 feet, 249 Squadron led the way.[30]

Fifteen thousand feet became 20 000. They were shadowed by Me109s. George Barclay, who estimated hundreds of the intruders, considered it 'an awful trip as we were quite helpless, just waiting to be attacked'. The enemy bombers slipped by to drop their loads on London. The pilots didn't even glimpse them, so intent were they on watching for the 109s, with 46 Squadron's weavers taking the main responsibility for keeping their eyes open. Then, with little warning and obscured by cloud, the Messerschmitts pounced. 'Probably our snake saved us', Barclay later recorded, but the weavers were vulnerable.[31]

John Crossman's Hurricane was jumped. Witnesses claimed he engaged 20 fighters, exhibiting 'stupendous courage' as he did so. He flew in and out of the clouds, ducking and weaving, to elude his attackers, turning, then sheering away to create an advantage. Those on the ground watched as he manoeuvred onto the tail of one of the Messerschmitts. He fired, 'shooting down one which fell over the [Ashdown] Forest'. But he in turn became the victim of the stricken Me109.

V6748 plummeted. Eye-witnesses considered that John 'must have been killed as the machine came down in "full throttle"'. Tom Neil saw a 'flurry of activity against the blue followed by a thin trail of smoke as an aircraft curved away downward to its death'. Then he saw a parachute. 'Whose? No one knew. Not one of ours, we hoped.' Barclay also saw 'a parachute above us, possibly a Jerry' and 'a Hurricane going down in flames'.[32]

It was all over in less than 40 seconds. Six months earlier, John had confided to his diary, 'When I go out I pray God it will be in the air'. With a quick bullet in combat, he had been granted his wish. And he had perhaps been granted another. He had mused during training that it would be a pleasure to be killed 'if I only get two – one to equal me and one to justify myself'.[33] But if, as witnesses attested, the Australian had shot down the Messerschmitt that claimed his life, he was not credited with it in 46 Squadron's operations record book or by post-war researchers.

Shortly after 1.30 p.m., young Peter Wheeler, who had been playing with his brother, Richard, in the garden of their mother's cottage while John's final dogfight roiled above, saw a Hurricane emerge from the clouds and plunge to the ground in 'an almighty wallop'. V6748 had crashed in a field at Tablehurst Farm near Forest Row, in East Sussex, about 60 miles from Stapleford Tawney. Peter's mother, Dorothy, who had been chatting with a neighbour, watched the Hurricane explode then burst into flames. Wreckage scattered across a wide area, and the engine was deeply buried. Locals came running from all directions to help but were held back from the burning machine by exploding ammunition. Even so, Dorothy's brother, Raymond Brown, identified the aircraft as RAF and was close enough to see the stripes on John's jacket sleeve.[34]

Edmund Wimperis, a gifted architect and son of watercolourist Edmund Morison Wimperis, lived at nearby Holly Cottage. He arrived about half an hour after the crash. He was astonished. He had been sketching that morning, just 20 yards away. It had been quiet, with nothing but rural sounds to intrude, as he drew the autumn scene of mown field, bordering bushes and the brown and green mottled hill in the background. Now, all was a-chatter as the villagers talked about the dogfight above and the pilot's last moments. He was so moved by the accounts of the pilot's bravery that he decided to work up the finished sketches into a watercolour of John's last moments as a tribute. He attempted to return to his earlier sketching spot but was turned away – a guard had been mounted by the remains of the Hurricane to watch for souvenir hunters.[35]

As Wimperis returned to Holly Cottage, William Clark, the village pharmacist, who ran the local first aid and rescue unit, was picking through the debris. He had been about to sit down to his birthday lunch when he was called to the scene. His wife had scrimped her rations for months and he was looking forward to apple dumpling – his favourite. As he rushed off, she put the meal back into the oven to keep warm.

One of Clark's responsibilities was to identify the bodies of dead pilots. This was one of his first call-outs, and he had seen nothing like it before. He was appalled. John's body was strewn over the field, and as he searched for something to identify the dead airman he steeled himself to pick up the young Australian's body parts. It took some time.

Clark's daughter Anne, who had been watching the much-awaited apple dumpling spoil after her mother put it back in the oven, took it out then put it in again, eagerly awaiting his arrival. 'Eventually', she recalled, 'my father returned looking ashen and refusing to eat anything'. He was too shaken.[36]

John's remains were removed, and his squadron received word that he had been killed in action. That evening, Jackie Bush listened for the sound of his auto rattling up the street. 'I waited and waited … I couldn't make it out. He'd never let me down before.' Pat Pattullo, still recovering from his injuries, wrote to her as soon as he heard that his new friend had died. 'Such a sweet letter, breaking the news. I just couldn't believe it. I was so upset, I went nearly frantic.' She contacted the aerodrome to find out more. She asked for John's wallet, which contained the treasured photos of his mother and sister, but was told it had burned. Turning over their last hours together in her mind, recalling their laughter and unful-filled plans to meet, Jackie realised that 'I was possibly the last girl to talk to John. He rang me about an hour before he was killed'.[37]

'Laid at ease as one of us'

When John had first arrived in Britain, his Aunt Ann had told him to provide her details to the RAF. On his last visit, he had said to her, 'Don't worry if you don't hear from me. You would get a telegram if anything were amiss'. But when the wire arrived, they assumed it was from John announcing an imminent visit. Plans to entertain her nephew were already running through Ann's mind as she opened the envelope. And then she read it. 'Request details of funeral arrangements you desire to be made etc.'[38] She could not comprehend it. 'I was struck dumb and numb.' Will Brawn tried to send a response but there was an air raid on. 'Everywhere there was disconnection.' It wasn't until 5.30 a.m. the next day that he succeeded. He sent one telegram, then another. 'No reply. He went everywhere to try and find someone to take him over, but private people had no petrol and garage people not enough for so long a journey (50 miles).'

Will reached Stapleford Tawney on the morning of 3 October and discovered that his telegrams had gone astray. He spoke to the squadron's commanding officer and the adjutant and arranged for John's body to be brought to Chalfont St Giles. He also sent a telegram to Ted and Mick Crossman back in Australia, advising that their son's death had been 'instantaneous'. They received it on 4 October, the day of their son's funeral. John's commanding officer promised to send an officer and six bearers from North Weald for the ceremony. 'Everyone spoke most highly of him', Will told Ann and her sister Mabel when he returned. 'Said he was so keen they could not keep him out of the air and he was popular with everyone.' And yet the squadron

FUNDS MAY BE QUICKLY, SAFELY AND ECONOMICALLY TRANSFERRED BY MONEY ORDER TELEGRAM. (PLEASE TURN OVER.)

COMMONWEALTH OF AUSTRALIA.—POSTMASTER-GENERAL'S DEPARTMENT.

RECEIVED TELEGRAM

The first line of this telegram contains the following particulars in the order named.

Office of Origin. Words. Time Lodged. No.

Remarks. Sch. C.1672.—11/1936.

This message has been received subject to the Post and Telegraph Act and Regulations. The time received at this office is shown at the end of the message. The date stamp indicates the date both of lodgment and of reception unless otherwise shown after the particulars of time lodged.

William Brawn's telegram advising the Crossman family of John's death in action, received 4 October 1940. Courtesy of the Bowden family

diarist did not record the death of their only casualty that day.

John's aunts and Uncle Will 'met him at the Church'. He 'was enclosed in a plain oak coffin with Pilot Officer John Dallas Crossman, Died September 30th, on the plate and a large Union Jack was used as a pall'. They had arranged for him to 'be laid at ease as one of us'. They thought John's parents would prefer him to be 'here than among strangers', next to his Aunt Florence, whose grave he had visited during his Christmas visit. It was a privilege readily accorded, and the rector had waived the usual £50 fee. John's aunts were 'so glad we had that comfort, just to know he is near us'.

'All our little village were shocked' at the loss of someone who was as good as their own, Ann reported afterwards, 'and he is the first soldier of this war to find rest here'. The crowded church was full of autumn flowers. Ann and Mabel had made 'a lovely cross

… of laurel leaves, white chrysanthemums and red carnations' on behalf of John's parents. They also sent one of bronze chrysanthemums, and Ann 'made two beautiful sprays – white and pink Michaelmas daisies from Joan and white and mauve from Pat [Foley] and several of our dear friends sent flowers too'. The floral masses reminded Mabel of the last time she saw John, three weeks earlier. 'I see him through the flowers – and his face all smiles.'

The promised bearers did not arrive. 46 Squadron had carried out a standing patrol over convoy 'Bosom', not returning to base until 12.30 p.m., and the sole representative was Pat Pattullo, his 'face very cut and glass in it still', who brought with him a 'beautiful wreath from the squadron'.

After the service, they invited Pat to a late lunch, and he told them about John and his brief time on the squadron. Despite their nephew's fastidious care with his Hurricane, they discovered that 'he didn't play for safety. He was so keen on his work and a good pilot'. And now, 'the dear lad has flown away and left us so unhappy'.

John Crossman was the 11th Australian to die in the Battle of Britain. He was only 22 years of age. Considered by his mother to be 'more English than the English', John had been 'so proud to be with the RAF', and 'the greatest honour in his life was to be allowed to fight with the English Air Force'. John was loved, and even those who had known him only briefly grieved deeply. 'We loved him so', admitted his Aunt Mabel. 'He was so dear to us.' His parents mourned 'the loss of a beloved only son'. But John had been doing what he had always wanted: 'I don't care about anything so long as I can fly'.

17

1–31 October

'The most difficult to counter'

RAF deaths mounted, including that of 248 Squadron's Clarence Bennett, of Mallala, South Australia, who, along with his crew, failed to return from a photographic reconnaissance operation to the Norwegian coast on 1 October. He was the 12th Australian to die in the Battle of Britain. The Luftwaffe's casualties were also high. Seven weeks had passed since Adlertag, and as his air force had not achieved air supremacy Goering changed tactics again. He still hoped Britain would capitulate if key industrial targets were destroyed. Heavy raids were largely restricted to night. With the deteriorating weather during autumn's second month, intense daylight operations were reduced but not abandoned as Goering maintained the pressure on Fighter Command. They became the remit of Me109 and 110 fighter-bombers, which had been fitted with bomb racks. Smaller formations soon became the norm, with modified Me109s flying at 25 000 feet and escorts at 30 000 feet.

Air Chief Marshal Sir Hugh Dowding later acknowledged that of all Luftwaffe tactics this was 'the most difficult to counter'.[1] Without the promised Hurricane IIs, 249 Squadron strove to meet the challenge of high-level operations and during one early October sortie climbed to 28 000 feet. As well as being too high for successful dogfighting, this created a new danger, as one pilot at least discovered: his radiator froze up.[2] The increased altitude also made the observer corps's radar and visual tracking harder. Without the lumbering bombers to slow them down, the smaller, faster formations arrived on Britain's doorstep with only about 20 minutes' warning. The escorts were free to attack the defenders rather than cling to their charges, who, once rid of their load, could join in the fight.

'Point blank range'

The results of the Luftwaffe's decreased daylight operations were fewer interceptions, more nil-report sorties and the pilots of 249 Squadron wondering where the bombers had gone. In spite of John Crossman's death, 249 and 46 squadrons continued to implement the new formation tactics. George Barclay considered them 'quite a success'. Tom Neil, however, who had thought Beamish to be 'talking nonsense' when he championed the wing formation, now '*knew* it to be nonsense' after they had experimented with his idea.

Halfway around the world, news of Bill Millington's achievements had spread. His sister Eileen received a letter from the president of the Streaky Bay branch of the South Australian Country Women's Association congratulating her 'on the wonderful achievements of your famous brother Pilot Officer Millington'. He may have been fighting the war in a different land, but the association was 'proud and grateful for what the Air Force are doing and you must indeed be proud of your distinguished brother'. The letter concluded with the 'sincere wish' that 'he be long spared to enjoy the laurels he has earned'.[3]

Bill flew six patrols on the first two days of October, each over an hour long, with less than an hour on the ground in between. Bad weather followed, and his flying time decreased until the clouds disappeared on 7 October, when he carried out four sorties. The first three were uneventful. Shortly after landing from his third patrol, he and the squadron were off to Maidstone. 46 Squadron led the wing, and 249, with Bill in V6692, flew above as their weaving escorts. North of Ashford, they saw 20 to 30 Me109s flying in a loose formation between 20 000 and 30 000 feet. A squadron of Spitfires was also in the vicinity and had already engaged the enemy fighters. At about 4.15 p.m., the wing joined the dogfight at 21 000 feet. According to Tom Neil, it became a 'streaming mêlée of Huns, Spitfires and Hurricanes'. Bill, who was Green One, 'chased an Me109 which dived steeply down'. Rather than continue his pursuit, he 'left him to a Spitfire and climbed back to about 22 000 feet into the sun'. He selected another free-ranging Me109 which was harassing one of the RAF fighters and hurtled down. 'It broke off his attack and turned steeply in front of me, offering a plain view of his underside at point blank range.' Bill did not hesitate. 'I gave him a short burst.' The Messerschmitt 'turned on his back and dived steeply down, emitting black smoke'. Bill did not see his target crash. Such was the confusion, he was 'tackled by two Spitfires so broke off the engagement'.[4] He may not have seen the fate of his 109, but the black smoke was a clear sign that it was out of the battle. He was credited with a probably destroyed.

'Keen on animals'

On 8 October, flying V6692 on every occasion, Bill carried out four patrols, but only one offered any excitement. Flight Lieutenant Robert 'Butch' Barton of B Flight was leading, but Bill scrambled before him. Not surprisingly, everyone thought Bill had taken the lead so formated on him. This was not an unreasonable notion, as he was one of B Flight's section leaders. As soon as the Australian realised what was happening, he 'tried to buzz off', as George Barclay, who was Yellow Leader, put it. The others then thought that Barton's radio telephone must be unserviceable, because he appeared to be indicating for someone else to take over. Barclay assumed the role but discovered his radio telephone was out of order. He signalled Sergeant John Beard to take over. It was such a muddle that Barclay later commented waggishly that they would have been fine targets if any enemy aircraft had been about.

Over the next four days, Bill carried out five more patrols, as well as one cancelled after 10 minutes in the air. The lack of aerial activity enabled him to enjoy the companionship of some new friends. Tom Neil recalled that the young Australian was 'keen on animals', and, perhaps missing his collie, Prince, Bill introduced to the squadron 'a little black and white terrier of indeterminate ancestry' named Pipsqueak. He was followed a short while later by a white duck dubbed Wilfred, which, according to Barclay, joined their menagerie of dog and kittens to satisfy Butch Barton's 'craving for duck'.

Wilfred was considered 'a great character'. He was relatively tame and when not paddling in the ditch bordering the aerodrome would tag along to the pub with his canine friend and off-duty masters. The duck apparently had a taste for the hostelry's best bitter and, after taking his full, would deposit what the squadron historian coyly referred to as 'his calling card'. Pipsqueak also had his unsavoury moments, favouring Barton's bed for a private lavatory. Disconcerting sanitary habits aside, photos reveal the obvious fondness of Bill and his comrades for their bewhiskered and feathered friends.

'Enemy aircraft unaware of my presence'

Despite inclement weather on and off throughout October, 249 Squadron continued to fly. Not only did they have to contend with freezing cockpits and the possibility of combat with more agile fighter-bombers, but they managed with aircraft at the limit of serviceability. The ageing Hurricanes sprung oil leaks in the air and an opaque film would spread over the windscreen, thus precipitating an early return to base. As the Hurris submitted more frequently to the ministrations of the ground crew, it became harder to mount full squadron sorties. Bill flew a number of different Hurricanes during October, indicating that pilots weren't always able to fly 'their' machines. It was frustrating. The pilots considered the state of their aircraft so bad that they, and perhaps every other squadron, claimed they would be grounded within the first hour of an invasion. They were only half joking.

What with faulty Hurricanes, bad weather, a spot of leave and few sightings of the enemy, it was a quiet time for Bill since his success of 7 October. He was in the air three times on 25 October, but the second outing of the day, when 249 teamed up with 46 Squadron over North Weald, proved to be the most dramatic. B Flight took off at 11.25 a.m. with A Flight following 5 minutes later. Bill, flying Hurricane P3463, was Blue Leader, and his section was to join 46 Squadron's weavers as the protective rearguard.

The wing climbed to 25 000 feet and at noon spotted a formation of Me109s below. Bill could not estimate the total and later plumped for 'innumerable' on his combat report, but it was generally agreed that there were 15 enemy aircraft. The Messerschmitts made no effort to engage and, in the words of the squadron diarist, 'turned and fled for the coast'. But not all. Some lurked above, hidden in the cloud. About 12 miles north of Hastings, they pounced on the rearguard.

Most of the wing pursued the Me109s. The rearguard pilots scattered. Bill dived to 20 000 feet and found himself up-sun of one of the intruders. 'Enemy aircraft unaware of my presence.' Bill took the advantage and 'carried out an astern attack from slightly below Me109 firing from about 50 yards'. His bullets struck true. 'Large pieces flew off and enemy aircraft dived steeply through clouds' with 'quantities of black smoke pouring from it'. The stricken Messerschmitt 'presumably crashed in vicinity or in sea near Hastings'.[5] He claimed it as a probable.

The Australian emerged from battle unscathed, but two of his comrades weren't so lucky. Sergeants Beard and Henri Bouquillard, both flying in the rearguard, were wounded in combat. Beard was admitted to hospital after baling out, as was Bouquillard after he force-landed. Pat Pattullo, one-time member of 249 Squadron and friend of John Crossman, was also bounced. His Hurricane was damaged and he attempted to put down at Maylands Aerodrome, at Harold Park, Romford. He didn't have enough height and crashed into a house in Woodstock Avenue, quite close to Jackie Bush's home in Beaumont Close. He died the next day. John had been sure that he and Pat would not survive the war. 'Poor darling', their young friend noted. 'Little did he know how true his words were.'[6]

Bill carried out seven patrols on 26 and 27 October. The shortest was 55 minutes long, and the others were of at least 1 hour 25 minutes' duration. One was 1 hour 45 minutes. Longer patrols were now the norm, and the majority were of the usual 'nothing to report' persuasion.[7]

Mid-morning on 28 October, 249 Squadron was detailed to a standing patrol over North Weald. Bill, flying V7677, was again Blue One and weaving above the main squadron formation. They were patrolling above the clouds when a solo Do17 snuck in below them, dropped its load and disappeared. At about 10.10 a.m., 'control reported bandit coming southwest about 10 miles northeast of us'. It had been raining earlier, but flying at 16000 feet they found themselves in bright sunshine above what Tom Neil termed 'a carpet of small white dumplings'. They were north of Hastings when Bill sighted the Dornier crawling above the clouds. He dived towards it. 'Two bursts of anti-aircraft fire close to enemy aircraft drew attention of Red One', and he sent three Hurricanes to Bill's aid, but the Do17 was the Australian's. He dived 'from above and behind, opening fire at about 200 yards'. He saw his bullets penetrate. He then 'closed to about 50 yards before breaking away'. As Pat Hughes had demonstrated, the enemy machine was a dead cert at that distance, and so it proved for Bill. There was no more machine gun fire, which 'leads me to believe that rear gunner was killed'. This was fortunate, because at 50 yards the young Australian would have been an easy target. He followed the Dornier, which 'streamed white smoke and vanished in clouds'.[8]

While Bill was dealing with the Dornier, Tom Neil had plunged into the cloud. When he emerged, he saw a Hurricane above. He rose towards it. 'As we banked and curved on collision courses, I recognised the other aircraft as Bill Millington's. Straightening up at the last minute, we drifted together and looked about.' The controller instructed them to circle 12 000 feet over Dungeness. It wasn't long before Bill and Neil espied a Ju88 breaking from the cloud, coming from the north. The Junkers hadn't seen them, and they took advantage of its blindness. Neil came in behind and Bill 'carried out a quarter attack from above, allowing full deflection and, with a long burst, fixed his starboard engine'. His guns were now empty, but that did not stop him. 'I made a few dummy attacks from above to keep gunner engaged while Yellow One continued' to blast away and killed the rear gunner. 'There appeared to be a small explosion in rear of fuselage.' Bill and Neil followed the Junkers, which trailed smoke as it headed southeast. Neil fired until he too ran out of ammunition. Then, as he recalled it, 'with a final forlorn glance and by mutual consent', disappointed they could not finish off the Ju88, they broke away and made for home. Yellow Section's pilot officers McConnell and Thompson lost no time in bringing down the Junkers.[9]

Bill had perfected his art. His combat the day before had seen him climbing to take advantage of height and sun, then diving and firing at point blank range. This battle demonstrated that he was prepared to go in for a close attack and to continue feinting to keep an enemy gunner occupied so his partner could have his chance at it. It was a team effort, and Bill was credited with the damaged Dornier and a one-quarter share in the Ju88. This was the second of two memorable days – the first being 27 September – when Bill and Neil had teamed up. Neil recalled 'reliving these and other events … when we discussed them later, he being especially animated'.

'With cheerful willingness'

There was no let-up. Bill had already been in the air three times on 29 October when he was ordered to carry out an afternoon base patrol. It was not a full squadron effort, as some of the A Flight pilots, including Tom Neil, had been released after their early morning sorties. Just as they and their wing partners, 257 Squadron – who had recently arrived at North Weald – were taking off, 12 fighter-bomber Me109s made a hit-and-run attack on the station.

A 500-pound bomb exploded in the middle of the aerodrome. Flying Officer Keith Loft's Hurricane was knocked by debris but landed safely after the raiders disappeared, as did Tich Palliser's, even with part of the propeller missing. 257 Squadron's Sergeant Alexander 'Jock' Girdwood's machine was struck by a bomb splinter and crashed outside 249 Squadron's dispersal hut. As the fuel tanks burned, 'whoofs of flame' leaped up and ammunition exploded. The fuselage and wings bent and disintegrated. The blazing beacon, reminiscent of John Crossman's fire-engulfed Hurricane less than a month earlier, could be seen by those above.

Red Section navigated through enemy machines and exploding bombs, as did Blue Leader, Bill Millington, who 'took off as quickly as possible behind Red Section'. As Red Section gave chase, Bill followed closely in V7677. He was trailing Red, which was catching up with the Me109s, so 'opened up to maximum speed'. By about 5 p.m. he had 'gradually overhauled enemy aircraft which had climbed to 3000 feet' above the coast west of Southminster, about 40 miles from North Weald. He saw 'four Me109s in front with two He113s [sic] weaving slightly behind'. One Me109 lagged on the right, so Bill 'formated on him line astern and opened fire at about 100 yards'. Yet again, Bill's bullets found their target. The Messerschmitt 'immediately dived for haze over the sea'. Bill followed 'close behind, firing continuous burst'. Large pieces shattered off the intruder, which plunged to about 500 feet 'emitting large quantities of black smoke'. The Me109 disappeared, but Bill thought it would crash into the sea.[10]

The battle was over within 15 minutes. Bill landed 5 minutes later to an aerodrome which resembled Biggin Hill in the waning days of August. Between the two squadrons, 19 men had been killed and 42 injured. Bill's probable Me109 was added to Butch Barton's one destroyed and two damaged, Sergeant Michal Maciejowski's one destroyed, and the probables of sergeants George Stroud and Henry Davidson. The jubilation of their success soon faded. As Bill picked his way through the rubble, he could not have avoided the ashes of Girdwood's Hurricane outside the dispersal hut, a stark reminder of the fiery death of his 79 Squadron comrade Edward Mitchell, and his own narrow escape from flames on 31 August. More than anything, it would have reinforced his belief that he couldn't 'expect to get away scot free' during this war.

It was cloudy and drizzly on 30 October, 'a miserable, bitty and perfectly bloody day', as Tom Neil put it. The weather didn't improve, and 249 Squadron's pilots were surprised when they received orders to patrol North Weald at 20 000 feet. Neil's Hurricane sprung a leak, obscuring his view through the windscreen, and he had to retire. Bill, in V7536, and the rest disappeared southward. Over the coast, they sighted eight or ten Me109s at 28 000 feet. The enemy aircraft scattered. Bill and his friends gave chase, and sporadic swooping and dogfighting ensued. The pilots noticed that the 109s 'repeatedly flew out to sea and then turned back again as if to entice' the Hurricanes further from the coast. Bill was last seen dashing over the Channel. It seems he succumbed to the temptation.[11] Later analysis of Luftwaffe claims indicates that he may have fallen victim to a Messerschmitt's guns; one of the German pilots claimed a Hurricane at about the time of the 23-year-old's disappearance. Bill was the 13th Australian to die in the Battle of Britain.

As he had averred in his 8 July letter that was published in the *Advertiser*, Bill had gone down fighting. But his actions had been contrary to directions. Just before he bowed out of 79 Squadron operations, Bill and his confreres had been ordered to break off Channel engagements before reaching mid-point. He would have been aware of Air Vice-Marshal Keith Park's instructions to controllers to avoid engagements with small formations over the sea. Indeed, Tom Neil was surprised the Australian had chased the Me109s. He did not recall Bill ever forsaking normal fighter practice, 'being particularly individualistic' or going off 'on special lone forays'. Yet the next-of-kin letter sent to the Millingtons stated that 'when things were quiet with the squadron he would sneak off in a Hurricane and prowl around hunting Jerries'. Not only that, but 'he would always be the last to return to the base after a battle because, if petrol and ammunition remained, he would go alone hunting trouble. His favourite area was the French coast'.[12] The squadron's operations record book does not support this assertion, but perhaps it is true, as, in the majority of cases, pilots were neatly and coincidentally noted as landing at the same time or within five minutes of each other. True or not, it would have been a comforting thought to a family whose kith and kin were in the Luftwaffe's bomb sights to know that their son had been actively trying to protect them.

And if Bill wasn't 'hunting for trouble', why did he disregard orders? Why did he fall to the lure of the enemy fighters when he did not have the advantage of height and surprise? Did his determination to fight at all costs overtake common sense and experience? Or did he suffer hypoxia-induced euphoria and increasing confusion as his oxygen ran out at an altitude of over 20 000 feet? This was a possibility for a squadron coping with under par Hurricanes, and indeed, Sergeant Edward Bayley had vanished during a patrol of Rochford on 10 October after flying at 24 000 feet; it was believed at the time that he had lost consciousness because either he ran out of oxygen or the supply failed.[13]

Tom Neil hoped Bill would turn up, but 'the fact that he had been over the Channel seemed to reduce that possibility'. The young Australian did not reappear in the mess, and no word came through that he had been plucked from the water. In retrospect, Neil admitted that with so many deaths in action 'we quickly became inured to them. It sounds a heartless thing to admit now, but we lived hour to hour, day to day, and some colleagues, even close friends, came and departed almost unnoticed and were soon relegated to the past, if not forgotten. Sadly, in war it happens'. Even so, he remembered 'feeling very upset at the time about [Bill's] loss, but mainly for the sadness it would cause his parents'. Tich Palliser recalled that 'the whole squadron was sick' when Bill didn't return. 'He had been well liked, was a nice lad and had made a great impression on the squadron. He was very much missed.'[14] George Barclay, who returned from leave on 4 November to the news that the Australian had not survived his final combat, recorded the details in his diary. 'Bill is a great loss – he was a grand fellow, one of the most likeable in the squadron.' In dispersal, Bill's furred and feathered friends 'wandered about, mournful reminders of their absent master. If only they knew!' exclaimed Tom Neil. 'But, perhaps they did.'

From his first victory, on 9 July 1940, Bill had accumulated a total of nine and two shared destroyed, four probables and three damaged. His squadron attributed him with an official score of 'ten German aircraft but it is likely that he brought others down, which could not be confirmed during "private excursions"'.[15] Either way, he was a double ace – perhaps even a triple ace, like Pat Hughes, if we stretch the definition and count the probables – and the fourth highest scoring of those Australians acknowledged by the Battle of Britain Monument and the Battle of Britain Historical Society. Before going into battle for the first time, he had determined to live up to his high standards of honour, chivalry and Scout Law. In a final accolade from Tom Neil, it is clear he did: 'I knew him to be a brave and capable colleague and friend, who fought with distinction and was a credit to himself, to his parents, and to all who were close to him. He served both Britain and Australia well. He answered the call to arms and gave all he had to give – with good grace and with cheerful willingness'.

18

Loss

'Your son's noble sacrifice'

Just as there was no initial agreement on exactly when the Battle of Britain began, there was no immediate consensus on when it ended. There was no great speech from Churchill declaring it was over, but in its 24 October 1940 issue *Flight* magazine asserted that 'the Battle of Britain has been won by the Fighter Command, and … what is now going on is mere nuisance raiding, not intended to prepare the way for an invasion of this island'. The Air Ministry later declared in its official account that 'by 31st October, the Battle was over. It did not cease dramatically. It died gradually away; but the British victory was nonetheless certain and complete'. Dowding concurred.[1]

Des Sheen survived the world's first great aerial combat. Thirteen Australians did not. Their war was over, but it still raged for their loved ones. All pilots had to nominate their next of kin as well as an address to which a telegram could be sent. Some designated an additional person to receive the news. Jack Kennedy requested that his godfather, Pat Bray, be contacted, and Dick Glyde wanted Reverend Canon Bell of Christ Church to be advised. John Crossman stipulated that Pat Foley be told.[2] She received the devastating news at work. It would have been impossible to hide her shock and grief from workmates and

T.G. 42 A

FUNDS MAY BE QUICKLY, SAFELY AND
ECONOMICALLY TRANSFERRED BY
MONEY ORDER TELEGRAM.
(PLEASE TURN OVER)

COMMONWEALTH OF AUSTRALIA·POSTMASTER-GENERAL'S DEPARTMENT.

RECEIVED TELEGRAM.
URGENT RATE.

The first line of this telegram contains the following particulars in the order named.

Office of Origin.   Words.   Time Lodged.   No.

Via Imperial 333. Priority LONDON 61/60 1st 11.07

Remarks.   Sch. C1672, 11/1936.

This message has been received subject to the Post and Telegraph
Act and Regulations.
The time received at this Office is shown at the end of the message.
The date stamp indicates the date both of lodgment and of recep-
tion unless otherwise shown after the particulars of time lodged.

To

Immediate.

G.E.Crossman Esq'

Villa Road

Newcastle NSW.

From Air Ministry P931 1/10 Deeply regret to inform you that your son
Pilot Officer John Dallis Crossman is reported as having lost his life
as the result of Air operations on September 30th/40 stop Letter follows
stop The Air Council express their profound sympathy stop Miss P.Foley
has been informed.

9am C8.

Air Ministry telegram notifying John Crossman's death, 2 October 1940. Courtesy of
the Bowden family

perhaps even from members of the public in the tourist bureau.

As a senior man at his place of employment, perhaps Frank
Glyde read that his only child was 'reported missing' in the privacy
of his own office. John Kennedy's telegram, however, was delivered 'personally to addressee or member of family' at his Bellevue
Hill home. As it arrived on a Monday, a normal working day,
Frances Kennedy was probably alone when she discovered that
her only son had died. It seems Mick Crossman may also have
received the telegram addressed to Ted at their Waratah home.
When Sir Donald Cameron, the chairman of the RAAF Recruiting Drive Committee, heard of the 'circumstances in which your
son's noble sacrifice was made known to you' he 'felt appalled'.[3]

As he tried to absorb the news that his youngest son was

324

'reported as having lost his life', Percy Hughes was assaulted by the advice that Pat's 'wife has been informed'. The reluctant letter writer had played true to form. He had regaled his mother with the adventures of Flying Officer Butch and apprised her of the Airedale's total flying hours but had told no one about Kay. 'The fact of my son's marriage has come as a complete surprise', wrote Percy. Jack Kennedy too had failed to tell his family about his engagement to Christine Jourd. They found out when Christine wrote to Frances Kennedy.[4]

'The world must mourn a lad like that'

After receiving the first of many condolences – 'Air Board joins with the Air Ministry in expressing profound sympathy in your sad bereavement' – John and Frances Kennedy placed a small notice in the paper which elicited many more. Masses were said for Jack at the family church, Beryl's old school and Waverley College.[5]

The Glydes advised the *West Australian* of Dick's death, and it reported that a 'distinguished West Australian' was missing. The August 1940 edition of Guildford Grammar School's magazine recorded both its pride in Dick's award of the DFC – the first old boy to receive this honour – and the sad news that he had been posted missing. William Millington, who had joyfully passed on so many of Bill's letters to his local paper, advised the *Advertiser* that his son was missing in action. A month later, he shared with readers a letter from 'a fellow officer' of 249 Squadron who praised Bill as a 'grand, fearless and unquenchable fighter'.[6]

The *Sydney Morning Herald* was prompt in advising Pat Hughes's death, as was Perth's *Daily News*, which quoted Caroline Hughes's assertion that 'my pride in my son is beyond description'. Three days after Ken Holland's cremation, a small notice appeared in the *Sydney Morning Herald*'s roll of honour:

'September 25, 1940, killed in action. Sgt-Pilot Ken C. Holland RAF, only son of Mr and Mrs H.G. Holland'. Its appearance in a daily (except for Sundays) paper ten days after Ken's death indicates that the Hollands weren't listed as Ken's next of kin. Their son's emotional estrangement was absolute. Eight days later, the members of the Tamarama Surf Life Saving Club moved that 'the committee express their great sorrow on learning of the death of Ken Holland and that letters of sympathy be forwarded to his parents and Major Ripley'. The motion was carried by members 'standing in silence'.[7]

Less than two months after a photo of John Crossman and his fellow trainees at Cranwell appeared in the *Newcastle Morning Herald & Miners' Advocate*, the Crossmans received a myriad of letters and floral tributes. On the day their son was buried in Chalfont St Giles, the masters and pupils of his old school observed 2 minutes' silence. The school captain was asked to write to John's parents expressing the school's sympathy and the 'pride with which the students regard' John's 'great sacrifice'. That 'supreme sacrifice' was toasted at the annual dinner for leaving students.[8] Within months, John was recognised by Newcastle's aviation enthusiasts through the Australian Air League's Crossman-Fairbairn Division, which was named in honour of the Hamilton branch's former member and James Valentine Fairbairn, minister for Air, who died a few weeks before John, in the Canberra air disaster of 13 August 1940. (The Crossmans were honoured guests at the division's parade on 20 June 1941.)

Pat Foley was recognised as a grieving fiancée, and Mick Crossman's status as a mother in mourning was acknowledged when a social planned by the Australian Flying Corps Comforts Association (of which Mick was one of the most active members) was cancelled. After standing in silence in memory of her son, the association's patron 'paid a tribute to the courage Mrs Crossman has shown'.[9] The public recognition tempered their grief; when

Mick told Mabel Crossman of it, she responded sympathetically, 'I can imagine how you all feel the world must mourn a lad like that'.

The Crossmans' sorrow, however, was exacerbated as one by one John's letters arrived. On reading his letter of 22 September – his last letter home – Mick would have been comforted knowing that her hours of knitting had been appreciated and that John would be 'very glad of the pullover when it arrives'. (What happened to it? Did a friend appropriate it? Did it keep another mother's son warm?) But could she accept that he was satisfied with a life that had brought about his death? And how long after glancing at his farewell – 'I must close now so until next week, All my love, John' – did she give up hope of receiving that next promised letter?[10]

Dorothy Foley typed up and distributed the letter John had written her in confidence. Like his last letter, it was received weeks after his burial. How did Mick Crossman react to the knowledge that her only son could not confide in her, but had turned to another woman? How did Ted Crossman react to John's seeming prediction of death, 'I shall probably never see my people and friends again'? Certainly, Ted blamed himself for his son's death, and those words would have done nothing to allay his guilt. As he saw it, he had taught John to be fearless, had bought the balsa-wood from which he had fashioned his model aeroplanes, had taken him up on his first flight, and time and again had withheld permission for John to learn to fly before the war. Ted's sister, too, blamed him. After John's brief Christmas visit, Ann had written, 'If only we could see ahead or rather that you had been able to Ted. He would have trained young and would now be instructing at a good salary and not so likely to have to fight'. John had also told Ted that he regretted not learning to fly earlier: 'It would have made all the difference in the world'. Ted's self-reproach lasted a lifetime. It was a heavy burden.[11]

'I have not heard further from you'

Printed notices gave no hint of the anguish Percival and Florence Walch experienced over not knowing what had happened to their son. Two days after the *Mercury* advised its readers that Stuart was missing, it revealed their 'anxiety'. In deference to Percival's hopes that his son would turn up alive, J. Walch and Sons failed to record Stuart's loss in the company minute books. As time passed and he heard nothing, however, Percival became fretful. On 6 November 1940, he wrote to Air Board expressing his 'surprise' that 'I have not heard further from you … neither have I heard from the Air Ministry'. He stated that 'I am rather constrained to remark that I consider there is something lacking in supplying information to the parents of a young man who has been apparently killed in the service of his country'. He appreciated that there were postal delays so asked Air Board to 'cable for some information from the Air Ministry concerning my son'.[12]

Such was his grief, Percival could not comprehend the numbers of deaths in action that had to be notified and the numbers of missing investigated by the Red Cross. The 43rd Air Ministry casualty list, for instance, published in Australia on 26 August, contained 292 names, of which 107 had been killed and eight – including Stuart Walch and Dick Glyde – had gone missing during the lead-up to Adlertag.[13] More had occurred since, and to those were added Bomber and Coastal command losses. The Air Ministry had more to cope with than just slow mail.

'He did not fail his ideal and his honour'

The RAF received no further information about Dick Glyde, Bill Millington or Stuart Walch. After some months' silence, their fathers received advice 'with deep regret' that 'all efforts to trace your son … have proved unavailing, and it is feared that all hope of finding him alive must be abandoned'. Action would now be taken 'to presume his death for official purposes'. Each father was asked that 'you be good enough formally to confirm that you have received no further evidence of news regarding this'. Each responded that he had not. William Millington had to do this twice, once in May 1941 and again on 11 September. With no word for almost 11 months, he was 'still hoping that eventually something will be heard of him'.[14]

Within weeks, the Millingtons, Walches and Glydes were advised that 'in view of the lapse of time and the absence of any further news regarding your son ... must regretfully conclude that he has lost his life'. Death was presumed to have occurred on the day their sons had gone missing.[15]

With her special relationship with the RAF, Miss Celia Macdonald of the Isles was advised by the Air Ministry that Bill had been presumed dead. Bill had given her his 'last letter' for safekeeping and had entrusted her with gathering up 'any of my personal effects ... in the event of some untoward incident'. She had carried out that duty, as well as 'the sad job of unpacking the Christmas parcels which had come to him from Australia and sending them off again to be divided among his friends'. She wrote to Elizabeth Millington to pass on the letter Bill had written before his first operational sortie, telling her she had not sent it sooner 'because I knew you had such a strong feeling that he would still turn up and, like you, I hoped and hoped'. But they, like she, 'must presume that he was killed'. Miss Macdonald could 'not bear to write the words', but she knew that 'Bill would want us to be brave and face facts with as much courage as possible'. Despite the tragedy of losing someone so young, she believed 'that he died gloriously' and that he had forfeited 'his life for his friends'. She also offered the comfort that 'he was happy. I can assure you of that'. She, as 'one of his many friends', was 'grateful for his trust and affection and for the inspiration and help I gained from his great unselfish spirit'. She knew that 'his mother can indeed be proud of him'.[16]

As they read their son's letter, William and Elizabeth Millington recognised that he had lived true to his principles; they were indeed proud. On 13 December 1941, the *Advertiser* printed extracts from Miss Macdonald's letter along with Bill's 'last' words. The next day, Reverend John H. Crossley of Adelaide's Pirie Street Methodist Church held up Bill as one of the world's 'truly great ones'. He considered him 'one of the finest young men of this city' and claimed that 'no odds were too great for him, no risks too many. No reckless, daredevil, unreflective youth, love for his home, people, and country, was the inspiration of his breath-taking power-dives and blazing guns … He did not fail his ideal and his honour'.[17]

'We did not know how our son had died'

Over time, Percival Walch discovered more about Stuart's last battle as squadron friends wrote to him with details. Knowledge did not assuage grief, however. He destroyed objects and mementos relating to his son's earlier life. He grasped at any straw relating to his son and in 1944 made a number of entreaties to the Department of Air for details of a broadcast a friend had heard which purportedly mentioned Stuart's name. He was adamant that a transcript would reveal something of his son, but no such broadcast had been made.[18]

The squadron's next-of-kin letter usually provided broad brushstroke details about the circumstances of a pilot's last combat. Dick Glyde's, written by Widge Gleed, who had briefly assumed command following Squadron Leader Terence Lovell-Gregg's death in action two days after Dick's, combined warranted praise with a handful of inaccuracies. He said that Dick had 'died in combat with a German bomber, which was shot down by his comrades' and erroneously advised that he 'fell with his plane in the sea off Portland Bill'. In an attempt to give their son's death some meaning, Gleed concluded by stating that 'I am very pleased to say that our squadron has over 100 confirmed victories to our credit, thanks to magnificent fighters like your son'. Errors aside, Gleed's sentiment was sound, and Dick's parents would have taken comfort in knowing how 'popular and happy in the squadron' their son had been.[19]

Edmund Wimperis completed three watercolours portraying Forest Row before and after John Crossman's crash. He wanted to gift them to John's next of kin 'as a token of the sympathy and gratitude felt by those for whom he died'. The paintings were sent to Australia along with Wimperis's note describing them. The first, entitled *The Last Flight*, showed 'the countryside over which your gallant son made his last flight, in freedom's cause'. The second, *The Journey's End*, depicted where John's 'plane made its final descent' and a trail of almost submerged wreckage. The third, also called *The Journey's End*, was a different perspective of the crash site, which Wimperis hoped would be 'acceptable to Miss Foley'. He offered the works 'in grateful homage to the memory of one of the bravest of the brave' and told Ted Crossman about his son's last moments, as reported to him by eye-witnesses, in the hope that they would afford 'some consolation to those whom he left behind and so far away'. He related how, 'with the same expressions of intense admiration and sorrow', they had told him of how the brave airman 'attacked a group of enemy fighters, some say 20 in number, single handed, the clouds concealing him from his comrades in the air'.[20]

Such knowledge was overwhelming. 'Words fail', Ted explained to Wimperis. 'We did not know how our son had died'. The Brawns had sent him a copy of the *Daily Telegraph* of 1 October 1940 so he and Mick could gain a sense of John's last battle but it had provided little context. It was not until

Wimperis's letter, which indicated that eye-witnesses believed their son had 'brought down his last antagonist' even as he fell, that the Crossmans realised John had accounted for one of the '49 Nazis down over S. England' in the *Telegraph*'s headline and that he had indeed participated in the 'best fighting of the day'. 'You have made us very proud', Ted revealed to Wimperis.[21]

John and Frances Kennedy had been troubled by their son's lack of correspondence during his time in Britain. Even after James Fairbairn's intervention, Jack still did not write – any free moments were spent scribbling hurried notes to Christine Jourd. They accepted their son's death but not the dearth of information surrounding it. John wanted more. He wrote to 238 Squadron 'hoping to hear from someone' who had flown with Jack. The squadron had lost many in the Battle of Britain, including Jack's Red Three, Sergeant Cecil Parkinson, who had been shot down in flames a week after Jack. But Pilot Officer Charles Davis, Red Two, who knew 'how you must feel about the whole affair being so far away and cut off from definite news', responded, even though 'I cannot give you precise details'. He did his best, telling John how his son had 'succeeded in disabling one motor with his first burst' before he and Parkinson finished off the enemy aircraft. At that point, Jack 'went off to look for more Huns', and, as he had been out of sight, Davis could only relay eye-witness reports. He knew it was inadequate but he hoped 'this effort will enlighten you somewhat'.[22]

Davis, who crashed into a hill on 26 March 1941, aged 20, was unable to offer further insight, and what he was able to share was not enough. For more information, John contacted the External Affairs Department, which referred the request to the Air Ministry. Their August 1941 response added little extra, but it was as much as the Kennedy family would ever know. From the RAF's perspective, that was the end of the matter.[23]

'I hated doing it at all'

A week after John Crossman's funeral, Ann Brawn received a parcel of photos along with her nephew's diary and flying log. The remainder of John's belongings weren't released, as 'a certain lot of formalities have to be gone through'.[24] This included ensuring that John's financial affairs were in order, and Ann had to sign an undertaking that all outstanding accounts would be settled, including one for £48 19s 3d from Gieves Ltd, who had supplied his uniform. John had been granted a subsidy from the RAF to cover his costs, but he had not paid the original November 1939 account, or for additional items ordered in May and June 1940, which included 'best ivory visiting cards' and a wings brooch for his mother. The outfitters had not heard from him since their last communication in July and, unaware of John's death, had sent a polite reminder on 8 October.[25]

'It quite upsets us', wrote Ann to Ted Crossman, as 'he hadn't the money to pay'. This was painful for a family who considered thrift a virtue. She concluded that he had 'an entire disregard for money. I don't know how he proposed to carry on'. And yet, she conceded that he had kept his cheque book in order when he first arrived in England, and even though he had been disorganised towards the end with no balances recorded, 'of course pay was due to him'. Putting aside her disappointment that her nephew died in debt, Ann readily forgave him. 'Bless him. He had no vices', other than this one. 'His heart was kindly towards everyone.'

Ted could not comprehend the magnitude of what John owed, and it rankled that Ann had had to promise to settle those obligations before the RAF would release his possessions. He considered it 'dishonourable', whereas Ann believed they had 'a debt of honour' to pay the accounts.

In the end, all but £10 of outstanding bills was covered through monies owed to John by the RAF and the sale of his books, golf clubs, uniform and even underwear. Because he was so slight, it was difficult to find someone his clothes would fit, so his aunts inflated the coffers. They paid 18s 6d for three sets of pyjamas, 'there are still two sets of winter underclothes which Will will pay for if they fit him and that can be added as an asset', and Mabel paid 50s for a radio John had gifted her. 'I hated doing it at all', Ann told her brother. It took over a year to settle, and despite the distress, Ted's sister was still able to sign off as 'your loving Ann' and offer solace. 'You can be comforted in the thought that John did all, dared all. Will never know want or sorrow.'

'Brave and so perfect young man'

Christine Jourd was ill for a year after Jack Kennedy's death, 'unable to cope with the terrible grief'. She recovered, but her deep depression continued; the 'most wonderful year of my life' was over.[26] She was called up by the army's auxiliary services in 1942, but her father was able to pull strings to get her into the WAAF. She trained as a driver and was posted to a Yorkshire aerodrome, where she spent much of her time driving an open truck refuelling Spitfires. She soon regretted it. 'I was always searching the pilots' faces to see if it might have been him and there had been a terrible mistake.'[27] It was 'a great ordeal'.

Her grief took nothing away from her beauty. Many men fell in love with her, but she turned them all down until 1944, when she met Geoffrey Stanley-Hughes, an Australian-born captain in the army. (He was born in Brisbane and schooled in Sydney. He left Australia in his early twenties.)[28] They had a short engagement, as he expected to be deployed to France as part of the invasion forces. He was wounded after D-Day and spent two years recovering in hospital. On one of her visits, Christine, who was seven months pregnant, went into labour. Their first child lived for three months. When Geoffrey was released, the couple moved to London and he took a job in property. A daughter was born in 1946 and twin sons in 1956.

Before he died in 1951, John Kennedy went to England to meet Christine and to visit his son's grave. He told Christine he would have been proud to have her as his daughter-in-law. She developed a close albeit long-distance friendship with Beryl Kennedy, and they wrote or spoke to each other weekly throughout their long lives.

After living in Kensington for 40 years, the Stanley-Hugheses returned to Whitstable, so Christine could care for her mother, who died in 1998.[29] Geoffrey, who died in 1992, was a good man and they shared many happy times. He always knew about Jack and how his wife had felt about him. Christine never forgot her 'brave and so perfect young man'. She treasured the silver and marcasite wings brooch Jack had given her and in the weeks before her death, in September 2013, gifted it to a friend who treasures it also.

'Pat told me to marry again'

Like Christine Jourd, Kay Hughes took to driving for her war work. Instead of a refuelling truck, she drove ambulances.[30] She continued to grieve for her dashing husband, but 'Pat told me to marry again so I did, three times'. In 1946, she met her second husband, a former prisoner of war and director of Hull-based brewery Moors' and Robson's. They had three or four years of happiness and saw the birth of 'two lovely sons'. Then 'disaster set in'. Henry Moor went to Australia without his wife and children. Kay was penniless and had to move out of the company house and back into her mother's. She divorced him in the early 1950s. When she met Victor Marchant, 'I just wanted someone to love me', but 'he didn't'.

After the failure of that 1954 marriage, Kay looked after her mother, who suffered from rheumatoid arthritis, and also worked for 14 years in an old people's home, first as deputy then as matron. 'I was happy doing that.' Pat had taught her to live for the day; tomorrow would take care of itself. She had a restless energy and couldn't sit still. She always had to be doing something, but cramming her life with activity did not fill the hole left by her young Australian husband. She was lonely.

She married Darcy Wray in 1978 'for companionship', and both were aware of previous claims on each other's heart. Darcy had been married before and often visited his former wife's grave. Kay understood his abiding affection for her, just as he accepted her deep-seated tie to Pat. Darcy died in January 1983, and Kay had a massive stroke after the funeral. She died on 28 June that year.

Kay's sons always knew she wanted her ashes buried with Pat. She believed that 'the first person I'll meet will be Pat, not grown old or changed at all'. She had no idea 'what he'll make of me' but was convinced he would 'understand everything just as he always did, and we'll have time together, at last'. Her sons honoured her wishes, and Pat's headstone was amended to include the inscription 'In loving memory of his wife Kathleen'.

In love to the last

When Pat Foley received the telegram notifying John Crossman's death, she was overwrought with grief. Although she and John had not settled on when they would marry – and John did not mention wedding arrangements in his diary – all her future had been wrapped in the thought that she would be his wife and mother to his children. Those plans might have been dashed, but she was mindful that too many women had struggled with a solitary existence after the Great War. As a Catholic, she felt great pressure to marry, and she feared being alone. She also wanted children. Still in mourning, she accepted that she would have to marry.

She left the tourist bureau and worked as a Voluntary Aid Detachment and later joined the Australian Women's Army Service. The useful war work kept her occupied but did little to ease her anguish. She met Allan Caban in 1942 and they married soon after, but Pat later admitted that she had been on the rebound. She was discharged from the army during her first pregnancy, and their son was born in August 1943. Pat, who had been living with her parents, moved to Sydney for a time but returned to Newcastle before her daughter was born in November 1944. The marriage did not last. Caban worked in the Australian Army Canteen Service, and the longest they spent together was three weeks.[31] He left her soon after their daughter's birth.

The Foleys supported their daughter after the breakup of her marriage and in her decision to sue for divorce in 1947, despite the strong stigma regarding divorce at the time. They, and the Crossmans – who considered Pat to be an honorary member of their family – offered continuing support as she built a new life for herself and her children. She had left school after sitting for the Intermediate Certificate and had no formal qualifications, but that did not deter her from higher education. She studied speech and drama through Trinity College, London. While her children attended Sydney boarding schools, she taught in private schools, including Jack Kennedy's alma mater, Waverley College, as well as Santa Sabina, Strathfield, and a number of schools in the Southern Highlands. Later, she was engaged as a managing clerk in a Sydney law firm and in the 1960s passed several stages of law through the Solicitors Admission Board before letting it go because of the stress of study and work.

Pat led a full life but never forgot John. She visited his grave many times and on one occasion was given a fragment from his Hurricane, which had been recovered from the crash site. It was just a manufacturer's label from the oleomatic strut of the main undercarriage leg, but she cherished it as a tangible reminder of her fiancé. She also treasured Edmund Wimperis's watercolour, along with the portrait photos John had sent. But John's death remained a central sadness from which she could never move on. When she was diagnosed with terminal cancer, her attitude was that she would soon be with her Johnny. She died in May 1997, in love to the last.[32]

'Professional and capable'

Although she had agreed to her father's demands to break off with Alex Hutchison, Seina Haydon determined never to be bullied again. She developed a high degree of moral courage and learned to rely on her own resources.[33] The result was a strong, independent woman who carved out a fulfilled professional and personal life.

She left Torbay Hospital and worked as a radiographer at the Royal Marsden, in London. She never married but developed a close friendship with radiologist Leo Feuchtwanger, whom she met in 1942 when he was employed with the Emergency Medical Service at Bodmin. She acted as his housekeeper and, although not Jewish, maintained a Kosher house. She often spoke of his kindness to her over the 22 years they were together before his death, in 1966. From London she moved to Tunbridge Wells, then to Burton and Highcliffe in Dorset. She was a dedicated gardener and proud of her garden in Tunbridge Wells. She travelled extensively and indulged her passion for walking and bird-watching. She would often joke that she had tramped so often through the New Forest, which extends through southwest Hampshire into southeast Wiltshire and towards the eastern reaches of Dorset, that she knew every square foot of it. A keen genealogist, she joined the Bournemouth Family History Society, in which she was known as a 'lovely lady, professional and capable'.[34]

Seina may have become engaged to Ken Holland for less than

passionate reasons, but she kept his photo tucked into her hand-bag until she misplaced it in old age as a consequence of memory loss. She did not speak of him to her family and shared details of their relationship only late in life, when early memories flooded back at the expense of recent experiences during the onset of dementia. Her smile endured even through her final illness. She died in June 2012, shortly after her 93rd birthday, when her long, full and active life was celebrated.[35]

19

In memoriam

'I know how much you will value it'

Military medals provide a tangible connection to the recipient. They are a visual symbol of contribution. In 2005, Bill Bond of the Battle of Britain Historical Society invited Beryl Kennedy to the dedication of the Battle of Britain Monument in London. She organised an invitation for Christine Stanley-Hughes and they attended the reception together. Beryl brought along Jack's medals in honour of the important occasion of remembrance. As the elderly women showed the medals to Prince Charles and the Duchess of Cornwall, Christine explained how a 23-year-old boy had 'shot one of the buggers' who had been harassing their country. It was a proud moment.[1]

John Crossman's family treasures his medals. They are carefully tucked away, but in 2011, for the Battle's 71st anniversary commemoration in Newcastle, John's nephew and great-nephew gave them a public airing. They spoke of John's love of flying and his willing death in battle and impressed those present with the significance of the Battle of Britain clasp.

When Dick Glyde's possessions were gathered up after his death, 87 Squadron's adjutant, Pilot Officer Sutton, separately sent his DFC to Phillis Glyde stating he was 'afraid it might go astray if left with his other personal kit'. He assured Phillis that the award of the DFC was 'an honour he well and truly earned, and I know how much you will value it'. Dick's parents never applied to receive his campaign medals or the precious clasp which signified that he was one of 'The Few'. Dick's cousin wrote to the British Ministry of Defence and claimed the medals on behalf of his family. In 1980, he decided to donate them to the Western Australian branch of the RAAF Association so they could be included in its Aviation Heritage Museum's Battle of Britain display. They were stolen in the early 1990s but resurfaced in 2006, when they were spotted in an auction catalogue. They were returned to the museum and are once again part of its collection.[2]

Pat Hughes's medals also found their way into public hands. Kay Hughes cherished the DFC and Pat's service medals, but in the early 1950s, because of a misplaced sense of guilt, she entrusted them to Pat's sisters Midge and Valerie, who were visiting Britain, so they could take them to Percy Hughes. Percy later gave them to his son Charles for safekeeping. During the 1960s, Pat's brother Fred, who had been a prisoner of the Japanese, decided to wear them as well as his own at an Anzac Day march. The medals slipped off his jacket and disappeared during a post-march reunion. They were handed in to the *Sydney Morning Herald*, and Midge noticed a small piece about their return to the family. She decided that she should have the medals, but Charles wanted to retain them. This precipitated heated discussions and threats of legal action. Charles and his wife, Heather, suffered much anguish over it. In the end, Charles relented and passed them to Midge.[3]

Forty years after Pat's death, Kay decided to find out what had happened to the medals. She had lost contact with the Hughes family, so on 15 September 1980 – Battle of Britain Day – she wrote to Geoff Hartnell, an old friend of Pat's from Point Cook, to elicit his assistance. It was a pleasant surprise for Geoff to hear from her, as they had been out of touch since the mid-1950s.

'I think of you often', he wrote. He had never forgotten his old friend. 'Pat still has a particular place in my heart and his photo is located where I can see him even as I write this letter.'

Many of Pat's siblings had died, including Valerie and Midge, in 1951 and 1977 respectively, Fred in 1971 and Charles in 1977. Geoff had retired from the RAAF after attaining the rank of air vice-marshal so put Kay in touch with Fred's son, Air Vice-Marshal Henry 'Bill' Hughes. Bill advised her that 'so far as I know', Pat's brother John 'may be in possession of the DFC but I am not sure'. John, however, did not know where the medals were. By May 1982, Bill had discovered that the medals had been with Midge at the time of her death. The Hughes family then assumed they had passed to relatives of her husband, Tom, when he died, in early 1978. Kay suspected they might have been taken to Britain, and this seemed to have been confirmed by an anonymous note sent to her after she advertised in the Manchester area (where Tom's family came from): 'Please Kathleen leave it as it is'.[4]

Kay was so upset at the disappearance of Pat's medals that her sons applied to the Central Chancery of the Orders of Knighthood for replacements. In 1985, Charles's son, Greg, wrote to the Australian Department of Defence requesting Pat's service medals but was advised that they were the responsibility of the British Ministry of Defence.[5]

That seemed to be the end of it, until the day Pat's brother William visited Christ Church, Kiama. He wanted to photograph the brass plaque in memory of Pat that Midge had placed on the churchyard wall. (The house at which Pat had enjoyed his sun-filled holidays was next door to the church.) A woman who had been arranging flowers in the church came up to him and he told her the young airman had been his brother. She asked William to go with her to the Country Women's Association rooms, as there was something there that would interest him. William followed and met one of the committee women, who opened a safe.

Nestled inside were Pat's medals. Midge had forgotten them. William spoke to his siblings and extended family. His nephew Bill had always been keen for Pat's artefacts to be placed with the Australian War Memorial and had told Kay that if she did locate the medals 'this would be a fitting place for his decoration to reside in posterity'.[6] The family agreed. In 1990, the medals were donated to the memorial and are on permanent display in Anzac Hall's Courage Column.

'He was such a character and he died so young'

As well as the memorial plaque at Christ Church, Kiama, Pat is honoured in Cooma by a memorial instigated by the local Returned and Services League club, at Monaghan Hayes Place, which depicts his Spitfire and major sorties. On the 65th anniversary of his death, a wall plaque was placed at 16 Main Road, Sundridge, Kent, in memory of 'an Australian who fell in the garden here'. It was initiated by Desmond and Tony Hall, who had been having tea at their grandmother's during Pat's final combat. Throughout their school years they had walked past the sites where Pat had fallen and his Spitfire had crashed. Their father never forgot witnessing Pat's demise, and Desmond and Tony continued to live 'the excitement of it all'. With the assistance of the Battle of Britain Historical Society they decided to honour the Australian who had died in battle close to their home.[7]

Bob Doe was present when the memorial was unveiled, and in recollection of the man who had saved his life on at least one occasion, he remarked that Pat had 'earned his place in our history as one without whose efforts we would not be free today'. He went on to add that 'I saw some of the things he did and know that he was fully qualified to enter our history's Hall of Fame'. He concluded with his heartfelt gratitude for 'an Australian who came to help us when we needed him, God bless him'.[8]

On 23 August 2008, as part of Shoreham Aircraft Museum's Local Memorials Project, a commemorative stone was dedicated to Pat at Sundridge. Bob Doe gave the eulogy and again remembered his former flight commander with admiration and affection, praising his flying skills and leadership abilities. On 2 June 2013, Joe Roddis, Pat's one-time fitter, visited the Shoreham memorial. Joe was overcome by memories of that long ago time and moved by the memory of the death of someone so vibrant. 'I can still picture Pat at Middle Wallop', he recalled. 'He was such a character and he died so young.'[9]

'In memory of Sergeant Kenneth Christopher Holland'

In Australia, Ken Holland is remembered on a memorial at the Tamarama Surf Life Saving Club. Despite his pre-war ties to the area, he was not considered a man of Camelford. He is not included on the local war memorial, which was unveiled in 2006 (although it does include the name of Ian Haydon, brother of Ken's fiancée, Seina).

There are two memorials to the young man in Cornwall, both commissioned by Toby Ripley and both in the name of Kenneth Christopher Holland Ripley. Although Seina believed Ken had been formally adopted, he did not refer to an adoption in his diaries; nothing more was written on the matter after his 8 September 1939 entry noting 'difficulties abound' regarding a potential name change. Ken, however, had 'expressed the wish several times' that his surname be legally changed to Ripley, but according to Guy Ripley, Toby 'did not agree'. Indeed, Ken was cremated under the name of Holland, and his RAF service record, death certificate and probate notice are all in his birth name. Why, then, were the memorials to Kenneth Christopher Holland Ripley? Guy Ripley believed it was 'purely out of sentiment'.[10] Whatever the reason, the gesture revealed the depth of Toby's love for his ward.

Toby placed the first memorial, a Saint Christopher statue, in the Parish Church of St Materiana, Tintagel, where Ken was baptised. It was dedicated 'in memory of my dearly loved, adopted son'. The other was a memorial stone constructed from silver-grey Cornish granite, which he erected in a field at Church Farm, Woolverton, to mark the site of Ken's crash.

Ken's beloved guardian continued to grieve. Such was the depth of his sorrow that he relinquished his RAF commission in July 1941 because of ill-health. He returned to Australia after the war and contemplated adopting a young girl, but that did not come about. He later moved to South Africa and died there, on 17 June 1963. He did not forget his young ward, but Ken passed from Woolverton's memory. His stone was later removed and abandoned because it had not been maintained and was inconveniently located for the farmer. It was largely forgotten until the Rode branch of the Royal British Legion brought it to the attention of the Frome branch of the RAF Association. Those who rescued it and rededicated it in 1976 did so because they thought the removal and abandonment a disgrace, as Ken 'was an orphan with no one to care about him and … his adoptive father Flight Lieutenant [sic] Ripley was also dead'. The stone was refurbished and resited at Woolverton, against a low wall bordering a field on the grassy verge on the A36 road (opposite the Red Lion Inn). It is just to the right of a lane that leads to the former St Lawrence Church. On the opposite side of the lane is Woolverton's war memorial.[11]

Aviation writer Jonathan Falconer lives near Ken's crash site. 'Having a natural curiosity for the unexplained, I wanted to discover more about the memorial stone beside the A36 road.'[12] As it happened, a former girlfriend's grandparents had lived on Church Farm, so he knew the basics. He researched, wrote an article or two and was so moved by Ken's story that he dedicated his *Life of a Battle of Britain Pilot* 'in memory of Sergeant

Kenneth Christopher Holland, RAFVR Spitfire pilot'. Chris Taylor of Australia was also captivated by the mystery of the Woolverton memorial. He stumbled across it in 2006. Although he had lived in the area for the first 20 years of his life, he had never stopped to look at it before. This time he did. He started researching and wrote a brief account of Ken's life.

'Proud thanksgiving'

The first significant memorial to 'The Few' was instigated even before the end of the war. During the Blitz, London suffered many architectural casualties. Westminster Abbey's Lady Chapel – now more commonly known as the Henry VII Chapel – was one of them. When the dean of Westminster was approached about a memorial to those who fought and died in the Battle of Britain he suggested the Lady Chapel. Lords Trenchard and Dowding (the latter was honoured with a peerage in 1943) headed the committee to raise funds to restore the chapel and to commission a new stained-glass window. It would incorporate the crests of participating squadrons and the furled flags of the 'Dominions and Allies whose sons were slain or mortally wounded in this great Battle'. Specific reference to each of the Allied nations would be included. In October 1944, the Australian government decided that a sprig of wattle would symbolise the contribution of Australian pilots.[13]

As part of the memorial, a roll of honour containing 1497 names was placed in the Battle of Britain Memorial Chapel. The roll was not limited to the men of Fighter Command. It listed those killed or mortally wounded from all commands, including 24 Australians.

The next of kin of airmen killed in the Battle were invited, at their own expense, to the unveiling by King George VI of the Battle of Britain Memorial window on 10 July 1947. Families based in Australia unable to be present could appoint a relative or friend living in Britain as their representative. If that were not possible, an officer from RAAF Overseas Headquarters in London would attend for them.[14]

The Air Ministry issued direct invitations to Kay Hughes, Ann and Will Brawn and Toby Ripley in Britain. Frank Glyde died on 17 February 1947 and Phillis Glyde was represented by Mr E. Tennant. Frances Kennedy had been ill for some months. Despite the expense, John Kennedy would have gone but could not leave his dying wife. Frances died on 20 June 1947 so Squadron Leader John Herington, the official historian of the RAAF's activities in Europe during the Second World War, attended in her memory.[15]

Percival Walch had closely followed the memorial's progress. He first heard about it unofficially in early 1944 and wanted specific details. He also 'would appreciate some official recognition of my son's devotion of duty'. Even though he was desperate for his son to be honoured, he was unable to attend, and Major H. Walch stood in his place. The family would not have known it, but also present was Group Captain Colin Hannah, who was representing Clarence Bennett. Like Stuart, Hannah was a former Point Cook cadet and had been in his senior term when Pat Hughes and Des Sheen commenced, in January 1936. He graduated in June 1936 and was commissioned in the RAAF the following month. On 12 August 1940, he was air duty officer at the Department of Defence Coordination. At 8.32 p.m. he took a call from the Department of Air and was told that Acting Flight Lieutenant Stuart Crosby Walch was missing. He was asked to inform the next of kin.[16]

When William Millington learned that the governor of South Australia, Sir Willoughby Norrie, would be attending, he asked him to represent him and his wife. Sir Willoughby agreed, but on the day when 'every seat in nave, choir and Henry VII's Chapel was filled', Miss Macdonald was among them in the Millingtons' stead, listening to the archbishop of Canterbury's moving sermon of dedication. He addressed the relatives of 'The Few' who 'not less than others, though with deeper emotion' joined in the 'proud thanksgiving and grateful recollection with which this chapel is to be set apart for all time to make remembrance before God of the immortal act in which these young men purchased with their lives this England, and so much besides'.[17]

Although the Australian families could not attend, their representatives provided mementos of the ceremony. Miss Macdonald saved a program for the Millingtons. The Brawns sent the order of service along with postcards of the window and altar to Mick and Ted Crossman. Herington wrote to John and Beryl Kennedy afterwards, describing what he had witnessed and enclosing treasured photographs.

Two months after the unveiling of the window, those Australians who had not been able to attend had an opportunity to remember their 'Few'. In ceremonies throughout Australia on 15 September 1947, the RAAF Association inaugurated Air Force Day to annually commemorate the RAAF's war dead. Bill Millington's parents – with Elizabeth wearing a wings brooch her son had given her – attended Adelaide's service. Holding the brochure for the Battle of Britain window in Westminster Abbey that Miss Macdonald had sent them, they remembered their son and his sacrifice. During the following year's Air Force Week, Bill's young nephew, Kenneth, son of his sister Eileen, placed a posy on the state war memorial in memory of his uncle. Percival Walch did not attend Hobart's commemoration. Never accepting that his youngest child would not return, he died on 13 July 1948. His obituary claims he died after a short illness, but the family believes Stuart's death broke his heart.[18]

'His spirit ... lives on'

'The Few' continued to be remembered either as part of the collective fallen during the world wars or in specific memorials. In April 1942, Bill Millington's headmaster Thomas Nevin presented to Edwardstown Primary School a photograph of his former pupil framed with a copy of his 'last letter' and a news clipping of his DFC citation. Nevin lauded the young man who 'gave his life that we might live in security and happiness. His spirit, however, lives on and we will forever reverence his memory'. He quoted Sir Cecil Spring Rice's 'I Vow to Thee My Country', which refers to a sacrifice made in the name of unwavering love. In doing so, he placed Bill's death within the noble tradition of sacrifice. This notion of sacrifice for the greater good was reinforced by the King and Queen, who, from September 1947, sent scrolls to next of kin commemorating the men who gave their lives 'to save mankind from tyranny. May his sacrifice help to bring the peace and freedom for which he died'. The framed tribute to Bill is still on display. His name also appears on Adelaide Technical High School's Second World War honour board.[19]

The Crossmans continued to grieve. Mick Crossman was of German extraction, but she harboured a life-long hatred of the Germans because of what they had done to her son. Portraits of John dominated the house. When Mick received Edmund Wimperis's watercolours, she was not able at first to look at them but knew 'the time will come when they will be of infinite comfort and happiness to me'. So too, perhaps, were John's letters. She had kept them all. Also safely stored away was a recording John had made at the HMV studios in London on 29 January 1940 while he was on leave and recovering from his broken collar bone. He wasn't overly happy with it, or with the one he made for Pat Foley. 'They just didn't sound like me.' He told them of his sightseeing, his trip to the Windmill Theatre, the food, the warm weather

– little more than what he would have included on a postcard, really. But the concluding words, in their son's voice, would have meant the world to them: 'I do think of you often and I love you very, very much'.[20]

Private and public grief continued to mingle for the Crossmans. In 1952, Ted planted a commemorative pine at the front of Newcastle Boys' High School, as part of the ceremony unveiling a memorial entrance dedicated to the school's Second World War veterans. John Crossman's name is recorded on one of the two remembrance plaques. (John's school no longer exists. It is now Waratah High School, the junior campus of Callaghan College. The memorial plaques are still mounted there.)

The Glydes belonged to Christ Church parish in Claremont, Perth. They commissioned a stained-glass window to replace a window on the north side of the church. Its iconography reveals how the Glydes viewed their son's life, service and death. The Lamb of God represents a willing sacrifice, indicating that they recognised Dick's death as a sacrifice within the Christian tradition of battle against evil. Did the Glydes know that Dick had refrained from shooting at enemy parachutists? Even if they didn't, the inclusion of two patron saints of chivalry, Saint George and the archangel Michael, shows that they perceived their son as a chivalrous knight of the air. At the bottom of the window is the RAF badge, its spreading eagle wings iconographically linking it to Saint Michael's wings and representing Dick's passion for service flying. The Glyde Window was dedicated at Evensong on 15 December 1946. The service was attended by 470 people, including the window's benefactors, Phillis and Frank Glyde; the latter was in his final illness. He was frail and weak, and it isn't hard to imagine his pride and joy, intermingled with renewed grief, as he witnessed the dedication of the remembrance window.[21]

In 1956, Guildford Grammar School's Memorial Science Block was inaugurated in honour of the Old Guildfordians who had been lost during the Second World War. The honour roll, which includes Dick Glyde's and Frank Cale's names, is mounted near the entrance. Phillis Glyde died on 19 April 1962. Seventeen years later, as part of Western Australia's sesquicentenary celebrations, commemorative plaques, one for each year of Western Australia's settlement history, were laid on St George's Terrace. Dick is remembered on the 1940 plaque.

Stuart Walch's links to The Hutchins School were strong. In his will, he bequeathed £50 towards construction of a planned chapel. It seems he had been deeply impressed by Geelong Grammar's chapel when he visited in 1933 and wanted to ensure that Hutchins would be a few bricks closer to dedicating its own. He joined Hutchins's old boys on the school's honour roll and was held as an example to others. The Old Boys' Association ordered a new racing four for the school, which was delivered in 1949. When it came to name the boat, the committee decided it should 'perpetuate the memory of a prominent oarsman of the school who had given his life in the service of his country'. They decided that 'no one was more deserving of this tribute than Flight Lieutenant Stuart Crosby Walch'. In 1967, the boat shed burned down. The *Stuart C. Walch* was salvaged and restored, and when the school's museum was inaugurated, it was mounted there.[22]

On 15 August 2011, Stuart was inducted as a Hutchins School Old Boys' Association 'Lion', the highest honour conferred by the school on former teachers and students who have excelled in their chosen professions or fields of endeavour and who provide clear examples of inspiration. Six days later, Hutchins was presented with a Battle of Britain Historical Society school plaque to honour Stuart.

'Help remember those men'

Des Sheen's stiff knee – injured after his second bale-out – loosened up and he rejoined his squadron in mid-October 1940. He was appointed commander of A Flight and then commanding officer on 28 March 1941, shortly after claiming a destroyed Junkers Ju88 on the night of 13–14 March, which he felt 'evened up an old score because I owed Jerry one' for taking him out of action on 5 September the year before. Des found his commanding officer duties 'rewarding, but demanding. There's quite a lot of responsibility'. He established a good relationship with his men, which was exemplified on 29 August 1941. During an operation escorting bombers to Hazebrouck marshalling yards, he led the squadron into a fierce running battle and claimed a damaged 109. After they returned, his pilots recommended 'that Squadron Leader Sheen be awarded a bar to his DFC for his conspicuous bravery, coolness and initiative in saving his squadron from suffering very heavy casualties and in inflicting them on the enemy'.[23]

Air Vice-Marshal Trafford Leigh-Mallory, who took command of 11 Group soon after the end of the Battle of Britain, wrote to Des. He offered his congratulations on being awarded the bar, 'which you have so very well earned', then went on to state that 'I always feel that the thing which really matters in the Service is what those who are serving under you think of you'. He enclosed the squadron's recommendation, which he believed 'you would be likely to value for the rest of your life'.[24] The bar was gazetted on 21 October 1941, the second anniversary of Des's first combat and victory.

Des was posted from 72 Squadron on 3 November 1941, a month after claiming a probable Me109 on 2 October, his 24th birthday. It was his final combat claim. His official total for the war was four and one-third destroyed, two damaged and two probables. Including his partial claims, if not the Heinkel for which he received no credit on 7 December 1939, he would be deemed an ace. He attained his final wartime rank of acting wing commander on 29 January 1942 and enjoyed a varied wartime career which included command and administrative posts.

Like Pat Hughes, Des willingly succumbed to the charms of a young Englishwoman. He met Muriel Russell, known as Rusty because of her glorious tresses, while working with the photographic development unit. She had enlisted in the Women's Royal Army Corps based in a signals unit at Heston. The squadron sanctioned their marriage on 16 July 1941 by emblazoning their wedding car with a '72'. Des knew it was not overly sensible to marry during wartime, especially when he was in charge of an operational squadron – he even had to fly on their wedding day – but sometimes love is more powerful than common sense. In Des's case, marrying young after a whirlwind romance was 'one of those things'. Interestingly, given the frankness of his letters to his parents during the Battle of Britain, like Pat Hughes and Jack Kennedy he did not reveal the details of his growing love. He eventually broke the news by post. No details, not even a photo. Even so, Harriet Sheen was over the moon, and although she knew nothing of her new daughter-in-law, she trusted Des 'would pick out a nice girl'. Her grandson, young Des, was born in October 1941, and her granddaughter, Diana, arrived in January 1943.[25]

In 1942, amid calls to formally establish 15 September in the British 'national calendar' to annually commemorate the Battle, Des and ten other fighter pilots charged with defending Britain in 1940, along with a WAAF, joined Sir Hugh Dowding to 'toast the Battle of Britain'.[26] All had lost friends and comrades during the Battle and were committed to remembering their service. Battle of Britain Sunday is now annually marked by a formal service of thanksgiving and rededication in Westminster Abbey.

Des was repatriated to Australia in July 1946. His brother, Gordon, also returned safely from the war. (He had enlisted in

July 1943 and served with the 2/2nd Pioneer Battalion in New Guinea. He later served with the battalion's intelligence section at Tarakan and Balikpapan.) Des and his young family moved in with Harriet and Walter, and he resumed employment in the public service, this time in the Immigration Department. He joined the RAAF Association and was elected president of the Canberra branch in September 1946. Almost immediately, he opened an appeal to raise money to establish a fund which would provide facilities and treatment for those suffering war neuroses. He announced that 'it is not enough to celebrate the anniversary of the Battle of Britain. We must honour its obligations, particularly to the airmen who won this and other battles leading to victory'. On 14 September 1947, Des, along with former Point Cook course mates Gordon Olive and Richard Power, and John Pain, John Crossman's friend from the RMS *Orama*, training days and 32 Squadron, paid homage to their fallen comrades at the Brisbane commemorations.[27]

The Sheen family left Australia in November 1947; Des had accepted a consular job in San Francisco. The air force was still in his heart, however, and when his old flying friends told him the RAF was recruiting he applied for and was granted a permanent commission on 14 July 1949. He retired on 2 January 1971 as a group captain, after a fulfilling career which included command of a fighter squadron in Northern Ireland, wing commander flying at RAF Leuchars, in Scotland, command of RAF Odiham, in Hampshire, and postings in Germany and India. He 'enjoyed every minute' of his extensive and varied service life. 'I was lucky all the way through with postings and I wouldn't have missed it for anything.'[28] He remained active in the aviation industry after he retired, working for the British Aircraft Corporation (later British Aerospace) on the BAC111 and Concorde marketing teams.

In 1984, Des returned to Australia. In his suitcase were three souvenirs. One was a bullet-damaged earphone cover, and the others were a pair of stainless-steel parachute harness 'D-ring' ripcords with connecting wires. It was time to put the mementos of his wartime near-death experiences aside. He decided to donate them to the Australian War Memorial, in Canberra, where he had spent most of his boyhood and had first been struck with a lifelong passion. In a sense, his aviation life had come full circle. He and Rusty enjoyed a long marriage and celebrated their 60th anniversary. Rusty died in December 2000 and Des just five months later, on 24 April 2001. He was 83.

Squadron Leader Bob Cowper DFC and bar, Legion of Honour (Fr) (Retd) was one of Australia's most distinguished night fighter aces. He was invited to represent the Australians who flew in the Battle of Britain at the 65th anniversary commemorations in London. 'It was the most moving experience of its kind I ever attended', he recalled. He also went to the opening of the Battle of Britain Monument. As he read the names of the Australians, 'I decided then and there that I would see if we had a similar tribute to them in Australia'. We don't. The names of the former Point Cook–trained pilots are recorded on the Australian War Memorial's Roll of Honour wall, and the memorial's Commemorative Roll lists those who served with the RAF. The names of those Australians who helped defend Britain are not grouped together in recognition of a shared service.

Cowper, who was appointed representative of the Battle of Britain pilots in South Australia after the death of Desmond Fopp, the last Australian who had fought in the Battle, decided an honour board listing those Australians who fought in the Battle would be the most appropriate memorial. He sought support from the chief of air force Air Marshal Mark Binskin AM, received funding from the Department of Veterans' Affairs, and commissioned a firm to construct the board. On 15 September 2011, it was unveiled at RAAF Edinburgh, South Australia. Also attending the ceremony was Cowper's wife, Kay, a member of the

WAAF stationed in the operations room at RAF Kenley, London, during the Battle. (Kay, recognised as the last surviving Australian-born Battle of Britain veteran, died in late 2013.) The board now hangs in the officers' mess. Cowper was 'glad that my efforts have contributed in a small way to help remember those men to whom the whole world owes a debt'.[29]

'It's good to know our service is appreciated'

Des Sheen reported to his parents on the day after Black Thursday, 'It's good to know our service is appreciated'. And indeed it was, and is. The importance of the Battle of Britain cannot be overestimated. Fewer than 3000 men – including '30 or so' Australians – denied Hitler his prerequisite for invasion. An unconquered Britain was able to take the offensive in air operations to the continent and successfully prosecute the Battle of the Atlantic and the naval blockade of Germany as well as frustrate the German navy's counter-blockade. After the United States entered the war, Britain provided a base from which the D-Day landings and final battles could be launched. As historian Adam Claasen points out, without D-Day the Soviet Union might have won the European battle, with the inevitable consequence of one form of totalitarianism being replaced by another. It is not too much to say that the Battle of Britain ensured post-war democratic security in Western Europe or, as Bill Millington had hoped, 'a greater freedom, democracy and peace among nations'.[30]

Epilogue

'He ... died so far from home'

In 2006, Pat Hughes's great-niece Louise Bladen – granddaughter of Fred and Ruby – visited his grave. Her father was a commissioned officer and one of Australia's original Special Air Service members. His great-uncle James Winning, of the 11th Battalion, was killed at Leane's Trench, Gallipoli, and his grandfather Albert Percy Bladen served as a padre attached to the 23rd Battalion at Gallipoli and in France. War was never far from Louise's mind. Even so, her childhood was idyllic, with lots of outdoor adventures at a host of army camps. She rode in tanks, rushed to Santa arriving in a helicopter at the annual Christmas party, and made new friends on each army posting. When her father was sent to Vietnam, when she was nine, she realised for the first time the possibility that he might not return.

The Vietnam War and war in general left a significant emotional legacy on Louise's formative years. She developed a keen interest in discovering the experiences of other serving family members, such as her grandfather Fred Hughes, who had survived Changi and the Burma Railway, and her mother's two brothers, who both served in the RAAF. One of these was Bill Hughes, who, like his Uncle Pat, was an air cadet. (He attended the RAAF College at Point Cook and received the DFC for outstanding service with 77 Squadron in Korea.)

Louise was particularly 'moved by Uncle Pat's story, especially as he was so young (and the youngest of a large family) and died so far from home'. It was a great thrill and a moving experience to stand at his grave 'both as a family member and as an Australian'.

She felt that 'to visit his final resting place was a way of saying thank you and in some small way to show the respect and absolute awe I have for people who are prepared to die to protect those who cannot defend themselves'. As she placed a bouquet of lilies in front of his headstone, she mused, 'There he is lying in British soil after giving his life for the defence of that country – and ours indirectly – at such a critical and dangerous time'.[1] Men like Pat Hughes and his confreres will never be forgotten. Their service will continue to be honoured, and we will long regret their deaths and the loss of unfulfilled futures.

Acknowledgements

Many people have shared their stories, records and photos. I appreciate all who took the time to assist me in writing the story of eight Australian pilots. Thank you, Steve Allan and Greg Gilbert (Office of Air Force History), Mike Andrews (Christchurch History Society), Daniel Brackx (Belgian Aviation History Association), Major Nigel Chamberlayne-Macdonald, Dr Chris Clark (former RAAF historian), Gordon Cooper (archivist, Sydney Grammar School), Esther Davies (archivist, Telopea Park School), Glenys de Wit (finance officer, Edwardstown Primary School), Kim Eberhard (archivist, Waverley College), Anne Harrap, Peter Hodge, Flight Lieutenant M. Hudson (Air Historical Branch, RAF), Jeroen Huygelier (historian, Belgian Military Archives), Ian Johnson, Mervyn J.S. Knowles, Margaret Mason-Cox (archivist, The Hutchins School), Judy McKeough (archivist, Adelaide Technical High School Old Scholars' Association), Harold O'Keeffe, John Park (RAAFWA Aviation Heritage Museum), Winston Ramsey (editor-in-chief, *After the Battle*), Andy Saunders (Battle of Britain historian), Gordon Shanahan, Kathleen Van Acker (chief, ad interim, Belgian Military Archives), Reg A. Watson (Tasmanian historian and author), Rosemary Waller (archivist, Guildford Grammar School), Catherine Webb (Bereavement Services officer, Weymouth and Portland Crematorium), Wing Commander Greg Weller (commanding officer, 87 Squadron, RAAF Edinburgh), Victoria Wells (Hawkhurst History Society), and Peter Wimperis, who provided me with copies of his grandfather's records.

I am also grateful for the support and friendship of members of the worldwide Battle of Britain community, including especially Bill Bond and the late Mark Andrew of the Battle of Britain

Historical Society and Edward McManus of the Battle of Britain Monument. If I have forgotten anyone, I apologise.

Official records are readily available from public record holders, and I am indebted for the assistance I received over the years from curators and representatives of Australian, British and Belgian institutions. Such a personal work as this, however, could not have been written without the close support and confidence of the pilots' family members and loved ones. All opened their hearts and archives to me, and I will be forever grateful. All have kept the flames of memory burning and continue to cherish letters, photos and other records of their Battle of Britain pilots. Through their dedication to family record keeping, these men still live. My sincere and profound gratitude goes to the late Beryl Kennedy, William Stanley Hughes, Ann Walter, John Walch, Bob Glyde, Keith Glyde, Diana Foster-Williams, Peter Bowden, Chris Bowden, Denise Maguire, Geoffrey Caban, the late Greg Hughes, Stephanie Bladen, Louise Bladen, David Hughes, David Moor, Bruce Robinson, Simon Robinson, Carolyn and Sam Evans, Sir William Ripley Bt, and John Hodges, who kindly scanned Ken Holland's diaries on Sir William's behalf. Thank you, especially, to the late Christine Stanley-Hughes, who gifted me a most precious remembrance of Jack Kennedy.

In addition, I wish to express thanks to my friend Jean Main, who helped obtain secondary records and continued to watch (and listen) with interest as I wove the official records into (I hope) a richer tapestry; Squadron Leader Bob Cowper DFC and bar, Legion of Honour (Fr) (Retd), who told me the story of the Battle of Britain honour board; Group Captain Patrick Tootal, who put me in touch with Tom Neil; Tom Neil, who shared his memories of Bill Millington; the late Tich Palliser, who astounded me with his sharp memories of Bill Millington and Ken Holland and happily chatted to me about his encounters with two cheery young men; Keith Lawrence and Joe Roddis for giving me a better

Acknowledgements

understanding of Pat Hughes the fighter pilot and respected and beloved leader; and Tim Elkington, who responded to a number of queries relating to fighter pilots and John Crossman's training days, and provided me with pertinent extracts from his diary. I also wish to thank Erik Mannings, the 72 Squadron historian; Nigel Walpole, the 234 Squadron historian, who helped obtain an important photo of Pat Hughes; and Dr Michael Molkentin, who willingly visited Kiama to take the photo of Pat Hughes's memorial plaque. (I must add that I enjoyed my e-conversations with Michael about chivalry and appreciate his assistance with Great War fighter pilot recruiting.)

Thanks also to Helen Doe for her insight into the relationship of her father, Bob, and his former flight commander; Steve Ruffin, who provided copies of his articles about the physiological and psychological aspects of combat flying; Mike Donaghue for his invaluable comments on my analysis of fear and anxiety; Tony Hall for sharing his late brother Desmond's memories of 7 September 1940; Andrew Fletcher for additional information relating to the photographic development unit; Ronald Lees for scanning relevant pages of his father's log book; Joel Diggle and Andrew Rennie, biographers, respectively, of William Pattullo and Richard Reynell; Jonathan Falconer and Chris Taylor, who generously shared their research regarding Ken Holland; Tom Berekally, who sent me extracts of pilot biographies when I couldn't obtain my own copies; Jon Fenton for sending me a copy of Jim Fenton's memoir and putting me onto a significant source document; Graham Wilson for assistance with honours and awards; Diane Bricknell for her brilliant maps, which look as if they come straight from 1940; Garth O'Connell for showing me the symbols of Des Sheen's good luck; and Andy Wright, Charles Page and Owen Zupp, who have offered advice and support over the years and answered technical questions. Andy Wright also, along with Bob Livingstone, cast eagle eyes over the final draft to eliminate any remaining technical errors. My friend Jill Sheppard also read the final draft and offered valuable advice from the perspective of a lay reader.

Six people have my deepest gratitude: my husband, David, for always being there, loving, supporting, cooking and listening to me rattle on about the lives and loves of eight special men; Peter Stanley, perhaps the greatest support throughout my writing life, who hinted strongly that it was about time I found my voice and introduced me to my agent, Diana Hill; Diana, who embraced my work enthusiastically and found it a publishing home; Phillipa McGuinness, my publisher, who welcomed the story of eight young men to that publishing home, thrilled me by 'getting' the emotion behind it and entrusted it to the care of her dedicated editorial team; and Geoff Simpson, historical advisor to and trustee of the Battle of Britain Memorial Trust, who has acted as my unofficial mentor and guide, official 'reader' and critic since responding to my first enquiry in April 2011, and who has since become a friend. And Jill Sheppard, my dearest friend, to whom I have dedicated this book. Thank you all.

Notes

Full details of all sources cited in the Notes, except personal communications and newspaper articles, can be found in the Bibliography.

Abbreviations
AWM Australian War Memorial
IWM Imperial War Museum
NAA National Archives of Australia
NAUK National Archives, United Kingdom
OAFH Office of Air Force History

Author's note
1 Dr C. Clark, pers. comm., 27 Oct. 2011.
2 G. Simpson, pers. comm., 20 Apr. 2011.

Introduction
1 Bishop, *Battle of Britain*, p. 226.
2 Air Ministry Order A544/1946, Section 12, quoted in Newton, *A Few of 'The Few'*, pp. 263–64.
3 Wynn, *Men of the Battle of Britain*, p. 2; *Battle of Britain: Roll of Honour*; *Allied Aircrew in the Battle of Britain*; Battle of Britain Historical Society website; Simpson, 'Battle of Britain', pp. 67–69; G. Simpson, pers. comm., 20 Apr. 2011.
4 Herington, *Air War against Germany and Italy*, p. 35; Newton, *A Few of 'The Few'*, p. 284; *Battle of Britain*, AWM; *Battle of Britain: Roll of Honour*; *Allied Aircrew in the Battle of Britain*; Battle of Britain Historical Society website; Bishop, *Fighter Boys*, p. 242; Claasen, *Dogfight*, p. 14; Alexander, 'Battle of Britain Revealed', pp. 54–58; Dr C. Clark, pers. comm., 27 Oct. 2011.
5 Millington to his parents, June 1940; and to Robinson, 22 May 1940; and S. Robinson, Robinson collection; [Millington], NAA.
6 Bush, 30 Sept. 1941, Bowden collection.
7 C. Stanley-Hughes, 9 Apr. 2010; and B. Kennedy, 11 Mar. 2010, pers. comms.
8 Deacon Elliott, RAF Museum, p. 8; Price, *Spitfire Mark I/II Aces*, pp. 44, 93; D. Foster-Williams, pers. comm., 14 Sept. 2009.
9 Hughes, Bowden collection; K. Lawrence, pers. comm., 18 May 2011.
10 Holland, diary, 2 Aug. 1939, Ripley collection; Davey, Falconer collection; C. Palliser, pers. comm., 6 Oct. 2009.

Prologue
1 Millington to his parents, June 1940, Robinson collection.

1 Australia's 'Few'

1 S. Robinson, Robinson collection.
2 B. Robinson, pers. comm., 14 June 2012; *Advertiser*, 11 Aug. 1926.
3 S. Robinson, Robinson collection.
4 *Children's Hour*; Nevin; E. Robinson; and S. Robinson, Robinson collection.
5 Millington, diary, 1, 15 Jan., 12 Feb., Aug. 1939; photos; and to Robinson, 31 Dec. 1939, Robinson collection; *Advertiser*, 8 Aug. 1934, 26 Sept. 1940; B. Robinson, pers. comm., 30 Aug. 2013.
6 Nevin; and S. Robinson, Robinson collection; J. McKeough, pers. comm., 5 Dec. 2012; Millington, school records, Glenunga International High School collection.
7 Millington, school records, Glenunga International High School collection; E. Robinson, Robinson collection.
8 S. Robinson; and E. Robinson, Robinson collection; *Advertiser*, 8 Aug. 1934, 11 Sept., 20 Oct. 1940.
9 E. Robinson, Robinson collection.
10 *Sydney Morning Herald*, 11 Jan. 1939; *Barrier Miner*, 17 Jan. 1939; Millington, diary, Jan. 1939, Robinson collection.
11 Millington, RAF service record, Robinson collection; *Advertiser*, 10 May 1939.
12 E. Robinson; and S. Robinson, Robinson collection.
13 Millington, diary, Jan. 1939; and E. Robinson, Robinson collection.
14 Armitage, *Newcastle High School*, p. 118.
15 ibid., pp. 55, 117–18; Crossman, NAA; P. Bowden, pers. comm., 8 Dec. 2010.
16 P. Bowden, 8 Dec. 2010; and C. Bowden, 29 Nov. 2011, pers. comms.
17 G. Crossman, Bowden collection.
18 P. Bowden, pers. comm., 8 Dec. 2010; Brawn to Crossmans, 6 Oct., 16 Dec. 1940, Bowden collection.
19 Brawn to Crossmans, 9 Nov. 1940; Bush, 30 Sept. 1941; and Mabel Crossman, 10 Nov. 1940, Bowden collection.
20 P. Bowden, pers. comm., 8 Dec. 2010, 27 Aug. 2011.
21 Bentley; and J. Crossman, Intermediate Certificate; newspaper article; and school reports for first year at Newcastle Boys' High School, June, Dec. 1930, with comments by Mr H. Jurd (who knew John in 1930 and in 1933 when he sat for his Intermediate), Bowden collection.
22 P. Bowden, pers. comm., 8 Dec. 2010; Crossman, NAA; J. Crossman, reference from A. Goninan & Co., Bowden collection.
23 J. Crossman, references from Australian Institute of Industrial Psychology; and from C.W. Nicholls, Bowden collection.
24 Crossman, NAA; Brawn to Crossmans, 30 Dec. 1939, Bowden collection.
25 C. Palliser, pers. comm., 6 Oct. 2009; Taylor, *Life and Times of Kenneth Holland*, p. 7; Haydon, Evans collection.
26 Holland, NAA; H. Holland; and I. Holland, Department of Veterans' Affairs.
27 Haydon, Evans collection.
28 H. Holland, Department of Veterans' Affairs.
29 Taylor, *Life and Times of Kenneth Holland*, p. 8; *Sydney Morning Herald*, 25 Jan. 1936; Holland, nomination form; and examination report, Taylor collection.
30 Sir W. Ripley Bt, pers. comm., 9 Sept. 2009; Hodges, *Bedstone Court*, pp. 92, 95; *West Australian*, 22 Apr. 1926; Sheldon, Taylor collection; Haydon, Evans collection.
31 Holland, baptismal certificate, Taylor collection.

32 R. Glyde, 9 May 2010; and K. Glyde, 7 May 2010, pers. comms.
33 Golding, *Wonder Book of Aircraft*, p. 29; Newton, 'Flg Off Richard Glyde DFC', p. 87; R. Glyde, pers. comm., 19 May 2010.
34 Glyde, school records; and *Swan*, May 1931, Guildford Grammar School collection; White, *Go Forward*, p. 143.
35 Research project; and photos, Glyde collection; Glyde, photos, Guildford Grammar School collection; R. Glyde, pers. comm., 5 May 2010, 22 Apr. 2011.
36 Glyde, enrolment form; and job application, Guildford Grammar School collection; R. Glyde, pers. comm., 18 June 2010.
37 *Daily News*, 5 June 1940; *West Australian*, 6 June 1940; Newton, 'Flg Off Richard Glyde DFC', p. 87.
38 B. Kennedy, pers. comm., 11 Mar. 2010.
39 K. Eberhard, 17 Sept. 2009; and B. Kennedy, 11 Mar. 2010, pers. comms; *Christian Brothers' College Waverley Record*, 1927, 1932, 1934, 1940, Waverley College collection.
40 G. Shanahan, 1 Apr. 2010; and B. Kennedy, 11 Mar. 2010, pers. comms.
41 *Christian Brothers' College Waverley Record*, 1933, 1934, 1940, Waverley College collection; B. Kennedy, pers. comm., 11 Mar. 2010.
42 *Sydney Morning Herald*, 11 Jan. 1933; *Christian Brothers' College Waverley Record*, 1935, 1940, Waverley College collection; B. Kennedy, 11 Mar. 2010; and H. O'Keeffe, 7 Mar. 2010, pers. comms.
43 J. Walch, pers. comm., 3 Apr. 2011.
44 Walch, enrolment record, Hutchins Archives and Heritage Collection.
45 *Hutchins School Magazine*, Dec. 1940, June 1949, Hutchins Archives and Heritage Collection; *Mercury*, 22 Nov. 1934.
46 *Hutchins School Magazine*, Dec. 1933, Hutchins Archives and Heritage Collection; *Mercury*, 29 June 1933.
47 *Mercury*, 24 May, 12 July 1935, 8 Apr. 1936. Also refer to guest lists in various editions of the *Mercury*'s 'Women's Realm', 1935–36.
48 *Mercury*, 15 Sept. 1987; Walch, NAA, B4747.
49 Sheen, IWM, 18375; and 12137.
50 Sheen, National Library of Australia; 'Mr W.E. Sheen', obituary, *Canberra Times*, 5 Feb. 1974; Sheen, enrolment record, Telopea Park School collection.
51 Sheen, IWM, 12137; *Canberra Times*, 24 Mar. 1928; *Barrier Miner*, 17 Mar. 1928.
52 Sheen, IWM, 12137.
53 *Canberra Times*, 24 July 1946; M.J.S. Knowles, pers. comm., 7 Aug. 2009; H. Sheen, typewritten note in scrapbook, Foster-Williams collection; *Telopea School Magazine*, no. 5, Dec. 1932, Telopea Park School collection.
54 D. Foster-Williams, pers. comm., 10 Nov. 2009; *Canberra Times*, 3 Nov. 1932.
55 M.J.S. Knowles, 7 Aug. 2009; and D. Foster-Williams, 10 Nov. 2009, pers. comms; *Telopea School Magazine*, no. 4, May 1932, Telopea Park School collection; *Canberra Times*, 6 Apr. 1935.
56 Sheen, 'In England Now', AWM; Golley, *So Few*, p. 219.
57 *Fortian*, Fort Street High School collection.
58 Schofield & Numeralla and District, *'In Those Days ...'*, pp. 89–90, 93, 100; S. Bladen, pers. comm., 3 Mar. 2011; Hughes to Hughes, RAAF Museum.
59 Schofield & Numeralla and District, *'In Those Days ...'*, p. 94; Hughes, NAA, A9300. (NSW historical birth certificates are available only after 100 years.)
60 S. Bladen, pers. comm., 10 Feb. 2009.

61 Hughes, AWM, PR87/142, 19 Jan. 1936; *Cooma-Monaro Express*, 14 Aug. 2008.
62 D. Hughes, 30 Oct. 2013; and S. Bladen, 6 Mar. 2009, pers. comms.
63 *Cooma Express*, Fort Street High School collection; *Cooma-Monaro Express*, 14 Aug. 2008; Hughes, AWM, PR87/142, 19 Jan. 1936; S. Bladen, pers. comm., 3 Mar. 2011.
64 D. Hughes, 5 Mar. 2011; and S. Bladen, 3 Mar. 2011, pers. comms; Hughes to Hughes, RAAF Museum.
65 Hughes, NAA, A9300.
66 ibid.; Hughes to Hughes, RAAF Museum; *Cooma-Monaro Express*, 14 Aug. 2008.
67 Hughes, enrolment form, Fort Street High School collection. Pat's RAF service record (Hughes, RAF Disclosures) states that he attended Sydney Grammar School, 1932–35, but he was never a student there. G. Cooper, pers. comm., 3 Aug. 2011; Hughes, NAA, A9300.
68 *Cooma-Monaro Express*, 14 Aug. 2008; S. Bladen, 10 Feb. 2009; and D. Hughes, 30 Oct. 2013, pers. comms; Hughes, AWM, PR87/142, 27 Apr., 1, 14 May 1936; Hughes, NAA, A9300.

2 RAAF cadets

1   Hughes, NAA, A9300.
2   Research project, Glyde collection.
3   Operations record book, OAFH, 5 Mar. 1934; Glyde, 'Certificate of Character', Guildford Grammar School collection.
4   *Canberra Times*, 8 July 1936; B. Kennedy, pers. comm., 11 Mar. 2010; *Christian Brothers' College Waverley Record*, 1940, Waverley College collection.
5   Hughes to Hughes, RAAF Museum; Hughes, NAA, A9300, reference; cadet application; and interview assessment notes; Hughes, AWM, PR87/142.
6   Hughes, AWM, PR87/142, note in preliminary calendar and daily entry, 17, 18 Jan. 1936.
7   ibid., 20 Jan. 1936; Hughes, NAA, A9300; S. Bladen, pers. comm., 10, 15 Feb. 2009; Olive & Newton, *Devil at 6 O'clock*, p. 4.
8   Quotations to the end of this section that are not attributed in a note come from Hughes, AWM, PR87/142, diary, Jan.–Apr. 1936; and reflection written after several months' service and positioned in the pages before the diary entries begin.
9   Kingsland, *Into the Midst of Things*, p. 19.
10 Dr C. Clark, pers. comm., 4 May 2011; course notes, OAFH, July 1937; Hughes, AWM, PR87/142, 23 Jan., 6 Feb. 1936.
11 Hughes, AWM, PR87/142, 27 Feb., 18 July, 8 Aug. 1936; Kingsland, *Into the Midst of Things*, p. 19.
12 Dr C. Clark, pers. comm., 4 May 2011; Coulthard-Clark, *Third Brother*, pp. 201–203.
13 Hughes, AWM, PR87/142, 31 Jan. 1936; Olive & Newton, *Devil at 6 O'clock*, p. 4.
14 Hughes, NAA, A9300; Sheen, IWM, 12137; Coulthard-Clark, *Third Brother*, p. 173; *Argus*, 3 June 1936; D. Sheen, flying log, Foster-Williams collection.
15 Hughes, AWM, PR87/142, 25 Feb., 27 July 1936.
16 Quotations to the end of this section that are not attributed in a note come from Kennedy, RAAF Museum, July–Aug. 1936.

17   Hughes, AWM, PR87/142, 11 Mar. 1936.
18   ibid., 12 Mar. 1936.
19   Olive, NAA; D. Sheen, flying log, Foster-Williams collection; Hughes, NAA, A9300; operations record book, OAFH; Kennedy; and Walch, RAAF Museum, 7 Sept. 1936.
20   Operations record book, OAFH, 10 Mar. 1936; Sheen, IWM, 12137.
21   Quotations to the end of this chapter that are not attributed in a note come from Hughes, AWM, PR87/142, 1936.
22   *Argus*, 17 Apr. 1936.
23   Olive & Newton, *Devil at 6 O'clock*, p. 5.
24   Coulthard-Clark, *Third Brother*, p. 207.
25   Sheen, IWM, 12137.
26   Operations record book, OAFH, 7 May 1936. Pat put in a request for the damaged propeller.
27   Hughes, NAA, A9300.
28   Operations record book, OAFH, 2 July 1936.
29   Sheen, IWM, 12137.
30   Hughes, NAA, A9300; *Canberra Times*, 29 Oct. 1936.
31   Sheen, IWM, 12137.
32   Operations record book, 10, 17 Dec. 1936; and course notes, Jan., Dec. 1936, OAFH; D. Sheen, flying log, Foster-Williams collection; Hughes, NAA, A9300.
33   *Sydney Morning Herald*, 15 July 1937; B. Kennedy, pers. comm., 11 Mar. 2010; course notes, OAFH, July 1937.

3   The great adventure

1   Sheen, IWM, 12137; Coulthard-Clark, *Third Brother*, p. 89.
2   Sheen, IWM, 12137.
3   ibid.
4   R. Lees, pers. comm., 19 July 2013.
5   Sheen, IWM, 12137; Docherty, *Swift to Battle*, p. 20.
6   Olive & Newton, *Devil at 6 O'clock*, pp. 17, 20; Sheen, IWM, 12137; Hughes, RAF Disclosures.
7   B. Kennedy, pers. comm., 11 Mar. 2010.
8   Kennedy, RAF Disclosures; Olive & Newton, *Devil at 6 O'clock*, p. 22; Kennedy, RAAF Museum, 26 Nov. 1936; B. Kennedy, pers. comm., 11 Mar. 2010.
9   Album and accompanying note, Walch collection; J. Walch, pers. comm., 30 Mar. 2011.
10   H. Sheen, newsclipping (unattrib.) in scrapbook, Foster-Williams collection.
11   Sheen, IWM, 12137.
12   NAUK, AIR 27/592, 10 June, 5 Aug. 1938; Smith, *Second to None*, p. 47.
13   Charman, *Outbreak 1939*, p. 8; Sheen, IWM, 12137; NAUK, AIR 27/589, 25, 27 Sept. 1938.
14   NAUK, AIR 27/589.
15   Bungay, *Most Dangerous Enemy*, p. 250; Sheen, IWM, 12137.
16   *Daily News*, 5 June 1940; Glyde, job application, Guildford Grammar School collection; *West Australian*, 11, 17 May 1934.
17   Glyde, job application, Guildford Grammar School collection.
18   ibid.; Freeth, Guildford Grammar School collection.
19   *West Australian*, 3, 7 Aug., 3 Oct. 1934; Glyde, RAF Disclosures.

20 Glyde to Freeth; and *Swan*, May, Aug., Dec. 1935, Guildford Grammar School collection.
21 Freeth, 'Reference'; Glyde to Freeth; and *Swan*, Aug. 1936, Guildford Grammar School collection.
22 Glyde, RAF Disclosures; *West Australian*, 6 June 1940; *Daily News*, 5 June 1940.
23 Quotations and information to the end of this section that are not attributed in a note come from Glyde, RAF Disclosures.
24 *Swan*, Aug. 1939, Guildford Grammar School collection; Phillis Glyde, letter, n.d., in Glyde, AWM.
25 *Swan*, Aug. 1939, Guildford Grammar School collection.
26 Glyde, 22 Nov. 1939, Glyde collection.
27 B. Kennedy, pers. comm., 11 Mar. 2010.
28 ibid.; Fairbairn, 1, 3 Apr. 1940, Kennedy collection; Hughes, Hughes collection.
29 Hughes to Hughes, RAAF Museum.
30 Stokes, *Wings Aflame*, p. 61; NAUK, AIR 27/589; K. Lawrence, pers. comm., 18 May 2011.
31 NAUK, AIR 27/589; Hughes, Hughes collection.
32 Hughes, RAF Disclosures.
33 Hughes to Hughes, RAAF Museum.
34 Hughes, Hughes collection.
35 *Mercury*, 21 May 1941; NAUK, AIR 27/1018, 1 Dec. 1938; Thomas, *RAF Top Gun*, p. 49.

4 War

1 Holland, diary, 27 Feb. 1939, Ripley collection. The formation of the volunteer reserve was announced in 1934 and came to fruition in August 1936.
2 *Prospectus*, Anderson collection.
3 Holland, diary, 24 Feb. 1939, Ripley collection.
4 Newton, 'Australians Lost in the Battle of Britain'. Quotations to the end of this section that are not attributed in a note come from Holland, diary, 1939, Ripley collection.
5 Newton, 'Australians Lost in the Battle of Britain'.
6 Newton, *Clash of Eagles*, p. 46; Crossman, NAA.
7 *Air League Journal*, vol. 2, Feb. 1942; Crossman, NAA.
8 Millington to Robinson, 7 July 1939, Robinson collection.
9 Quotations to the end of this section that are not attributed in a note come from Millington, diary, 15–23 June 1939, Robinson collection.
10 Millington to Robinson, 7 July 1939, Robinson collection.
11 Bill's welcoming letter is no longer extant but would have been similar to the one John Crossman received a few months later. Macdonald, Bowden collection.
12 Millington to Robinson, 7 July 1939; and to his parents, June 1940, Robinson collection; Major N. Chamberlayne-Macdonald, pers. comm., 12 Jan. 2012; *Australian Women's Weekly*, 13 Apr. 1940; Atkin, Chamberlayne-Macdonald collection.
13 *Sydney Morning Herald*, 2 Jan. 1937; Millington to Robinson, 7 July 1939, Robinson collection.
14 Charman, *Outbreak 1939*, pp. 20, 25.
15 Holland, diary, 18, 26 Apr. 1939, Ripley collection.

16 NAUK, AIR 27/592; Olive & Newton, *Devil at 6 O'clock*, pp. 50–51.
17 Olive & Newton, *Devil at 6 O'clock*, pp. 51–52; Kennedy, RAAF Museum, 17 Aug. 1936.
18 D. Sheen, flying log, Foster-Williams collection; Docherty, *Swift to Battle*, p. 229; Sheen, IWM, 12137; and 18375. Both watercolours were painted in 1939 by Pip de Markham (whose full name was Philip de Lacey Markham), Ken Holland's friend.
19 Holland, diary, 15, 29 June, 1, 5 July 1939, Ripley collection.
20 Quotations and information in this section that are not attributed in a note come from 'Christine's Story', Stanley-Hughes collection, with additional information from C. Stanley-Hughes, pers. comm., 9 Apr. 2010.
21 Kennedy, 14 Aug. 1939; 'Christine Darling I was awfully disappointed'; and 'Dear Christine I had hoped', Stanley-Hughes collection.
22 Millington, diary, 24, 25 July 1939, Robinson collection.
23 Millington to Robinson, 19 Aug. 1939, Robinson collection.
24 Holland, diary, 18–19 July 1939, with results written in 'Memorandum' section at rear, Ripley collection.
25 NAUK, AIR 27/592.
26 *Prince Alfred College Chronicle*, Prince Alfred College collection; NAUK, AIR 27/712; Charman, *Outbreak 1939*, p. 28.
27 NAUK, AIR 27/712, 28 Aug. 1939.
28 J. Crossman, diary, 19 July, 12 Aug. 1939; and to Crossman family, 13 Aug. 1939, Bowden collection.
29 G. Caban, 30 Nov. 2011; and D. Maguire, 5 Jan. 2012, pers. comms.
30 J. Crossman, diary, 13 Aug. 1939, Bowden collection.
31 Thomas, *RAF Top Gun*, pp. 51–52, 54–55; David, *Dennis 'Hurricane' David*, p. 18.
32 J. Crossman to Kennedy, 12 Sept. 1939; to Crossman family, 30 Aug. 1939; and diary, 2 Sept. 1939; and Brawn to Crossmans, 6 Oct. 1941, Bowden collection.
33 Millington to Robinson, 7 July 1939, Robinson collection.
34 Holland, diary, 31 Aug., 1 Sept. 1939, Ripley collection.
35 Millington, diary, 2 Sept. 1939, Robinson collection; Holland, diary, 2 Sept. 1939, Ripley collection; J. Crossman, diary, 2 Sept. 1939, Bowden collection.
36 Thomas, *RAF Top Gun*, pp. 53–54.
37 Sheen, IWM, 12137.
38 Hughes, Bowden collection.
39 NAUK, AIR 27/712; David, *Dennis 'Hurricane' David*, p. 18.
40 Holland, diary, 3 Sept. 1939, Ripley collection.
41 Millington, diary, 3 Sept. 1939, Robinson collection.
42 'Christine's Story', Stanley-Hughes collection; C. Stanley-Hughes, pers. comm., 9 Apr. 2010.
43 C. Stanley-Hughes, pers. comm., 4 Sept. 1939; Harper, *Twenty-Two Temporary Gentlemen*, p. 44; J. Crossman to Crossman family, 12 Sept. 1939; to Kennedy, 12 Sept. 1939; and diary, 4 Sept. 1939, Bowden collection.

5 First wartime operations

1 Quotations and information in this section come from Hughes, Bowden collection.
2 Sheen, NAUK, AIR 50/30/34; Price, *Spitfire Mark I/II Aces*, p. 80; Sheen, IWM, 12137; Sheen, 'In England Now', AWM.

3 NAUK, AIR 27/712; Beer, *A Salute to One of 'The Few'*, pp. 88–89; David, *Dennis 'Hurricane' David*, p. 18.
4 Cornwell, *Battle of France*, p. 108.
5 David, NAUK, AIR 50/37/7.
6 Jeff, NAUK, AIR 50/37/18; Glyde, 22 Nov. 1939, Glyde collection.
7 NAUK, AIR 27/712; David, *Dennis 'Hurricane' David*, pp. 19–20.
8 NAUK, AIR 27/712; Glyde, 22 Nov. 1939, Glyde collection.
9 Quotations and information in this section come from *Christian Brothers' College Waverley Record*, 1940, Waverley College collection; Kennedy, 'My darling you probably'; 'Christine Darling I've got your two letters'; and 'Dearest Christine I tried several times'; and 'Christine's Story', Stanley-Hughes collection; C. Stanley-Hughes, pers. comm., 9 Apr. 2010.
10 '1939', *World War II*, From Camel to Hawk website; Walch, State Library of Tasmania.
11 NAUK, AIR 27/1018.
12 Adams, *Hurricane Squadron*, p. 7. There is a discrepancy with the times. The operations record book (NAUK, AIR 27/712) notes that Dick and Joyce took off at 1.30 p.m., and Coope at 4.45 p.m. But Dick's letter home (Glyde, 22 Nov. 1939, Glyde collection) clearly indicates that Dick accompanied Coope on this sortie. Quotations and information in this section that are not attributed in a note come from Glyde, 22, 30 Nov. 1939, Glyde collection.
13 Adams, *Hurricane Squadron*, p. 7; Brackx, *Phoney War*. Cornwell (*Battle of France*, p. 115) notes that Coope landed at 5.10 p.m., and Dick at 2 p.m. The Belgian Aviation History Association (D. Brackx, pers. comm., 23 June 2010) advised that Dick landed at 3.30 p.m. The chronology of Dick's letter to his mother (Glyde, 22 Nov. 1939, Glyde collection) indicates they landed more or less simultaneously.
14 Phillis Glyde, letter, n.d., in Glyde, AWM; Adams, *Hurricane Squadron*, p. 7.
15 [Glyde], Belgian Military Archives.
16 Gleed, *Arise to Conquer*, p. 27. Gleed used noms de guerre, and Dick was dubbed 'Dusty Miller'.
17 Gleed, *Arise to Conquer*, p. 27.
18 Phillis Glyde, letter, n.d., in Glyde, AWM; J. Huygelier, 8 July 2010, 24 Apr. 2012; and K. Van Acker, 6 Aug. 2010, pers. comms.
19 Quotations and information in this section come from Sheen, IWM, 12137; Sheen, RAF Museum; Sheen, 'In England Now'; and 'Secret', AWM; D. Sheen, flying log, Foster-Williams collection.

6 Training for war
1 Quotations to the end of this section come from Millington, diary, 29 Sept. – 10 Oct. 1939, Robinson collection.
2 Quotations and information in this section that are not attributed in a note come from J. Crossman, diary, Sept.–Oct. 1939; and to Crossman family, 25 Oct. 1939, Bowden collection.
3 Brawn to Crossmans, 15 Oct. 1939, Bowden collection.
4 Quotations and information in this section that are not attributed in a note come from Holland, diary, 1939, Ripley collection.
5 C. Evans, pers. comm., 1, 8, 10 Oct., 5 Nov. 2012.
6 Haydon, Evans collection.
7 Walpole, *Dragon Rampant*, p. 12.

8   K. Lawrence, pers. comm., 18 May 2011; Walpole, *Dragon Rampant*, p. 13; Willis, *Churchill's Few*, p. 30.
9   Doe, *Bob Doe – Fighter Pilot*, p. 1; NAUK, AIR 27/1439, 11 Nov. 1939.
10   NAUK, AIR 27/1439, 25–30 Nov. 1939.
11   K. Lawrence, pers. comm., 18 May 2011; Doe, IWM.
12   Quotations and information in this section that are not attributed in a note come from Millington, diary, Oct.–Dec. 1939; and to Robinson, 25 Nov., 31 Dec. 1939, Robinson collection.
13   No. 15, course results, NAUK, AIR 29/568.
14   Quotations and information in this section that are not attributed in a note come from J. Crossman, diary, Oct.–Dec. 1939; flying log; and to Crossman family, 1, 7, 21, 26 Nov., 4, 20 Dec. 1939, 3 Jan. 1940, Bowden collection.
15   Brawn to Crossmans, 30 Dec. 1939, Bowden collection.
16   ibid.
17   Quotations and information in this section that are not attributed in a note come from Holland, diary, Oct.–Dec. 1939, Ripley collection.
18   C. Palliser, pers. comm., 6 Oct. 2009.
19   Palliser, *They Gave Me a Hurricane*, pp. 21–22.
20   Haydon, Evans collection.

7   The Phoney War continues

1   Millington to Robinson, 26 Feb. 1940, Robinson collection.
2   Sheen, 'Secret'; and 'In England Now', AWM.
3   '1940', *World War II*, From Camel to Hawk website.
4   Quotations and information in this section that are not attributed in a note come from *Woman*, *After the Battle* collection; K. Lawrence, 18 May 2011; D. Moor, 12 Mar. 2013; and J. Roddis, 5 Aug. 2013, pers. comms; Doe, 'A Recollection of Pat Hughes'; Ramsey, *Battle of Britain*, p. 746.
5   *Daily News*, 12 Sept. 1940.
6   *Hull Daily Mail*, 4 Sept. 2000.
7   Doe, *Bob Doe – Fighter Pilot*, p. 12; Roddis, *In Support of The Few*, p. 15.
8   Kennedy, 'Dear Christine I tried several times', Stanley-Hughes collection.
9   Kennedy, 'Dear Christine I had hoped'; 'Christine Darling I've got your two letters'; and 'Christine Darling I was awfully disappointed', Stanley-Hughes collection.
10   Olive & Newton, *Devil at 6 O'clock*, p. 60; NAUK, AIR 27/592.
11   C. Stanley-Hughes, pers. comm., 9 Apr. 2010.
12   Kennedy, 'Dearest Christine I rang last night'; and 'Christine's Story', Stanley-Hughes collection; C. Stanley-Hughes, pers. comm., 9 Apr. 2010.
13   Ramsey, *Battle of Britain*, p. 746; *Woman*, *After the Battle* collection; Walpole, *Dragon Rampant*, p. 15; Doe, *Bob Doe – Fighter Pilot*, pp. 12–13.
14   Millington to Robinson, 26 Feb. 1940, Robinson collection; No. 15, course results, NAUK, AIR 29/568.
15   Millington to Robinson, 22 May 1940, Robinson collection.
16   NAUK, AIR 27/1439; Walpole, *Dragon Rampant*, p. 18; Hughes, NAA, A9300; Willis, *Churchill's Few*, p. 30; Hughes, AWM, PR87/142, 16 Aug. 1936.
17   Roddis, *In Support of The Few*, p. 17; NAUK, AIR 27/1439.
18   Quotations and information in this section that are not attributed in a note come from J. Crossman, diary, 1940; and to Crossman family, 3, 18 Jan., 22 Feb., 4, 12, 17 Apr. 1940, Bowden collection.

19 Millington to Robinson, 26 Feb. 1940, Robinson collection.
20 J. Crossman, flying log, final instructor's assessment, 9 EFTS, 9 Apr. 1940, Bowden collection.
21 Hudson, Bowden collection.
22 Quotations and information in this section that are not attributed in a note come from Holland, diaries, Dec. 1939 – May 1940, Ripley collection.
23 Palliser, *They Gave Me a Hurricane*, p. 32.
24 ibid., p. 12.
25 NAUK, AIR 27/712.
26 Gleed, *Arise to Conquer*, pp. 26–27.
27 Beamont, *My Part of the Sky*, p. 22.
28 NAUK, AIR 27/712.

8   The Battle of France
1   Beamont, *My Part of the Sky*, p. 25.
2   David, *Dennis 'Hurricane' David*, pp. 1, 24; Cull, Lander & Weiss, *Twelve Days in May*, pp. 35, 55–56.
3   NAUK, AIR 27/1439; J. Crossman, diary, 10, 16 May 1940, Bowden collection; Holland, diary, 10 May 1940, Ripley collection.
4   'Christine's Story', Stanley-Hughes collection; Olive & Newton, *Devil at 6 O'clock*, p. 152; C. Stanley-Hughes, pers. comm., 9 Apr. 2010.
5   NAUK, AIR 27/1453, 16 May 1940.
6   Millington to Robinson, 22 May 1940, Robinson collection.
7   Cull, Lander & Weiss, *Twelve Days in May*, pp. 84, 107.
8   Quotations and information to the end of this section that are not attributed in a note come from Glyde, NAUK, AIR 50/37/51.
9   Ward, NAUK, AIR 50/37/32. Ward's report records the time of attack as 8.15 a.m., but other details correspond to the dawn attack.
10 Ward, NAUK, AIR 50/37/32, 10 a.m.
11 Beamont, *My Part of the Sky*, p. 34.
12 Gleed, *Arise to Conquer*, pp. 39, 40; Beamont, *My Part of the Sky*, pp. 37, 39; David, *Dennis 'Hurricane' David*, p. 28; Cull, Lander & Weiss, *Twelve Days in May*, p. 176.
13 NAUK, AIR 27/712.
14 Franks, *Fighter Leader*, pp. 66–68.
15 Gleed, *Arise to Conquer*, pp. 46–47, 48–49.
16 NAUK, AIR 27/712.
17 Cull, Lander & Weiss, *Twelve Days in May*, pp. 306–307. Experts differ on Dick's Battle of France score. Shores & Williams, *Aces High*, p. 289, does not include Dick's victory of 12 May. It was published the year before Cull, Lander & Weiss, *Twelve Days in May*. Shores did not include it in his 1999 *Aces High*, vol. 2. Shores and Williams record Dick's victories in France as one-quarter share of a Hs126, a 109E probable and a 109E destroyed. In his article 'Flg Off Richard Glyde DFC', Newton records the He111 destroyed on 12 May and a shared destroyed Hs126, a probable 109E and a destroyed 109E on 19 May.
18 Barker, *Aviator Extraordinary*, p. 154. Quotations and information in this section that are not attributed in a note come from Sheen, IWM, 12137; D. Sheen, flying log; and to Sheens, 7 May, 18 July 1940, Foster-Williams collection; Sheen, 'Secret', AWM.

19   Deacon Elliott, RAF Museum, p. 17.
20   Barker, *Aviator Extraordinary*, p. 158; A. Fletcher, pers. comm., 3 Jan. 2014.
21   NAUK, AIR 2/9398.
22   Newton, *Australia in the Air War*, p. 97.
23   Barker, *Aviator Extraordinary*, p. 197.

9   Action at last
1   NAUK, AIR 27/1439.
2   K. Lawrence, pers. comm., 18 May 2011.
3   D. Moor, pers. comm., 15 Mar. 2013.
4   *Woman, After the Battle* collection; Ramsey, *Battle of Britain*, p. 746.
5   Quotations and information in this section that are not attributed in a note
     come from J. Crossman, diary, May–June 1940, Bowden collection.
6   J. Crossman to Crossman family, 6, 12 June 1940, Bowden collection.
7   Quotations and information in this section come from Holland, diary, May–
     June 1940, Ripley collection.
8   Millington to Robinson, 22 May 1940; and RAF service record, Robinson
     collection.
9   *Times*, 18 June 1940; E. Robinson, Robinson collection.
10   Millington to his parents, June 1940, Robinson collection.
11   NAUK, AIR 27/1453, 15–18 May 1940.
12   'Christine's Story', Stanley-Hughes collection.
13   Batt, *Scramble!*, p. 22.
14   NAUK, AIR 27/1453; Batt, *Scramble!*, p. 23.
15   'Christine's Story'; and Kennedy, 'Dearest Christine I rang last night', Stanley-
     Hughes collection; C. Stanley-Hughes, pers. comm., 9 Apr. 2010.
16   C. Stanley-Hughes, 9 Apr. 2010, n.d. [postmarked 19 Apr. 2010]; and
     B. Kennedy, 11 Mar. 2010, pers. comms; Kennedy, 'Dear Christine I tried
     several times', Stanley-Hughes collection.
17   'Christine's Story'; and Kennedy, 'Christine Darling sorry'; and 30 June 1940,
     Stanley-Hughes collection.
18   Ramsey, *Battle of Britain*, p. 218; 'Christine's Story'; and Kennedy, 'Dearest
     Christine this is a different letter', Stanley-Hughes collection (the polite
     omission in 'f— all' was Jack's); extract from letter by Flight Lieutenant S.C.
     Walch, dated 26 June 1940, in *Hutchins School Magazine*, Dec. 1940, Hutchins
     Archives and Heritage Collection.
19   Kennedy, 'Christine Darling this letter is long overdue', Stanley-Hughes
     collection.
20   Addison & Crang, *Listening to Britain*, p. 121; D. Sheen to Sheens, 18 July
     1940, Foster-Williams collection; Millington, letter published in *Advertiser*,
     11 Sept. 1940.
21   Addison & Crang, *Listening to Britain*, pp. 147, 179; *Rise and Fall of the German
     Air Force*, p. 79.
22   Kennedy, 'Christine Darling sorry', Stanley-Hughes collection.
23   NAUK, AIR 27/1453, 2 July 1940; Kennedy, 'Christine Darling this letter is
     long overdue'; and 'Christine Darling I've got your two letters', Stanley-Hughes
     collection; Mason, *Battle over Britain*, p. 105.
24   NAUK, AIR 27/1439.
25   Blue Section, combined combat report, NAUK, AIR 50/89, 8 July 1940.
26   NAUK, AIR 27/1439; K. Lawrence, pers. comm., 18 May 2011.

27 Quotations and information in this section that are not attributed in a note come from Millington, letters published in *Advertiser*, 11 Sept., 18 Oct. 1940.
28 NAUK, AIR 27/664.
29 Millington, NAUK, AIR 50/33/35.
30 Morris, IWM.

10 10 July – 7 August
1 *Battle of Britain, August–October 1940*, pp. 3, 6; 'Despatch on the Conduct of the Battle of Britain', p. 4544; *Battle of Britain*, Air Ministry pamphlet, p. 41.
2 James, *Battle of Britain*.
3 Holland, diary, 10 July 1940, Ripley collection.
4 Kennedy, 'Christine Darling sorry', Stanley-Hughes collection.
5 J. Crossman, diary, 6–8 July 1940; Brawn to Crossmans, 16 Dec. 1940; and Parkes, Bowden collection.
6 J. Elkington, pers. comm., 5 Feb. 2012, 14 Mar. 2013; J. Crossman, diary, 8 July 1940, Bowden collection.
7 An edited extract of the 11 July narrative was published in Alexander, 'Australian Hurricane Pilots'.
8 Jay, NAUK, AIR 50/37/17, 11 July 1940, 12 p.m.; Dewar, NAUK, AIR 50/37/49, 11 July 1940, 12 p.m.
9 Jay, NAUK, AIR 50/37/17, 11 July 1940, 12 p.m.; Glyde, NAUK, AIR 50/37/53, 12 p.m.; NAUK, AIR 27/712, 11 July 1940.
10 Glyde, NAUK, AIR 50/37/53; NAUK, AIR 27/712, 11 July 1940.
11 Walch, NAUK, AIR 50/91/41; NAUK, AIR 27/1453, 11 July 1940. Walch and Considine are credited with the one-third share in Shores, *Those Other Eagles*, pp. 118, 616; and Urwin-Mann is credited with his one-third share in Shores & Williams, *Aces High*, p. 601.
12 NAUK, AIR 27/1453, 12 July 1940; Kennedy, 'Christine Darling this letter is long overdue', Stanley-Hughes collection.
13 NAUK, AIR 27/1453, 12–13 July 1940.
14 Dorset County Council, Dorset History Centre.
15 Davis, Kennedy collection; NAUK, AIR 27/1453; Davis, NAUK, AIR 50/91/38.
16 Acutt, *Brigade in Action*, p. 94.
17 Davis, Kennedy collection.
18 Marsh, IWM; Batt, *Scramble!*, p. 45; Davis; and Kavanagh, Kennedy collection; NAUK, AIR 27/1453, 13 July, 11 Aug. 1940.
19 'Christine's Story'; and air liaison officer, Stanley-Hughes collection.
20 Information to the end of this section that is not attributed in a note comes from C. Stanley-Hughes, pers. comm., 9 Apr. 2010.
21 Kennedy, 'Christine Darling this letter is long overdue', Stanley-Hughes collection.
22 Kennedy, 'Christine Darling I've got your two letters', Stanley-Hughes collection.
23 Kavanagh, Kennedy collection; NAUK, AIR 27/1453, 15 July 1940.
24 Addison & Crang, *Listening to Britain*, p. 210; NAUK, AIR 27/1439, 20, 25 July 1940.
25 James, *Battle of Britain*, p. 39.
26 Hughes, combat report, NAUK, AIR 27/1439, 27 July 1940; Connor, NAUK, AIR 50/89/3; NAUK, AIR 27/1439, 27 July 1940; Franks, *Fighter Leader*, pp. 157–58.

27   Hughes, combat report, NAUK, AIR 27/1439, 28 July 1940; NAUK, AIR 27/1439, 27 July 1940; Franks, *Fighter Leader*, p. 158.
28   Walpole, *Dragon Rampant*, p. 29; K. Lawrence, pers. comm., 18 May 2011.
29   *Woman, After the Battle* collection.
30   Ramsey, *Battle of Britain*, p. 747; *Woman, After the Battle* collection.
31   Beamont, *My Part of the Sky*, p. 53. Beamont has mixed up his dates. He attributes this event to 11 Aug. 1940, but his description of 'a bullet had smashed his hood only an inch or so from his head' clearly relates to the 11 July incident. Gleed, *Arise to Conquer*, p. 64.
32   Gleed, *Arise to Conquer*, p. 64.
33   D. Sheen to Sheens, 18 July 1940, Foster-Williams collection.
34   Sheen, IWM, 12137; Nelson-Edwards, *Spit and Sawdust*, p. 64; Morris, IWM.
35   Quotations and information in this section that are not attributed in a note come from J. Crossman to Crossman family, 15 May, 15, 24–31 July, 2 Aug. 1940, Bowden collection.
36   J. Crossman, diary, 11, 14 July 1940, Bowden collection.
37   Quotations and information in this section that are not attributed in a note come from NAUK, AIR 27/1453, 17, 20, 21 July 1940; Walch, NAUK, AIR 50/91/21, 20–21 July 1940.
38   Fenton, RAF Museum, p. 46.
39   Walch, NAUK, AIR 50/91/47.
40   Walch, letter, 29 July 1940, quoted in *Hutchins School Magazine*, Dec. 1940, Hutchins Archives and Heritage Collection.

11   8–18 August
1   Bishop, *Battle of Britain*, pp. 95–97; *Rise and Fall of the German Air Force*, p. 79.
2   Bishop, *Battle of Britain*, p. 146.
3   NAUK, AIR 27/1453; Fenton, RAF Museum, pp. 48–50.
4   *Hutchins School Magazine*, Dec. 1940, Hutchins Archives and Heritage Collection.
5   NAUK, AIR 27/712; Gelb, *Scramble*, p. 120.
6   Gelb, *Scramble*, p. 120; NAUK, AIR 27/712.
7   *Hutchins School Magazine*, Dec. 1940, Hutchins Archives and Heritage Collection; Pidd, NAUK, AIR 50/91/43, 10.35 a.m.; Urwin-Mann, NAUK, AIR 50/91/42, 10.35 a.m.
8   Herington, *Air War against Germany and Italy*, p. 36; *Hutchins School Magazine*, Dec. 1940, Hutchins Archives and Heritage Collection; NAUK, AIR 27/1453.
9   NAUK, AIR 27/1453.
10   Jay, NAUK, AIR 50/37/17, 13 Aug. 1940, 7.35 a.m.; Dewar, NAUK, AIR 50/37/49, 13 Aug. 1940, 7.35 a.m.; NAUK, AIR 27/712.
11   Gleed, *Arise to Conquer*, pp. 63–64.
12   Glyde, NAA; Beamont, *My Part of the Sky*, p. 53.
13   *Woman, After the Battle* collection.
14   NAUK, AIR 27/1439, 13 Aug. 1940; Willis, *Churchill's Few*, p. 103.
15   Doe, 'A Recollection of Pat Hughes'; K. Lawrence, 18 May 2011; and J. Roddis, 5 Aug. 2013, pers. comms; Roddis, IWM; Willis, *Churchill's Few*, p. 87.
16   *Woman, After the Battle* collection.
17   Ramsey, *Battle of Britain*, pp. 220, 222; NAUK, AIR 27/1453, 13 Aug. 1940; Arthur, *Last of The Few*, p. 172.
18   Price, *Spitfire Mark I/II Aces*, p. 82; Sheen, RAF Museum.

19   Price, *Spitfire Mark I/II Aces*, p. 83; Sheen, combat report, NAUK, AIR 27/627, 15 Aug. 1940; Sheen, RAF Museum.
20   Nelson-Edwards, *Spit and Sawdust*, p. 65; NAUK, AIR 27/664.
21   NAUK, AIR 27/664.
22   ibid.; Doe, NAUK, AIR 50/89/73.
23   Sheen, IWM, 12137; Burgess, *'Bush' Parker*, p. 25; Wynn, *Men of the Battle of Britain*, pp. 216–17, 388. As for Bush Parker's claim of the Me110, none from his squadron could verify this; they hardly knew what had happened to him, let alone that he had added to the squadron tally – if indeed he had.
24   Wood & Dempster, *Narrow Margin*, p. 209.
25   Arthur, *Last of The Few*, p. 173; Doe, *Bob Doe – Fighter Pilot*, p. 21; K. Lawrence, pers. comm., 18 May 2011.
26   *Woman, After the Battle* collection.
27   Hughes, NAUK, AIR 50/89/83, 16 Aug. 1940; Doe, NAUK, AIR 50/89/73.
28   Doe, *Bob Doe – Fighter Pilot*, p. 23.
29   Bungay, *Most Dangerous Enemy*, p. 223.
30   *Woman, After the Battle* collection; K. Lawrence, pers. comm., 18 May 2011.
31   K. Lawrence, pers. comm., 8 May 2011.
32   NAUK, AIR 27/1439.
33   Hughes, NAUK, AIR 50/89/89; O'Brien, NAUK, AIR 50/89/18.
34   Bungay, *Most Dangerous Enemy*, p. 231; Price, *Spitfire Mark I/II Aces*, p. 9; Price, *Battle of Britain*, p. 158.

12   19–31 August
1   D. Sheen to Sheens, 16 Aug. 1940, Foster-Williams collection.
2   K. Lawrence, pers. comm., 18 May 2011; Hughes, NAUK, AIR 50/89/89.
3   J. Crossman, diary, 18 Aug. 1940, Bowden collection.
4   Van Sickle, *Modern Airmanship*, pp. 268–70, 272; J. Crossman, diary, 25 July, 18 Aug. 1940, Bowden collection.
5   Quotations and information in this and the following section that are not attributed in a note come from Holland, diary, Aug. 1940, Ripley collection.
6   Hillary, *Last Enemy*, pp. 70–71.
7   Haydon, Evans collection.
8   Hall, *Spitfire Pilot*, pp. 23, 44.
9   Haydon, Evans collection.
10   NAUK, AIR 27/1025; [Marrs], 'One of The Few', part 1.
11   Hughes, NAUK, AIR 50/89/83, 26 Aug. 1940.
12   Walpole, *Dragon Rampant*, p. 32.
13   NAUK, AIR 2/9398, 29 Aug. 1940.
14   [Marrs], 'One of The Few', part 2.
15   Holland, will and probate, Evans collection (original emphasis).
16   J. Crossman to Crossman family, 11 Aug. 1940, Bowden collection.
17   J. Crossman, flying log, Bowden collection.
18   J. Crossman, diary, 28 Aug. 1940; and to Crossman family, 28 Aug. 1940, Bowden collection.
19   Quotations and information in this section that are not attributed in a note come from Morris, IWM; NAUK, AIR 27/664.
20   Millington to Robinson, 14 Sept. 1940, Robinson collection; *Advertiser*, 9 Sept. 1940.

21 Parker, *Battle of Britain*, pp. 250–51; *Examiner*, 3 Sept. 1940; *Mercury*, 3 Sept. 1940, 19 May 1942.
22 Nelson-Edwards, *Spit and Sawdust*, pp. 66, 67; NAUK, AIR 27/664.
23 Quotations and information to the end of this chapter that are not attributed in a note come from Millington to Robinson, 14 Sept. 1940, Robinson collection.
24 *Advertiser*, 9 Sept. 1940; NAUK, AIR 27/664.
25 *West Australian*, 5 Apr. 1941; NAUK, AIR 2/9398, 8 Sept. 1940; Ramsey, *Battle of Britain*, p. 811; *Advertiser*, 9 Sept. 1940.
26 Austin, *Fighter Command*, p. 193; NAUK, AIR 2/9398, 10 Sept. 1940; V. Wells, pers. comm., n.d. [received 9 Mar. 2011].
27 *Alexander*, 'Australian Knights of the Air'; Cull, Lander & Weiss, *Twelve Days in May*, p. 318.
28 *Daily Express*, 13 Aug. 1940; *Alexander*, 'Australian Knights of the Air'. Also killed when Grice kept at the controls rather than let his Blenheim crash on a shopping centre were his crew, Sergeant Frank Keast and Aircraftman 1st Class John Warren.
29 Deacon Elliott, RAF Museum, p. 42.
30 Townsend, *Duel of Eagles*, p. 375.
31 NAUK, AIR 2/9398, 10 Sept. 1940.

13 1–6 September

1   *Advertiser*, 9 Sept. 1940.
2   Sheen, RAF Museum; D. Sheen to Sheens, 4 Sept. 1940, Foster-Williams collection.
3   NAUK, AIR 27/624; Deacon Elliott, RAF Museum, p. 43.
4   'In Memoriam'.
5   NAUK, AIR 27/624.
6   *Swift to Battle*, p. 110; Sheen, RAF Museum; Sheen, IWM, 12137.
7   D. Sheen to Sheens, 4 Sept. 1940, Foster-Williams collection; 'Despatch on the Conduct of the Battle of Britain'.
8   Sheen, RAF Museum.
9   D. Sheen to Sheens, 4 Sept. 1940, Foster-Williams collection; Hughes, Hughes collection.
10 D. Sheen to Sheens, 4, 10 Sept. 1940, Foster-Williams collection; Sheen, RAF Museum; *Swift to Battle*, p. 114; NAUK, AIR 27/624; Shores & Williams, *Aces High*, p. 544.
11 Lees, Lees collection; 'In Memoriam' (which also notes that Ronald Lees's Battle of Britain actions took place on 1 Sept. 1940); R. Lees, pers. comm., 17 July 2013.
12 Sheen, combat report, NAUK, AIR 27/627, 4 Sept. 1940.
13 Sheen, RAF Museum.
14 Sheen, IWM, 12137; NAUK, AIR 27/624; Deacon Elliott, RAF Museum, p. 47.
15 Quotations and information in this section that are not attributed in a note come from D. Sheen to Sheens, 10 Sept. 1940; and flying log, Foster-Williams collection; Sheen, IWM, 2308.
16 Sheen, RAF Museum. In D. Sheen to Sheens, 10 Sept. 1940, Foster-Williams collection, Des states that he was descending at 600 miles per hour. In Sheen, IWM, 2308, he states that it was 400 miles per hour.
17 H. Sheen, newsclipping (unattrib.) in scrapbook, Foster-Williams collection; Sheen, IWM, 18375; Sheen, RAF Museum.

18   Quotations and information in this section come from J. Crossman, diary, 23–24 Aug., 2 Sept. 1940; and to Foley, 1 Sept. 1940, Bowden collection.
19   J. Crossman, diary, 3 Sept. 1940, Bowden collection; Hughes, NAUK, AIR 50/89/83, 4 Sept. 1940; combined combat report, NAUK, AIR 50/89, 4 Sept. 1940.
20   Hughes, NAUK, AIR 50/89/83, 4 Sept. 1940.
21   NAUK, AIR 27/1439.
22   Franks, *Wings of Freedom*, p. 162.
23   Combined combat report, NAUK, AIR 50/89, 4 Sept. 1940; Shores & Williams, *Aces High*, p. 343.
24   *Woman, After the Battle* collection.
25   Hughes, NAUK, AIR 50/89/83, 6 Sept. 1940.
26   Wells, *Courage and Air Warfare*, pp. 61–62, 68; Van Sickle, *Modern Airmanship*, p. 270; Ruffin, 'Flying in the Great War', part 2.
27   Willis, *Churchill's Few*, p. 128.
28   Clostermann, *Big Show*, p. xii.
29   Francis, *The Flyer*, pp. 112–13, 115–16, 118–19, 124; Wells, *Courage and Air Warfare*, pp. 69, 117; Ruffin, 'Flying in the Great War', part 2.
30   K. Lawrence, pers. comm., 18 May 2011; Francis, *The Flyer*, p. 116; Symonds & Williams, *Psychological Disorders*, pp. 51–53.
31   Wells, *Courage and Air Warfare*, p. 63; *Woman, After the Battle* collection.
32   Willis, *Churchill's Few*, p. 136; Francis, *The Flyer*, p. 114; Symonds & Williams, *Psychological Disorders*, pp. 35–36; Doe, *Bob Doe – Fighter Pilot*, p. 42.
33   Willis, *Churchill's Few*, pp. 128, 135–36; K. Lawrence, pers. comm., 18 May 2011.

14   7–13 September

1   *Rise and Fall of the German Air Force*, p. 82.
2   Bishop, *Battle of Britain*, p. 289; *Rise and Fall of the German Air Force*, p. 85.
3   Bungay, *Most Dangerous Enemy*, p. 308; *Woman, After the Battle* collection.
4   J. Roddis, pers. comm., 5 Aug. 2013.
5   Hall, Hall collection; T. Hall, pers. comm., 6 Aug. 2013; Ramsey, *Battle of Britain*, p. 45.
6   Orange, *Park*, p. 104; J. Roddis, pers. comm., 5 Aug. 2013; Bungay, *Most Dangerous Enemy*, p. 309.
7   Hall, Hall collection.
8   A. Rennie, pers. comm., 2 Sept. 2013.
9   Hall, Hall collection.
10   Stansky, *First Day of the Blitz*, pp. 37–38.
11   Lawrence, NAUK, AIR 50/89/37; K. Lawrence, 18 May 2011; and T. Hall, 21 May 2011, pers. comms; *Sevenoaks News*, 12 Sept. 1940; Hall, Hall collection.
12   Doe, NAUK, AIR 50/89/35; Harker, NAUK, AIR 50/89/36; combined combat report, NAUK, AIR 50/89, 7 Sept. 1940; A. Saunders, pers. comm., 6 Aug. 2013.
13   T. Hall, pers. comm., 21 May 2011; Hall, Hall collection; A. Saunders, pers. comm., 6 Aug. 2013.
14   *Hull Daily Mail*, 4 Sept. 2000; Doe, IWM.
15   Pat Hughes, 'An Autumn Evening', *Fortian*, Fort Street High School collection.
16   Combined combat report, NAUK, AIR 50/89, 7 Sept. 1940; K. Lawrence, pers. comm., 18 May 2011.

17 Shores & Williams, *Aces High*, p. 343; Franks, *Wings of Freedom*, pp. 163–64.
18 Lists differ. *The Few*, Wikipedia, last modified 24 Feb. 2014, <en.wikipedia. org/wiki/The_Few>, has Pat Hughes as the ninth highest scorer of the Battle of Britain, with '14 + ' victories. In *A Few of 'The Few'*, p. 283, Dennis Newton ranks him sixth, with 14 plus three shared or 15 plus three (the difference here depended on whether or not he was credited with the final Do17). In *Fighter Aces of the RAF*, pp. 201–205, E.C.R. Baker ranks Pat 47th of all RAF aces, with 16 and one half. The variation attests to the difficulty in determining exact scores.
19 Willis, *Churchill's Few*, p. 136.
20 D. Sheen to Sheens, 19 Sept. 1940, Foster-Williams collection; Olive & Newton, *Devil at 6 O'clock*, p. 153.
21 J. Roddis, 5 Aug. 2013; and K. Lawrence, 18 May 2011, pers. comms; Walpole, *Dragon Rampant*, p. 22; NAUK, AIR 2/9398, 29 Aug. 1940.
22 Doe, IWM; *Woman*, *After the Battle* collection; D. Moor, pers. comm., 12 Mar. 2013; Willis, *Churchill's Few*, p. 135.
23 Hughes, newsclipping (unattrib.), n.d., AWM, PR87/180.
24 Doe, IWM.
25 *Woman*, *After the Battle* collection.
26 Walpole, *Dragon Rampant*, pp. 40–41.
27 Hall, Hall collection.
28 Addison & Crang, *Listening to Britain*, p. 408.
29 Quotations to the end of this section that are not attributed in a note come from D. Sheen to Sheens, 10, 14, 19 Sept. 1940, Foster-Williams collection.
30 Holland, diary, 8 Sept. 1940, Ripley collection.
31 Townsend, *Duel of Eagles*, pp. 399–400; Millington to Robinson, 14 Sept. 1940, Robinson collection.
32 J. Crossman, diary, 7 Sept. 1940, Bowden collection; Holland, diary, 6–7, 9–13 Sept. 1940, Ripley collection.
33 Orange, *Park*, pp. 108, 200.

15 14–24 September
1   Quotations and information in this and the following section that are not attributed in a note come from J. Crossman, diary, 12–14, 21 Sept. 1940, Bowden collection.
2   J. Diggle, pers. comm., 27 Oct. 2011; Jennings & Walton, *Search for One of The Few*, pp. 26–31; Brawn to Crossmans, 4 Oct. 1940, Bowden collection.
3   J. Diggle, pers. comm., 27 Oct. 2011; Brawn to Crossmans, 4 Oct. 1940, Bowden collection.
4   Mabel Crossman, 4 Oct., 10 Nov. 1940, Bowden collection.
5   J. Crossman, flying log, Bowden collection.
6   C. & P. Bowden, pers. comm., 23 Oct. 2013.
7   NAUK, AIR 27/460; James, *Battle of Britain*, p. 258.
8   Neil, *Gun-Button to 'Fire'*, p. 107; NAUK, AIR 27/460.
9   J. Crossman, diary, 15 Sept. 1940, Bowden collection. John's combat report (Crossman, NAUK, AIR 50/20/13), however, states he saw about 20 Dorniers.
10 NAUK, AIR 27/460.
11 Barclay, *Battle of Britain Pilot*, pp. 49, 51.
12 NAUK, AIR 27/460.
13 J. Crossman, flying log; and Brawn to Crossmans, 4 Oct. 1940, Bowden collection.

14   James, *Battle of Britain*, p. 266.

15   Quotations and information in this and the following section not attributed in a note come from [Marrs], 'One of The Few', part 1; combined combat report, NAUK, AIR 50/64, 15, 17 Sept. 1940; Holland, diary, 14–20 Sept. 1940, Ripley collection; Holland, NAUK, AIR 50/64/90, 17, 19 Sept. 1940.

16   Shores, *Those Other Eagles*, pp. 276, 625. There is no entry for O'Brian. Wynn (*Men of the Battle of Britain*) also does not accord any of Green Section with their shared probable.

17   Bungay, *Most Dangerous Enemy*, p. 332.

18   Addison & Crang, *Listening to Britain*, pp. 423, 425; D. Sheen to Sheens, 19 Sept. 1940, Foster-Williams collection.

19   Ken stated Green Section in his diary (Robinson collection), but both his individual combat report (NAUK, AIR 50/64/90, 17 Sept. 1940) and the combined report (NAUK, AIR 50/64, 17 Sept. 1940) state Blue Section.

20   *Advertiser*, 11 Sept. 1940; Nelson-Edwards, *Spit and Sawdust*, p. 64.

21   Cull, *249 at War*, p. 21; NAUK, AIR 27/1498.

22   T. Neil, pers. comm., 7 Oct. 2011; Neil, *Gun-Button to 'Fire'*, p. 118.

23   C. Palliser, pers. comm., 6 Oct. 2009; Palliser, *They Gave Me a Hurricane*, pp. 84, 98.

24   NAUK, AIR 27/1498; Barclay, *Battle of Britain Pilot*, p. 59.

25   J. Crossman to Crossman family, 22 Sept. 1940; and Brawn to Crossmans, 4 Oct. 1940, Bowden collection.

26   Francis, *The Flyer*, pp. 115–16; Wells, *Courage and Air Warfare*, p. 117.

27   J. Crossman, diary, 20, 21 Sept. 1940; and to Crossman family, 22 Sept. 1940, Bowden collection.

28   J. Crossman to Crossman family, 22 Sept. 1940, Bowden collection.

29   [Marrs], 'One of The Few', part 1; Holland, diary, 21 Sept. 1940, Ripley collection.

16   25–30 September

1   NAUK, AIR 27/1025; Devitt, NAUK, AIR 50/64/82; Bayles, NAUK, AIR 50/64/3.

2   Devitt, NAUK, AIR 50/64/82; James, *Battle of Britain*, p. 274.

3   [Marrs], 'One of The Few', part 1; Bayles, NAUK, AIR 50/64/3; Wakefield, *Luftwaffe Encore*, pp. 95–96; 'Report', Ripley collection; Hawkins, *Somerset at War*, p. 30.

4   'Report', Ripley collection.

5   Hawkins, *Somerset at War*, p. 30; NAUK, AIR 27/1025.

6   'Report', Ripley collection. Bayles's combat report (NAUK, AIR 50/64/3) noted a one-half claim for the destruction of the Heinkel. In *Aces High*, Shores and Williams note that Urwin-Mann destroyed two Heinkels that day, and in *Men of the Battle of Britain*, Wynn notes that Little was credited with the Heinkel.

7   Haydon, Evans collection.

8   Sir W. Ripley Bt, 9 Sept. 2009; and C. Webb, 21 Sept. 2009, pers. comms.

9   *Rise and Fall of the German Air Force*, p. 86; Orange, *Park*, p. 112.

10   J. Crossman, diary, 23 Sept. 1940, Bowden collection; Orange, *Park*, pp. 112–13.

11   Bush, 30 Sept. 1941, 31 Mar. 1943, Bowden collection.

12   J. Crossman, diary, 24–26 Sept. 1940, Bowden collection; NAUK, AIR 27/1498, 27 Sept. 1940.

13 NAUK, AIR 27/1498, 27 Sept. 1940; Millington, NAUK, AIR 50/96/10, 27 Sept. 1940.
14 Neil, *Gun-Button to 'Fire'*, p. 133; Millington, NAUK, AIR 50/96/10, 27 Sept. 1940.
15 T. Neil, pers. comm., 7 Oct. 2011.
16 NAUK, AIR 27/1498, 27 Sept. 1940.
17 J. Crossman, diary, 27 Sept. 1940, Bowden collection; NAUK, AIR 27/460, 27 Sept. 1940.
18 Bush, 31 Mar. 1943, Bowden collection.
19 J. Crossman, diary, 28 Sept. 1940, Bowden collection.
20 Quotations and information in this section pertaining to the evening with Jackie Bush come from Bush, 30 Sept. 1941, 31 Mar. 1943, Bowden collection.
21 NAUK, AIR 27/1498.
22 Quotations and information to the end of this section that are not attributed in a note come from Neil, *Gun-Button to 'Fire'*, pp. 137, 139.
23 Barclay, *Battle of Britain Pilot*, p. 65.
24 Cull, *249 at War*, p. 41.
25 Barclay, *Battle of Britain Pilot*, p. 65.
26 J. Crossman, diary, 29 Sept. 1940, Bowden collection.
27 J. Elkington, pers. comm., 25 Sept. 2013; Ruffin, 'Flying in the Great War', part 1.
28 Barclay, *Battle of Britain Pilot*, p. 65; J. Crossman, flying log, Bowden collection; NAUK, AIR 27/1498, 30 Sept. 1940.
29 Bush, 30 Sept. 1941, Bowden collection.
30 NAUK, AIR 27/460; Cull, *249 at War*, p. 41.
31 Barclay, *Battle of Britain Pilot*, p. 65.
32 Wimperis, Wimperis collection; Neil, *Gun-Button to 'Fire'*, pp. 140–41; Barclay, *Battle of Britain Pilot*, p. 65.
33 Brawn to Crossmans, 4 Oct. 1940, 6 Oct. 1941; and J. Crossman, diary, 9 Mar., 20 May 1940, Bowden collection.
34 *East Grinstead Courier and Observer*, 8 Oct. 2012; *East Grinstead Observer*, Sept. 1996 (date not on clipping); *East Grinstead Courier*, 27 Sept. 1996.
35 Wimperis, Wimperis collection.
36 A. Harrap, pers. comm., 12 Jan. 2012.
37 Bush, 30 Sept. 1941, 31 Mar. 1943, Bowden collection.
38 Quotations and information to the end of this chapter come from Brawn to Crossmans, 4 Oct., 16 Dec. 1940, 2 Apr. 1941; and Mabel Crossman, 4 Oct. 1940, Bowden collection; Mick Crossman, Wimperis collection.

17 1–31 October
1 'Despatch on the Conduct of the Battle of Britain'.
2 Quotations and information in this chapter that are not attributed in a note come from Barclay, *Battle of Britain Pilot*, pp. 65–82; Neil, *Gun-Button to 'Fire'*, pp. 139–75; Cull, *249 at War*, pp. 43–50; T. Neil, pers. comm., 7 Oct. 2011.
3 Gibbs, Robinson collection.
4 Millington, NAUK, AIR 50/96/10, 7 Oct. 1940.
5 ibid., 25 Oct. 1940.
6 Jennings & Walton, *Search for One of The Few*, pp. 34–35; Bush, 30 Sept. 1941, Bowden collection.

7 NAUK, AIR 27/1498.
8 Millington, NAUK, AIR 50/96/10, 28 Oct. 1940.
9 ibid.
10 ibid., 29 Oct. 1940.
11 NAUK, AIR 27/1498; M. Hudson, pers. comm., 21 Nov. 2012.
12 Millington, letter published in *Advertiser*, 11 Sept. 1940; Morris, IWM; *Advertiser*, 6 Dec. 1940.
13 Ruffin, 'Flying in the Great War', part 1; NAUK, AIR 27/1498.
14 C. Palliser, pers. comm., 6 Oct. 2009.
15 *Advertiser*, 6 Dec. 1940.

18 Loss

1 *Battle of Britain, August–October 1940*, p. 31; 'Despatch on the Conduct of the Battle of Britain', p. 4557.
2 Kennedy; Glyde; and Crossman, NAA.
3 Cameron, Bowden collection.
4 *Daily News*, 12 Sept. 1940; Hughes, NAA, A705, 163/36/115; B. Kennedy, pers. comm., 11 Mar. 2010.
5 B. Kennedy, pers. comm., 11 Mar. 2010.
6 *West Australian*, 16 Aug. 1940; *Swan*, Aug. 1940, Guildford Grammar School collection; *Advertiser*, 4 Nov., 6 Dec. 1940.
7 *Sydney Morning Herald*, 11 Sept., 5 Oct. 1940; *Daily News*, 12 Sept. 1940; Tamarama SLSC, Taylor collection.
8 *Newcastle Morning Herald & Miners' Advocate*, 7 Aug., 26 Oct. 1940; Harper, *Twenty-Two Temporary Gentlemen*, p. 57; Crossman, newspaper article (unattrib.), Bowden collection.
9 *Newcastle Morning Herald & Miners' Advocate*, 3 Oct. 1940.
10 Mabel Crossman to Crossmans, 22 Sept., 27 Oct. 1940, Bowden collection.
11 J. Crossman to Foley, 1 Sept. 1940; and to Crossman family, 26 Nov. 1939; and Brawn to Crossmans, 30 Dec. 1939, Bowden collection; C. & P. Bowden, pers. comm., 23 Oct. 2013.
12 *Mercury*, 14, 16 Aug. 1940; *Argus*, 20 Aug. 1940; J. Walch, pers. comm., 21 Apr. 2010; Walch, NAA, A705, 166/43/934.
13 *Examiner*, 26 Aug. 1940.
14 [Millington], NAA.
15 Walch, NAA, A705, 166/43/934.
16 Millington to his parents, June 1940; and Macdonald, Robinson collection; *West Australian*, 5 Apr. 1941.
17 *Advertiser*, 15 Dec. 1941.
18 J. Walch, pers. comm., 21 Apr. 2010; Walch, NAA, A705, 166/43/934.
19 Glyde, NAA.
20 Langslow; and Wimperis, Bowden collection.
21 T. Crossman, Wimperis collection; Wimperis, Bowden collection; *Daily Telegraph*, 1 Oct. 1940.
22 B. Kennedy, pers. comm., 24 July 2010; Davis, Kennedy collection.
23 Clark, Kennedy collection.
24 Quotations and information in this section that are not attributed in a note come from Brawn to Crossmans, 11 Oct. 1940, 2 Apr., 15 May, 6 Oct. 1941, Bowden collection.
25 J. Crossman, Gieves Ltd, Bowden collection.

26 Quotations and information in this section that are not attributed in a note come from C. Stanley-Hughes, pers. comm., 9 Apr., 19 June 2010, 24 June 2013.
27 'Christine's Story', Stanley-Hughes collection.
28 W. Stanley Hughes, pers. comm., 27 Mar. 2010, 10 Oct. 2013.
29 *Whitstable Times*, 10 Jan. 2002; W. Stanley Hughes, pers. comm., 11 Oct. 2013.
30 Quotations and information in this section come from D. Moor, pers. comm., 10, 11 Oct. 2013; *Woman, After the Battle* collection.
31 D. Maguire, pers. comm., 5 Jan. 2012; *Sunday Mail*, 18 May 1947.
32 D. Maguire, 5 Jan. 2012; and G. Caban, 30 Nov. 2011, pers. comms.
33 Haydon, Evans collection.
34 Feuchtwanger, Evans collection; M. Andrews, pers. comm., 27 July 2012.
35 C. Evans, pers. comm., 1 Oct. 2012.

19 In memoriam
1 B. Kennedy, 11 Mar. 2010; and C. Stanley-Hughes, 9 Apr. 2010, pers. comms.
2 Glyde, NAA; R. Glyde, 14 Nov. 2008, 5 May 2010; and K. Glyde, 9 Apr. 2010, pers. comms.
3 Wray, *After the Battle* collection; S. Bladen, 31 Oct. 2013; G. Hughes, Nov. 2008, with undated note and news article; and D. Hughes, 31 Oct. 2013, pers. comms.
4 Hartnell; H. Hughes, 23 Dec. 1980, 12 May 1982; and J. Hughes, 30 Mar. 1981, *After the Battle* collection; anonymous note and advertisement, courtesy of *After the Battle*.
5 D. Moor, pers. comm., 14 Mar. 2013; Hughes, NAA, A9300.
6 S. Bladen, pers. comm., 31 Oct. 2013; H. Hughes, 23 Dec. 1980, *After the Battle* collection.
7 T. Hall, pers. comm., 1 Nov. 2013.
8 Doe, 'A Recollection of Pat Hughes'.
9 J. Roddis, pers. comm., 5 Aug. 2013; 'Battle of Britain Groundcrew'.
10 Taylor, *Life and Times of Kenneth Holland*, p. 33; Holland, diary, 8 Sept. 1939; and Ripley, Ripley collection. RAF Disclosures advises that Ken's RAF service record notes Toby's guardianship but not an adoption. M. Hudson, pers. comm., 3 Nov. 2009.
11 Davey, Falconer collection; *Somerset Standard*, 19 Nov. 1976; J. Falconer, 18, 19 Nov. 2013; and G. Simpson, 20 Nov. 2013, pers. comms.
12 J. Falconer, pers. comm., 2 Sept. 2009.
13 Perkins, *Westminster Abbey*, p. 25; War Cabinet, NAA; *Argus*, 6 Nov. 1944.
14 *Advertiser*, 7 June 1947.
15 *Mercury*, 11 July 1947.
16 Walch, NAA, A705, 166/43/934.
17 *Advertiser*, 7 June 1947; *Times*, 11 July 1947; *Mercury*, 11 July 1947.
18 *Advertiser*, 16 Sept. 1947, 16 Sept. 1948; *Mercury*, 14 July 1948; J. Walch, pers. comm., 21 Apr. 2010.
19 *Mercury*, 11 Apr. 1942; *Times*, 25 July 1947; G. de Wit, 3 May 2012; and J. McKeough, 7 Nov. 2013, pers. comms.
20 P. Bowden, pers. comm., 8 Dec. 2010; Mick Crossman, Wimperis collection; J. Crossman, diary, 29 Jan. 1940; and recording, Bowden collection.
21 Alexander, *Australian Eagles*, pp. 71–73; Alexander, 'Australian Knights of the Air'.

22   *Hutchins School Magazine*, Dec. 1933, 1940, Hutchins Archives and Heritage Collection; Watson, 'Battle of Britain Claimed Tas. Pilot', *Advocate*, 15 Sept. 1990.
23   Sheen, IWM, 2308; and 12137. The recommendation is pasted in H. Sheen's scrapbook, Foster-Williams collection.
24   Leigh-Mallory, Foster-Williams collection.
25   D. Foster-Williams, pers. comm., 19 Nov. 2009, 26 Nov. 2012; Sheen, IWM, 18375; *Canberra Times*, 14 Oct. 1941.
26   *Daily Mail*, 15 Sept. 1942.
27   *Canberra Times*, 12, 17 Sept. 1946; *Courier-Mail*, 15 Sept. 1947.
28   D. Foster-Williams, pers. comm., 17 Nov. 2009; *Canberra Times*, 9 Oct. 1947; Golley, *So Few*, p. 220.
29   B. Cowper, pers. comm., 28 Oct. 2011.
30   Claasen, *Dogfight*, p. 185; Millington to Robinson, 26 Feb. 1940, Robinson collection; D. Sheen to Sheens, 16 Aug. 1940, Foster-Williams collection.

Epilogue
1   L. Bladen, pers. comm., 3, 24 Nov. 2013.

Bibliography

Newspapers, magazines, school magazines and personal communications with the author are listed separately in the Notes. Newspaper articles not provided by families were accessed via the National Library of Australia's Trove resource, <trove.nla.gov.au/newspaper>. All internet sources were accessed on 19 April 2014.

Official archive collections

Australian War Memorial (AWM)
Glyde, R.L., in Official History, 1939–45 War, Biographical Files, AWM76, B204.
Hughes, Paterson Clarence, papers, 1936–45, PR87/142.
Hughes, Patterson [*sic*] Clarence, newspaper cutting and papers, n.d. [1939–40], PR87/180.
Sheen, Desmond Fred Bert [Burt], paper files and documents, 1940–43, including 'In England Now'; 'Secret, 23 June 1943', AWM65, 4654.

Belgian Military Archives
Dépôts d'Internement, Militaires des Armées Belligrantes [*sic*] Internés en Belgique, Correspondence, Oct.–Nov. 1939, papers relating to Pilot Officer Glyde's internment.

Department of Veterans' Affairs
(formerly Repatriation Department)
Holland, Harold G., pension files, n.d. [1920–57], NC138282.
Holland, Ina G., medical and hospital files, n.d. [1962–68], NMB138282.

Dorset History Centre
Dorset County Council, daily reports of chief constable on air raids and crashed aircraft, 1940–44, DCC/CD 1/3.

Imperial War Museum (IWM)
Doe, Robert Francis Thomas, interview, 2004, 26964.
Marsh, Henry James, microfilm copy of diary, Jan. 1932 – Aug. 1940, in Private Papers of H.J. Marsh, Documents.12822.
Morris, E.J., Private Papers of Air Commodore E.J. Morris CB CBE DSO DFC, 1945–75, Documents.8231.
Roddis, Joe, interview, 2004, 26966.
Sheen, Desmond Frederick Burt, 'Experiences of a Night Fighter Pilot', 17 Apr. 1941, 2308.
——interview, 1 July 1991, 12137.
——interview, 1995, 18375.

National Archives of Australia (NAA)

The physical format of all sources listed is paper files and documents.

Crossman, John Dallas, 1939–48, A9300, Crossman J D.

Glyde, Richard Linsday [sic], 1939–42, A705, 163/34/110.

Holland, Harold George, 1914–20, B2455, Holland H G 8868.

Hughes, Paterson Clarence, 1939–48, A9300, Hughes P C.

——1940–42, A705, 163/36/115.

Kennedy, John Connelly [sic], 1929–45, A705, 32/4/71.

[Millington, Bill], RAAF: Directorate of Personnel Services: Casualty Section: Pilot Officer W.H. Millington DFC DP Air Operations: RAF, 1940–44, A705, 106/6/115.

Olive, Charles Gordon Challoner, 4 Dec. 1943 – 4 July 2005, A12372, R/17934/H.

Walch, Stuart Crosby, 1929–60, A705, 166/43/934.

——1935–46, B4747, Walch/Stuart Crosby.

——1939–48, A9300, Walch S C.

War Cabinet, Minute 3857, Memorial Window in Westminster Abbey, 18 Oct. – 4 Nov. 1944, A2676, 3857.

National Archives, United Kingdom (NAUK)

Sources are listed by file number. Numbers in brackets denote individual items within the file. Unless otherwise stated, individual items are from 1940. 'CR' denotes combat report, and 'ORB' operations record book.

AIR 2/9398: Decorations, Medals, Honours and Awards (Code B, 30), 3 Sept. 1939 – 29 Feb. 1940.

AIR 27/460: 46 Squadron, ORB, Apr. 1916 – Dec. 1943.

AIR 27/589: 64 Squadron, ORB, Mar. 1936 – Dec. 1940.

AIR 27/592: 65 Squadron, ORB, Sept. 1934 – Dec. 1940.

AIR 27/624: 72 Squadron, ORB, July 1917 – Dec. 1942.

AIR 27/627: 72 Squadron, Appendices Y, 1 Oct. 1939 – 30 Apr. 1942.

AIR 27/664: 79 Squadron, ORB, Mar. 1937 – Dec. 1941.

AIR 27/712: 87 Squadron, ORB, May 1937 – Dec. 1943.

AIR 27/1018: 151 Squadron, ORB, Aug. 1936 – Dec. 1940.

AIR 27/1025: 152 Squadron, ORB, Oct. 1939 – Dec. 1943.

AIR 27/1439: 234 Squadron, ORB, Oct. 1939 – Dec. 1943.

AIR 27/1453: 238 Squadron, ORB, May 1940 – Oct. 1944.

AIR 27/1498: 249 Squadron, ORB, May 1940 – Dec. 1943.

AIR 29/568: 10 Flying Training School, Jan. 1936 – Oct. 1940.

AIR 50/20: 46 Squadron, CR, Oct. 1939 – Oct. 1944 (13: Crossman, 15 Sept.).

AIR 50/30: 72 Squadron, CR, Oct. 1939 – July 1942 (34: Sheen, 21 Oct. 1939).

AIR 50/33: 79 Squadron, CR, Nov. 1939 – May 1943 (35: Millington, 9 July).

AIR 50/37: 87 Squadron, CR, Nov. 1939 – Apr. 1942 (7: David, 2 Nov. 1939; 17: Jay, 11 July, 13 Aug.; 18: Jeff, 2 Nov. 1939; 32: Ward, 19 May; 49: Dewar, 11 July, 13 Aug.; 51: Glyde, 19 May; 53: Glyde, 11 July).

AIR 50/64: 152 Squadron, CR, Jan. 1940 – Dec. 1941 (3: Bayles, 25 Sept.; 82: Devitt, 25 Sept.; 90: Holland, 17, 19 Sept.).

AIR 50/89: 234 Squadron, CR, July 1940 – Feb. 1945 (3: Connor, 27 July; 18: O'Brien, 18 Aug.; 35: Doe, 7 Sept.; 36: Harker, 7 Sept.; 37: Lawrence, 7 Sept.; 73: Doe, 16 Aug.; 83: Hughes, 16, 26 Aug., 4, 6 Sept.; 89: Hughes, 18 Aug.).

AIR 50/91: 238 Squadron, CR, July 1940 – Mar. 1941 (21: Walch, 20, 21 July;

38: Davis, 13 July; 41: Walch, 11 July; 42: Urwin-Mann, 11 Aug.; 43: Pidd, 11 Aug.; 47: Walch, 26 July).
AIR 50/96: 249 Squadron, CR, July 1940 – Dec. 1943 (10: Millington, 27 Sept., 7, 25, 28, 29 Oct.).

National Library of Australia
Sheen, Walter Ernest, 'Reminiscences', [19—], MS 3908.

Office of Air Force History (OAFH)
1 Flying Training School, Point Cook, operations record books and course notes, 1934, 1936, 1937, in Flying Training Courses, 1923-65, Historic Photos and Notes box file.

RAAF Museum
Hughes, Pat, letter to Marjorie Hughes, n.d. [early 1939]; Point Cook photo album, 1936.
Kennedy, Jack; and Walch, Stuart, Point Cook cadet assessment records, first term, 20 Course, 1936–37.

RAF Disclosures
(RAF Cranwell)
Crossman, John Dallas; Glyde, Richard Lindsay; Hughes, Paterson Clarence; Kennedy, John Connolly; and Walch, Stuart Crosby, RAF service records.

RAF Museum
Deacon Elliott, Robert, *72 Squadron World War II, Dec 1939 – Dec 1940*, photocopy of typescript, 1961, X002-5542.
Fenton, H.A. 'Jim', *Aquarius: The Man Who Holds the Watering Pot; A Flying Memoir, 1928–1945*, privately published, 1992, 025376.
Sheen, Wing Commander Desmond, to Alexander McKee, 1959, AC/94/18/1.

State Library of Tasmania and Tasmanian Archive and Heritage Office
Walch, Stuart Crosby, will, 9 Jan. 1942, in Probate Book 48, p. 551, will 24752, AD960/1/66.

Private archive collections
Due to space constraints, private individuals' collections are cited in the Notes and below by their surnames. They belong to John Anderson (vice-president, Nevil Shute Norway Foundation), the Bowden family, Major Nigel Chamberlayne-Macdonald, Carolyn and Sam Evans, Jonathan Falconer, Diana Foster-Williams, Robert Glyde, Tony Hall, Greg Hughes, Beryl Kennedy, Ronald Lees, Sir William Ripley Bt, Simon Robinson, Christine Stanley-Hughes, Chris Taylor, John Walch, and Peter Wimperis.

***After the Battle* collection**
(Winston Ramsey)
Anon. to Kay Wray (note with advertisement).
Hartnell, Air Vice-Marshal Geoff, to Kay Wray, 22 Oct. 1980.
Hughes, Air Vice-Marshal H.A. 'Bill', to Kay Wray, 23 Dec. 1980, 12 May 1982.

Hughes, John, to Kay Wray, 30 Mar. 1981.
Woman, 15 Nov. 1980.
Wray, Kay (written on behalf of), to *Hull Daily Mail*, 26 May 1982.

Anderson collection
Airspeed Aeronautical College, *Prospectus*, 1936.

Bowden collection
Bentley, Godfrey, to Mrs Crossman, 8 Nov. 1941.
Brawn, Ann, to Joan Bowden, 15 Dec. 1940; to Ted & Mick Crossman, 15 Oct.,
    30 Dec. 1939, 4, 6, 11 Oct., 9 Nov., 16 Dec. 1940, 2 Apr., 15 May, 6 Oct. 1941.
Bush, Jacqueline, to Crossman family, 30 Sept. 1941, 31 Mar. 1943.
Cameron, Sir Donald, to Mrs Crossman, 28 Nov. 1940.
Crossman, George Edward 'Ted', 'Ted's Story', May 1962.
Crossman, John: diaries (1939, 1940); flying log; Gieves Ltd (account and
    correspondence); Intermediate Certificate; letters to Crossman family,
    13, 30 Aug., 12 Sept., 25 Oct., 1, 7, 21, 26 Nov., 4, 20 Dec. 1939, 3, 18 Jan.,
    22 Feb., 12, 17 Apr., 15, 25 May, 6, 12 June, 11, 28 Aug., 22 Sept 1940; letter
    to Dorothy Foley, 1 Sept. 1940; letter to Aunt Nell Kennedy, 12 Sept. 1939;
    newspaper article (unattrib.) from after John's death; photo albums; recording
    (HMV studio, 29 Jan. 1940); references (Australian Institute of Industrial
    Psychology, 19 June 1936; A. Goninan & Co., 17 Aug. 1938; C.W. Nicholls,
    rector, St Philip's Church, 29 July 1936); school reports.
Crossman, Mabel, to Ted Crossman, 4 Oct., 10 Nov. 1940; to Ted & Mick
    Crossman, 22 Sept., 27 Oct. 1940.
Hudson, Flight Lieutenant M., Air Historical Branch, Ministry of Defence, to Chris
    Bowden, 10 Jan. 2012.
Hughes, Pat, to William Hughes, 6 Sept. 1939.
Langslow, M.C., secretary of Department of Air, to Ted Crossman, 10 June 1941.
Macdonald of the Isles, Miss Celia, to John Crossman, 26 Oct. 1939.
Parkes, Mrs 'Granny Mary', to John Crossman, 14 July 1940.
Wimperis, Edmund, to Ted Crossman, 6 Nov. 1940.

Chamberlayne-Macdonald collection
Atkin, Ronald William Mein MBE, 'In Memoriam: Celia Macdonald, 1889–1976',
    funeral oration.

Evans collection
Feuchtwanger, Jacob Leo, 'Last Will and Testament', dated July 1958.
Haydon, Seina, to Carolyn & Sam Evans, 21 Sept. 2002.
Holland, Ken, will, signed 28 Aug. 1940; probate, dated 11 Jan. 1941.

Falconer collection
Davey, Canon F.H.D., chaplain, RAFA, Frome, to the editor, *Weekly Newspapers*,
    Sept. 1987.

Fort Street High School collection
Cooma Express, Sept. 1940 (not fully attrib.).
Fortian, June 1934.
Hughes, Paterson Clarence, enrolment form; school records.

Bibliography

Foster-Williams collection
Leigh-Mallory, Air Vice-Marshal Trafford, to Des Sheen, with attached
    recommendation, 9 Oct. 1941.
Sheen, Desmond, flying log; interview by Diana Foster-Williams & Erik Mannings,
    72 Squadron historian, 18 Nov. 1994; letters to Walter & Harriet Sheen, 7 May,
    18 July, 16 Aug., 4, 10, 19 Sept. 1940; photos.
Sheen, Harriet, scrapbook, n.d.

Glenunga International High School collection
(via Adelaide Technical High School Old Scholars' Association)
Millington, Bill, enrolment form; school records.

Glyde collection
Family research project, n.d.
Glyde, Dick, to Phillis Glyde, 22, 30 Nov. 1939.

Guildford Grammar School collection
Freeth, Rev. Robert Evelyn, MA, letter to Dick Glyde, 17 July 1934; 'Reference for
    Mr R.L. Glyde', 12 May 1936.
Glyde, Richard Lindsay, 'Certificate of Character on Discharge'; enrolment form; job
    application to Rev. Robert Evelyn Freeth MA, 13 July 1934; letter to Rev. Robert
    Evelyn Freeth MA, 13 May 1936; school records; sporting records and photos.
Swan, various issues.

Hall collection
Hall, Desmond, to Herr Bauman (representing Herr Schneider, father of a crew
    member of the Dornier Do17 which crashed in Sundridge, 7 Sept. 1940), n.d.
    [late 1980s].

Hughes collection
Hughes, Pat, to Charles & Heather Hughes, July [1939].

Hutchins Archives and Heritage Collection
(The Hutchins School)
Hutchins School Magazine, various issues.
Walch, Stuart Crosby, enrolment record; photos; school records.

Kennedy collection
Clark, St. E.F., for director of Personal Services, Air Ministry, to J. Oldham,
    Australian External Affairs Department, 1 Aug. 1941.
Davis, Pilot Officer Charles Trevor, DFC, to John Kennedy, 9 Dec. 1940.
Fairbairn, J.V., minister for Air, to John Kennedy, 1, 3 Apr. 1940.
Kavanagh, Arthur, CFRC, to John Kennedy, 20 July 1940.

Lees collection
Lees, Ronald, flying log.

Prince Alfred College collection
Prince Alfred College Chronicle, no. 185, Sept. 1939.

Ripley collection
Holland, Kenneth, diaries (1939, 1940).
'Report in Connection with the Aerial Engagement over Woolverton on Wednesday
    25th September 1940 from Information Collected by Fl Lt Hudson Who
    Investigated It Immediately Following the Crash', n.d.
Ripley, E. Guy, memo, Sept. 1940.

Robinson collection
Gibbs, Phyllis, president, Streaky Bay branch, to Eileen Robinson, 1 Oct. 1940.
Macdonald of the Isles, Miss Celia, to Elizabeth Millington, n.d.
Millington, Bill, diary (1939); letters to his parents, 10 Oct. 1939, June 1940; letters
    to Eileen Robinson, 7 July, 19 Aug., 31 Dec. 1939, 26 Feb., 22 May, 14 Sept.
    1940; photos; RAF service record.
Nevin, Thomas, speech, Edwardstown Primary School, 10 Apr. 1942.
Robinson, Eileen, biographical notes on Bill Millington, n.d.
Robinson, Simon, biographical essay on Bill Millington, n.d.

Stanley-Hughes collection
Air liaison officer, Australia House (telegram), to Christine Jourd, n.d.
'Christine's Story', n.d.
Kennedy, Jack, letters to Christine Jourd, 14 Aug. 1939, and nine others, n.d.
    (commencing 'Christine Darling I've got your two letters', 'Christine Darling I
    was awfully disappointed', 'Christine Darling sorry', 'Christine Darling this letter
    is long overdue', 'Dear Christine I had hoped', 'Dear Christine I tried several
    times', 'Dearest Christine I rang last night', 'Dearest Christine this is a different
    letter', 'My darling you probably'); photos, 1939–40; telegram to Christine Jourd,
    30 June 1940.

Taylor collection
Holland, Ken, baptismal certificate, Parish of Tintagel, 13 Sept. 1936, copy issued
    7 Dec. 2009; death certificate, 5 Oct. 1940, copy issued 1 Feb. 2007; probate,
    11 Jan. 1941; nomination form, 6 Oct. 1935, and examination report for
    examination on 20 Dec. 1936, for Tamarama Surf Life Saving Club and Surf
    Life Saving Association of Australia.
Sheldon, Richard, former secretary, Tamarama Surf Life Saving Club, to Chris
    Taylor (email), 22 Apr. 2008.
Tamarama Surf Life Saving Club, minutes of meeting, 13 Oct. 1940.

Telopea Park School collection
Sheen, Desmond Frederick Burt, enrolment records; school records.
Telopea School Magazine, various issues.

Walch collection
John Player & Sons, 'Aircraft of the Royal Air Force' album, issued 1938, with
    accompanying note to Walch's niece Ann, n.d.
Photos.

Waverley College collection
Christian Brothers' College Waverley Record, various issues.
Kennedy, John Connolly, enrolment record; school records; sporting records.

Bibliography

Wimperis collection
Crossman, Mick, to Edmund Wimperis, 29 July 1941.
Crossman, Ted, to Edmund Wimperis, 20 July 1941.
Wimperis, Edward, 'Notes for Future Reference', 4 Oct. 1940.

Books, articles and internet sources
Acutt, Private D.G.F., *Brigade in Action: The History of the Origin and Development of the St John Ambulance Brigade in Weymouth and of Its Co-operation with the Civil Defence Services during the War 1939–1945*, Sherren & Son, Weymouth, [c. 1945].
Adams, P., *Hurricane Squadron: No. 87 Squadron at War, 1939–1941*, Air Research Publications, New Malden, 1988.
Addison, P., & J.A. Crang (eds), *Listening to Britain: Home Intelligence Reports on Britain's Finest Hour, May to September 1940*, Bodley Head, London, 2010.
Alexander, K., *Australian Eagles: Australians in the Battle of Britain*, Barrallier Books, Geelong, 2013.
——'Australian Hurricane Pilots: First Blood in the Battle of Britain', *Flightpath*, vol. 25, no. 3, Feb.–Apr. 2014, pp. 58–61.
——'Australian Knights of the Air and Their Little Touches of Chivalry', *Sabretache*, vol. 53, no. 4, Dec. 2012, pp. 4–14.
——'Battle of Britain Revealed: New Information on Australian Pilots', *Britain at War Magazine*, no. 75, July 2013, pp. 54–58.
——'Miss Celia Macdonald of the Isles "Who Has Been a Particularly Good Friend"', *Sabretache*, vol. 55, no. 3, Sept. 2013, pp. 15–25.
Allied Aircrew in the Battle of Britain, Battle of Britain London Monument, n.d., <www.bbm.org.uk/participants.htm>.
Armitage, A.M., *Newcastle High School: The First 75 Years*, 75th Anniversary Committee, Newcastle, 1983.
Arthur, M., *Last of The Few: The Battle of Britain in the Words of the Pilots Who Won It*, Virgin/Random House, London, 2010.
Austin, A.B., *Fighter Command*, Victor Gollancz, London, 1941.
Baker, E.C.R., *The Fighter Aces of the RAF, 1939–1945*, William Kimber, London, 1962.
Barclay, G., *Battle of Britain Pilot: The Self-Portrait of an RAF Fighter Pilot and Escaper*, ed. Humphrey Wynn, Haynes, Yeovil, 2012.
Barker, R., *Aviator Extraordinary: The Sidney Cotton Story*, Chatto & Windus, London, 1969.
Batt, L.G., *Scramble! A Flying Memoir of One of 'The Few'*, Battle of Britain Historical Society, Gunthorpe, 2001.
Battle of Britain, Air Ministry Pamphlet 156, His Majesty's Stationery Office, London, 1943.
The Battle of Britain, August–October 1940: An Air Ministry Account of the Great Days from 8th August – 31st October 1940, His Majesty's Stationery Office, London, 1941.
Battle of Britain, Australian War Memorial, n.d., <www.awm.gov.au/encyclopedia/battle_of_britain>.
'Battle of Britain Groundcrew Member Visits Pilot's Memorial', *Britain at War Magazine*, no. 75, July 2013, p. 8.
Battle of Britain Historical Society, <www.battleofbritain1940.net>.
Battle of Britain: Roll of Honour, Royal Air Force, n.d., <www.raf.mod.uk/history/

BattleofBritainRollofHonour.cfm>.

Beamont, R., *My Part of the Sky: A Fighter Pilot's Firsthand Experiences, 1939–1945*, Patrick Stephens, Wellingborough, 1989.

Beer, S., *A Salute to One of 'The Few': The Life of Flying Officer Peter Cape Beauchamp St John RAF*, Pen & Sword Aviation, Barnsley, 2009.

Bishop, P., *Battle of Britain: A Day-by-Day Chronicle, 10 July to 31 October 1940*, Quercus, London, 2009.

——*Fighter Boys: Saving Britain, 1940*, HarperCollins, London, 2003.

Brackx, D., *The Phoney War (Sept 39 – May 9, 40)*, Belgian Aviation Historical Society, last updated 6 Nov. 2011, <www.belgian-wings.be/Webpages/Navigator/Belgian_Aviation_History/interbellum/ThePhoneyWar%2002.htm>.

Bungay, S., *The Most Dangerous Enemy: A History of the Battle of Britain*, Aurum, London, 2000.

Burgess, C., *'Bush' Parker: An Australian Battle of Britain Pilot in Colditz*, Australian Military History, Loftus, 2007.

Charman, T., *Outbreak 1939: The World Goes to War*, Virgin, London, 2009.

The Children's Hour, vol. 54, no. 605, grade 7, June 1942.

Claasen, A., *Dogfight: The Battle of Britain*, Exisle, Wollombi, 2012.

Clostermann, P., *The Big Show*, Cassell, London, 2005.

Cornwell, P., *The Battle of France: Then and Now*, Battle of Britain International, Old Harlow, 2007.

Coulthard-Clark, C., *The Third Brother: The Royal Australian Air Force, 1921–39*, Allen & Unwin, Sydney, 1991.

Crang, J.A., 'Identifying the "Few": The Personalisation of a Heroic Military Elite', *War & Society*, vol. 24, no. 2, Nov. 2005, pp. 13–22.

Cull, B., *249 at War*, Grub Street, London, 1997.

——, B. Lander & H. Weiss, *Twelve Days in May: The Air Battle for Northern France and the Low Countries, 10–21 May 1940*, Grub Street, London, 1995.

David, D., *Dennis 'Hurricane' David: My Autobiography*, Grub Street, London, 2000.

'Despatch on the Conduct of the Battle of Britain Submitted by Air Chief Marshal Dowding to the Air Ministry in August 1941', *Supplement to the London Gazette*, no. 37719, 11 Sept. 1946, pp. 4543–71, digitised copy of pp. 4544, <www.london-gazette.co.uk/issues/37719/supplements/4544> and 4553, <www.london-gazette.co.uk/issues/37719/supplements/4553>.

Docherty, T., *Swift to Battle: No. 72 Squadron RAF in Action*, vol. 1, *1937 to 1942: Phoney War, Dunkirk, Battle of Britain, Offensive Operations*, Pen & Sword Aviation, Barnsley, 2009.

Doe, B., *Bob Doe – Fighter Pilot: The Story of One of The Few*, Spellmount, Tunbridge Wells, 1991.

——'A Recollection of Pat Hughes', in service booklet for the Commemoration Service and Memorial Unveiling for Flight Lieutenant Paterson Clarence Hughes DFC, 234 Squadron, Royal Air Force, Sundridge, 7 Sept. 2005, p. 8.

Falconer, J., *Life of a Battle of Britain Pilot*, Sutton, Stroud, 2007.

Francis, M., *The Flyer: British Culture and the Royal Air Force, 1939–1945*, Oxford University Press, Oxford, 2008.

Franks, N., *Fighter Leader: The Story of Wing Commander Ian Gleed*, William Kimber, London, 1978.

——*Wings of Freedom: Twelve Battle of Britain Pilots*, William Kimber, London, 1980.

From Camel to Hawk: A Diary History of 151(F) Squadron RAF, <www.151squadron.org.uk>.

Gardner, J., *Blitz: The British under Attack*, HarperPress, London, 2010.

Gelb, N., *Scramble: A Narrative History of the Battle of Britain*, Michael Joseph, London, 1986.

Gleed, I., *Arise to Conquer*, Severn House, n.p., 1975.

Golding, H. (ed.), *The Wonder Book of Aircraft*, Ward Lock, London, 1927.

Golley, J., *So Few: A Folio Dedicated to All Who Fought and Won the Battle of Britain*, So Few, Chichester, 1992.

Hall, R., DFC, *Spitfire Pilot: An Extraordinary True Story of Combat in the Battle of Britain*, Amberley, Stroud, 2012.

Harper, H., *Twenty-Two Temporary Gentlemen*, n.p., Goulburn, n.d.

Hawkins, M., *Somerset at War, 1939–1945*, Dovecote, Stanbridge, 1990.

Herington, J., *Air War against Germany and Italy, 1939–1943: Australia in the War of 1939–1945*, vol. 3, Series Three Air, Canberra, 1962.

Hillary, R., *The Last Enemy*, Macmillan, London, 1978.

Hodges, J., *Bedstone Court: The Story of a Calendar House*, J. Hodges, n.p., 2006.

Holland, J., *The Battle of Britain: Five Months that Changed History, May–October 1940*, Bantam, London, 2010.

'In Memoriam: Air Marshal Sir Ronald Lees KCB CBE DFC RAF (Ret)', *AFSA*, 29 May 1991, p. 6.

James, J., *The Paladins: A Social History of the RAF up to the Outbreak of World War II*, Macdonald, London, 1990.

James, T.C.G., *The Battle of Britain*, ed. and introduction by S. Cox, Frank Cass, London, 2000.

Jennings, N., & G. Walton, *The Search for One of The Few*, Redden Court Enterprises, n.p., 2001.

Kingsland, Sir R., *Into the Midst of Things: The Autobiography of Sir Richard Kingsland*, Air Power Development Centre, Canberra, 2010.

Legg, R., *Dorset's War Diary: Battle of Britain to D-Day*, Dorset, Wincanton, 2004.

Marchant, D.J., *Rise from the East: The Story of No. 247 (China-British) Squadron Royal Air Force*, Air-Britain (Historians), Tunbridge Wells, 1996.

[Marrs, E.], 'One of The Few', 2 parts, *Aeroplane*, 14 Sept. 1945, pp. 299–300, 21 Sept. 1945, pp. 338–39.

Mason, F., *Battle over Britain: A History of the German Air Assaults on Great Britain, 1917–18 and July–December 1940, and the Development of Britain's Air Defences between the World Wars*, Aston, Bourne End, 1990.

Middleton, D.H., *Airspeed: The Company and Its Aeroplanes*, Terence Dalton, Lavenham, 1982.

Neil, T., *Gun-Button to 'Fire'*, William Kimber, London, 1987.

Nelson-Edwards, G., *Spit and Sawdust: The Story of a Fighter Pilot Turned 'Cordon Bleu' Cook Licensee and Restaurateur*, Air Forces, Swindon, 1995.

Newton, D., *Australia in the Air War of World War 2*, vol. 1, *1939–40*, First Impact: Combat Diary Series, Banner Books, Maryborough, 1997.

——'Australians Lost in the Battle of Britain: SGT K.C. Holland 152 (Spitfire) Squadron RAF', *Aviation Heritage*, vol. 39, no. 1, Apr. 2008, pp. 17–20.

——*Clash of Eagles*, Kangaroo, Kenthurst, 1996.

——*A Few of 'The Few': Australians and the Battle of Britain*, Australian War Memorial, Canberra, 1990.

——'Flg Off Richard Glyde DFC', *Aero Australia*, no. 18, Apr.–June 2008, pp. 86–91.

Olive, G., & D. Newton, *The Devil at 6 O'clock: An Australian in the Battle of Britain*, Australian Military History, Loftus, 2001.

Orange, V., *Park: The Biography of Air Chief Marshal Sir Keith Park GCB KBE MC DFC DCL*, Grub Street, London, 2001.

Palliser, C., *They Gave Me a Hurricane: From Fighting in the Battle of Britain to the Defence of Malta and Sabotage in South Africa*, Fighting High, Hitchin, 2012.

Parker, M., *The Battle of Britain, July–October 1940: An Oral History of Britain's 'Finest Hour'*, Headline, London, 2000.

Perkins, J., *Westminster Abbey: The Royal Air Force Chapel with the Battle of Britain Window in the Chapel of King Henry VII*, H.B. Skinner, London, n.d.

Price, A., *Battle of Britain: The Hardest Day, 18 August 1940*, Macdonald & Janes, London, 1979.

——*Spitfire Mark I/II Aces, 1939–41*, Osprey, Oxford, 2005.

Ramsey, W.G. (ed.), *The Battle of Britain: Then and Now*, Mk V edn, Battle of Britain Prints International, London, 1996.

Rawlings, J., *Fighter Squadrons of the RAF and Their Aircraft*, Macdonald & Janes, London, 1976.

The Rise and Fall of the German Air Force (1933 to 1945), Air Ministry Pamphlet 248, Air Ministry, [London], 1948.

Roddis, J., *In Support of The Few: From an 'Erk' to Chief Technician the Diary of Joe Roddis*, with M. Hillier, Yellowman, n.p., 2013.

Ruffin, S.A., 'Flying in the Great War: Rx for Misery; An Overview of the Medical, Physiological and Psychological Aspects of Combat Flying during the First World War', 2 parts, *Over the Front*, vol. 14, no. 2, 1999, pp. 115–25, vol. 17, no. 2, 2002, pp. 21–40.

Schofield, E., & Numeralla and District Community History Group, *'In Those Days …': Numeralla-Countegany-Peak View and Surrounding Areas*, Numeralla, 1996.

Shores, C., *Fledgling Eagles: The Complete Account of Air Operations during the 'Phoney War' and Norwegian Campaign, 1940*, with J. Foreman, C.-J. Ehrengardt, H. Weiss & B. Olsen, Grub Street, London, 1991.

——*Those Other Eagles: A Tribute to the British, Commonwealth and Free European Fighter Pilots Who Claimed between Two and Four Victories in Aerial Combat, 1939–1982*, Grub Street, London, 2004.

——& C. Williams, *Aces High: A Tribute to the Most Notable Fighter Pilots of the British and Commonwealth Forces in WWII*, Grub Street, London, 1994.

Simpson, G., 'The Battle of Britain: Counting The Few', *Britain at War*, no. 30, Oct. 2009, pp. 67–69.

——*A Dictionary of the Battle of Britain*, Halsgrove/Battle of Britain Memorial Trust, Wellington, 2009.

——*A Good Aggressive Fighter Pilot: The Story of One Airman Who Fought in the Battle of Britain*, G. Simpson, Stockport, 2000.

Sims, E.H., *The Fighter Pilots: A Comparative Study of the Royal Air Force, the Luftwaffe and the United States Army Air Force in Europe and North Africa, 1939–45*, Cassell, London, 1967.

Smith, R.C., *Second to None: A Pictorial History of Hornchurch Aerodrome through Two World Wars and Beyond, 1915–1962*, Grub Street, London, 2004.

Stansky, P., *The First Day of the Blitz, September 7 1940*, Yale University Press, New Haven, 2007.

Stokes, D., *Wings Aflame: The Biography of Group Captain Victor Beamish DSO and Bar DFC AFC*, William Kimber, London, 1985.

Bibliography

Sturtivant, R., J. Hamlin & J.J. Halley, *Royal Air Force Flying Training and Support Units*, Air-Britain (Historians), Tunbridge Wells, 1997.

Symonds, C.P., & D.J. Williams, *Psychological Disorders in Flying Personnel of the Air Force Investigated during the War*, Air Ministry Publication 3139, His Majesty's Stationery Office, London, 1947.

Taylor, C., *The Life and Times of Kenneth Holland: The Spitfire Pilot from Waverley*, C. Taylor, Gosford, 2010.

Thomas, N., *RAF Top Gun: The Story of Battle of Britain Ace and World Air Speed Record Holder Air Cdr E.M. 'Teddy' Donaldson CB CBE DSO AFC* LoM (USA)*, Pen & Sword Aviation, Barnsley, 2008.

Townsend, P., *Duel of Eagles*, Weidenfeld & Nicolson, London, 1971.

Van Sickle, N.D., *Modern Airmanship*, Van Nostrand, Princeton, 1967.

Vasco, J.J., & P.D. Cornwell, *Zerstörer: The Messerschmitt 110 and Its Units in 1940*, JAC, Norwich, 1995.

Wakefield, K., *Luftwaffe Encore: A Study of Two Attacks in September 1940*, William Kimber, London, 1979.

Wallace, G., *RAF Biggin Hill*, Putnam, London, 1957.

Walpole, N., *Dragon Rampant: The Story of 234 Fighter Squadron*, Merlin Massara, London Colney, 2007.

Wells, M.K., *Courage and Air Warfare: The Allied Aircrew Experience in the Second World War*, Frank Cass, London, 1995.

White, M., *Go Forward: Guildford Grammar School, 1896–1996; A History*, Guildford Grammar School, Guildford, 1996.

Willis, L., *Churchill's Few: The Battle of Britain Remembered*, Michael Joseph, London, 1985.

Wood, D., & D. Dempster, *The Narrow Margin: The Battle of Britain and the Rise of Air Power, 1930–1940*, Tri-Service, London, 1990.

Wynn, K.G., *Men of the Battle of Britain: A Biographical Directory of 'The Few'*, CCB, Croydon, 1999.

Index

Index